FIRST HAND KNOWLEDGE

How I Participated in the CIA–Mafia Murder of President Kennedy

ROBERT D. MORROW

A division of Shapolsky Publishers, Inc.

S.P.I. BOOKS

A division of Shapolsky Publishers, Inc.

For any additional information, contact:

S.P.I. BOOKS/Shapolsky Publishers, Inc.
136 West 22nd Street
New York, NY 10011
(212) 633-2022
FAX (212) 633-2123

ISBN: 1-56171-179-9

10 9 8 7 6 5 4 3 2 1

Design and typesetting by Smith, Inc., New York
Printed and bound in the United States of America

In Memoriam

This book is dedicated to the memory
of two persons, without whose dedication
to finding out the truth surrounding the death
of John F. Kennedy this book would not have been possible.

BERNARD (BUD) FENSTERWALD
Founder & Director of the
Assassination Archives and Research Center

"TINY" HUTTON
Former Deputy Director of the
House Select Committee on Assassinations

CONTENTS

ACKNOWLEDGMENTS

To former Representative Thomas W. Downing, first Chairman of the House Select Committee on Assassinations, who had the courage to push for its formation.

To my good friend and associate, Robert Eickelberger, without whose help I could not have undertaken this project.

To Douglas Sandbag, publisher and editor of the Cincinnati *East Side Weekend* who believed in me and my story enough to publish it.

To my wife, Jeanne D. Morrow, who suffered along with me on this project.

And to the two wonderful editors JoAnna Cimino and Ann Cassouto who made the job possible under unbelievable time constraints, and last but not least—Skipper Morrow who kept me company the whole time.

AUTHOR'S NOTE

I have always been a person with a strong sense of patriotism. So much so, that I unwittingly placed myself, in the eyes of some, in the position of committing treason.

Whether I can be indicted for it so many years later is a matter of conjecture. But I am willing to take that chance.

One month before his predestined death, President John F. Kennedy said, "The highest duty of the writer is to remain true to himself and to let the chips fall where they may. In serving his vision of the truth, the artist best serves his nation."

I devoted several years of my life to the nation's clandestine intelligence operations, and even committed two major felonious acts because I believed them to be essential to the preservation of a free society here at home and elsewhere in the world. My view and my values have remained unchanged.

Today, I cannot undo what I have done, nor can I continue to rationalize the reasons I was given so long ago as to why the President had to be killed.

I wanted to speak out when the Warren Commission was in session in 1964, but my connection at the CIA told me—using the following words which I will never forget—"You have signed a secrecy agreement with your government. It is your government that is responsible for what has transpired. You are part of that government, and you have a solemn commitment to it and its national security. I agree, the act of murder can never be justified . . . unless it's done for the good of the country. This was one of those instances."

Marshall Diggs, a prominent Washington attorney, told me this. It was the same rationale used by the people responsible for the murder of the President. Diggs may not have believed his own words, but I clearly understood his meaning to be for me to keep my mouth shut, or I could end up dead too.

Today, most of the people who got me involved in the CIA conspiracy have passed away. I hope the surviving participants in the assassination plot will now see their way clear to come out of hiding and join me in telling the world the truth.

Robert D. Morrow
1992

PREFACE

More than half the characters about to come to life on these pages have already been put to death, tortured, exiled or silenced in strange and horrible ways. They knew too much about the corruption, deception and Mafia connections that led to the assassination of President John F. Kennedy.

I was one of the first people to obtain first hand evidence of Soviet missiles in Cuba (evidence that was presented to President Kennedy in 1961 and ignored for political reasons).

I made the counterfeit money for the Cuban underground resistance which was trying to put an end to Castro's communist regime in Cuba.

I bought the three Manlicher rifles that would be used to shoot Kennedy.

I supplied Kennedy's three hit squads with communications devices more sophisticated than any previously designed.

I knew that the Mob, the leaders of our nation, and our government's intellignece agencies conspired together to asassinate very important people, including the President.

I was there, and now you will be, too, as the deadly truth is uncovered here. You may initially not believe what you are reading, but by the end of this book the overwhelming facts leave no room for doubt.

I realize how impossible and illogical it sounds to assert that the CIA would orchestrate the assassination of the president of the United States. After all, the CIA is supposed to protect our nation and its leaders from their enemies. To comprehend why the CIA found it necessary to commit the seemingly treasonous act of murdering the country's Commander-in-Chief, one must understand the political climate of that age. The circumstances that led up to the assassination were set in motion prior to Kennedy's election.

As a CIA operative, I witnessed first hand the events that let to the murder. Although the assassination may seem outrageous when considered in isolation, at the time, it really did not come as such a surprise. I do not mean to defend or condemn the murder of President Kennedy, I just hope to explain how and why it happened. The assassination made some sense to me at the time, and it still does to this day. My goal in this book is to put you in my shoes so that you too can make sense of the events that transpired in November 1963.

The justification for what happened is best understood by reliving the months leading up to it, focusing on the political climate of the era. I will now take you through my turbulent years with the CIA so that you will understand why the United States intelligence community concluded that the President had to be eliminated.

INTRODUCTION

by

John H. Davis

The John F. Kennedy assassination case has, in recent months, become an investigative Tower of Babel, thanks largely to Oliver Stone's controversial film on the assassination, *JFK*, which was released, with much fanfare, in December, 1991. For, after the *JFK* bombshell exploded, a discordant chorus of new voices suddenly rose up across the land presenting a bewildering variety of assassination scenarios.

One book held that Kennedy was killed accidentally by a bullet fired by a Secret Service agent in one of the motorcade's back-up cars. Another asserted that the assassination was initiated, planned and then covered up by Kennedy's successor, Lyndon B. Johnson. Still another, citing alleged evidence of forgery of crucial autopsy x-rays and photographs, pinned the blame for the crime on a vast conspiracy comprised of elements of the Secret Service, the Ultra Right Wing, the CIA-sponsored Cuban exiles, the FBI, the Dallas Police, and medical personnel at Bethesda Naval Hospital.

The most responsible writers on the assassintaion, however, have leaned toward the belief that organized crime was a major force behind the Kennedy murder, with perhaps the CIA and the Cuban exiles playing supporting roles. This was essentially the conclusion of the House Select Committee on Assassinations which in 1979 identified Teamsters chief Jimmy Hoffa, Florida Mafia boss Santos Trafficante Jr., and Gulf Coast Mafia boss Carlos Marcello as the most likely suspects in a plot to kill the President. This scenario found strong resonance in books by G. Robert Blakey, David E. Scheim, Anthony Summers and myself, and, most recently by Mark North, who added Lyndon Johnson and J. Edgar Hoover to the mix as accessories before and after the fact. Then, in January, 1992, Frank Ragano, a former attorney for Santos Trafficante Jr. (27 years), and Jimmy Hoffa (15 years) and occasional advisor to Carlos Marcello, came forth and alleged publicly that he was the intermediary in a plot to assassinate President Kennedy composed of Jimmy Hoffa, Santos Trafficante, and Carlos Marcello. So sure of his position was Mr. Ragano that he volunteered to testify under oath on what he knew about the assassination before a congressional committee, provided he would be granted immunity. Not long after this offer, Representative Louis Stokes of Ohio, former Chairman of the House Assassinations Committee, recommended to the Justice Department that it conduct a full investigation of Ragano's allegations.

Proponents of the Mafia-Did-It theory of the assassination, including Mr. Ragano, have, however, been unable to identify the Mafia's long suspected co-conspirators in the CIA and the Cuban exiles community.

Now along comes the author of this book, Robert D. Morrow, former CIA contract employee from 1959 through 1964, with a book that purports to fill in the missing links in the Mafia-Did-It scenario: first hand knowledge of the additional involvement of the CIA and the Cuban exiles in plotting the crime.

According to Mr. Morrow, who in this book describes his participation in the original planning for the assassination, certain elements of the CIA and their allies among the Cuban exiles in the CIA's secret war against Fidel Castro, learned about the Mafia contract to assassinate President Kennedy put out by Carlos Marcello, and reacting to what they perceived to be Kennedy's betrayal of the CIA-Cuban exiles campaign to overthrow Castro and re-take Cuba, decided to join forces with Marcello, Trafficante et al. to assassinate President Kennedy. The Cubans believed that only through this action could Castro be defeated and Cuba freed from bondage.

Robert Morrow is not new to the Kennedy assassination case. In 1976 he published *Betrayal: A Reconstruction of Certain*

*Clandestine Events from the Bay of Pigs to the Assassination of
John F. Kennedy.* This book was a partially fictionalized account
of what Mr. Morrow knew and personally experienced of the
Mafia/CIA/Cuban Exiles plot to assassinate President Kennedy.
Morrow and his book were instrumental in persuading the U.S.
House of Representatives to establish the Select Committee on
Assassinations which then conducted a three-year investigation into
the Kennedy murder.

Now, in *First Hand Knowledge,* Mr. Morrow has abandoned
his fictionalized approach to the Crime of the Century and has given
us a first hand, factual account of the plot to assassinate President
Kennedy, as he experienced it, while working as a CIA contract
employee responsible for providing sophisticated electronic
services for covert CIA operations.

It must be emphasized at this point that Mr. Morrow was not
a conspirator in the plot to assassinate the President, but an
unwitting accessory who became privy to the plotting but was not
a willing participant in it. For example, when he was ordered by
his CIA case officer Tracy Barnes to purchase four 7.35 mm
surplus Mannlicher-Carcano rifles he was not informed of their
intended use in the JFK assassination.

Robert Morrow identifies the major players in the plot to
assassinate President Kennedy: his CIA case officer, Tracy Barnes;
Marshall Diggs, an attorney and former Comptroller of the U.S.
Treasury under Roosevelt; New Orleans mob boss Carlos Marcello
and his associates Guy Bannister and David Ferrie; New Orleans
businessman Clay Shaw; Mario Kohly, a leader in the Cuban
resistance movement; Cuban exile leaders Sergio Arcacha Smith,
Eladio del Valle and Rolando Masferrer; and Florida Mafia boss
Santos Trafficante Jr. By inference Morrow also involves CIA Agent
William Harvey, who had been in charge of the abortive CIA-Mafia
plots to assassinate Fidel Castro.

In addition, Morrow names one of the shooters in the ambush
of the President, John Michael Mertz, who he identifies as a former
French mercenary and "an assassination expert who worked on the
CIA's official hit squad."

One of Morrow's most significant revelations is his firm belief that the principal operations planner in the assassination conspiracy was David Ferrie. Morrow knew Ferrie well and flew with him on a number of covert CIA missions into Cuba. Morrow is convinced that Ferrie, working under Carlos Marcello and Guy Bannister, was the brains, the "mastermind," behind the assassination.

Long suspected by many writers on the assassination to have been a major player in the plot to kill the President, David Ferrie has remained until now a shadowy, elusive figure. Circumstantial evidence of his possible involvement cried out for verification but no one ever came forward to vouch for his participation in the plot. Now Robert Morrow has placed him, from first hand knowledge, at the center of the web of intrigue that saw two Mafia bosses conspire with elements of the CIA and the Cuban exile community to assassinate President Kennedy. This revelation alone makes Robert Morrow's *First Hand Knowledge* one of the most important works on the Kennedy assassination in recent years.

One of Robert Morrow's most salient points is that the conspir-. ators plotted the assassination in such a way as to give the American public the impression that Fidel Castro, or at least his supporters, planned the killing of Kennedy. The purpose of this ruse was to outrage the public sufficiently to induce them to call for another U.S. invasion of Cuba to overthrow the Castro regime. This view, supported by Mr. Morrow, confirms one held by many assassination investigators. At a conference of Kennedy assassination researchers and writers held at the State University of New York at Fredonia on June 28–30, 1991, it was concluded that "The assassination of President Kennedy was, to put it simply, an anti-Castro 'provocation,' an act designed to be blamed on Castro to justify a punitive American invasion of the island. Such action would most clearly benefit the Mafia chieftains who had lost their gambling holdings in Havana because of Castro, and CIA agents who had lost their credibility with the Cuban exile freedom fighters from the ill-fated Bay of Pigs invasion."

One of the chief merits of *First Hand Knowledge* is that it successfully argues the point that the assassination of President

Kennedy was not merely an act of revenge, or blind hatred, but a *political act*, one designed to effect profound political change: the liberation of Cuba from a tyrannical Communist dictator.

In *First Hand Knowledge*, Robert Morrow ably shows how the government, fearful of having the CIA's involvement in the assassination exposed, managed to manipulate the Warren Commission's investigation of the crime so that it came to the conclusion that there was no conspiracy in the case, that Lee Harvey Oswald, the accused assassin, had acted alone, and managed also to thwart New Orleans District Attorney Jim Garrison's abortive investigation in 1968.

But the government has not been able to thwart the investigations of intrepid writers like Robert Morrow. Against dangerous odds, he has accomplished an important breakthrough in the Kennedy assassination case. His book presents the only believable first hand knowledge we have of the involvement of the CIA and the Cuban exile community in the tragic assassination of President Kennedy.

John H. Davis
New York
1992

John H. Davis is the author of several best selling books including *THE KENNEDYS: DYNASTY & DISASTER, MAFIA KINGFISH: CARLOS MARCELLO & THE ASSASSINATION OF JFK, THE GUGGENHEIMS* and *THE BOUVIERS*. A *cum laude* graduate of Princeton, he studied in Italy on a Fulbright scholarship and served as a naval officer with the Sixth Fleet.

1

JANUARY 1959–MARCH 1960

My initial contact and employment with the CIA commenced
without either my knowledge or my consent. At the time, I
was engaged by the Martin Aircraft Company as a project engineer.
A significant percentage – if not perhaps the total sum – of Martin's
annual revenue was acquired through lucrative United States
Government contracts, particularly contracts originating in the
Department of Defense for the Air Force and Navy. While it was
obvious that most of our engineering work had military applications, it was not so obvious that we were servicing government agencies other than the Defense Department; one would
be the just-formed National Aeronautics and Space Administration (NASA).

The projects undertaken by Martin at the behest of the Department of Defense were numerous and varied. Most projects,
however, bore a common characteristic. In addition to stringent
security and confidentiality requirements, they were also "pilot"
programs for advanced concepts. In other words, they were
projects wherein the concept, or theoretical ideas, were resolved
on paper. The next developmental stage was pragmatic: the actual
hardware was created and made to function within the parameters
established by its conceptual designers. This is where Martin
engineers entered the picture; their engineers and scientists not
only created the actual product, but made the product work and
function in the manner envisioned by its designer.

1

During my employment with Martin, I had acquired a certain reputation as a creative but pragmatic engineer who eagerly responded to challenging and provocative ideas. Consequently, I was frequently assigned to work on jobs that required a particular expertise in creative but immensely practical engineering problem solving. I had also developed a reputation as a distinctly non-bureaucratic, non-corporate individual who preferred to work independently and outside of the bureaucracy typical of large corporations. Consequently, I began to gradually divorce myself from Martin's corporate hierarchy and found myself increasingly more productive while working out of my home laboratory in Baltimore. The environment I had created there was precisely the type of work situation I needed—uncluttered by administrative protocols and maintained exclusively for the expedient resolution of engineering problems.

Eventually my reputation as a competent scientist began to attract other solicitations for my engineering services. As I became increasingly more reliant on the quiet concentration I could achieve in my home laboratory, my work habits reached a point wherein the maintenance of a salaried employee relationship with Martin was decidedly counterproductive to my growth and development as an engineer. Consequently, I left my position at Martin and, in January 1958, proceeded to establish an engineering consultancy in Washington, D.C.

In Washington, I became closely associated with another former Martin engineer, Dr. Stan Clark, who was considered one of the finest minds in the field of radiation effects. He had left Martin's employ in their Nuclear Division concurrent with my departure from the aircraft side. He was then employed by a "Company" in Washington, D.C. engaged in work on a top secret project for an unknown government agency. I would subsequently learn that the project was for the CIA.

Clark requested that I join him in his work and the two of us collaborated on an extremely ambitious assignment we named the Doomsday project. "Dr. Strangelove" lore aside, this was a serious government program whose directive was the development of a device which rendered an enemy population alive but helpless and did minimal physical damage to real property.

Our solution was as heinous as the directive. We determined that the optimum solution to the first mission was to enslave the hypothetical enemy population and render them totally dependent on their attackers. We then determined that enslavement could be accomplished by the utilization of a compound which would cause death if not treated with an antidote. We had done extensive research on hyperthyroidism and the role radioactive iodine played in reducing the amount of vital thyroxin produced by the thyroid gland. We also discovered the antidote to this condition, which was called thyroxin.

We therefore chose an isotope known to destroy the human thyroid gland and whose physiological effect can be controlled by the utilization of thyroxin. The weapon created would be on the order of a neutron bomb surrounded by a compound which, when exposed to radiation, would produce the thyroid-destroying isotope. The attacker would, of course, be the sole supplier of the antidote — in this scenario, thyroxin. The hypothetical victims would thus be utterly dependent on the perpetrators for the antidote. Without the antidote, the enemy population would die a quick and certain death.

I was stunned at the hypothesis. There would be no explosion, no buildings destroyed, just people dying an expedient and sterile death unless they had the antidote.

Using his hypothesis, Dr. Clark and I came up with a device that could be towed behind a jet plane constantly irradiating an unsuspecting population below. Unfortunately, because of his close proximity to the device, the pilot would have a very short life expectancy, no matter how well he was shielded. The consequence of using such a weapon is obvious: those who control the antidote can control the target population without bloodshed. To this day I don't know what happened after Dr. Clark submitted the results of our work to his clients.

My work with the Doomsday project was concluded in July 1958. Throughout the summer, I was employed as a a consultant for various companies engaged in the creation of several new electronic devices. While in the midst of doing some basic research for a project exploring new transducer devices, I came across an interesting process, the Ranque Hilsch effect.[1] This process enabled me to develop a unique furnace capable of maximizing heat efficiency to an unbelievable 96%. By February 1960, I had designed and built the first prototype of my furnace and had started testing it in my home in Baltimore.[2]

During that same period of time, I set up a meeting with my Washington attorney, Darwin Brown. We discussed the potential for the furnace and I asked if he could arrange a meeting with the United Mine Workers, who were looking to find ways to encourage the use of electricity for home heating. Darwin said he could set it up, and that he also had numerous clients who had large amounts of investment money available. He seemed quite pleased to see me and said he would extend his best efforts to assist in my commercial ventures.

Immediately following my meeting with Darwin, an episode occurred that would change my entire future: I spotted my old buddy, Ross Schoyer, who I hadn't seen for years, walking down K Street in Washington. The last time I had heard about him, he was married again, living in Connecticut, and employed by Landers, Ferry & Clark.

At first he didn't appear to hear me calling his name as I followed him across "K" Street toward the 16th Street entrance to the Carlton Hotel. Then, suddenly, he stopped. When I caught up with him I was utterly shocked. He looked terrible. He was unshaven and his clothes looked as though he had been sleeping in them. "Why the hell are you trying to avoid me?" I asked.

For a moment he didn't say anything. "For Christ's sake, Robert, look at me."

Ross and I spent several hours together as he relayed what had happened to him since the last time we had met. It was not a pretty story. Finally I said, "I've been contemplating getting an office/apartment in Washington. I'll need somebody I can trust to man it. Would you be interested?" He looked at me unbelievingly and said, "If you're serious, hell yes."

Within a week, Ross had found a respectable address within a block of DuPont Circle, at the corner of "19th" and "R." As it turned out, Ross had chosen the location for my apartment/office well. It was in the heart of an area where upwardly mobile young politicians were locating, and just a few blocks from Embassy row on Massachusetts Avenue. As Ross would also discover, it was around the corner from the newly formed National Police Academy, where Joe Shimon—one of the liaisons for the CIA with the mob—headed the Agency training school for foreign police officials. It was this organization that would train selected agents in the finer arts of torture, interrogation, and covert activities. By the end of April, we had completely moved in and my activities were keeping me in Washington for five days a week.

Despite Ross's series of bad luck, I found that he was well connected in Washington through his affiliations with his former employer, Landers, Ferry and Clark. As we settled into life in D.C., he introduced me to a number of people who were strangely interconnected with the flow of Washington events.

Concurrent with the improvements in my social affiliations, my reputation as a scientific electronics expert and my various commercial successes had brought both my name and expertise to the attention of numerous influential and highly respected individuals in Washington. One person particularly would be my ticket to meeting members of the House and Senate. Her name was Frances Russell, an attorney for the House Ways and Means Committee. As my professional reputation grew, I was asked by my corporate attorney, Darwin Brown, if I would be interested in undertaking a project for a friend of his, Marshall Diggs. As the former Deputy Comptroller of the U.S. Treasury under the Roosevelt Administration, Marshall Diggs was, according to Brown, intimately familiar with the august luminaries who comprised the treacherously sophisticated world of international corporate finance and banking, the peculiarly rough and tumble milieu of Wall Street and the international bourses, and the Byzantine domain of international politics. It so happened that at present Diggs had an equally influential and respected client who required my communications expertise.

I met Diggs and his client in an office Diggs occupied with several associates at 1025 Connecticut Avenue, at the corner of Connecticut and "L." Mario Garcia Kohly was as impressive as his prestigious international counsel. Known to certain Cuban political factions as the next president of Cuba, he enjoyed valuable patronage from certain members of the Eisenhower administration's elite inner circle. He and his family were established members of the Cuban aristocracy and prominent in the Cuban banking, financial and political arenas. I learned that his father had distinguished himself throughout his twenty-three year tenure as the Cuban Ambassador to Spain and in his retirement was a statesman of impeccable repute and an orator and writer with profound insight on the Cuban political situation.

Mario Kohly's resume was equally illustrious as that of his father and the other members of his family. A distinguished statesman and diplomat, Kohly was also one of the most illustrious members of Cuba's investment banking elite. He enjoyed a distinguished reputation in the world of international finance, corporate finance and business. As an international investment banker, Kohly was Cuba's premier trade and financial representative to the international community at large and major American energy-related industries in particular. I was to find out much later that he represented, in Cuba, an extraordinary number of prominent American corporations in industries as diversified as banking and energy, foodstuffs and finance, corporate finance and real estate development.[3]

When Castro "nationalized" Cuban industries, the Cuban economy was devastated. He had taken over stock holdings, assumed ownership of private property, appropriated bank accounts—essentially wrested all control of proprietary assets from all existing corporations, foreign or Cuban. Billions of dollars in assets were confiscated. Castro's nationalization program not only brought all business dealings in Cuba to a grinding halt, but effectively destabilized the Cuban economy. Prominent American and European multinational corporations, financial institutions and banks suffered heavy losses.

Kohly brought suit against Castro's government on behalf of both Cuban and foreign interests whose contractual rights or ownership had been usurped by Castro's government.[4] Numerous foreign corporations had executed contracts under the Batista regime which provided them with legal recourse against the Cuban government for infringement of contractual rights and non-performance of contractual obligations under the tenets of the signed agreements. Some multinationals holding total proprietary rights under international trade agreements which provided one hundred percent ownership of Cuban companies by non-Cuban nationals brought suit against Castro's government for full restitution of loss of revenue, capital and profits as the result of the nationalization program.

Kohly's primary interest in Cuba's economic disaster lay signficantly beyond his own personal losses and those of his clients. Kohly wanted restitution for much more than that. He was propelled by a driving nationalist concern for the economic health of his homeland. He wanted to return stability to the Cuban economy and re-establish Cuba as a viable econmic power. Castro had thrown the economy in an uproar. Kohly's nationalist pride would not tolerate this insult to Cuban economic integrity. Imperative for both the economic and political survival of Cuba was the destruction of the Castro regime. For Kohly this translated into one overriding directive: destroy Castro's communist regime and oust the dictator from Cuban soil.

In his excellent English, and with his sophisticated, politic manner, Kohly described in detail this dramatic situation and convinced me to help him and the members of his Cuban resistance movement engineer Castro's political demise. Having eloquently established his position, Kohly politely left Diggs and me to iron out the details.

As persuasive as Kohly was, it really didn't take much rhetoric to convince me of the concept's validity and judiciousness. I had never been able to conjure up a kind thought for Castro or his communist ideology. I was also flattered that this freedom-fighting Cuban resistance leader was interested in employing me and, in the bargain, entrusting me with such an important role in this quest to overthrow Castro's regime. My moment of self-reflection and congratulation was cut short by Diggs's commanding voice.

Amenities completed, Diggs cut right to the meat of the matter, briefing me on the project's specifics. "We need someone who is not connected wth any intelligence agencies or Cuban nationals, but who is qualified to do a variety of unusual and extremely important technical jobs. A certain government agency had embarked on a project to oust Fidel Castro from power in Cuba. He's a dangerous and lethal communist of the first order and a direct threat to the sovereignty of the United States. We're bombarding the Cuban airways with messages of freedom right now. We need your expertise for several vital communication projects immediately."

This was indeed a surprise, and I was stumped by the identity of Diggs's "we." "What makes you think I'm the man?" I asked.

Diggs gave a sly grin. "Aren't you the Robert Morrow with a variety of patents; the senior project engineer of the Martin Company in Baltimore who came to Washington to work on Dr. Clark's Doomsday project, and whose father was John Sandels Morrow, a member of military intelligence during World War II?" I was surprised. It was obvious Diggs had done some extensive homework. I never mentioned my father's background to anyone.

"Well . . . as a matter of fact, yes," I answered, while trying to appear nonchalant.

"Then you're our man."

It was a heady moment. Diggs and Kohly had expertly tapped into my firmly anti-communist sympathies. With my pride significantly bolstered by Kohly's interest and Diggs's knowledge of my past accomplishments, I was ready to actively help the Cuban freedom fighters.

Within a week, I was making feverish plans to supply Kohly's Miami resistance forces with communications gear and more. His men were successfully raiding Cuba daily. They were tough. Kohly was also. Manners and diplomacy aside, he held the line and accepted nothing less from those who worked with him. Since we spent the next several months working closely with one another, I gained his respect and we both grew to trust each other implicitly.

CHAPTER ONE NOTES:

1. See Appendices.
2. It was applied for in May of 1960 and issued in 1963, and can be seen in the Appendices.
3. As clarified in a subsequent memorandum written by Diggs, "He had established a brokerage business which included transactions in real estate, mortgages and insurance. From this he had gotten heavily involved in finance, putting together syndicates for the financing of large government projects such as the French Key Project of building roads to the seaports, land reclamation projects, small housing projects and culminating in 1956 with the financing of the Hilton Hotel. He was working on an 80 million dollar project, Canal Via Cuba, when Castro began his activity."
4. See Appendix *** for list of companies for whom Kohly brought suit against the Csatro government and for whom he acted as a representative.

2

March–September 1960

On March 17, 1960, President Eisenhower, at the urging of the National Security Council, authorized the formation of a top secret committee allowing the CIA to conduct a *Program of Covert Action Against the Castro Regime*. This committee became known as the *5412 Committee*, its formation having originated with the implementation of *National Security Council Directive 5412/2*. As stipulated by the *Directive*, the committee employed a four-point program designed to achieve the following:

1. Create a Cuban government in exile.
2. Start a powerful propaganda offensive.
3. Create a covert intelligence and action organization inside Cuba.
4. Create a paramilitary force outside of Cuba for future guerilla action.

With the exception of points 2 and 4, the CIA knew that Mario Garcia Kohly had everything else in place. The Agency fulfilled the two remaining items of the *Directive*'s agenda. The propaganda broadcasting was assigned to David Atlee Phillips. The creation of a non-Cuban based paramilitary force—the future *2506 Brigade*—was placed in the capable hands of my future case officer Tracy Barnes, and E. Howard Hunt.

11

* * *

Ross Schoyer, my business associate, had nearly completed organizing our new Washington apartment complex on 19th Street. Ross was preparing to take over most of my commercial projects. My work with Kohly and the CIA was escalating, and demanded increasingly more of my time.

In addition to assisting in my commercial projects, Ross was also helping me with my social life. He introduced me to a vibrant young girl named Amy. My marriage to Cecily, my wife of five years, had lost its fire. Cecily had never quite recovered from her father's suicide in 1956. Since that time, she and I had become more like friends than a married couple. After our introduction, Amy quickly became a welcome distraction and a shot in the arm when I needed one. She was a secretary for the Marine Corps, but I lured her to my office. She eventually took up residence with me and was both my secretary and lover. At the time I didn't tell Cecily about Amy; it would have added to her depression.

At the end of March I was contacted by Marshall Diggs and given a special assignment. Diggs instructed me to deliver a truckload of electronic equipment—designed to teach radio operators—from Miami to the west coast of Florida. I was to make the delivery, unpack the gear, install it and ensure its smooth operation.

My destination on the west coast of Florida was Useppe Island. It was located on the intracoastal waterway opposite Cabbage Key, between Charlotte Harbor and Captiva Island. In the late 1800's it was a millionaire's resort and sported a hotel, swimming pool, golf course, and isolated cottages. When I saw it, it was over-grown, dilapidated, and the first training facility for the *2506 Cuban Brigade.*

It took me three days to reach my destination. I collected the gear in Miami and transported it by truck across the Everglades on the Tamiami Trail. I arrived at Ft. Myers and rented a boat for the last leg of my journey. My third day was spent unloading the equipment at the ancient dock of the Useppa Island training center. When I had finally finished unloading my cargo, a man who resembled a Cuban hit-man, and not a stevedore, signed the consignment papers. After my delivery was complete, I thought about my encounter with the "receiving agent" cum Cuban hit-man. For the first time, I began to wonder who was financing all this equipment and activity. I knew Kohly was being backed by someone, but didn't know who. I would learn very soon.

In June, three months after my initial meeting with Diggs, I received a strange phone call. It was Diggs. He requested that I come to his home for a meeting. He also requested that I say nothing about the meeting to Mario. When I arrived, Diggs greeted me at the door and guided me to his study. Seated in a large leather chair was a man I had never seen before. Diggs introduced him to me as Mr. Brown from New York. Mr. Brown didn't rise to greet me. When I reached over to shake his hand, he presented his left one to me. I immediately noticed that the thumb and index finger of his right hand were missing. Eventually I learned that Mr. Brown was actually the infamous New York Mafia don, Thomas Luchese.

Diggs explained that Brown was a friend of Mario Kohly's, with close ties to the United States government. He indicated that Brown wished to query me about Kohly's activities, since Kohly and I were working together on an almost daily basis. I was somewhat surprised by Diggs's request and responded with a quizzical look. He nodded his approval to proceed.

In Diggs's presence, I told Brown about the arrangements for the Cuban operation's communications equipment. I also spoke about other communications projects, such as building a jamming device to confuse Castro's field operations. Neither seemed to be overly enthused about my presentation, or for that matter, even interested. The entire discussion had taken all of ten minutes.

When I finished, Diggs thanked me and said he appreciated my stopping by. I was both angry and a little confused. I had given up a dinner date with Al DeBacker and some friends, after having been given the impression that the meeting would require several hours of my time. I shook Brown's hand again, received his thanks for coming, and was escorted to the door by Diggs. Sensing my agitation, Diggs, as we were saying good-bye, explained the importance of my introduction to Brown and the meeting we had just completed. Mr. Brown—or more accurately, Mr. Luchese—represented one of the financial backers who was providing Kohly with funds—the Mafia.

My second meeting with Diggs was quickly followed by a third encounter. Two days after the meeting with Luchese and Diggs, I was contacted by Diggs. He requested that I meet him at his office around 5:30 P.M. It was a Friday and I was preparing to go back to Baltimore for the weekend. I did not want to leave Amy, but Cecily had invited Fred and Jean Weisgal, a prominent Baltimore criminal attorney and his wife, over for a cookout. Diggs assured me that our meeting would be brief. I took him at his word and arrived promptly at the appointed time. Diggs met me at the door and escorted me into his suite of offices.

Initially, I thought Diggs was alone. As we walked further into his office, I heard voices coming from the direction of the law library. Upon entering the library, I saw two men; both stopped speaking as we walked in. I recognized Mr. Brown immediately; the other gentleman was introduced to me as Tracy Barnes. Barnes was employed by the CIA as a deputy to the Deputy Director of Plans and head of the CIA's Covert Operations, Richard Bissell. He was extremely articulate and had a relaxed, self-assured manner about him.[2] Brown excused himself and, nodding goodbye to me, went into Diggs's office.

After we all sat down at the conference table, Barnes asked about my background. I briefly gave him my resumé, including my present projects. I did not make any reference to my association with Mario Kohly's activities. He seemed to approve of my discretion. It was obvious from his demeanor that he was well-informed of both the Cuban's activities and my association with him. After I had completed reciting my employment history, Barnes asked if I would be interested in doing some special projects for Kohly. I told him I would be honored to do anything for my government that would help eliminate the communist threat to our country. Perhaps my statement now sounds a bit trite, but in that day and age, we were all naive and I possibly more so than many.

At any rate, Barnes seemed to approve of my reply and told me to contact Diggs if I thought of anything that might help accomplish our mission more expeditiously and effectively. Our meeting complete, Barnes and I shook hands and I prepared to leave. Diggs escorted me to the door and requested that I say nothing about this meeting to anyone. His request was graciously made, but I received the message loud and clear. I wondered why it had been made. A few days later, I would find out.

I proceeded to keep my appointment in Baltimore and had time on the way to reflect on my two encounters with Luchese and my discussion with Barnes. I was delighted to comply with Barnes's request to assist in "special projects" for Kohly. I was somewhat confused, however, by the very obvious connections between the CIA and at least one Mafia family. At the time, I accepted the CIA's complicity with organized crime by rationalizing that our government had to use every possible weapon at its disposal to fight the communist threat. If achieving victory over communism meant temporarily making a pact with the Devil, well, so be it. Certainly this wouldn't be the first time necessity had made strange bedfellows. I also wondered about the size and the dimensions of the special projects Barnes had mentioned. I wouldn't find out until Tuesday just how big and extensive those projects actually were. At that moment, the cookout in Baltimore had seemed a welcome relief, even if I had had to leave Amy behind.

When I returned to Washington on Monday morning, I received another call from Diggs. He requested that we meet on Tuesday at his home. He told me that "something big was on" and that I would receive my first exposure to one of Kohly's "special projects." When I hung up the phone that Monday after Diggs's call, I did not know that on Tuesday I would receive my first exposure to what would eventually become known as the Bay of Pigs invasion.

When I arrived at Diggs's house on Tuesday afternoon, the place was surrrounded by a swarm of parked cars that jammed both the street and the drive. As I was escorted into the house, I saw men in the study. Several chairs brought in from the dining room accommodated the entire group. The man who spoke was a Cuban whose face I did not recognize. His name, according to the man next to me, was Eladio del Valle. Interspersed among the Americans were Kohly, Bill Grosh, and several other members of Kohly's Cuban entourage. Del Valle introduced to the assembled group several Cubans who had recently escaped from Castro's clutches. These men eventually became the nucleus of Kohly's *United Organizations for the Liberation of Cuba.*[3]

When he completed his introduction, del Valle launched into a loud, passionate speech. Immediately after he finished his speech, he introduced Kohly—the obvious leader of the gathering. Mario had an important announcement to make, and his presence before the gathering brought a silence that quickly enveloped the room. It was very clear that his announcement was not unexpected.

Kohly's speech was as memorable to me as our first meeting. Although the entirety of his speech escapes me now, I remember some of it quite well.

For the past several weeks, members of the administration have been reviewing my plans for the future government of our beloved country. As some of you know, it includes the proposed names and future titles of many of you here. More importantly, it reinstates our 1940 Constitution. I've just received wonderful news today. I am going to form a de facto government in exile for the approval of our hosts and benefactors, the United States of America!

The room erupted with applause. When at last it was quiet enough to continue, Kohly went on.

"This can only mean that now we'll be given the real help we need to regain our homeland. You must use extreme caution in deciding whom you tell about this. Castro's agents are all over Miami and some are probably your friends. My son has infiltrated the Cuban Consultate in Miami and has compiled a list of the most senior agents. I will pass this list on to you before you leave today. I thank you all for coming. We will meet again in a few weeks."

As people made their way to the door, I realized that I had witnessed a truly historic moment. In fact, I realized that I would help make a portion, albeit very small, of American political history. The covert projects Kohly and I were working on (with the CIA) would now receive the full backing and support of the American government.

I remember reflecting upon the historic implications of this meeting when Tracy Barnes excitedly pulled me into the next room and asked, "Well, what do you think?"

Unsure what reaction he expected of me, I asked him to explain the whole speech in his words. His answer contained the first mention I had heard of a plan that eventually evolved into the disastrous Bay of Pigs invasion.

Barnes in a serious tone declared, "It means the CIA is going to strongly recommend Kohly's ideas to form a provisional government after Castro is gone. Kohly's plans have already been given to the powers that be. . . . And that means *all* his plans, including his preparations and actual strategy for the invasion." Barnes hesitated momentarily before plunging forward. "We have a slight problem. The Cuban leaders selected by the State Department vehemently oppose the idea of Kohly as the next Cuban president. The CIA is in favor of Kohly's presidency. Actually, we intend to actively support it. That's why you were chosen to work with Mario; you are there for us."

Barnes stopped speaking for a moment and gave me an opportunity to take in all that he had just conveyed to me. I understood everything he had said, but was puzzled by the overall management of the situation and the role I was expected to play. I looked at Barnes and said, "There are several items I don't understand. If Kohly's plan is approved by the Administration, what's the problem? Why do you need me?"

Barnes looked somewhat exasperated. "I can answer both questions; in order to do so, I must give you some background."

He then proceeded to give me a short snyopsis of Kohly's political history and his plans for orchestrating the Bay of Pigs invasion. According to Barnes, Kohly was a conservative—right-wing,

actually—Cuban banker. He began his political career a year prior
to my meeting him. It seems that he was inspired by the defection
of a friend of his to the United States: Pedro Diaz Lanz,
Commander of Castro's Air Force. Once safe in America, Kohly's
friend denounced Castro for infiltrating the Cuban government with
communists.[4]

When he learned of his friend's actions, Kohly drafted a plan
for a new, provisional Cuban government. With his plan completed,
he then proceeded to establish a Cuban-based resistance movement. He made several trips to Havana—risking his life doing so—
to recruit reliable personnel for his resistance force in Cuba. In the
United States, he created the *Cuban Liberators*—an organization
comprised of former Cuban Army, Navy and Air Force personnel.
At the time of our meeting, Kohly was fortifying his Cuban and
U.S.-based forces, strategically positioning them for deployment
in stage two of the plan. Stage two called for an amphibious landing
of exiles near Trinidad. The landing force would be joined by
Kohly's three-hundred-man guerilla army in the Escambray
Mountains just north of the city.[5].

Barnes maintained that the CIA learned of Kohly's plan
through Marshall Diggs, the influential Washington attorney
responsible for introducing me to Kohly. Richard Bissell, Barnes's
boss, was very excited by Kohly's plan.

I interrupted Barnes's commentary at that point and queried
what the Agency had done so far. Barnes continued enthusias-
tically, "Bissell has set the wheels in motion to implement Kohly's
plan. As of today, we've arranged for aircraft, pilots, the training
of saboteurs and infiltrators, and are ready to recruit and train an
actual invasion force."

I interrupted him to ask if Kohly knew of the resources the CIA
was prepared to place at his disposal.

"Don't tell Kohly about the last part. He's dead set against the
CIA controlling his operations. Our money is welcome, not our
control."

In his commentary, Tracy Barnes neglected to tell me that that
CIA had commandeered Kohly's plan to implement the NSC

Directive 5412/2. I would not discover this until much later; the implications of the CIA's actions would only be made fully manifest after the assassination of John F. Kennedy. Barnes continued with his explanation of the Agency's involvement—what I later learned to be its manipulation—with Kohly.

"The Agency needed Kohly to finalize our plans. Since Kohly is Marshall Digggs's client, we asked Diggs to introduce him to the Vice President. Kohly will do anything for Richard Nixon. He knows the V.P. is the man chairing the Administration's apparatus to see Castro defeated (Nixon was the White House Action Officer heading the 5412 Committee). When Nixon saw Kohly's invasion plans, he was impressed and gave us the go-ahead; once we assured him it could be easily pulled off. The Vice President agreed to give Kohly encouragement. You see, Bob, the project's escalated to the point where we've committed ourselves to following through. We simply can't turn back."

I was still confused. Barnes had mentioned the problem with the State Department and other Cuban exiles and . . . a piece of the puzzle seemed to be missing. I decided to ask the question that might lead me to the missing piece of the puzzle.

"Mr. Barnes, maybe I'm missing something. If you've got the Vice President behind you, and the Administration is satisfied, why is there a problem with other exiles?"

Barnes paused a minute, smiled and said, "There is also one critical person in the Administration who doesn't know our complete plans . . . it's the President!"

All I could reply was, "Uh huh."

Barnes took this as either acknowledgment or acceptance and continued. "But, that doesn't matter. Within a few months Mr. Nixon will be elected, and Kohly will be his choice to head a Cuban government in exile. Then, after a successful invasion, he'll be the next president of Cuba. The problem . . . we can't accomplish any of this without Kohly's forces in the Escambray and his underground."

As I digested all the amazing information Barnes had just relayed to me, he interrupted my thoughts and explained my role in the Agency's plans. "To ensure that our plans are not disrupted, the Agency needs you. Kohly needs an advisor and consultant who he thinks is not involved with the Company. He distrusts our government. We know he trusts you and your good suggestions have helped to calm him down. Keep it up. You must continue to give him good advice . . . especially now that another problem has arisen. The State Department has thrown a monkey wrench into our plans. Kohly is unaware of the situation, but Mr. Nixon can't remedy the problem without divulging our plans. If Kohly gets out of control it could blow everything. So to keep him happy, we'll arrange for you to introduce him to friendly politicians, media people . . . whatever it takes to satisfy him that everything is under control . . . even when it isn't. Like Mr. Nixon, the Company can't do anything to intercede with the Department of State. Now, do you understand, and will you do it?"

I felt flattered that Kohly trusted me and held my advice in high regard. I could also understand the CIA's rationale. I had some qualms about the mission, but understood the Agency's position; it wasn't an easy one. After a few moments I replied with a grin, "Do I have any choice?"

In the weeks that followed my discussion with Tracy Barnes, the CIA's "problem" with the State Department became significantly more difficult and thorny. My problems increased as well; the State Department was complicating Kohly's implementation of his plans against Castro. By August the situation with the State Department was almost too hot to handle. The source of the problem and the primary obstacle to implementing Kohly's plan was William Wieland, Castro's man in our own U.S. State Department. Wieland, seeing Kohly's rise to power within the administration, accused him of being a "Batistaite."[6] The result of Wieland's accusation was the issuance of a State Department directive to Kohly that ordered the immediate cessation of any activity regarding Cuban real estate claims and other legal or fiduciary matters Kohly then had pending against Cuba. He would then be permitted to resume his legal actions against the Cuban government after the presidential elections in November 1960.[7]

The State Department's directive initiated Wieland's campaign to undermine Kohly. Wieland's next maneuver was the establishment of the *Cuban Revolutionary Front (FRD)*. He achieved this by convincing a liberal faction in the CIA to assist in the formation of the *FRD* and to install, as its leaders, former members of Castro's cabinet. The leaders of the *FRD*, according to Wieland's plan, would form their own Cuban government in exile, and thereby destroy Kohly's leadership of the Cuban exile community in the United States. Consequently, Kohly would be deposed as the president of the Cuban government in exile.

When he leared of Wieland's plan, Kohly contacted Diggs and requested that his concern about Wieland's campaign and its liberal supporters in the CIA be conveyed to Nixon. In October, Kohly, while consolidating his political position with the Cuban exile community in Florida, was called back to Washington. He was to meet with General Robert E. Cushman Jr., Nixon's military adviser.

When Kohly arrived in Washington at the scheduled meeting place, General Cushman wasn't there. In his place was a CIA man who claimed that he represented both the General and Vice President Nixon. The CIA representative attempted to convince Kohly to give his allegiance, albeit superficially, to the new *Front*. He attempted to justify his request to Kohly by claiming that the *Cuban Revolutionary Front* was to be chaired by E. Howard Hunt, a man whose sympathies were in complete accord with Kohly.

Unfortunately, Kohly was unimpressed with the CIA representatives arguments and refused to cooperate. Kohly's refusal was predicated upon his knowledge of the *Front* members'[8] former status as constituents of Castro's government hierarchy and as known socialist and communist sympathizers.

Immediately after his October meeting and prior to leaving Washington, Kohly contacted Marshall Diggs. He briefed Diggs on the meeting and requested a personal interview with Richard Nixon, the Vice President. Kohly, confident he could straighten the matter out with Nixon personally, told Diggs that he was returning to Miami and could be contacted there. Upon his return to Florida, Kohly proceeded with his preparation of his Cuban guerilla invasion force. He forgot about Wieland and the bureaucrat's maneuvering with both the State Department and the CIA. Unfortunately for Kohly's cause, bureaucrat Wieland and his CIA cohorts had not forgotten about Kohly.

By the end of October, with plans for the invasion proceeding at a rapid pace, Wieland, acting on behalf of the State Department and against the wishes of Nixon and *FRD* Coordinator E. Howard Hunt, exerted more influence on the CIA to accept additional leftist leaders in the *FRD*. Wieland's idea was to have the *FRD*'s new leftist Cuban leaders head both the impending invasion of Cuba and, upon the invasion's success, the future Cuban government. His rationale for promoting the leftist Cubans was simple: "Kohly's conservative Cubans would be classified automatically as former Batistaites . . . not acceptable to the Cuban people."

As a result of Wieland's pressure and the political force he mustered from the State Department, the more naive liberal elements in the CIA managed to outmaneuver E. Howard Hunt. The *FRD* was then replaced with the liberal CIA faction's own organization, the *Cuban Revolutionary Council (CRC)*. The *CRC*'s membership was composed entirely of the most extreme leftist members of the *FRD*. Their sole purpose was to control the *FRD* and sabotage, if not destroy, Kohly's efforts. Wieland had been shrewd to sidestep Hunt. Hunt never would have accepted the *CRC*'s new leader in the *FRD*. The man selected to head the newly formed council was José Miro Cardona, Fidel Castro's first Prime Minister.[9]

The *Front*, or *FRD*, was now under the complete control of the *CRC*. Only two *FRD* members could be considered moderates, Carlos Prio Socarras and *FRD* director Sergio Arcacha Smith. Smith was directly associated with Louisiana Mafia leader Carlos Marcello. His association with Marcello was the result of his ties with both former FBI agent, Guy Banister and Banister's rabid anti-Castro investigator—who was also Marcello's pilot—David Ferrie.[10]

William Wieland's maneuver, executed with the CIA's liberal faction's assistance, forced Kohly to take a subordinate position to

former members of the Castro regime. This move resulted in both
the isolation of the moderate Cuban exile leader from his own plan,
and the exacerbation of friction between Kohly and the CIA.
Further, Wieland's maneuvering substantially altered the previously smoldering division of the CIA into conservative and liberal
factions; a one time management rivalry had now been escalated
to a war between the two camps. The only saving grace for Kohly
and his plan in this political morass was the appointment of E.
Howard Hunt as the invasion coordinator.

* * *

As a result of my affiliation with the Agency I was well aware of
the internal strife; the political machinations adopted by the
conservative and liberal partisans in their handling of Mario Kohly
and his invasion plan had split the Agency in two. Kohly was caught
between the two factions, and my job, which was becoming
increasingly more difficult to perform, was to walk the tightrope
between Kohly and both factions of the CIA.

When Kohly became aware of the CIA's in-fighting, and the
manner in which he was being used by both factions, his wrath was
nearly uncontrollable. It didn't take long for me to become its
target. In the midst of the drama with both the Agency and the State
Department, Kohly accused me of being a CIA operative. Of
course, he was correct; I could not allow him to realize how much
so. It took me nearly a week, but I did eventually manage to
convince him that my loyalties were completely aligned with his
cause. Admittedly, I felt disgusted with the dissembling I was
forced to do; I had made my promise to Barnes and intended to
keep my word. I did, however, inform Barnes of Kohly's reaction.
He was not surprised; he was both expecting it and worried about
it. I was actually glad to see he was. . . . He should have been.

* * *

Kohly's plans for an invasion of Cuba and the subsequent
establishment of a provisional government committed the Agency
to utilizing Kohly's U.S.-based exile organization, his underground

force inside Cuba, and his guerrilla army hiding in the Escambray Mountains.

The problems caused by Wieland, resulting in the establishment of the CRC, were problematical for the Vice President. As a result of the impending elections and John F. Kennedy's exploitation of the Cuban controversy, Nixon could not publicly endorse Kohly, his plan for the invasion of Cuba, or his provisional government in exile. The CIA decided to assist Nixon in his quandry. The Agency moved to rid Cuba of Fidel Castro in a more direct way: assassination.

As the new invasion coordinator, E. Howard Hunt attempted to save the Kohly plan and recommended the assassination of Castro as an integral part of the overall Cuban operation. To set the wheels in motion, he submitted a memorandum to Tracy Barnes. The memorandum was explosive material, and Barnes had it in my hands within hours. He wanted me to be convinced, after my prevarication to Kohly about my non-CIA involvement, that I could now assure the Cuban exile leader that he had not been betrayed by the United States government. I was to cite Kohly's attorney, Marshall Diggs, as my source of information. Diggs would confirm to Kohly that the promise to assassinate Castro and invade Cuba came directly from Nixon. Barnes would contact Diggs and inform him of the role he was to play. I was convinced. The memorandum was succinct and to the point. I remember seeing it quoted ten years later in Hunt's book *Give Us This Day*.[11] It said: "Assassinate Castro before or coincident with the invasion (a task for Cuban patriots)."

Upon receiving Hunt's memo, Barnes immediately submitted it to his boss, Richard Bissell. Bissell assigned the project to Colonel Sheffield Edwards, the Agency's Director of Security.[12] Edwards gave the assignment to his Operational Support Chief, a former FBI man named James O'Connell.

In August, O'Connell reported to Edwards who then reported to Bissell that the Cuban Mafia was best suited to carry out the mission. Bissell agreed; he rationalized that the syndicate would be highly motivated to salvage their Cuban investments. He commissioned Edwards to proceed. Edwards, in turn, gave O'Connell the go ahead.[13] It was a wild daisy chain of command. No one in authority would take responsibility for implementing the assassination plan. Neither would O'Connell; directly, that is. For him, however, implementation was simple. He knew his old FBI colleague, Robert A. Maheu, the former FBI special agent who had worked for Guy Banister in Chicago, was tough enough to handle the mob. He also knew whom to call to arrange the Mafia hit. It was Las Vegas Mafia don, Johnny Roselli.

Maheu had known Johnny Roselli since the late 1950s and considered him well qualified to finger an assassin to hit Castro. When he met with Roselli at the Brown Derby restaurant in Beverly Hills, however, Roselli seemed reluctant to accept the assignment. His hesitation dissipated quickly when Maheu explained, ". . . high government officials needed his cooperation to recruit Cubans who would eliminate Castro."

With these magic words, Roselli eagerly agreed to assist the CIA. He, like New Orleans Mafia don Carlos Marcello, currently faced deportation proceedings for illegal entrance and domicile in the United States. The proceedings were the result of the unrelenting efforts of then Senator Robert Kennedy.

Roselli made one condition to his acceptance of the assignment: confirmation of his mission of murder with an official representative of the United States Government. On September 14, 1960, Maheu and Roselli met with James O'Connell at the Plaza Hotel in New York.[14] There would be no problem. Roselli knew O'Connell. They had met socially at Maheu's home in Washington.

While Roselli and Maheu were meeting in New York, Deputy Director of Plans Richard Bissell and CIA Security Director Sheffield Edwards were briefing Allen Dulles and CIA Deputy Director General Charles Cabell on the Agency's assassination plans. It was a meeting that would join the CIA and Mafia in a partnership with the Devil.

By the end of September, Roselli, at the request of Maheu, had asked the number-two man in the syndicate, Chicago's Sam

Giancana, to seek the help of Roselli's old Havana boss, Florida's top mobster, Santos Trafficante, Jr.

A few days after Sheffield Edwards and Richard Bissell briefed Dulles and Cabell, Bissell and Cabell briefed Vice President Richard Nixon about the plans to assassinate Fidel Castro. Nixon, unlike President Eisenhower, thoroughly understood the policies of assassination.[15] The plan to assassinate Castro, coupled with his acute political understanding of the expediency of assassination, allowed Nixon to formulate a solution to the problems caused by Wieland's and the liberal faction of the CIA's formation of the *CRC*, their utilization of former Castro cabinet members, and their attempt to form a leftist Cuban government in exile which would ulimately depose Mario Kohly.

It was just after this briefing, and with his plan now formulated, that Nixon, with neither Eisenhower's knowledge nor consent, took action. In October, just a few weeks before the national elections, Vice President Nixon and CIA Deputy Director Cabell met secretly with Mario Kohly on the golf links of the Burning Tree Club in suburban Washington. There a deal was consummated which finally satisfied Kohly. Officially it was to be known as *Operation Forty*.

Although I more or less knew the substance of the meeting from Tracy Barnes, Kohly disclosed the details to me. In simple terms, the Vice President had agreed that Kohly could terminate all of the prominent Cuban leftist leaders of the *CRC* after a successful invasion of Cuba. Kohly was thus assured of becoming the new president of Cuba.[16]

Operation Forty was set up in the belief that it would be in the best national interest and that Nixon, as the next president of the United States, would be in a position to justify such an action. At the time, it was an understandable decision. Kohly claimed that the agreement was reached only after his guarantee to the Vice President that the invasion would be supported with his large Cuban underground and guerilla army.[17]

To accomplish this scheme of mass murder, the leftist *CRC* and *FRD* leaders were to be held prisoners by the CIA until the landing had been secured. They were then to be delivered to the beach and assassinated by Kohly's men.

Shortly after Kohly's meeting with Nixon and Cabell, I again asked Tracy Barnes, in the presence of General Cabell, if in fact Kohly had made a deal with Vice President Nixon. Both men confirmed that an arrangement had been made for Kohly to take over Cuba once the invasion had been successful.

Operation Forty would surface at the fiasco we historically refer to as the Bay of Pigs.

CHAPTER TWO NOTES:

1. He was referring to Swan Island, where CIA's David Atlee Phillips would set up a 50 kilowatt transmitter for bombarding Cuba with propaganda.
2. Tracy Barnes graduated from Harvard Law School and practiced with Carter, Ledyard & Milburn on Wall St. In the OSS, he worked with Allen Dulles in Switzerland, parachuted into occupied France and won two Croix de Guerre's, one with palm and the other with star.
3. The list of these organizations would eventually number over 115 and constitute thousands of persons. See appendices.
4. This was done before the Senate Internal Security Subcommittee on July 11, 1959.
5. In an October 18, 1960 memorandum, Kohly claimed to have 6,000 men organized in the U.S. and 12,000 inside Cuba. See appendices.
6. Nixon was no stranger to using political assassinations as a means of achieving his ends. A Warren Commission document [WCD 279, still classified], disclosed that on January 1, 1955, Nixon attended a meeting in Honduras at which the planned assassination of President José Antonia Remon of Panama was discussed in detail. The hit team hired to kill the Panamanian leader was among those present at the meeting. The following day, Remon was machine-gunned to death at a racetrack outside Panama City.
7. For further illumination of Kohly's legal and fiduciary matters against Cuba, see appendices.
8. Hunt, completely agreed with Kohly. In his book, "Give Us This Day," he reiterated this position continually.
9. In Exhibit Number 28 of the Senate Select Committee on Internal Security, date January 23, 1959. See Appendix, No. ***. José Miro Cardona's name is signed as Cuba's Prime Minister. In an attempt to show the close bond that existed between Cardona and Wieland, ambassador Earl T. Smith would later state in testimony before the Senate Select Subcommittee on Internal Security that: "Many of these people, who later became members of the first Cabinet of Castro were asylees in the United States. They had close contacts with members of the State Department.

   "To name a few: Urrutla, the first President of Cuba, Agramonte, the first Foreign Minister of Cuba, the first Prime Minister of Cuba, Miro Cardona. As a matter of fact, the first time that I met Cardona was after Batista had left the country. It was about the 4th of January of 1959 in the Presidential Palace. He turned to me and said, 'I am a good friend of William Wieland, a very good friend of William Wieland.' "

10. Throughout the latter part of World War II and the late 1940s, Guy Banister was special-agent-in-charge of the Chicago FBI office. Twelve years later, one of Banister's former agents became the CIA's assassination coordinator whose assignments sometimes involved working with the Mafia's assassination coordinator, Sam Giancana. This former FBI agent turned CIA assassin was Robert A. Maheu.

    Guy Banister Associates, a New Orleans private detective agency, owned and operated by Guy Banister, was the employer of several of Marcello's close associates. David Ferrie, Banister's investigator and a CIA operative, would eventually be called upon to plan, coordinate and implement the assassination of John F. Kennedy. Ferrie would be positively identified as a companion of Lee Harvey Oswald.

11. New York: Popular Library Edition, 1973, pg. 38.

12. Senate Intelligence Committee Report on Foreign Assassinations, 1976, pp. 94–96.

13. Ibid.

14. Senate Intelligence Committee Report on Foreign Assassinations, pg. 76.

15. In a Warren Commission document [WCD 279, still classified], Marlon Cooper, a former CIA operative, disclosed that on January 1, 1955, he attended a meeting in Honduras with Vice President Richard Nixon, at which the planned assassination of Prsident José Antonio Remon of Panama was discussed in detail. Among those present: the hit team hired to kill the Panamanian leader. The following day, Remon was machine-gunned to death at a racetrack outside Panama City.

    The author found out about this in early July of 1975, when he was called to testify before the staff of the Senate Select Committee on Intelligence Matters to tell what he knew about Richard Nixon and his association with Mario Kohly. During the course of the hearings he was asked if he knew Marion Cooper. He told them he didn't know Cooper, but had heard his name mentioned in reference to the Vice President on several occasions around 1960.

    The Committee was interested in Nixon because Cooper had appeared on the Lou Staples talk show in Dallas, Texas, a week earlier and had told the story about the meeting of January 1, 1955, on KRLO Radio, June 6, 1975.

    Subsequently, the author was informed that Cooper's statements were validated by a polygraph examiner "of the highest rating." In addition, newsman Joe Pennington of Chicago said he had been able to verify most of the details of Cooper's story in an interview with B. Gary Shaw, February 18, 1983, in Cleburne, Texas.

16. Kohly, in a recorded deathbed statement made in my presence said:

> I had arranged to recruit or to enlist better than three-hundred
> boys who, on a set signal once we took over the island, would meet
> with me and arrange for the overthrow of the CIA-inspired council
> of Miro Cardona and the rest of them. If this had been successful,
> they would have been eliminated almost at once, and I would have
> come into Cuba and taken over. . . . This can be confirmed
> through Mr. Sourwine, in the U.S. Senate, who called me one day
> to meet with one of the troopers who had come out of the Bay of
> Pigs alive and back to the States. And it was this trooper who very
> discreetly divulged our plans to former Senator Owen Brewster
> and stated that each one of them [Kohly's men] was wearing a
> yellow handkerchief around their collar to show who was who and
> to know who each other was, so that at the proper time they could
> communicate. Yellow was chosen because it fitted in with the
> uniforms and would not attract attention as they were current army
> handkerchiefs or bandanas, whatever you wish to call them.

17. Confirmation of this uniform style was also made in Haynes Johnson's
    Book, "The Bay of Pigs," published in 1964 by W.W. Norton, pg. 87.
    Referring to their uniforms:

> As they neared the cargo vessels in the small outboard-motor
> launches, the officers saw the men of the Brigade lining the
> railings, singing and cheering. Each battalion had been issued a
> different colored scarf. Now they were waving them — blue, yellow,
> white, black, red — from each ship.

3

OCTOBER 1960–APRIL 1961

By mid-autumn of 1960, frightening instruments of horror and mass destruction were casting their shadows over Cuba; their ominous presence would eventually contribute to the death of President John F. Kennedy.

British Royal Air Force reconnaissance flights detected unusual military construction while flying over Cuba from Nassau; they increased their surveillance. By the end of October 1960, their aerial photographs revealed sufficient data to ascertain that Russian offensive missile installations were being built on Cuban soil and, further, British Intelligence reported their findings through diplomatic channels to the United States State Department, and the CIA started its evaluation of the information.[1] On the domestic front, the upcoming national elections were giving candidates both the forum and the reason to commence slinging mud at opponents.

Issues involving Cuba were not confined to the usual oblique discussions on foreign policy typical of election year rhetoric. Rather, Communism and the Castro regime took center stage in the battle for the White House. The anti-Castro propaganda disseminated throughout the United States as a result of the extensive efforts expended by CIA man David Atlee Phillips was, by the end of October, increasing the sensitivity of the American people to the threat of communism and communist domination only ninety miles from the American shore.

31

Vice President Nixon, as Action Officer in the White House (chairing the 5412 Committee), decided it was time to once again try and suppress the ex-communist leaders of the *Cuban Revolutionary Council (CRC)*. Nixon alerted Bissell of his intent to suppress the CRC. Bissell briefed Barnes who, in turn, informed both Diggs and me. Diggs and I were briefed so that, in the event of a problem developing in Nixon's plans, we could handle Kohly. Barnes's decision was wise. Problems did develop and something went terribly wrong.

John F. Kennedy was briefed on the Cuban situation by Allen Dulles on July 23, 1960. His briefing by Dulles was limited to a succinct presentation of *National Security Council Directive 5412/2*. Dulles felt that Kennedy was not a serious political threat to Richard Nixon in the upcoming presidential elections. Further, giving classified information to a member of the Kennedy family, particularly with their reputation—established by Joseph P. Kennedy Sr. when Ambassador to the Court of St. James—could be tempting history to repeat itself at an accelerated pace. Unfortunately, in the case of JFK, history did precisely that. Dulles was right.

For John F. Kennedy, the plight of the Cuban exiles was a political weapon to be selectively employed against his opponent Richard Nixon; its proper and most effective utilization dependent upon the information available to him at the time. JFK had such a source of data on the Cuban situation. It was William Wieland, Kohly's old nemesis and Castro's friend in the State Department.

Wieland had nothing to lose by covertly leaking information to Kennedy. If Nixon was elected and Wieland's activity for Kennedy was discovered, he could be branded a communist, lose his job, or even worse, go to jail. On the other hand, if JFK was elected, Wieland would be well-protected against his growing number of conservative enemies in both the State Department and the CIA. Wieland, unlike Allen Dulles, was a Kennedy supporter. He clearly placed his chips on JFK as the winner of the 1960 presidential campaign. To hedge his bet, Wieland, unbeknownst to the CIA, Kohly, and Nixon, introduced the *Cuban*

Revolutionary Council's leftist leaders to Kennedy at the time of the Democratic National Convention. The *CRC* leaders gave the presidential nominee what details they had on the planned Cuban invasion.

On October 17, 1960, Nixon, unaware of Wieland's treachery and the information now in JFK's hand, announced at an American Legion convention in Miami that his "patience with Castro was over; it was time to eradicate this 'cancer' from the American hemisphere to prevent further Soviet penetration. The government was already planning a number of steps."

To create an image of Nixon as a politician who reneged on his promise to the Cuban exile community in particular and the American people in general, Richard Goodwin – an abrasive, pockmarked, twenty-eight-year old former clerk for Supreme Court Justice Felix Frankfurter, and recently hired Kennedy political writer – released a story to *The New York Times* on the day before the last political debate. The *Times'* front page headline screamed: "KENNEDY ASKS AID FOR CUBAN REBELS TO DEFEAT CASTRO. URGES SUPPORT OF EXILES AND FIGHTERS FOR FREEDOM."[3]

The release of *The New York Times* headline and story was a great political coup. Kennedy knew that Nixon, abiding by security restrictions he could not disavow, was bound to limit his debate discussions to the official government line: there was to be no U.S. intervention in Cuban affairs.

Nixon was angry, especially when convinced by a surprised and shaken intelligence community that Kennedy's *New York Times* announcement, obviously made with sufficient knowledge of the facts, jeopardized the security of a United States foreign policy operation.

Nixon's fury stemmed largely from his awareness that the secrecy of the planned invasion and operations to assassinate Castro must remain inviolate. Secrecy must be maintained at all costs. Nixon therefore chose to uphold the official United States position. He deferred to the *Organization of American States'* treaties and international law and attacked Kennedy's proposal as wrong and irresponsible on the grounds that, ". . . it would violate our commitments."

In the debate, Nixon labeled Kennedy's scheme, ". . . the most shockingly reckless proposal ever made by a presidential candidate." Frustrated by the need to remain diplomatic and circumspect, Nixon went on to remind Kennedy of his proposal's flagrant disregard of United Nations mandates which the United States, by virtue of its membership, had agreed to uphold. He stated, "If the United States backed the Cuban freedom fighters, we'd be condemned in the United Nations . . . and wouldn't accomplish our objectives." Kennedy's proposal would be . . . an open invitation for Khruschev to come into Latin America and engage us in . . . a civil war or something worse."

At the time Nixon made this statement, he had been informd of the Soviet's deployment of IRBM missiles into Cuba. With this knowledge, coupled with his obligation to retain the secrecy of the covert Cuban operation, Nixon was forced into a softer public stance on the issue of Cuba. He resolved the dilemma posed by Kennedy by suggesting a quarantine of the island. Ironically, this quarantine plan was later adopted as Kennedy's official policy during the Missile Crisis of 1962. Nixon's presentation of the quarantine at the time of the debate, however, appeared a weak and non-committal response in comparison to Kennedy's forthright and aggressive Cuban policy publicized in *The New York Times*. Kennedy's strategy obviously paid off. The unsuspecting public thought him to be the tougher of the two candidates and declared him the winner of the debate. Nixon's softer stance, though born of secrecy's necessity, may very well have cost the Republican party their seat in the Oval Office. As for Richard Goodwin, Kennedy's political writer, he was impressed by the inadvertent assistance his timely article gave Kennedy: the political destruction of Nixon, a man Goodwin detested.

Political strategists atribute Kennedy's very narrow November 1960 victory as the result of highly diverse elements: the first, as we have seen, was *The New York Times* headline and article proclaiming the plight of the Cuban exile community; the second, not so well-publicized, was the contribution of Chicago Mayor Richard Daley's political machine. Sam Giancana had bought Mayor Daley and his extraordinary political network. Giancana also had enormous and unquestioned control over Cook County. It has long been believed, and Giancana himself intimated, that Giancana helped deliver the state of Illinois to Kennedy.

Appreciative of the helpful information provided by the Cuban leftist leaders of the *CRC*, President-elect John Kennedy became an ally of the *CRC*. He also defended Wieland, who was considered by some members of the Senate to be a communist security risk.[4] Kennedy's close association with the wrong group of Cuban exiles (Castro's ex-associates) continued for the next couple of years.

Kennedy's support of the *CRC* and Wieland were extremely harmful to Kohly. By supporting the *CRC*, Wieland continued to prevent Kohly and his forces from achieving significant power, and obtaining his goal. Kohly and his followers were absolutely frantic, and neither Diggs nor I could calm their panicked fears. At the time, I did everything possible to convince Kohly of continued United States support and loyalty. I had even considered revealing to Kohly both Diggs' and my association with the CIA, thus firmly assuring him of the Agency's solid support. When I suggested my idea to Diggs, his response was an emphatic no. Diggs maintained that he could neither jeopardize his friendship with the Agency nor the new administration. He suggested that I handle Kohly in the manner I deemed most appropriate. From that day forward, my relationship with Kohly became one of genuine trust and respect. I never directly revealed my association with the Agency to him, but I never denied it when he asked. Sensing a change in me, Kohly became more calm. I assured him of my fidelity to the bitter end. Little did I know then how much my assurance would cost.

Shortly after Kennedy's presidential inauguration, CIA Director Allen Dulles and Deputy Director of Plans Richard Bissel briefed the new president about the Cuban exile training operations currently set up in Florida and Guatemala. Kennedy was also informed of the plan to invade Cuba, using the Cuban exiles as an informed of the plan to invade Cuba, using the Cuban exiles as an expeditionary force, with additional support to be provided by Kohly's guerilla fighters and underground resistance, presently in place on Cuban soil. The President was told that these plans had been sanctioned by the National Security Council and President Eisenhower. He was not informed about Nixon's *Operation Forty* or the secret deal struck between Nixon and Kohly. Concerned about Kennedy's support of his leftist associates on the *Cuban Revolutionary Council*, the two intelligence chiefs opted not to inform him of the Nixon-Kohly arrangement. To do so would potentially jeopardize Kohly and his vital underground, and the participation of the underground was essential if the invasion were to be successful. Neither Dulles nor Bissel briefed Kennedy on the British sightings of suspected Soviet missile sites, then under construction in Cuba, or the CIA-Mafia plan to assassinate Fidel Castro.

Kennedy's unbelievable reaction to Dulles' and Bissel's briefing on the Cuban invasion shocked and dismayed both men. The President demanded that the CIA "put a temporary hold on the invasion." His rationale for ordering a momentary hold on the operation was quite simple: he wanted a second opinion. The shift of power from the Eisenhower to the Kennedy Administration was rendering Washington even more chaotic and treacherous than usual. Kennedy was adding fuel to a fire already burning nearly beyond control. The President's "hold" may only have been temporary, but his order clearly signaled a warning to the operation's coordinators and leaders: the new man in charge may not allow business to continue as usual. To make assumptions contrary to Kennedy's obvious assertion of power would be a very foolhardy, if not dangerous, undertaking.

With his temporary "hold" in place, and against the CIA's wishes, JFK sent some leftist Cuban leaders from the *CRC* to the Guatemalan military training center. His intent was to take control of the invasion operation by putting his own team in place—a plan consistent with the earlier machinations of William Wieland and the conservative faction in the CIA. The result of the *CRC*'s leaders' presence in Guatemala was the near-destruction of both the invasion force and the very operation they were sent to command. Upon their arrival, JFK's men attempted to usurp the authority of the *Brigade* commander who, along with half of the 500 men stationed there, resigned from the force. By late January, the remaining members of the invasion *Brigade* were ready to mutiny.

Once again, I was placed in the position of reaffirming the United States Government's support to Kohly and winning back his cooperation. Without Kohly's men in Cuba, the invasion did not stand a chance. With behind-the-scenes assistance from the CIA, a new invasion *Brigade* leader was announced. Barnes contacted me prior to the announcement and requested that I secure Kohly's approval of the new *Brigade* commander. The new leader, Manuel Artime, although a former Castro officer, eventually became a trusted associate of Kohly's. Predictably, he was not well received by Kennedy's left-leaning Cubans who controlled the operation. Kohly was momentarily appeased by our move to wrest the leadership of the *Brigade*'s command from Kennedy's henchmen and our assurances that *Operations Forty*'s secrecy would remain impenetrable by the Kennedy administration.

The leaders of the *CRC* did not take the replacement of the *Brigade*'s leadership in mute silence. They complained to Kennedy, and claimed that their control of the invasion operation had been usurped by the CIA. Ever watchful of any slight to his authority, Kennedy responded vindictively at the Agency's insubordination; he stubbornly refused to set a date for the invasion to commence. JFK had clearly decided to show the CIA who was Commander-in-Chief.

Kennedy's ire did not remain dormant with the CIA's insubordination, unfortunately. It was soon to be substantially escalated—and to include the wrath of Robert Kennedy, the Attorney General, as the result of further political machinations by both William Wieland and the *CRC* leadership.

Wieland and the leftist faction of the Cuban exile community—in addition to the *CRC*—were dismayed by the CIA's usurpation of the *Brigade* leadership. The new *Brigade* commander was clearly a threat to the power the *CRC* exercised. To redress the power imbalance caused by the conservative faction of the CIA's appointment of Manuel Artime, Wieland and his compatriots told JFK and his brother Robert that the invasion *Brigade* was partially funded by the Mafia in an attempt to secure the return of their Cuban holdings. Cuba had been a significant profit-producing center for the Mafia under Batista's regime, and prior to Castro's revolution. The Mob, through their Cuban syndicate affiliations, had controlled the major portion of many bordellos, gambling houses and drug operations. The contents of Wieland's disclosure infuriated the Kennedy brothers, particularly Robert, who was actively implementing enforcement of his campaign against organized crime; a campaign which commenced in 1957 when he was chief counsel of the McClellan Committee. The involvement of the Mafia with sanctioned government operations threatened the fulfillment of the Attorney General's first priority: the destruction of the Mafia in the United States. Politically, the Mafia-CIA connection, in addition to being another example of the CIA's position of total autonomy, rendered the Kennedy administration's credibility vulnerable to attack by both the media and the public. Further, in the eyes of the Kennedys, it provided a potential vehicle with which both Kennedys could be rendered vulnerable to pressure from Mafia leadership. The wrath of the Kennedys was equal in intensity to that of the CIA. Wieland and his colleagues' disclosure threatened the exposure of the Mafia-CIA plan to assassinate Castro, the revelation of which would disrupt, if not destroy, the planned invasion of Cuba.

The president, in response to Wieland's accusation, placed the invasion on hold for yet another month. By late February, a frustrated Dulles warned JFK that a further delay in the implementation of the invasion would be fatal. His warning went unheeded; Robert and JFK both agreed to order Dulles to cease all anti-Cuban operations until such time as their advisors could be consulted and opinions from less biased parties heard. Although JFK's request made sense, he had waited too long to solicit the opinions of other advisors. Castro, anticipating a move by the resistance forces already operative in Cuba, had launched an offensive against all resistance in an effort to solidify and secure his regime. Kohly's guerilla army, as one of the resistance movement's operatives in Cuba reported at the time, was being chewed up in the Escambray Mountains.[5] The underground radio reports from Cuba looked dismal. Tracy Barnes told me that the situation was beyond control; there was nothing more he could do.

Wieland and his colleagues' exposure of the Mafia-CIA association was well-timed. Robert Kennedy, empowered with this new information, could expeditiously kill two birds with one stone: embarrass the CIA, and accelerate his campaign against organized crime. As at that point neither Kennedy was informed about the CIA-Mafia collaboration to assassinate the Cuban dictator, Robert naively dug himself in for a major assault against the Mafia. By doing so, he sabotaged Kohly's underground with even greater expediency than Wieland's behind-the-scenes maneuvering could ever achieve.

RFK's first target was Carlos Marcello, the New Orleans crime boss who had financed a significant portion of the anti-Castro exiles' expenses in his territory, the states of Louisiana and Texas. Marcello's Mafia empire had been identified by the McClellan Senate Committee as the key distribution point for drug shipments entering the United States.[6] Therefore, to remain consistent with the administration's directive to cease all anti-Castro aid, RFK's decision to target Carlos Marcello was the most logical and expedient means by which to stop Mafia funds from reaching the Cuban exile organizations.

As Robert Kennedy proceeded with his pursuit of Carlos Marcello, John F. Kennedy initiated actions within another domain. On March 11, 1961, he called a White House meeting on the subject of the invasion. The following members of the administration and adjunct agents were present: the Secretary of State, the Secretary of Defense, three members of the Joint Chiefs of Staff, numerous assistants, CIA Chief Allen Dulles and the Agency's Head of Covert Operations, Richard Bissell. After a lengthy debate, the President scrapped Trinidad as the landing site for the invasion of Cuba, claiming it to be too spectacular. He proposed that an intensive search for a new site be pursued, and directed that the meeting's attendees commence their search and report their conclusions to him in fourteen days. JFK requested that the site to be selected facilitate two prerequisites; a quiet landing at night and a landing which did not necessitate American intervention. Fourteen days later three choices were presented to the president; from these, the site selected was the Bay of Pigs, one hundred miles west of Trinidad, in Las Villas Province.

By the time this March 11 meeting had taken place, Kennedy's consistent delay of the invasion had caused the near-decimation of Kohly's 300 man army in the Escambray Mountains.[7] The delays had given Castro ample time to seek out and destroy the resistance fighters. Unbeknownst to Kennedy, the movement of the invasion away from the Trinidad site had caused the destruction of this armed guerrilla force and rendered the proposed invasion of Cuba without air cover doomed before it began. Kohly's force in the Escambray was the only immediate aid the invading Cuban exiles would have received and were, therefore, one of the necessary ingredient for the success of the invasion.

Although the decimation of Kohly's force in Cuba was an enormous setback for the Cuban exile community, the information transmitted to Kohly by his men, prior to their demise, was of extraordinary significance to the security of the United States. Their sacrifice was not in vain.

Kohly's men uncovered hard evidence of Soviet missile site construction before they were completely decimated by Castro's troops. Kohly, immediately upon his reception of this information, contacted Marshall Diggs and relayed the information to him. Diggs contacted the Attorney General and arranged a meeting between Kohly and RFK. Kohly later informed me of his meeting with the Attorney General and his surprise with the manner in which RFK handled Kohly's presentation of the evidence. According to Kohly, the Attorney General was uninterested in Kohly's men's evidence of Soviet activity in Cuba. RFK politely dismissed Kohly and the evidence he presented with the usual bureaucratic brush-off, "We'll look into it" – a sure indication that the matter would be shelved in some forgotten tomb, housing equally uncomfortable situations which the Justice Department thought inconvenient to address. Unfortunately, this missile problem would not remain buried in one of RFK's back rooms and, after the Bay of Pigs fiasco, would rear its ugly head quite noticeably.

After Kohly's discussion with the Attorney General, and while JFK's staff sought an alternative landing site for the invasion, RFK made his first big strike against the Mob: twelve days before the Bay of Pigs invasion, he had Carlos Marcello seized by Federal agents while walking along a street in New Orleans. The crime czar was driven to a waiting jet liner, in which he was the sole passenger, and flown to Guatemala.

Marcello was given no chance to pack a bag, call his wife or, more importantly, his lawyer.

The deportation – or a more appropriate term, kidnapping – at the hands of Robert Kennedy enraged the New Orleans Mafia leader. He declared war on both Kennedy brothers. Friends and associates of Marcello stated that he spoke of little else for weeks.

With Marcello's seizure and arrest by RFK, Kohly lost his financing for the Cuban underground. This, coupled with the decimation of his guerilla force in the Escambray Mountains of Cuba, prompted Kohly to fear that he was in danger of losing CIA funding for his Cuban underground and his invasion plan.

In a desperate bid to relieve his precarious financial situation and continue supporting his Cuban underground resistance, he solicited the aid of two Mafia dons: Meyer Lansky and Santos Trafficante. Against my advice, he promised, upon becoming President of Cuba, a reinstatement of the Mafia's Cuban casino rights in exchange for immediate financial assistance. This accord was reached, in my presence, at Kohly's Washington, D.C. residence and was finalized in the offices of Marshall Diggs. C. H. Polley, the Washington liaison "officer" for Lansky and Trafficante, represented the two absent Mafia dons at the meeting with Marshall Diggs.

With the finalized accord between Kohly and the Mafia dons Lansky and Trafficante in place, Trafficante immediately set to work. He understood that the financial interests of the Mafia would be best served with the expeditious replacement of the Castro regime. The obvious means by which to achieve this end was a successful invasion of Cuba followed by the establishment of Kohly's provisional government. As Trafficante knew of the Kennedy administration's delays in granting consent to proceed with the invasion, he pressured CIA assassination coordinator Robert Maheu into using the Agency's clout with the administration to present the urgency of a quick and incisive plan of action.

It is unknown what effect Trafficante's pressure actually had on the CIA, if any. On April 10, however, President Kennedy made a complete reversal of his formerly held position and gave his consent to proceed with the invasion of Cuba. His consent was given, ostensibly, as the result of a massive briefing by attendees of the March 11 invasion site meeting: representatives from the departments of State and Defense, the Joint Chiefs of Staff, the Senate Foreign Relations Committee, and the CIA (Bissell).

According to Tracy Barnes, my case officer, Richard Bissell informed JFK of a key factor in the invasion unknown to anyone save CIA Director Allen Dulles, General Cabell and Bissell: The Bay of Pigs invasion was designed to cover a flying mission into Cuba's Camaguey Province. The mission's objective was to assess the progress made by the Soviets on the construction of their missile installations. To cover this operation, a secondary invasion was to take place concurrent with the primary invasion landing. The purpose of this secondary invasion was twofold: it was to be a diversion for the main assault and to divert Castro's troops from the site of the clandestine aircraft's landing.[9]

This diversionary force was slated to land thirty miles east of the U.S. naval base at Guantanamo. It would be under the command of Nino Diaz, a young Cuban exile from New Orleans. The men who comprised the diversionary force were trained in New Orleans by Sergio Arcacha Smith. Smith was the associate of New Orleans' Mafia leader Carlos Marcello and ex-FBI man Guy Banister. The pilot selected to fly the clandestine mission into Cuba, with myself on board, was Dave Ferrie, Carlos Marcello's personal

pilot.[10] Ferrie and I would be briefed when the mission was
declared a "go."

On Friday evening, April 14, 1961, I received a call from
Diggs at my home in Baltimore. He informed me the mission into
Cuba was a "go," and requested I meet him at 8:00 A.M., on
Sunday at his home. When I replied affirmatively, he said that I
would be gone for several days. After concluding my conversation
with Diggs, I attempted to contact Kohly. I had spoken to him
earlier, prior to leaving Washington, but was unable to reach him
on Friday evening. I thought it strange that Kohly was not available,
but decided to try again later. On my second attempt I was able
to reach Mario's wife, Doris. She informed me that Mario had been
called out of town early. I requested that she inform him of my
call and ask him to call back upon his return. Saturday arrived
quickly and was soon followed by my early Sunday departure for
Diggs's home in Washington. Our appointment was scheduled
for 8:00 A.M.

By the time I was ready to depart for Washington, I had still
not heard from Kohly. I arrived at at Diggs's home at the scheduled
time. Tracy and Diggs were in front of the house, awaiting my
arrival. Tracy was to drive me to my briefing. He greeted me
cordially and said, "Give Diggs your car keys while I throw your
bag in my car. The General's waiting." Diggs told me he would take
good care of my new car and wished me luck. Barnes and I quickly
took our leave of Diggs and headed to our destination. In the rush,
I had forgotten to call Kohly.

On the way to the briefing, we stopped to pick up an unusual
looking man who was waiting for us in front of the Washington
Hotel. Barnes introduced him to me as Dave Ferrie, the pilot who
would fly the mission I was to undertake. With Ferrie aboard, we
continued on our way to the briefing.

The briefing took place at a Naval Research Facility across the
street from the State Department. We were briefed by General
Cabell who was casually dressed in a sports shirt and slacks.
Cabell's presentation was quick and to the point: "Your destination
will be the Camaguey mountains, where you will be met by your

friend Kohly's guerillas. You will fly due south from the mouth of the Caloosahatchee River at an airspeed of 160 knots for fifteen minutes, then onto a heading of 128 degrees, at which time, if you are in your proper position, you should pick up the Key West beacon twenty-five miles to your left at 222 degrees. Key West will not be visible at your altitude. Maintain your 128 degree heading for another ten to fifteen minutes; you should then pick up the guerilla radio beacon located on the beach. If you don't pick it up within eighteen minutes, scrub the mission and return home. If you don't exceed an altitude of 100 feet, you'll be flying beneath the range of Castro's radar, as well as ours at Guantanamo. Frequency for the guerilla locator beacon will be given to you just before you take off. Needless to say, you are to maintain complete radio silence.

"Now comes the clincher. It's likely that no one will detect you because we have arranged a sizeable diversion. Two guerilla assault forces, one staged and launched from Central America and the other from the Florida Keys, will be going ashore about an hour before you take off. One will land approximately fifty miles south of your beacon location, across the island at a place called Bahia Cochinos—the Bay of Pigs. The other will land near Guantanamo at Pinar del Rio. If all goes as planned, this affair should keep the Cubans busy while you complete your mission, pick up a passenger, turn tail, and get the hell out."

When neither Ferrie nor I said anything, Cabell continued, watching us intently to be sure we were reading him, "Once you have passed over the locator beacon, it will be turned off. You should then spot an arrow-shaped line of burning smudge pots which will give you your first overland heading.

"Your checkpoints, if not full arrows, will be groups of smudge pots spaced every seven to ten miles. The number of pots will give you your altitude; or, if they manage an arrow, separate pots off to one side will indicate what your minimum altitude should be in hundreds of feet. For example, if three pots are lit, you should fly at an altitude of 300 feet or more; four, 400; and so on. You should maintain an airspeed of ninety knots once you have crossed over the beach. Your landing strip will be about forty-five miles inland. It will be marked on each side by a row of electric lanterns. I don't know how long the strip will be, but we're making sure it'll be more than enough to land safely."

Ferrie interrupted. "How much is enough, General?"

"We'll try to give you 1800 feet. Remember, you've got a Super G model with tricycle gear."

"Great!" Ferrie said sarcastically.

Concerned by the risks of the flight, I was annoyed by his attitude. Cabell ignored it and came to the point.

"The purpose of your mission is twofold. For some time Guantanamo has been monitoring unusual pulse transmissions that appear to be coming from Camaguey. They are too weak to be identified by Guantanamo, but we suspect they are the sort associated with guidance systems for drone aircraft or similar devices."

"Your job, Robert, will be to try to record or analyze those transmissions and identify their precise function and, hopefully, their source. You will also bring out one of Mario Kohly's principal lieutenants, Eladio del Valle, who may have some additional information."

Our briefing took no longer than one hour. Tracy Barnes, Ferrie and I dropped General Cabell off at Quarter's Eye—the CIA Operations center—and then continued toward our next destination: National Airport. Ferrie and I had a flight to catch. Our journey to Cuba would begin in Miami.

CHAPTER THREE NOTES:

1. I have in my possession a memorandum that quotes a former R.A.F. squadron leader and later MI-6 (British Intelligence) man as saying: "The R.A.F. knew of the missiles as early as October of 1960, and the British government passed the information on to our State Department." See Appendices.

2. Wieland, in August of 1960, was being investigated by the Senate Subcommittee on Internal Security for his communist leaning by chief counsel for the committee, Julian G. Sourwine.

3. *The New York Times*, October 19, 1960.

4. As late as January 25, 1962, President Kennedy continued to defend Wieland, even though he was considered a security risk by the Senate Subcommittee on Internal Security matters. In an article of that date entitled "President Rebukes a Reporter," the President's reply to the accusation of Wieland and a State Department associate being a security risk was: "In my opinion, Mr. Miller and Mr. Wieland, the duties they have been assigned to . . . they can carry out without detriment to the interests of the United States and I hope without detriment to their character by your question."

5. Barnes told me that the information regarding Kohly's guerilla army was conveyed to Castro agents in Miami from some of the leftist CRC members. They felt its destruction would help stop Kohly's influence with the CIA.

6. Senate Committee on Government Operations, Organized Crime, and Illicit Traffic in Narcotics, 88th Congress, pp. 800–801.

7. On March 23, 1961, Captain Enrique Lianso picked up the last 12 survivors of the Escambray and took them to the U.S. They had fought their way out of the mountains and were wounded, starved, and defeated.

8. This information was confirmed, in an interview with Mario Kohly, Jr., on October 11, 1977.

9. Wynden, Simon & Schuster, p. 170; Johnson, Norton, p. 96; Morrow, Regnery, pg. 4.

10. Ferrie, as a contract agent for the CIA, claimed to have flown on several hazardous missions into Cuba, one on the night of the Bay of Pigs where he landed. Ferrie's role as a CIA agent was confirmed in 1975 when Victor Marchetti, former Deputy Assistant to Richard Helms, told Robert Sam Anson that Helms disclosed, in executive discussions during the Garrison investigation, that Ferrie had in fact been employed by the CIA.

4

APRIL 17–24, 1961

On Sunday April 16, 1961, at 1:30 P.M., while Dave Ferrie and I met at the Miami airport, the members of the *Cuban Revolutionary Council* began what was publicly announced as a long afternoon session at the Lexington Hotel in New York. The previous day, the Council introduced the new cabinet posts of the Cuban provisional government in exile: Tony Verona, Secretary of War; Antonio Maceo, Secretary of Health; Manuel Ray, Chief of Sabotage and Internal Affairs; Justo Carrillo, Economic Administator; and Manuel Artime, "Delegate in the Invading Army." It was not surprising that Kohly's two friends in the CRC, Carlos Prio Socarras and Sergio Arcacha Smith—neither of whom were present at the April 16 meeting—had not been assigned cabinet posts. Nor was it shocking that Manuel Artime, the man commanding the *Brigade* and about to invade Cuba, was assigned the temporary post of delegate to the Council; this post, of course, a gesture of political goodwill and applicable only for the duration of actual invasion of Cuba. At 3:30 P.M., with the exception of the three members just mentioned, the remaining *CRC* members attending the meeting were escorted by five Americans in plain clothes through a back delivery entrance of the Lexington Hotel. The press was informed that the meeting was to be continued at a secret location. In point of fact, the *CRC* members were escorted to a waiting plane, taken to Opa Locka Naval Air Base in southern Florida, and placed upon their arrival under house arrest. True to their word and the provisions of Nixon's *Operation Forty*, the CIA was preparing the promised delivery of the *CRC* members to their murdurous fate. If the invasion of Cuba was successful the *CRC*

47

members would meet their deaths on the beach in Cuba, having never served a day as cabinet members of the Cuban provisional government in exile. The political machinations of William Wieland and his leftist supporters in both the State Department and the CIA would come to naught; that is, if the invasion of Cuba was successful.

*   *   *

Concurrent with the meeting and abduction of the *CRC* members in New York, was our arrival in Miami. We were met at the Miami airport by two men, neither of whom I had met prior to that first meeting nor would after. Our escorts quickly brought us to an awaiting car and drove, silently, to Opa Locka Naval Air Base. The base, surrounded by thick and lush vegetation, seemed abandoned. Our drivers brought us to a section of the field clearly isolated for the CIA's use. We arrived at what appeared to be an unused hanger. Our escorts told us to go inside, and quickly drove away.

The silence and inactivity of the hanger's surrounding area was certainly not reflected inside the hanger. Both Ferrie and I were shocked by the bustling activity. A tri-gear Twin Beech airplane seemed to be the focus of attention. Clearly it was the plane about which we had been briefed hours before in Washington. Men were hurriedly loading gear into its cabin, which had been converted into a cargo bay as Ferrie and I walked over to inspect the plane upon which the success of our mission, and our lives, were partially dependent.

Dave Ferrie, who had hardly spoken to me since our departure from Washington, dropped his gear and said, "Come on, let's check this baby out." He then started an intensive pre-flight check of the plane. As I followed him around, I could tell how conscientious he was. He pulled each prop through, checked the gear and all the flying surfaces, and last but not least, checked the fuel for water. Then we went aboard. Again he was satisfied; he nodded to himself and got out. I followed. The first thing he said, as we were walking toward a table with some charts on it, was, "It's the first time I've gotten a whole plane." He smiled at my expression.

"Usually there is something wrong. . . some instrument that's not working. . . ."

Ferrie paused and looked at me quizzically, before continuing, "I hear you're pretty important to this operation. In fact, I hear the whole reason we're going in is 'cause of the stuff you're testing over there."

"The stuff I'm going to test may be important. I doubt that I am, though—at least, not in the scheme of things going on here. Hell, I don't even see the gear I'm supposed to be using."

Ferrie responded quickly, "They're bring it in from Useppa Island. It's now waiting for us at Buckingham Field which is just outside of Fort Meyers. We'll pick it up, fill the tanks again and then, it's just you and me, Robert. Piece of cake!"

I would remember Ferrie's statement. At that moment, I wanted it to be the truth; my memory of it now is simply an ironic understatement which ominously foreshadowed the terror into which both Ferrie and I were plunged.

As we flew across the Everglades, Ferrie showed me the rudiments of flying the heavy twin engine airplane. I had previously flown a conventional gear Twin-Beech, but had never flown a tri-gear model. Aside from its also being the last and most modern of the Twin-Beech series, it was basically the same as the plane I had previously piloted. Our Twin-Beech must once have been an executive plan. The radar gear and other niceties had been stripped out, but it was clear that the plane still had a very modern and well-equipped instrument planel.

About forty-five minutes after take-off, we spotted the lights of Fort Myers; there weren't many at that time of night. I thought we would continue heading toward Fort Meyer. Ferrie, however, banked sharply and, before I realized what had happened or in what direction we were flying, pointed to a large runway surrounded by swampland, directly before us. There wasn't a building in sight.

"Welcome to Buckingham Field. It was an old Army Air Corps base during the 'Big One.' The only thing left of the base is this overgrown runway. Ten years from now you probably won't be able to find it."

Ferrie expertly landed our Twin-Beech and, as the two of us de-planed, we were promptly met with the lights of an ancient pick-up truck. Two Cubans wearing fatigues emerged from the truck and promptly transferred our gear into the cabin. Ferrie decided against adding fuel from an old rusty fifty-five gallon drum sitting in the back of the Cuban's truck. With our gear on board, Ferrie suggested that I relax and have a cigarette. Everything was ready; we would take off in thirty minutes.

Our thirty minutes had passed quickly. Airborne again, the reassuring drone of the engines penetrated the soundproofing of the twin Beech's cockpit. The red glow from the instrument panel confirmed that all was in order. From the right-hand seat, I could barely discern the dark outline of the Florida coast which was to my left. Occasionally the moonlight, breaking through a rift in the clouds, revealed the Gulf of Mexico rushing beneath us less than 50 feet below.

Ferrie had held a steady course 180 degrees due south since our departure from Buckingham Field. After checking our heading, I checked my calendar watch; it was 3:45 A.M., April 17, 1961.

I was glad it was Dave Ferrie at the controls of the Beech. In civilian life he was an Eastern Airlines pilot and I was comforted by his confident and conscientious manner at the controls. He was very thorough, and clearly very competent. We had been flying for about fifteen minutes when Ferrie, concentrating on resetting the gyro compass, banked to the left and took a 128 degree heading. The coast of Florida disappeared as we skimmed the Gulf's surface without lights; only the blue-white exhausts from our powerful engines were visible. When Ferrie changed our course I turned the ADF (Automatic Radio Direction Finder) to check the Key West beacon which had been approximately 45 degrees to my left. Now the indicator arrow swung directly to 222 degrees, indicating our new heading. The instruments confirmed what I immediately sensed when Ferrie changed our course. My shoulders twitched with apprehension; we were headed directly to the center of Cuba.

"We'll hold this course for another fifteen minutes until we pick up the guerrilla beacon on the ADF," Ferrie said, breaking a long silence. "It should be close to the beach." He reached over and turned to a new frequency.

"I suppose that's meant to be reassuring," I replied, "but what if it isn't there?"

"It will be. But if you really want something to be nervous about, remember Cabell's instructions. We go VFR[2] after that."

In just the short time I had flown with him, I knew that Ferrie was a top-notch pilot. After God knows how many clandestine missions he was still alive, so he had to be. Yet I couldn't recall our instructions without misgivings. Enough of these operations had ended up in disaster. The middle of Cuba was no place for an American to be.

Furthermore, the flight plan itself, however intimidating, was only the beginning. Although crude by today's standards, in the cabin behind me was a custom-built, battery-operated Tektronix spectrum analyzer with a Polaroid camera attachment. I also had a portable instrumentation tape recorder, with a frequency capability to record most electronic control pulses. I had used this gear before, but never under these conditions.

Before long, as I stared out the cockpit window, I began to see the phosphorescent glow of surf breaking along the Cuban beach, approximately seven miles in front of us. Focusing on the instrument panel, I saw that we were almost over the locator beacon. The luminous indicator needle of the ADF began fluctuating wildly, then stopped; the beacon had apparently been turned off. As we flashed low over the narrow strip of sand, blackness again engulfed us. Without changing power settings, Ferrie pulled up the nose of the Beech and took us to 250 feet. Levelling off, we spotted — slightly to the right of the Beech's nose — the faint glow of flickering lights in the distance. Soon we swept over a crude arrow made up of about twenty burning smudge pots, pointing approximately 30 degrees to our left. As Ferrie executed the left bank, the lights disappeared beneath our wings. Looking to my left, I saw that they had been promptly extinguished. As we flew inland, we repeatedly spotted the smudge pot arrows positioned as Cabell had described in our briefings.

We had changed our heading four times as directed by the
pots, and were now flying at an altitude of 1150 feet, only 100 feet
above the increasingly rough terrain below. As we crossed over the
fifth smudge pot arrow, Ferrie slowly eased the throttle back in
order to decrease the Twin Beech's airspeed. At seventy-five knots,
he lowered the flaps to 30 degrees and extended the landing gear.
Two minutes later, out of nowhere, about forty powerful lantern
beams drilled the darkness, feebly lighting up a flat area approximately a thousand feet in length. It was a quarter of a mile ahead
and no more than a hundred feet below. At the far end of a
makeshift runway, the headlights of a small vehicle suddenly
flashed on, the beams crisscrossed the lanterns and formed a series
of guides on the runway. Thirty seconds later we had landed; the
lanterns blinking out as we rolled past them. Ferrie cut the power,
and we rolled 800 feet to a gentle stop. He had made it seem as
simple as a landing at Washington's National Airport.

Within seconds of our landing, our plane was surrounded by
a group of bearded men in battle fatigues, carrying Thompson
submachine guns slung over their shoulders. For a wild moment,
I thought they might be Castro forces, until Ferrie anxiously
shouted out his open window to the man who was apparently their
commander. "For God's sakes, keep them back till the props stop."

"Okay, amigo."

The short, tough-looking Cuban commander, wearing a pair
of captain's bars pinned to the collar of his fatigues, was indis-
tinguishable from his men. I recognized him immediately but could
not recall where I had last encountered him. . . . I quickly
remembered; he was the man who introduced Kohly at the big
meeting held at Digg's home, Eladio de Valle. I was to learn
much later that he was formerly a wealthy Cuban congressman who
financed some of Ferrie's activities through his anti-communist
civilian and armed forces. Valle's organization would later become part of Kohly's United Organizations for the Liberation of
Cuba.[8]

As the engines were dying down, Ferrie turned to me and
identified the captain with whom he had spoken only moments

before as Pepe Arnez. He then said, "You get the hatch, and let's start unloading the cargo. We'll have to move to be out of here before daybreak."

Until these words were spoken, the mission had seemed somewhat unreal to me. Reality came quickly. It was only 4:25 A.M.; we had taken off from Florida less than one hour earlier. As I squeezed past Ferrie in the crowded cabin, he began unstrapping my gear which was lashed to rings on the floor. The hatch swung down to form the stair ramp. Before I could deplane, del Valle reached up, grabbed my hand, and announced with great dignity, "Welcome to Cuba, compadre. I take it you're the electronics expert the chief sent." This was real. I had arrived in Castro's Cuba.

I greeted "Arnez" standing in the middle of the stair ramp, "Right, Sir. My name's Bob Porter." It was the code name I had been assigned during my briefing with Barnes and Cabell in Washington.

As I continued to walk down the remaining stairs, Arnez said, "Pepe Arnez, here, and knock off the sir. No relation to Desi, I'm sorry to say. Please call me Pepe."

Arnez appeared to be about forty, but could have been older; I couldn't be sure as his trimmed beard hid many potentially revealing signs of age. His eyes were black in the dim light, all but a few lanterns near the Beech having been extinguished by Arnez's men.

Ferrie quickly deplaned, reached past me, and vigorously shook Pepe's hand. "Glad to see you," he said, "We don't have much time, so you and Bob had better get moving."

Pepe and I loaded my gear into a World War II-vintage jeep and began a grinding ride, without lights, up the nearby mountainside. At the top of the ridge, we reached a level plateau. Pepe cut the jeep's engine, jumped out, and began unloading my gear. While I opened the first container, he took a pair of night infrared binoculars from the jeep and surveyed the countryside. Then he pointed to a flat rock that could serve as a working surface. "It's best you set up here," he said. "We should be good for at least another forty-five minutes."

I worked feverishly to set up the sophisticated electronics gear.
A few minutes later, the first signals appeared on the screen of the
spectrum-analyzing oscilloscope. After sweeping the lower frequencies with negative results, I shifted to a higher range. Within
ten more minutes I had locked onto a very unusual transmission.
I knew at once that it was useless to attempt a tape recording
because the response of the recorder was far below what I was
receiving.

But what surprised me most was the intensity of the signal. It
had to be originating nearby. None of the reports from our naval
base at Guantanamo, about 175 miles southeast of our present
location, had indicated that we could expect to find signals of this
magnitude. Fascinated, I took photographs of the high-and low-
frequency segments of the pulses appearing on the oscilloscope
screen, snapping the shutter as rapidly as I could. I was so engrossed that I didn't notice that Pepe, lying beside me peering
through his night binoculars, had spotted something far down the
canyon near the top of the opposite slope.

"Madre de Dios!" he muttered under his breath as he tapped
me on the shoulder. "I think we may have been discovered."

Pointing in the direction from which we had come, he whispered, "I can see a line of men moving down the mountainside into
the canyon about three miles from your plane. They must be
government troops garrisoned at Puerto Marah. They probably
heard the plane and took the mountain highway toward Victoria
de las Tunas, hoping to spot something."

"How far is the highway?"

Pepe said softly, "Uno momento." He concentrated on his
binoculars. "On second thought, they never would have had time
to get here. It's at least thirty miles to Puerto Marah by air and
twenty miles from here to the highway. They must be from the
construction site? Would it be more southeast of here?"

"Si. That would be right. It is more southeast from this point.
How did you know?"

"Watch this," I replied. As I slowly turned the little antenna
on top of the spectrum analyzer, the train of pulses that had filled

the height of the screen contracted. As I continued to turn it through a full 360 degree circle, the screen was again filled with the unusual pulse train. I explained, "When the screen is full, the direction arrow on the base of the antenna points to where the signals are coming from, just like the old radio direction finders. Then you check the arrow in relation to your compass, and it gives you the heading."

He nodded. "Now," he said, "if you have enough data to work with, let's vamoose out of here as fast as we can. If those troops get between us and the plane, you can kiss your Yankee ass good-bye."

I began shutting everything down. "What time is sunrise around here?" I asked.

"About 6:00 A.M., but it will be light before then."

It was just a few minutes after 5:00 A.M. "We should take off within half an hour, to be sure of clearing the coast by sunrise."

"I agree, I'm going with you. I don't want to be nailed by one of Castro's fighters."

Alarmed, I remarked, "They were supposed to have been taken out on the first air strike."

"From what we heard on the radio, they weren't."

Pepe suggested that we save time by abandoning the gear and the jeep, and climb down the side of the canyon. His suggestion made sense, so I shoved the exposed film into the pockets of my leather jacket, and charged off with him through the surrounding thick brush.

When we reached the top of the ridge just above the plane, we saw no lights but faintly detected the Twin-Beech fuselage's white top and wings. Fortunately, the wind had shifted, and Ferrie had turned the plane around to face into it. This would enable us to avoid flying over the advancing Cuban troops and possibly exposing ourselves to their small arms fire.

Pepe and I hit the bottom of the canyon less than fifteen minutes after leaving the jeep, unscathed except for our brush-burned hands and faces. As we stopped to catch our breath, I saw Ferrie and a bearded stranger standing next to the Beach. Ferrie was looking at his watch. I didn't blame him for being restless; it was 5:35 A.M. and the sky was beginning to brighten overhead. As we approached the plane, I saw that the truck and the three soldiers who had greeted Ferrie and me with Pepe had disappeared. Only Ferrie, Pepe and I, along with the bearded stranger standing next to Ferrie, were left on the runway. As we approached Ferrie, Pepe waved and said to me, "Good, Manuel made it." He quickly introduced me to Manuel Rodriguez, one of Mario Kohly's principal lieutenants.[4]

Manuel Rodriguez was halfway through his forties. In the predawn light his dark penetrating eyes seemed almost unreal. Manuel asked me, "Did you receive the data you came here to receive?"

"I sure did," I told him. "It appears that the transmissions are coming from very near here. Pepe says there is some type of construction going on about seven miles southeast. Do you have any idea what it is?"

"No," he said quickly. "Now, you better get the hell out of here." With that, Quesada shoved a small package at Pepe and bid us a safe journey home.

Our good-byes said, Ferrie, Pepe and I scrambled into the plane. Pepe strapped himself into the single bucket seat just behind the pilot's cabin. Ferrie sat down and hit the start button in one swift movement. The starboard engine kicked over almost immediately, but the port engine wouldn't catch. As the starter labored, Manuel, who had been standing about twenty feet away from the plane and was looking skyward with his binoculars, suddenly lowered the binoculars and gestured wildly. He then stretched his arms straight out to emulate an airplane, warning us that he had spotted a Cuban plane close by.

"Christ, that's all we need!" Ferrie yelled. "This engine picked one hell of a time to fuck up." He turned to me and shouted, "You start pumping the fuel pressure pump. I'm going to put the starboard engine up to 1500 revs and hope the generator will juice up the port starter enough to get her going! We must have fouled a plug with the high manifold pressure and rich mixture coming in."

Our engine ground over, and a moment later the powerful roar of a 2500-horsepower Bristol Centaures engine streaked over our heads. Before it turned and disappeared over the rim of the canyon, I could see that it was a WW-II's British Sea Fury.

"Jesus," I thought. With a jet we might have a chance, but it was not likely against the slower, more maneuverable prop fighter.

"He must have seen us." I could barely hear Dave over the roar of our starboard engine and the starter of our left engine still relentlessly grinding away.

"It's unbelievable," I said. "Why didn't he fire?"

Ferrie yelled back, "The bastard saw we're in trouble and he's setting us up like a sitting duck." With that, the port engine sputtered into life for a few seconds, then died. "Damn! Damn! Damn!" Ferrie roared.

"We've got to gamble," I shouted. "We're pointing into the wind. Can we hack it with one engine?"

"We've got to," Ferrie screamed. "I don't want to die here!"

Suddenly, the fighter reappeared, flying down the canyon toward us at a much reduced airspeed. We could see him clearly against the lightening sky, preparing to make a strafing pass. When he was within 200 yards, he dropped the fighter's nose slightly and loosed a volley of .303-caliber bullets. Terrified, I could see the lattice trace along the ground in tiny puffs of dust as the bullets swept up to the front of the Beech and suddenly seemed to stop. Miraculous, I thought. My eyes followed the plane as it circled off to the left and then banked sharply out of the canyon.

Turning back to Dave, I noticed that his hand was no longer on the starter switch but was grasping his left shoulder. He was gritting his teeth and swearing under his breath. One of the heavy slugs had evidently richocheted off a rock right through his open window. I was really panicked and as I began to get out of my seat, Ferrie hollered, "Sit your ass down, Porter, and do what I say. Start cranking that engine over. That will give you enough oil pressure to feather it.[5] Unless you want to die in this miserable valley, you're going to take us out of here with the one engine." With that he closed his eyes and fainted.

"Oh, Christ," I thought, "I've never flown one of these from

the co-pilot's seat," and started to panic. I quickly realized I had
no choice and decided that the only way to stop the panic was to
act; I did.

Instinctively, I reached over and hit the starter switch for the
port engine. It responded feebly, and half-sputtered into life. I
quickly adjusted the fuel mixture to medium-lean as I eased the
throttle up. The engine continued to run half-heartedly. Pushing
hard on the toe brakes, I gave the Twin Beech a hard right rudder
and red-lined the starboard and port engines to their maximum;
the former responded with 2600 rpm and the latter, a sad 1700.
I knew that I must be well up over the danger line on the starboard
engine, but it was the only chance Ferrie, Pepe and I had. The port
engine had begun to develop some power. I released the brakes
and the Twin Beech began to move down the canyon. As we rolled
toward the end of the short airstrip, I realized that I had forgotten
to put down the flaps. In a panic, I reached down and shoved the
flap control to fifteen degrees. The airspeed indicator showed that
we were now rolling along at fifty knots. I had also used up most
of the runway. I remembered that all of my gear had been unloaded. Pepe, in a seat behind the pilot's cabin was a featherweight
and we had just enough fuel to get to Florida. The Twin Beech was
light without its cargo. All I had to do was fly the Beech and avoid
the Sea Fury that, I suspected, had set up and was ready to shoot
off our tail.

I checked the airspeed indicator. This time it registered sixty-
five knots. With the Beech at the end of the runway, I eased back
the wheel.

The Beech lifted off but veered sharply to the left. I gave her
a hard right rudder to straighten her out. Once airborne, I raised
the flaps, then reached down and got the landing gear up. It stayed
at fifty feet as our airspeed climbed at ninety knots and I had no
intention of going any higher as long as the Sea Fury was in the
vacinity. I eased back the throttle of the starboard engine and held
the port at its present setting. The plane was vibrating badly
because the props were not synchronized.

I kept out of sight below the canyon rim and had travelled

about 35 miles when, in a flash, the Sea Fury reappeared two miles ahead of me. He had lost us temporarily after our takeoff, but now was coming directly at us. Just as before, he approached me as if on a collision course, then sharply, with less than one hundred yards between us, pulled up and over our heads. He was so close, I could see the smile on his young Cuban face. I sensed that he was planning to attack my rear so I couldn't ram him.

Approximately one mile ahead of our position, the valley narrowed again into a deep ravine that dead-ended into another fairly wide valley. We were quickly approaching the area where Ferrie and I, upon entering Cuba hours before, had crossed over our first smudgepot arrow after leaving the guerrila beacon. This meant that the sea and beach were only a few miles away, possibly thirty degrees to our right. On our left. . . was great unknown. In another ten to fifteen seconds, the Sea Fury would attack again; my compatriots and I were going to become part of the Cuban countryside; I had to make a choice.

If I turned right once out of the narrow canyon, which would be what the young Cuban was expecting, the Beech could be shot down at leisure. If I gambled by making a 330 degree left turn, Castro's pilot might be sufficiently surprised and attempt to follow me. When he had passed overhead, a few minutes before, he was flying at maximum power. And now, anxious to make the kill, he wouldn't have decreased his airspeed. The Beech was travelling at less than half the Sea Fury's speed and, if I timed it just right, we might be able to make the sharp maneuver. If the Cuban pilot made the turn with me at his present velocity, the Sea Fury would crash into the hillside before its pilot realized what had happened.

I had no chance but to risk it. I put the Beech's nose down, gained airspeed, and dropped down to about a hundred feet off the canyon floor, well below its rim. To get a shot at us, the Cuban would have to follow. Waiting until the last possible minute, knowing that he was hurtling down behind me, I feigned a slight right turn by dropping my right wing slightly. Then, swiftly, I kicked the left rudder pedal hard and brought the right wing up close to a 45 degree angle. In combination with the superior power of

the starboard engine, the maneuver practically tore the wings off
the Beech as it went into a sharp left bank, slipping a few feet in
altitude. For a wild moment, I thought my left wing was going to
touch the ground.

Obviously confused, the young Cuban held his fire and started
to turn after me. As he hurtled past our tail, he tried desperately
to execute a climbing right-hand turn. His speed must have been
in excess of 300 knots. I heard the explosion behind me as the Sea
Fury buried itself in the hillside.

Flying up the rapidly narrowing valley, I had just about given
up trying to gain altitude when the port engine coughed once, then
regained full power. I had all I could do to compensate for the port
engine's gain but was thankful for its sudden resurrection; it
relieved the burden on its badly overheated starboard mate. I set
the engine to maximum cruising speed, set the mixtures, synchronized the props, and started the Beech into a tight vertical
climb. Within less than a minute, we had pulled out over the top
of the valley, now bathed in the first light of a magnificent sunrise.
Executing a 180 degree turn, I could see the white beach and the
blue waters of the Straits of Florida less than five miles ahead. Off
to the left, not quite a hundred feet from the top of the hill, a tall
column of thick smoke rose from the funeral pyre of the downed
fighter. Dropping into the valley, I followed it directly out to the
sea. I set the autopilot on a course of 308 degrees as we flashed
over the beach and headed for Florida at an altitude of seventy-
five feet.

Soon the sun's rays, glistening on the sands of Sanibel Island,
told me that I could gain altitude and fly inland over the swamp
to the abandoned government strip Ferrie and I had left a few
hours before.

We landed at the abandoned airstrip, Buckingham Field, at
6:42 A.M. A waiting CIA crew rushed Ferrie to Lee Memorial
Hospital in nearby Fort Myers. I was told later that a splinter of
rock over three-eighths of an inch in diameter had been removed
from Ferrie's upper left shoulder, just a fraction of an inch below
his neck. The doctor in the emergency room accepted the

explanation that the splinter had been kicked up by a passing truck along the Tamiami Trail.

With Ferrie incapacitated, I was the one who climbed aboard a National Airlines jet for Washington with the pulse train film taped to my belly. I also had, courtesy of the agents who had met us and brought me to the Miami airport, a new Walther PPK automatic in a spring holster tucked under my left armpit.

* * *

When I arrived back in Washington I went to my office on 19th Street and attempted to reach Tracy Barnes. As he was not available, I contacted Marshall Diggs at his law offices. Diggs answered immediately. Before I had a chance to open my mouth he asked, "have you heard the news?"

"No, not since this morning. The news was glowing in Miami."

"Well, you better get down here. Things are falling apart." He then hung up before I could even ask him about my car.

When I arrived at his office, Diggs was talking, or I should say arguing, with Mario. I could hear the two of them quite clearly while waiting in the reception area. Digg's secretary, Carol, interrupted the argument and announced my arrival. Almost immediately upon hearing my name, Diggs flung open the door of his office, pulled me, literally, through the doorway and said, "The fucking President has canceled the second air strike. We're being slaughtered on the beaches. The Navy is sitting off-shore prohibited from doing anything to help."

I was dumbfounded but recalled what had been said by Pepe Arnez (del Valle) before we had escaped from Cuba. "But that's impossible. They don't stand a chance." I had been so engrossed in my conversation with Diggs that I neglected to notice Mario who sat in a chair directly behind me. His face was livid and his voice full of fury as he said, "I found out about the Presidents treachery after the troops had sailed. Obviously, without air support I could not commit my underground. As it was, one of my underground leaders, Rogelio Corso (known as Francisco), was picked up by Castro and executed last night. We got the message by radio telling us it was all over. I honestly don't know how many we can save.

"My God, over two hundred thousand persons have been arrested in Havana alone. With luck, we may save one, maybe two-hundred out of thousands. It was received by our radio this morning."[5]

Mario stopped speaking for the moment, too upset to continue. Diggs took up the explanation. "Brewster—referring to former Senator Owen Brewster—called the first thing this morning to tell Mario."

"My God, what do we do?" I stupidly asked.

"I say we kill the son of a bitch."

I ignored Mario's remark, but could understand it. I readily understood the horror which resulted from JFK's actions. I simply could not understand what had prompted the President to go back on his word. Turning to Diggs I asked, "What happened? Why did Kennedy do this?" Diggs immediately launched into his analysis of the events which led to Kennedy's betrayal of the Cuban exiles. "The why is simple to answer: a combination of inexperience and cowardliness on Kennedy's behalf. The reason for this fiasco: last-minute restrictions imposed on the invasion plan by Kennedy; the restrictions resulting from a confrontation between Kennedy and U.N. Ambassador Adlai Stevenson. Their rationale can be summarized in one simple statement: 'No U.S. support or inter-vention to be provided, either prior to, or during, the initial land-ing.' Stevenson represented Kennedy's assurance of non-intervention on the behalf of the United States in Cuban affairs to the Cuban Ambassador to the United Nations. Then, thanks to our wonderful media, Stevenson was made to look like an ass in front of both the Cuban Ambassador and the U.N. General Assembly.

"It occurred when the plan to convince the world that attacks upon Cuban airfields were being conducted by defecting Castro aircraft, was called a hoax by reporters."

"How the hell did that happen?"

"Somebody at the Company didn't do their homework. A *Brigade* pilot was to fly one of the World War II B-26's with Cuban Air Force markings to Miami. His cover was that he was one of three pilots, all disenchanted with Castro, who had been planning to defect for months. On that particular day, he had been flying a routine patrol from his home base, San Antonio de los Banos, and decided to strafe the field. Then, after being hit by small-arms fire and low on fuel, he headed for Miami.

"To make the story authentic, thirty minutes from Miami, he opened his cockpit window and fired enough pistol shots into the port engine so that is had to be shut down. After landing, he gave out his cover story. In less than an hour, it was proven a hoax. Reporters noted that, not only had the plane's machine guns not been fired, but it had a solid metal nose; Castro's B-26's have plastic noses."

When the Cuban ambassador waved the damning photographs and news reports in front of the United Nations General Assembly, Stevenson reacted.

He intimidated Kennedy. He claimed he would inform the U.N. that the new chief executive had lied, then resign as ambassador. Obviously, our young new President — sufficiently coerced — was afraid to give any support orders. That included a formally pledged air strike by our Navy, in the event the exile air force was unable to knock out Castro's jets.

"It was all political image. Adlai Stevenson, for the most part, was responsible for the failure of the Bay of Pigs. Had John Kennedy not been cowed by Stevenson and just fired him, hundreds of Cubans would be alive today."[6]

At this point I was considering that I was damn lucky to be here. I told them both about my experiences over the past 30 hours.

As I would learn shortly after, the one man in the CIA who would suffer the most from the President's disastrous decision was Deputy Director General Charles Cabell. From the beginning, it was obvious that the Bay of Pigs operation would fail without U.S. air support, because Castro's air force had not been knocked out as planned on the first day. For that blunder, Cabell would be held accountable.

* * *

It occurred late on Sunday morning—about the time we were
arriving in Miami. After a round of golf at the Chevy Chase Club,
the former Air Force General decided to visit the Agency
Operations Center again, on his way home. He arrived just as the
Air Operations Officer was preparing to launch the clean-up air
strike, and inquired about what was going on, as he scanned U-2
photographs of the previous day's damage.

When the Air Operations Officer told Cabell that he was
readying another strike against the last of Castro's air force, Cabell,
in doubt as to what orders had been issued from the White House,
put a personal hold on the action, pending clearance for the action
from the White House. When clearance was denied, Cabell
realized what a terrible mistake he had made, and would repeatedly try to make up for it. He requested air cover for the invasion
on four separate occasions. His final attempt was at 4:00 A.M. on
the second day of fighting.

In a last, desperate effort to persuade the President to
reconsider his orders, CIA Deputy Director Cabell drove through
the darkened capitol to Secretary of State Dean Rusk's hotel. In
Rusk's apartment, Cabell again expressed his fears. Despite the
hour, the Secretary of State called the President once more. The
reply was still negative. The surviving Castro jets were free to
destroy the exile army and invasion fleet at will. The final blow for
the *Brigade* came when Kohly discovered that the air cover was
being withheld.

Kohly's immediate reaction was to stop his underground from
supporting the invasion force. What he didn't know at the time was
that his force had been sold out by the *CRC* weeks earlier. So,
without air protection or internal support, the invasion failed and
the *Brigade* was vanquished in a humiliating defeat.

Infuriated, the President promised to splinter the CIA into a
thousand pieces. Kennedy would not concede that withholding the
air strike had contributed to the invasion's failure, though his best
military advice had been that the operation would fail without it.

He would also soon learn that it had aligned the right-wing
elements of the CIA and the violent Cuban exile organizations

against him. In a bizarre twist of fate, however, his action had saved the lives of the leftist exile leaders.

Just hours after Ferrie and I left Opa Locka, the leftist *CRC* members were delivered there and placed under house arrest. They sat incensed for three days as the invasion raged on to its desperate conclusion. Then, on April 19th, Tony Verona managed to elude the guards surrounding the house by escaping through a bathroom window. Once free, he called the White House in a frenzy.

After hearing their story of captivity, Arthur Schlesinger Jr. advised the President to see the Cubans immediately, in order to smooth their ruffled feathers. The President dispatched Schlesinger and A.A. Berle to rescue the leftist Cubans. Within hours, they were headed toward Washington on an Air Force plane.[7]

Fortunately, my end of the operation was successful. The film had been delivered and processed, although I was not yet privy to the conclusions formed by the analyst responsible for reviewing the evidence I brought back from Cuba's Camagney Province. My state of ignorance would be short-lived, however, as I would soon be thoroughly briefed on the horrifying impact of my mission and the evidence which resulted from my night in Castro's Cuba.

CHAPTER FOUR NOTES:

1. Ferrie's maneuver is commonly referred to in aeronautic parlance as recaging the gyro compass. It refers to manually resetting a compass that is stabilized by a gyroscope.
2. Visual Flight Rules are flying by sight and not on instruments.
3. The United Organizations for the Liberation of Cuba was formed in October of 1961 and would consist of over 100 anti-Castro Cuban groups, a list which can be seen in the Appendices.
4. His full name was Manuel Rodriguez Quesada. He would head the group at the safe house in Dallas during the assassination of J.F.K. Quesada was killed by one of Kohly's lieutenants when he was about to talk. I have a transcript by Quesada's assassin describing the hit. See Appendices.
5. A radio message in reply to a CIA radio exhortation for the underground to rise, was met with: IMPOSSIBLE TO RISE, MOST PATRIOTS IN JAIL, THANKS FOR YOUR HELP. CLOSING TRANSMISSION.

   All over Cuba that day similar CIA messages were sent. But it was too late. As Felix Rodriguez, one of the underground leaders said: "The roads were closed, the houses were surrounded and they were arresting thousands of people. I cried."

   While the Castro radio played soothing music, a reign of terror had begun. In Havana more than two hundred thousand people were arrested. In theaters and ballparks, auditoriums and public halls, men, women and children were packed together indiscriminately. At the Blanquita Theatre, where more than five thousand citizens were confined, there were only two bathrooms.

   Of all the failures that day, the failure to alert the Cuban underground in time was one of the most damaging and certainly the most baffling. From the time when Artime had been smuggled out of Cuba to set in motion the events leading to this April 17, the underground had been a vital part of the CIA's plan. In the original plan the underground was to aid a guerilla force, which at this point was non-existent. Later it was to support and join the invasion. In any case its role called upon it to create confusion, sow discord and fashion an environment in which the populace would join the liberators. The diversionary landing at Oriente, the sabotage campaign through the island presaging the signal for a revolt, the propaganda broadcasts of Radio Swan, were all a part of the overall plan to distract attention from the invading army. And now those 1,500 invaders stood alone.
6. According to Tracy Barnes, Stevenson not only knew about the invasion but had been briefed by him, President Kennedy, plus others in the CIA. He would have had to be deaf, dumb and blind not to know all about the

upcoming action against Castro. Every exile was talking about it. In fact, open recruiting stations had been operating in Miami for months. It was the poorest kept secret in the world. Howard Hunt also claimed that he knew Stevenson was briefed by Tracy Barnes and even mentioned it in his book, *Give Us This Day.*

Although Stevenson would state he had been kept in the dark about the invasion preparations, Barnes would produce a record of his briefing of Stevenson well before to the invasion date. The Barnes-Stevenson memorandum was furnished to Lyman Kirkpatrick, the CIA's Inspector General at the time.

7 . When Representative Thomas Downing held his press conference on August 2, 1976, to motivate the House Rules Committee to reopen the Kennedy assassination investigation, he also told the story of the *CRC* leftist leaders being held captive as part of the Nixon/Kohly deal. As a result, Arthur Schlesinger, Jr., was contacted and, in a statement to Richmond Times Dispatch reporter Eston Melton, on August 3, 1976, Schlesinger confirmed the release of the Cubans from Opa Locka:

> Arthur M. Schlesinger, Jr., former special assistant to President John F. Kennedy, confirmed yesterday that that he freed "six to eight" Cuban exile leaders being held "under house arrest" at Opa Locka, Fla., by the Central Intelligence Agency during the 1961 Bay of Pigs invasion.
>
> Schlesinger said, "Kennedy was furious when he discovered this," referring to the Cuban exile leaders.

It was apparent that President Kennedy, even at that fateful point in time, had not been informed by the CIA hierarchy of the Kohly/Nixon arrangement or *Operation Forty.*

5

APRIL 1960

On Sunday April 24, 1961, one week after the fiasco on the beaches, I received a call from Tracy Barnes. In our conversation, Barnes seemed completely at ease and made no reference to the Bay of Pigs disaster. He requested that I meet him at the Golden Parrot in Washington for lunch on Monday, and indicated that Marshall Diggs would possibly join us. He also reaffirmed that, to the best of his knowledge, Kohly was still unaware of my involvement with the Agency. As I had not heard from Kohly since our meeting in Diggs's office a week earlier, I was concerned that, in the interim, he may have somehow learned of my CIA involvement. I was also concerned that he, as a consequence of his newly acquired knowledge, would hold me partially responsible for the disaster; thus destroying our many months of mutual trust, respect and comradeship.

While driving down the parkway into Washington, I reflected upon my harrowing mission into Cuba and wondered when I would learn about the conclusions drawn by the experts, to whom the electronic evidence I secured from the Camaguey Mountains had been given. I wondered if they had confirmed my initial suspicions that the patterns I had originally observed, were computer pulses designed to trim and guide an as yet unidentified type of high-speed space vehicle. If, indeed, I was correct in my assumption, the next pertinent query was why such sophisticated technology was in Cuba. I was still preoccupied with my reflections when, thirty minutes later, I pulled into the Golden Parrot's parking lot.

The Golden Parrot was a new establishment catering to sales-
men and influence peddlers who dealt with the DOD, FAA, CAB,
and other alphabetical benefactors of Washington representatives[1] Situated near the corner of R Street and Connecticut
Avenue, across the street from the gaily colorful carts of flower
peddlers, the restaurant was affectionately referred to by its
numerous patrons as the Dirty Bird.

As I opened the ornate double door of the converted brown-
stone mansion, I was immediately greeted by a rush of cool,
refreshing air. The day was blisteringly hot for April and I had a
feeling that it would quickly become hotter. Tracy Barnes and
Diggs were waiting for me in the lobby; in spite of the air condi-
tioning, I felt the temperature rise. The three of us were seated and,
after ordering our round of drinks, I asked Barnes, "What did the
experts make of my pulse train photos?"

"What I'm sure you suspected," he replied. "Castro and the
Russians are operating a control center in the Camaguey. The pulse
trains you photographed indicate computer-controlled digital
signals of the kind used to give inertial guidance direction to
ballistic missiles and space vehicles. But we have more evidence
than that."[2] After quickly looking around the room, he reached
into his inside coat pocket and drew out a small stack of 5x7
photographs. He handed them to me.

For a few moments, what I was looking at didn't register; the
photos were dim and slightly blurred. Then I realized they had
been taken at night with an infra-red camera. What I saw, I didn't
believe. Each of the six shots, taken from a different angle and
position, was obviously of the same subject. They were photos of
a launching pad for intermediate or long-range ballistic missiles.
"Jesus! These are in Cuba?"

"Less than seven miles from where you were standing." Tracy
replied. Stunned, I asked, "Who knows about this? How long have
they been in place?"

"Take it easy, Robert. Other than General Cabell, the Director,
Richard Bissell, and the three of us at this table, the only other
person who has been briefed is President Kennedy. Cabell

informed him of our suspicions in early March. When the underground informed Mario that they had these pictures, the first week
in April, we sent you in to secure the electronic data and bring
del Valle out with the pictures. We thought we might need him as
a witness."

"Who does del Valle think I'm working for?"

At that point Diggs spoke up. "He thinks you were hired as a
CIA consultant for this job only, just like Ferrie. I told him after
you left my office last week."

"You think he was stupid enough to believe it?"

"Only because you were sent in as a sacrificial lamb. He knows
you are smarter than that." Tracy Barnes blushed deeply at my
exchange with Diggs.

I thought for a moment about how close Ferrie and I had
come to not getting back at all, and began to feel the same anger
I had felt after my conversation with Diggs and Kohly in Digg's
office.

When I learned from Diggs of Kennedy's cancellation of the
second air strike, I realized that while Ferrie and I were in Florida
preparing for our night flight to the Camaguey, Tracy Barnes, my
case officer, knew that the strike had been canceled. He contacted
neither Ferrie nor me to warn us of the recent developments.
Diggs's choice of words was frighteningly on target. Indeed, I had
been set up as a sacrificial lamb and I still had not gotten over
either the anger or the sense of betrayal. In fact, I would hold
Barnes's remarks suspect here on out as it was very clear that
loyalty to the Agency superceded any loyalty he might feel toward
one of his operatives. I was glad Barnes was embarrassed.

My reflection was broken by Barnes's soft but firm voice, "And
now for the clincher. At the end of March, JFK ordered us to drop
the entire missile matter."

"Drop the matter?" I repeated, stupidly.

Barnes was grim as he said, "In fact, as of 10 A.M. today, the
President ordered all of our intelligence data, photos, the report
on your findings, and any other documents pertaining to the site,
turned over to the Attorney General."

He then asked that the names of all our personnel who had been working on the project be turned over to the DOD for transfer to a new agency.

I felt overwhelmed by the information Barnes threw in my direction. I needed time to digest its import and significance. I asked Barnes to slow down and then proceeded with the two queries uppermost in my mind. "A new agency? What new agency?"

Barnes's response was as rapid as his earlier delivery of Kennedy's demands, "Rumor has it that the new agency will be called the 'Defense Intelligence Agency.' It's to be formed when the CIA is—and I quote the President—'splintered into a thousand pieces.' Brother Robert, meanwhile, will ride herd on all our activities until Dulles, and whomever the Kennedy's so desire, are replaced."

I was incredulous. "Are you telling us that the White House knows that there are IRBM's located less than 100 miles from the continental United States, and they want the information turned over to Robert Kennedy to hush it up?"

"As near as we can tell, they want to bury it."

"But why? Sooner or later one of the U-2 overflies will detect it; then, the whole military establishment will know about it. I can't believe what you're saying."

"This missile site could take a year to detect from over 60,000 feet. Kohly's underground forces had to take their camera within 200 yards to penetrate the heavy camouflage." Of course, the Administration's action this morning could be strictly politcal. Our Bay of Pigs operation tarnished the Kennedy image and the President isn't apt to forgive us for the slight. Robert, you should know that it was absolutely necessary for us to insure the success of your mission using the exiled Cuban's diversionary force."

I snapped back, "It didn't seem to work too well, did it? What happened?"

"That's a little embarrassing. The men who comprised the diversionary group were trained at our facility in New Orleans, near Lake Ponchatrain. They were deliberately trained in the States and not in Guatemala for two reasons: they were never told they were a diversionary force, and the Agency wanted to keep them separated from the *Brigade*. Mario may disagree with me, but I think the real problem was one of leadership; our man, Nino Diaz, goofed. The force was never told how vital their mission was. Frankly, I don't think Diaz realized how vital his mission was and how much depended upon him. The upshot of this lack of communication and understanding, you lived through without knowing it; when the going got tough, Diaz and his men aborted the mission."

"And you still sent us in? You still let us go, knowing this?" I was becoming increasingly angrier. Barnes cut me off before I could say any more. He went on, "We had no choice, Robert. Diversion or no diversion, we had to get that data. Judging from the evidence you obtained, it was worth the risk." Barnes sensed my mounting fury and hurriedly continued, "Try to understand. The only course of action open to us was the one we chose to take. The risk had to be taken, regardless of the cost. For months, we'd heard rumors about the building of that site. It wasn't until the beginning of April that we could get any hard evidence to substantiate our suspicions. We had to be absolutely certain they were operational missile sites and that the pulses we had tracked earlier were the guidance system signals. The data you brought back was the conclusive evidence. Control systems, as you know, are almost impossible to identify positively unless you're right on top of them." I agreed, slightly mollified, and handed back the pictures he had passed to me earlier.

Barnes left me no time for further reflection, hurriedly continuing his case. He knew that he had calmed me down and that I was listening intently to his rationale. He continued, "The urgency was further compounded when the Agency was notified by Kohly's underground and told that hard evidence of the site's existence had been obtained. We were forced to act swiftly. The President was made aware of the Cuban missile situation the first week of April. Cabell briefed him immediately upon the Agency's reception of the information provided by Kohly's underground. Kennedy's response to Cabell's briefing was a directive which ordered that no further moves, at least none relating to missile intelligence, be undertaken by the Agency."

Hearing Barnes's latest remarks intensified the confusion and surprise I had experienced earlier. "You mean that the President, knowing that there might be missiles in Cuba, gave specific orders for us not to enter Cuba and secure information? Why?" I asked.[4]

Barnes understood my shock and the horror and disbelief which I felt growing within me. I suspect he also recognized a certain political naïvete and attempted to respond to my ignorance of power politics and its machinations. He continued, "The Agency would only assume that the President wanted to completely control any and all responses to the Cuban situation. The maintenance of that control is the ultimate reason to set up an alternative intelligence agency. It may be difficult to believe, but we strongly suspect that Kennedy wants to use this missle information for some future political advantage. If he wanted to, he could suppress this information long enough to facilitate its use as a point of political leverage and thereby influence the outcome of the 1962 Congressional elections. It is certainly a ploy that has been used very effectively by other administrations. . . . You know it; the 'don't switch horses in the middle of a crisis' school of presidential management. FDR, after all, was the Grand Master of that game. I know you remember your history, Robert."

I felt my ire rising again; I was angry with Kennedy and with Barnes. My next query revealed my agitation, "So you sent us in as sacrificial lambs for Kennedy and the Agency and a power struggle between the two. Have I got the picture?"

"Damn it, Robert, you weren't listening to me," Barnes bitterly responded. "We had to. From the information we received through the underground, we had estimated that one site is far enough advanced to be operational within six months—that's less than three months from now. We had no other choice, regardless of Mr. Kennedy's maneuvers."

I understood Barnes's words despite my resentment. He posed

a quick question before I had a chance to respond to his last statements.

"The General wants to see you. Are you up to it?"

I wasn't sure of my response, and decided to ask a question which had disturbed me throughout our entire meeting. Diggs had remained with us but had not uttered a word while Barnes and I spoke.

"Before I answer, whether I'm willing to see Cabell, I want to know what Digg's role has been in all this. He's said very little throughout our discussion. . . . What does he have to do with this?"

Barnes's response was quick and to the point. "He has to keep his sources apprised of what's going on."

Having met the people I had through Digg's intervention, I could only speculate on who those sources might be. I would find out soon enough, but I wasn't prepared to pose any more queries that afternoon.

I agreed to see General Charles Cabell and was in his office one hour after leaving the Golden Parrot. This was the second time Barnes, Cabell and I were together in Cabell's office; the first had been prior to my flight into Cuba. A third man was with Cabell when Barnes and I entered his office. He was introduced as the Deputy Director of Plans for the Agency, Richard Bissell.[5]

The General did not waste time with further amenities and chatter. He turned to Barnes and asked, "Have you brought Robert up to date?"

"Yes, sir," Barnes replied, smartly.

My turn was next. "Well, young man, I assume Tracy has told you about the Agency's problems with the White House."

"Yes, sir, he did. I understand that the Agency has been placed in a difficult position." Cabell shot a quick glance at Bissell and said, "Of course, we're all concerned. It isn't every day we are forced to act independently in such a crucial situation."

I asked the obvious question, "You'd act against the express wishes of the President?"

"In this case, yes. But, before you make any rash assumptions, take a look at this. After what you have done for us, you've earned the right to know."

He then reached into his top desk drawer, removed a large file folder and handed it to me.

The first item I removed from the folder was a memorandum, handwritten on the official stationary created exclusively for the Vice President of the United States. Beneath the stationary's engraved: "Office of the Vice President of the United States," the salutation read: "My dear Charles:"

Thirty years have passed since I read that memorandum, but its tone and message are indelibly marked on my memory. After a number of critical, self-serving comments about the intention of the President and his brother to build a Kennedy dynasty in the White House, Lyndon Johnson proceeded forthrightly to the crux of his message.

The Vice President had learned, "strictly by accident," of the secret directives issued to Defense Secretary Robert McNamara by President Kennedy. The directives were straightforward and brutal. McNamara was ordered to employ any and all means at his disposal, which would result in the revocation of the CIA's power and the usurpation of any and all control currently exercised by the CIA over its extant activities. McNamara was further authorized to establish an alternative intelligence agency which would perform the functions previously assigned to the CIA. The establishment of this new agency was to be undertaken upon the replacement of CIA Director Allen Walsh Dulles and Deputy Directory of Plans, Richard Bissell.[6] The final item mentioned in Johnson's memorandum was a brief summation of a meeting held between the President and the Chairman of the Senate Appropriations Committee. In this meeting, Kennedy had intimated the misuse of power he thought typical of the Agency, and requested that the Chairman initiate an investigation, which conclusions would result in a severe limitation of the Agency's unvouchered funds. In addition, he sought the repudiation of the CIA charter which placed Agency control over all United States intelligence activities under the auspices of the soon to be established DIA agency.[7]

The memorandum lacked a conclusion, abruptly ending with

the summation of Kennedy's meeting with the Chairman of the Senate Appropriations Committee. Immediately beneath the last written line were the Vice President's initials, "LBJ." The memorandum was not dated..

Feeling queasy, I looked up, and had the distinct impression that my reading of this memorandum was not accidental. A quick glance at the faces of Cabell, Bissell and Barnes told me that I was being intently studied—that, in fact, I was being *allowed* to view a document which I would otherwise never have been made privy. There was an obvious reason for the course of action Cabell had taken with me. My intuition told me I was being set up; the substantiation of this intuition would come much later—after the assassination of John F. Kennedy.

Cabell continued to watch me intently and then abruptly broke the silence which had fallen over all of us. "Read the next report," he said. "It was handed to us by one of the President's Secret Service bodyguards. If you accept another assignment, it will be important to you."

I opened the file folder again. On top of a stack of reports was a carbon copy of a handwritten memo. The memo was short, and I can remember almost all of its precise contents.

Memorandum to the Attorney General:

If possible, try to apprehend all Cuban and American personnel currently engaged in manufacturing bogus Cuban currency. As you know, in its efforts to overthrow the Castro regime, the CIA has disregarded our direct orders and placed us in a politically embarrassing position. The names of all the parties involved in the conspiracy should be in the Agency's file.

Also, you might consider leaking to the Cuban authorities that a massive counterfeiting scheme may be launched against them that could jeopardize the Cuban economy.

The memorandum was signed simply "Jack."

"When did you receive this?" I asked. "In some circles this would be considered treasonous."

Cabell listened to my remark and then replied, "Not necessarily. It could perhaps be justified as part of a diplomatic strategy. For the moment, we would like you to continue reading; as you can readily see, there's much more to review." During the next half-hour, I read through numerous reports dealing with everything from unsavory campaign tactics authorized by Kennedy to surveillance reports which explictily detailed the manner in which he occupied many of his nights.

When I completed my reading, I whistled in amazement; the data compiled on the President had been amazingly thorough and comprehensive. I turned to Cabell who had patiently waited with Bissell and Barnes for me to complete my reading and asked, "What now?"

"Well, young man," Cabell said, "this afternoon we have arranged through the intercession of Marshall Diggs a meeting between Kohly and Robert Kennedy. The purpose of this meeting is for Kohly to confront the Attorney General with the photos of the missile site and your electronic data report. If RFK reacts negatively to the data Kohly presents to him, Kohly will give a television interview and break the story. The threat of an interview should flush out both Kennedys out and force their hand. They will have no choice but to admit the Cuban missile site's existence. Since you are our only functioning operative within Kohly's inner circle, we want you to go with him to see the Attorney General.

"Our second request is a bit more complex. The Agency must continue a peso counterfeiting operation which was established as a means of destabilizing Cuba's economy through Kohly's underground prior to the invasion. The operation was initiated on a contract basis and can remain with that status. Fees will be paid in accordance with our previous arrangements and Kohly will also provide additional funding through his various sources.

"The thrust of the operation now is to completely destabilize the Cuban economy. With any luck, we will achieve the objective long before autumn and significantly prior to the Department of

Defense's usurpation of authority over the Agency's operation. Well, I've explained what we need; the whole point is, simply . . . will you continue to work with us?"

"How much time do I have?"

"Actually none. Kohly is scheduled to speak with the Attorney General this afternoon."

I knew that I had to be crazy to even consider continuing my association with the Agency. I did like the action, however, and the perks which accompanied the position were attractive—I had many opportunities to meet influential people which I might otherwise not have had. Without giving the matter any more reflection, I immediately responded to Cabells's query, "All right, I'll give it another shot."

"Fine, we'll go over your compensation and expense account later. The counterfeiting operation about which we spoke was shut down two days ago since we were warned of Kennedy's intent to arrest operatives associated with the venture. We want to move the entire operation, preferably to your lab in Baltimore."

I wasn't particularly sure that I found this idea very appealing, but responded by asking, "Isn't that dangerous?"

Bissell, for the first time since our meeting had commenced, fielded the question and jumped in, saying, "It will be an independent operation. Kohly will handle the politics and, as the General stated, provide enough cash to make him think it's his operation. Give him the idea. He'll bite."

"What happened to the original venture?"

Bissell continued, "We hired an outfit in New York to print up some phony pesos, tens and twenties. They looked great, but the ink was so bad it came off with a little spit. We had minted the equivalent of approximately five million dollars in pesos and given two million of the total to the underground before we discovered the problem with the ink. Can you alleviate this problem?"

"Hell, yes," I replied, "but what if the President or the Attorney General finds out?" Although I agreed with the tack the Agency had taken with respect to the Cuban underground, I was still very shaken to learn that the CIA would defy a direct presidential order.

"Who's going to tell them?" he asked sarcastically. "We want Cuba's economy broken before they discover what hit them. Then we can deal with Castro on our terms, despite his missiles. This time we'll plan it so no one knows anything about the currency operation except Kohly, Barnes, me, and the personnel directly involved in its manufacture.

When Bissell paused, Barnes entered our conversation, breaking the silence. "Not to change the subject, but what time this afternoon is the meeting between Kohly and Robert Kennedy scheduled to take place?"

Bissell responded, "Have Bob drive Kohly over in the next few minutes. If all goes well, Mario will simply cancel his TV interview. Now, show Robert to the car. He better get going or he'll be caught in the Monday afternoon traffic."

As Barnes and I headed toward the parking lot, Tracy said, "Your distinctive car has been taken back to the Golden Parrot's parking lot."

"My car! How? . . ." I stopped short as he waved a set of keys in my face and smiled. "For any car, Robert. You'll be equipped with a set of your own before long. For now you are to use the boss's souped-up model."

"Souped-up how?"

"Well, for openers, she's got a supercharged 300-horsepower overhead cam V-8; the individual coil springs have been replaced with torsion bars; and the Dynaflow drive train has been replaced with a four-speed box and dual-speed rear axle."

"I take it you mean an overdrive."

"You have it," Barnes replied. As we stepped outside, he pointed up the street and said, "There she is."

The yellow Buick looked just like any other 1961 model until you sat down inside. A panel of instruments just beneath the dash sported an electronic tachometer, a Rootes blower pressure gauge complete with engaging switch, and other goodies, such as a radio telephone. The speedometer indicated up to 160 miles per hour. The biggest surprise came when I started the engine; it didn't make any of the familiar noises I would have expected of a supercharged automobile. In fact, it sounded like any other piece of Detroit iron. I was amazed by the ingenuity of the instrumentation and the inconspicuousness of the automobile. Beyond any shadow of a doubt, it bore all the hallmarks of the agency for whom it was built.

As we entered the garage of the Justice Department, I knew things were going to be bad. Kohly had been late, and with the traffic, we were barely able to keep the appointment with the Attorney General. As I was leaving Mario at the garage entrance to the Justice Department, I was told that I must park outside. I told Mario I would meet him outside the front door once his meeting was completed. Mario left the car and I pulled out of the garage into a constant stream of traffic.

I didn't have long to wait. It was only my fifth time around the block when I spotted Kohly waiting by the curb. When he got in, he slammed his briefcase into the back seat and said, "Take me to the TV station."

Although the normally heavy Monday traffic had not hit its peak, it took me the better part of an hour to get to the studio, drop Kohly off at the front door and pull into a parking area reserved for visitors. As I pulled into one of the visitor slots farthest from the studio entrance, I was surprised to see Tracy Barnes getting out of a Chevy parked a few cars down. He walked over to the Buick and slid in. Wiping his brow with a large handkerchief, he said, "All hell's broken loose. Just after you left, Cabell got a call from the Attorney General. He has issued orders to have Kohly picked up. Cabell told him he didn't know where Mario was, but there's always the chance you may have been followed."

"What happened at the meeting? Kohly didn't say a word to me the whole time it took to get here."

"According to one of Cabell's sources inside of Justice, the Attorney General called Mario an unmitigated liar and accused him of making up the whole story about the missile site, and even went so far as to imply that Kohly had faked the photos."

"But the data on the pulse trains can't be denied."

"Robert, you and I know that neither the photos nor the data could have been faked in this instance. If the Attorney General knows it, he refuses to acknowledge it. Obviously something very strange is going on. My major concern, however, is Mario. As soon as he finishes here, you must get him the hell out of town. Cabell briefed me on your instructions. I'll try to keep the Justice Department bastards off your back long enough for you to get Kohly away. Damn, you would think we were in an enemy country."

"Do you think we'll have any trouble?"

"I hope not, but you should be prepared for the worst possible scenario. Cabell told me that Robert Kennedy was so furious he almost hit Kohly. Now, here's what Cabell has requested that you do. After Kohly's TV interview, you are to fly Kohly to Florida. A brand new 400-horsepower Comanche hangared at Friendship Airport's South Terminal is awaiting you."

He hesitated and, reading his thoughts, I said, "If there's trouble, I'll have a rough time getting to Friendship, especially in rush hour traffic and having to backtrack through town."

"You're right. I'll have the Comanche shuttled over to Montgomery County Airport at Gaithersburg. Here's a set of keys for the plane. I'll have the tanks topped off. And remember, this airplane is special. It has a 1200-mile range. Now, unless something changes, you will take Kohly directly to Gaithersburg and from there into Opa Locke. Upon your arrival, have the plane refueled. Eladio del Valle, the man you flew back from the Camaguay, will be awaiting your arrival. You'll receive further instructions from him. Incidentally, do not file a flight plan; the latest weather reports and a recommended VFR routing will be on the front seat of the Comanche. Do remember, Robert, we can't plan for every eventuality, so do keep your presence of mind. If the weather's good, you should make it in just under four hours. Now, get cracking." Smiling, he added, "Good luck!"

With his last statement, Barnes jumped out of the car. He started to move away when, as an afterthought, he stuck his head through the window and said, "You probably won't see me again. When Kohly's done, I'll tell him someone's waiting for him at the front door. He doesn't know me. Then, I'll race out the back door.

If anyone was following both of you, he'd expect that kind of maneuver and may choose to follow me instead. Wait here for ten minutes and then pull up in front of the entrance. Leave your engine running. I'll send Mario out fast so he can jump in quickly. Once he's in, you dig out. If they follow me, fine, and if anyone follows you, you should be able to lose them in this baby." Barnes slapped the side of the car door. "So long."

Before I could reply, he had disappeared between two parked cars. A moment later I saw him entering a side door of the studio building. I backed the Buick into a spot directly opposite the studio entrance; then I lowered the convertible's top. It was a full fifteen minutes before I spotted Kohly just inside the glass doors. Placing the Buick into first gear, I swung the powerful car out of the parking space and pulled up to the front steps.

As I screeched to a halt, a black Ford sedan surged out of another slot three cars down, cut in front of me and blocked the driveway. Instinctively, I threw the Buick into reverse, backed into the slot I had just vacated, cut the wheels hard, and headed out in the opposite direction. Fortunately, Mario had spotted what was happening. The little guy lunged headlong into the back seat as I gunned the Buick down the studio driveway. For the next ten minutes, heading away from Gaithersburg to avoid revealing our intended destination, the Ford and the Buick played tag, the two-way traffic being just heavy enough to deny either car an advantage.

Finally I spotted a short gap in the oncoming traffic. I engaged the blower switch, floored the accelerator, and pulled around the next three cars. By running a yellow traffic light it took only a fraction of a mile to lose our pursuers. The signal and the intervening autos tied them up long enough to enable us to get out of sight and cut into a side road.

After we rejoined the slow-moving northbound traffic, we arrived, thirty minutes later, at the Montgomery County Airport in Gaithersburg. As we entered the airport's parking lot, I spotted the Comanche on the ramp in front of the fuel pumps of Freestate Aviation. I pulled the Buick into a crowded rear section marked "Employees Only," and we walked casually to the plane.

I had flown a number of Comanches in the past, but this plane was, as Barnes had predicted, special. Her nose was a good foot longer than the other models with which I was familiar. Consequently, the plane resembled a German Messerschmitt 108 fighter trainer far more than it resembled a civilian plane. The Comanche also had wing-tip fuel tanks to supplement the four standard ones in the wings, and in front of her supercharged 8-cylinder power plant sat a three-bladed Hartzel prop. As with the Buick I had just left in the parking lot, the Agency clearly spared no expense in providing extraordinarily well-equipped means of transport. I was impressed. I unlocked the door of the cockpit and slid in to take a look. The engine time recorded registered eleven hours.

As I was climbing out of the cockpit to preflight the Comanche, a young pump attendant presented me with a fuel bill. It was made out to one of the many companies that Cabell used as covers. I signed it, asked him to pull the chocks from the wheels, and proceeded to preflight the plane. Mario was inside the terminal purchasing some sandwiches and a quart of milk for our journey.

At 7:30 P.M., with the sun low in the western sky, the Comanche ready and Mario comfortably seated, I pulled onto Runway 24. With less than half the runway gone, we rose swiftly into the darkening sky. Once we reached altitude, Mario finally spoke to me. "Well, Chico I guess it's time to clear the air. How long have you been working for the CIA?" He didn't turn his head to look at me, but I could tell he was smiling.

"I guess the car and the plane gave it away."

"I knew you were wealthy, Chico, but this kind of equipment requires very serious funds. Even I know that an aircraft like this costs many, many thousands of dollars."

"I can't deny it. I signed aboard as of today. It was the only way I could keep going, and simultaneously make sure your interests were being appropriately attended to."

"I suspected that might be your rationale. For the moment, however, we should carry on the charade a little while longer with my compadres. After the Bay of Pigs, they have no trust for anyone connected with the U.S. government."

"I understand, Mario, and I don't want anything happening to you because of the Kennedys."

"Good. I thank you and, Chico, I do trust I shall not be incarcerated at Opa Locke, like my leftist countrymen, upon our arrival there this evening."

I looked at Mario, grunted and said emphatically, "Over my dead body."

If all went well, I judged our estimated time of arrival at Opa Locke to be approximately 11:00 P.M.

CHAPTER FIVE NOTES:

1. DOD: Department of Defense; FAA: Federal Aviation Administration; CAB: Civil Aeronautics Board.
2. Inertial pre-programmed missile control systems, set by microwave links.
3. According to del Valle, the man who took the pictures was killed by Castro on Saturday, April 16, 1961, the day after giving del Valle the photos. His name was Rogello Gonzales Corso, head of the underground, whose code name was Francisco.
4. This event occurred more than eighteen months before the public was told there were Soviet missiles in Cuba. In 1969, a conference held between delegates of the U.S., Cuba, and the Soviet Union, finally divulged that the IRBM missiles had been in Cuba long before the crisis of October 1962.
5. Bissell was also head of Covert Operations.
6. Allen Walsh Dulles resigned as the Director of Central Intelligence in November of 1961 and Richard Bissell in December.
7. The DIA was set up by Robert McNamara under the auspices and control of the Department of Defense (DOD) in late fall 1961, about the time Allen Dulles was forced to resign as Director of the CIA.

6

MAY 1961

When Kohly and I arrived at Opa Locka, del Valle was waiting for us. He appeared to be very hurried. Amenities were exchanged and he quickly proceeded with our agenda. "I've got reservations for you in a motel in Lauderdale by the Sea. Barnes called. He wanted to make sure you got your stuff out of the plane. It's being used for a trip to New Orleans tomorrow." I was disappointed; I wanted to be able to fly the Comanche back north. Del Valle sensed my disappointment and quickly added, "It will be back in time for your next assignment."

"Very perceptive, Oscar."[1] It was the first time I had used del Valle's nickname. He didn't appreciate my reference. His displeasure was clearly evident as he continued relaying Barnes's instructions. "Barnes may be down tomorrow. He will be staying at the motel next door. I couldn't get reservations for both of you, as well as Mario, at the same place. Barnes also told me that you probably did not have time to bring any luggage. I've purchased a pair of pajamas, a sport shirt, slacks, some underwear, and shaving gear for you and Mario."

Kohly had remained silent during the entire conversation with del Valle. Finally, he entered our exchange and asked, "I assume the Agency man is going to finally provide some positive help?"

Del Valle replied somewhat dejectedly, "My friend, at this point, your guess is as good as mine."

I remained silent, knowing that the wounds shared by these two men over the Bay of Pigs fiasco were far better left alone.

* * *

Casa Verde, one of the newer and more exclusive motels in Lauderdale by the Sea, catered to the more extravagant life style of the rich and famous.[2] I was exhausted upon my arrival, and slept from the time I arrived at the motel until late afternoon the following day. I called Kohly and del Valle shortly after awakening from my restful sleep and invited them for drinks in my suite. The two Cubans were admiring the view from my window when Del Valle turned toward the bar where I was making a cocktail and said, "Mario is going to have to get out of the country to avoid being arrested."

Mario, who had chosen to seat himself in a massive chaise lounge, chuckled at del Valle's remark and said with a quiet venom, "The bastards may force me out of the country, but they will regret the day they sold out the Cuban patriots."

Del Valle, who was fixing himself a rum and coke, grinned at me. "I know we'd better get the old man out of the country. He could do something rash."

"Don't worry about me, amigo. I can take care of myself. Did Barnes say anything about the weapons we were promised?"

"Ah, yes," del Valle said. "I was coming to that. He said funds will be transferred sometime today from Mexico to your numbered account in Bimini." He looked at his watch. "In fact, they should already be there. Someone could probably catch a flight over and come back in the morning."

"No, tomorrow will do." Then, turning to me, he stood up and said, "Now, Chico, I'm going to have to borrow your services for another few days."

Surprised, I replied, "What do you need me for?"

"You can pick up the money." Then he reached inside his shirt, unstrapped a large money belt, brought it over and dropped it on the bar. "I certainly can't make the trip. I don't hold a U.S. passport and, with the Kennedys after me, I would be deported immediately into the loving arms of Fidel. If that happened, I wouldn't last an hour in one of his torture chambers."

"I agree. What precisely do you want me to do in Bimini?"

"You are to pick up a package containing approximately $250,000–$350,000. The money will be in relatively small denominations."[3]

"Quite a package," I replied.

"It will not be in your possession very long, Chico. Immediately after you collect the package you are to return here, deposit the cash with Eladio, pick me up and head for a little town called Peterboro, Ontario. We must make a deal to purchase weapons with a company located there.[4] The cash you are to bring from Bimini will be used principally to buy weapons, medical supplies, and communications equipment. When you return from Canada, you will go to Europe and complete the weapons transaction initiated in Canada. Barnes will give you your European itinerary."

Kohly's directions were clear, and after listening attentively, I asked any questions concerning details I thought pertinent to my assignment. The three of us had a few more drinks and then decided to have dinner together. By 10:00 P.M., we returned to my suite. After a full meal and with a full agenda to be accomplished the next day, I was exhausted. Mario, spotting my difficulty staying awake, broke up our meeting and suggested that we all retire. As they left the room, del Valle said, "Pleasant dreams and hasta la vista. If you want us, we're just down the hall." Too tired to ask the number of their room, I muttered my thanks to them and fell into bed without bothering to turn out the lights.

My phone rang at 7 A.M. the following morning. The operator reported that I had a long distance call and then I heard Barnes's cheerful voice, "We have a clear line. Now, I've got news for you. Don't say anything about it to our Cuban friends. As you know, Mario needs that package from Bimini. It's imperative you get it. We need to convert most of it to British Pound Sterling. Are you following me?"

"Yes, Tracy, Kohly requested yesterday that I collect the package. But why not make the exchange into sterling at the

Bimini bank?"

"First of all the bank does not have that much currency in sterling on hand. The U.S. dollars were transferred in cash from the Banco Nacional de Mexico. They originated in New Orleans.[5] Do I make myself clear?"

"Yes and no, but I'll find out later."

Barnes continued. "Kohly will use some of the money to buy supplies and equipment for his underground, and some to bribe selected personnel in Castro's military. We've got to know what's going on down there. Now, you're not to say anything about this to Kohly, but the rest is to be converted in Puerto Rico to Pound Sterling, so you can physically handle it on your person. Do you understand? It's all been arranged."

"I do now. But as far as the missile complex is concerned, we know where it is. Isn't there any chance for a U-2 overfly to get some immediate dope?"

"Damn, we went through this before. Nothing's changed."

"OK. So all that's left is Mario's underground?"

"That's it, Robert. Now get your tail in gear. Tell Mario that the package he was expecting arrived. The bank will be open by 10:00 A.M. With any luck at all, you'll be in Puerto Rico by mid-afternoon and back in Florida by nightfall. The Comanche should be back from New Oreleans and at Opa Locka. Your instructions will be on board. Also, I've ordered it refueled."

"That's good. I don't think my credit card to the Gaslight Club could handle it."

Barnes chortled. "I know the feeling. I understand Kohly wants you to fly him to Canada. That's fine, but in a single-engine plane, you won't be permitted to enter Canada until daylight. When you return from Puerto Rico, Kohly will have made arrangements for you to stay somewhere. I assume it will be in Coral Gables at his son's house. At any rate, do not check out of the Case Verde when you leave this morning; then no one will know that you've gone or be able to trace your movements. When you decide to leave for Canada, depart in the morning and be sure to file a flight plan for Rochester. Then you can fly on to Canada and simply tell the tower you are meeting friends for a fishing trip at Stony Lake, Ontario. I understand you own an island there."

"Actually, its my mother-in-law's. But where do I land in Canada?" I understand Kohly wants to go to Peterboro."

"There's an airport in Peterboro. The runways are long enough for the Comanche, and by the way, please tell Mario that Marshall Diggs contacted me. Kohly has been asked to meet with Maxwell Taylor, Kennedy's military advisor. I frankly don't know what they have up their sleeves, but apparently the President has calmed down the Attorney General. Call me in Washington if you run into any trouble, Robert."

"OK. I will."

Our conversation completed, there was a moment of silence. Hesitantly, Barnes added a rushed "Robert, take care," and hung up.

I could feel the adrenalin pumping through me; then I remembered that the $150 I was carrying would not get me very far. I would be fine for my short hops to Bimini and Puerto Rico but I would need a credit card before I took off for Canada. Thank God I would not be required to check out of the Casa Verde; the tariff was a minimum of seventy-five dollars a day if it was a cent, and I still had to worry about fuel for the Comanche. As economical as it was, those 400 "horses" ate up a great deal of fuel. Well, I smiled to myself. . .I really am covered; hell! I'd be carrying a quarter of a million dollars in cash in just a few hours. When I pulled back the draperies covering the large window, I noticed for the first time what a magnificent day it would be for flying.

Kohly and del Valle arrived just as I finished dressing. It was Kohly who asked, "So what's new, compadre?"

"Well, I heard from Barnes. The money will be available in Bimini at 10:00 A.M. I have been assigned to the ranks of the infamous; I'm part of your group, at least temporarily, and I'm all set to fly to Bimini to pick up the cash." I then proceeded to tell him about the need for the underground and the meeting with Maxwell Taylor. He mulled over my statements for a minute, grimaced and said, "The son of a bitch has decided he needs my underground."

"If you want my opinion," del Valle said, "I think the CIA Director finally got to the President and told him the facts of life. However, I would trust neither what the Kennedys say nor do, if my ass were on the line. They've both proven themselves untrustworthy once and they will do so again. Mark my words, Mario."

"I agree, my friend, but it will be most interesting to see what General Taylor has to say. When do they propose to hold this meeting?"

"Barnes didn't say; however, I would assume sometime soon. Now, I think we should have breakfast because I need to get going if I'm to accomplish everything I'm scheduled to do this afternoon. Also, before I forget, you'd better give me the documentation I will require in Bimini. Please make sure that I am identified as Robert Porter."

With breakfast completed, documentation in order and the Comanche pre-flighted, I was in the car and on my way to South Bimini Airport. I covered the sixty-three miles in about sixteen minutes, being careful to stay within sight of land. I touched down on the 5,000-foot Bimini runway. After clearing immigration and customs, I rode into town in the most dilapidated taxi I'd ever seen. The taxi, a Ford Anglia, creaked to a stop in front of the Island Bank in the center of town. At ten o'clock, Bimini was barely awake. The bank was completely deserted. I went in and asked to see the manager.

The manager's name was Alexander Westwood. He was a nattily dressed Englishman in a white linen suit and light blue shirt, impeccably bisected by a deep red silk tie.

"Mr. Kohly?" he asked, hesitantly.

"No, Sir. My name's Porter, Robert Porter. I'm here on Mr. Kohly's behalf."

"Fine," he replied as we shook hands. "I have been advised by our main office that a transfer was made to Mr. Kohly's numbered account from the Banco Nacional de Mexico. I presume you have the proper identification, along with a signed authorization to withdraw, of course. May I see it, please?"

"Certainly." Reaching into my wallet, I pulled out my Porter passport and drivers license, and a sheet of onion skin paper which had been carefully folded between two sheets of plastic. I presented the documentation to him.

After unfolding the paper, he opened the top drawer of his desk and removed a large manila envelope, with what I assumed was the account number printed at the top. After carefully checking each number, he opened the folder to compare signatures. Then he said, "All seems to be in order. We'll have to count the currency in accordance with the instructions. I would like you to count it with us. We wish to avoid any problem at the other end."

"Thank you. I appreciate that."

"Excellent. Shall we proceed? I have everything prepared in the vault."

As we walked out of his office, I saw him give a little nod to one of the girls seated near the entrance. She picked up a telephone as we walked toward the vault. In the next hour, we counted out $320,000.00 in denominations of twenties, fifties and hundreds. Upon completing our count I carefully placed the money in a briefcase. I signed the receipt, bid farewell to Westwood and left the bank.

Upon my arrival at the bank, I had spotted a taxi stand half a block away. Walking toward it, I could sense someone following me. Suddenly, I felt very naked without my Walther which would have been impossible to conceal under a loose sport shirt and no jacket. As I approached the cab stand, the first of the three taxis pulled out and the others moved forward.

I stopped to look into a shop window that displayed several parakeets and other tropical birds. The angled plate glass reflected a small, shabbily dressed man in a white cotton jacket and torn trousers, watching me from across the street. He was less than fifty feet away, holding a newspaper in front of his face as if he were reading it. I was ready to dash for the cabs when I caught the menacing reflection of two other swarthy men stepping out of a doorway between me and the taxi stand. I began panicking when I noticed, in the narrow alley next to the shop, a rusty rack containing three bicycles and a BSA motorcycle with its ignition switch unlocked. The owner had probably thought no one in his right mind would steal a motorcycle, or any other vehicle for that matter, on an island you could drive across in ten minutes. It was a straight shot to the airport, and I figured that with any luck at all I could get halfway there before my "shadows" could crank either of the rickety cabs into motion.

I turned and started walking back toward the bank, causing my "shadow" across the street to turn away so that he was not directly facing me. Making a quick about-face, I ran into the alley, and pulled the motorcycle off the stand. Thank God it was still warm. Two quick kicks and the engine came alive. Barely holding on to the briefcase, I roared out of the alley, careened across the sidewalk, over the curb, and into the street, and headed directly for the airport road.

Riding along, I wondered who was paying the three characters I had just eluded. Presumably no one except Kohly's immediate group and Cabell's group knew of my intended trip. Yet somebody must have tipped off Castro's men. The leak could only be from someone who knew that a large transfer had been made to Kohly from the Banco Nacional de Mexico. That must have been the connection. I had no doubt that the three men must have been on Castro's payroll, and for that matter, so must a bank officer.

As I approached the airport, I began feeling a little better, and was positively ecstatic when I slid to a stop next to the Comanche. There was no one in sight. After a quick pre-flight, I was sky borne and on a course to Puerto Rico.

My instructions were to exchange the U.S. dollars into British Pound Sterling at the largest Chase Bank office in San Juan. I assumed that I was ordered to do this as a viable means of laundering the money. I had no proof of this, of course, but strongly suspected that the money was acquired via activities which the Agency preferred remain untraceable.

After landing and checking through immigration and customs, I hailed a taxi and headed into San Juan. I asked the driver to take me to the main Chase Bank office in the city. I expected smooth sailing in U.S. territory. I quickly realized that this expectation was unrealistic. At the first light we encountered upon entering town, my driver turned to me and asked, "Are you expecting any company?" When I replied, "No. Why?" he said, "A car pulled out as soon as you got in. We're being tailed by these mean-looking "mothers" who always remain two car lengths behind us."

Startled, I instructed my driver to take me to the bank quickly and wait while I went inside. I exchanged $300,000.00 of the cash into British currency — not an easy feat, considering the amount — and hurriedly returned to my waiting taxi. The skids had obviously been well greased. My patiently waiting driver immediately pulled away from the curb, exclaiming, "They're still there, and from the looks of it they are getting ready to make some sort of move. Where to?"

I knew there was one possible sanctuary for an Agency employee in San Juan and told the driver, "The Villa Repose at Cerro Gordo near the Dorado Beach Hotel. If we make it, you will be fifty dollars richer than you are right now."

"Ah, Congressman Powell's new place. You're as good as there," he said with a chuckle, and pushed the accelerator to the floor.*

It took us a while to reach our destination. My driver was continually attempting to lose our unwanted tail and was forced to outmaneuver every attempt made to overtake us. Finally, we nearly flew up a white-graveled drive to the doorway of a sprawling, tropically modern house. Off to one side was an expansive green lawn flanking a terrace. I saw flashing black and white bodies and heard the sound of laughter and splashing water. The three men in the pursuing car had evidently been successfully evaded, or at least had chosen not to follow me to Powell's; they were no longer

*I had met Powell while dining with Fran Russell at the newly opened Jockey Club in the Fairfax Hotel. He was with Corinne Huff, a beauty queen from Ohio who was Powell's current secretary. He gave me his card and Fran later described the new home he had just finished in Puerto Rico.

in sight. Thanking the driver profusely, I paid him his well-earned fare and dividend. As he drove back down the drive, I turned and rang the doorbell. In a moment the door was opened by a gorgeous, bronze-skinned girl who wore a brief halter and a very short skirt.

"Good morning, sir," she said. "Can I help you?"

"I hope so," I replied. "My name is Robert Porter. I've had some trouble and would like to use your telephone." At that moment, my only thought was to let Tracy Barnes know what was happening.

"I assume you are an American," she said. I nodded. "Do you know whose residence this is?"

"I do indeed," I replied. "And if the Congressman is here I wonder if I might speak with him. My name is Robert Porter. And you might tell him I'm a friend of General Charles Cabell, Deputy Director of the CIA." Her response was a cynical smile and a brief pause. Then, staring directly at me she said, "If you will wait here for a moment, I will ask if someone can see you." She returned momentarily and said, "If you will follow me I will take you to the Congressman. He is having lunch by the pool." Then, almost as an afterthought: "My name, incidentally, is Françoise Manet."

As is sometimes the case, I found myself torn between my appreciation of beauty and my need for food. The mention of lunch stirred pangs of hunger. I had not eaten for more than twelve hours and hoped I might be invited to join the congressman. I had been admiring the handsome foyer of his palatial home, but now, as I followed Françoise to the terrace, I could hardly take my eyes off her. As I knew from our brief encounter in Washington, the Congressman's superb taste was clearly not confined to architecture and decor. Although all the windows and doors were open, the place was cool, but as we reached the terrace I once more felt the sun's heat.

Powell was seated at a canopied table covered with white linen and set with sparkling silverware. On the other side of the terrace was an Olympic-sized pool where his guests were clearly enjoying themselves. Powell remained seated when I was introduced to him but briefly shook my extended hand and pointed to the chair opposite him. Without looking at Françoise, he said, "Get our guest a drink and make sure we're not disturbed. Where's Yvette?"

"In town, sir. And what would you like to drink, Mr. Porter?"

"Ice tea would be just fine, thank you."

"Yes, sir," she said dutifully, and walked back toward the house. I watched her retreating figure as long as I thought I could without making a total ass out of myself, and then looked back at my host.

Powell had an amused smile. "You've gotten thinner." I suddenly realized he remembered me from Washington. Then he said, "Françoise is a lovely child, twenty-six and thoroughly corruptible. You may be my guest as long as you are my guest." I felt chagrined that I had been so obvious. "But no one need be lonely here," he continued, waving toward the pool. "As you can see, Yvette[6] and I maintain a bountiful supply of companions for our Washington friends.

For the first time I focused my attention on the group in the pool and recognized, at the shallow end, a respected and aging United States Senator, and the fortyish son of another prominent Senator, frolicking with Powell's bountiful supply of companions.

"Now, what brings you to Puerto Rico and what, if anything, can I do to help you? I presume there was a message in your reference to General Cabell?"

Suddenly I became uncomfortably aware of the bulging money belt stuffed with high denomination British Pound Notes and U.S. dollars around my waist. Completing my assignment and bringing it to Kohly was the most important thing in the world to me. Although the chairman of the powerful House Committee on Education and Labor was a good friend of the Kennedys, he was also anti-Castro. I had heard about some of his exploits in Washington from numerous sources during the Presidential campaigns of 1960. As a result, I had made a split-second decision that Powell might be the only individual on the island who could get me out alive. I decided to level with him.

In the next five minutes I gave him a full report on who I was, who I worked for, and what I had gone through, both here and on Bimini. He listened attentively, commended my frankness, and said, "Now, while you're having some lunch I'll see what I can do. When you have finished, Françoise will show you to some quarters where you can relax, or, if you wish, join the group at the pool. I don't think it advisable to leave before this evening. If you can give one or two of my guests a lift back to the mainland, they wouldn't dare touch you."

He left the table and in a moment Françoise reappeared with a servant who brought a feast that matched the surroundings: avocados stuffed wtih crabmeat, lobster topped with a creamy garlic sauce, cherries jubilee and Viennese coffee. When I had finished, Françoise, wearing a matching bikini swimsuit and short skirt, escorted me to a cool, spacious bedroom dominated by a huge canopied bed. She said, "You'll find robes and swimming attire laid out in the bath, sir, unless you would prefer to take a nap. I'll have a fresh suit for you soon. If there is anything else you need, please call me. The phone is beside your bed and my intercom number is seven."

I took a hot bath and relaxed. When finished, I realized that my only course of action for the moment was sleep. After putting the money belt under the pillows, I tumbled into bed. The last thought I had was the hell Barnes was gonig to give me for not being back in Miami this afternoon.

When I awoke, it was to the strains of soft music coming from the patio beneath my window and a cool hand lightly caressing my cheek. It was early evening.

Françoise, taking her hand from my cheek, said, "My, you're going to need a shave." Her hair, which had earlier been piled on top of her head, was now down around her shoulders, a thick, soft, and wavy chestnut coloured coif. She wore a superb long white sheath dress, cut to reveal her figure.

"My God, you're beautiful."

"You're not so bad yourself, cherie. I've laid your things out." Then, hesitantly, "I've been told that you are going back to Miami tonight. The Congressman has arranged everything. But before you leave, you will be having cocktails and dinner with him. If you'd care to escort me, I've been invited to attend . . . with you."

I reached up and took her hand. "It will be my pleasure, mademoiselle. By the way, where are you from?"

"New Orleans, and thank you, Robert. I'll wait downstairs for you until you're ready. The guests are already having cocktails, but we probably won't eat dinner much before nine o'clock."

"I don't have my watch on. What time is it?"

"Not quite 7:15. I'll be waiting."

With that she went out, closing the door quietly behind her.

As I swung out of bed, I noticed that my money belt was missing. Frantic, I looked around in the subdued light and sighed with relief when I saw it lying beside a pile of fresh linen, next to an unfamiliar white linen suit and shirt on a hanger.

Françoise had probably removed the belt. I checked the contents. It seemed to be as thick with bills as when I had exchanged the dollars into pounds that afternoon.

I quickly shaved and dressed. The suit fit. That was no surprise because I was a perfect size forty. Even the cuffs were the right length. I took a quick look in the mirror and, satisifed, walked down a long corridor to the cocktail party. Powell did things correctly and with great panache: the music I had been hearing was not from a stereo but from a small ensemble seated on the terrace.

As I walked into the room, Françoise appeared at the doorway of the library, a glass in each hand. Smiling, she handed one to me, then put her lips to my ear and whispered, "It's nonalcoholic. You're going to fly the Congressman's guests back to the mainland tonight, so I don't want anything happening to you." The warm, moist tip of her tongue darted into my ear.

She giggled quietly at my expression. Arm in arm, we walked through the library to the softly lighted terrace. The empty pool glowed with a blue fluorescence.

"Arrangements have been made to escort you to your plane. The Congressman is assuming you can carry two additional passengers?" She looked up at me expectantly, running the tip of her tongue across her lips.

"Of course." Then leaning down close to her, I said, "For God's sake stop it. Do you want to be dragged off into the bushes right now?"

"Sorry cheri, you seem so vulnerable. And you are carrying a lot of money." She reached over and tweaked my money belt. In response, I pulled her to me and kissed her.

The moment was suddenly broken by the harsh voice of Powell who was standing in the doorway. He sounded both bemused and irritated. "It appears that little Françoise has found a friend."

Startled, Françoise jumped away from me and said, "I'm sorry, sir." Then, with a quick glance at me, she hurried into the library.

After Françoise's hurried departure, Powell and I walked indoors. Near the library he introduced me to a man in uniform who had obviously been instructed to wait for us near the library door. The man was a police official. After our brief introduction Powell continued, "I've explained your situation to the captain. He agrees that with the amount of cash you are carrying, and the fact that Castro agents are on to you, it would be wise if one of his men accompanied you to your plane. It wouldn't be the first time something was hijacked between the customs gate and an aircraft."

"Why, yes," I said to the captain. "If those arrangements suit you, I'd be more than grateful."

He nodded and said, "Happy to, sir," then looked dubiously at the glass in my hand.

"Only fruit juice, Captain."

He smiled and said, "Of course, I should have known. At any rate, the aircraft is under guard and you may depart at any time."

"Right, Robert," Powell interjected, "but not before dinner, eh? There's a marvelous feast awaiting us. In fact, our guests are probably eating at this very moment. Why don't you join them? The Captain and I have a few things to discuss. When you're finished, you'll be driven to the airport."

"Thanks, I appreciate your kind hospitality."

I left them and walked through the library into the crowded dining room. A large buffet was in progress. I looked through the forty or fifty people, and spotted one of my intended passengers talking excitedly to Yvette Powell, the Congressman's new wife. Françoise was nowhere in sight. Feeling a little dejected, I ate. I had just completed my meal when a servant told me that the Congressman's Washington guests were ready to leave for the mainland. I asked if he would tell Miss Manet that I had to leave.

Smiling knowingly he said, "I believe that Miss Manet is already waiting in the car with the two gentlemen, sir. She will drive you to the airport. First, however, the Congressman wishes to see you in his private study."

He escorted me to the room where Powell was waiting.

"Well, I guess this is it," I said. "Good-bye, and thanks again for everything. I'll return the suit."

"Forget it," Powell laughingly replied as he shook my hand. "I was happy to help."

A Lincoln convertible, its top up, was at the entrance with its engine running. Françoise was at the wheel and the two inebriated Washingtonians were in the back seat. I slipped in beside her. As we started down the drive, she turned on the radio and set the controls so that music would come only from the rear speakers, preventing our passengers from hearing our conversation.

"Great," I said. "Now, I've got to ask, may we see each other again?. . . In Washington, perhaps?"

"I wish we could but it would be unwise. No matter what Adam says, he really would be upset if you attempted to encroach on his territory."

"Well. . .do you ever get to Miami?"

Her eyes brightened and she said, "Of course, how stupid of me. I'll be in Miami with the Congressman for the next few days. He's meeting with some constituents who are attending a convention and wants me to go along to assist."

"Can you get away while you are there?"

"Probably. I usually do some shopping while I'm on the mainland. It may even be possible to get away overnight." The implication was overwhelming. I leaned over and kissed her.

She quickly pulled away. "If all goes well, I can meet you in

Miami tomorrow night. The two men in the back seat will be staying at the Kenilworth, and Adam and I will be at the Fontainebleau. We can meet there after he leaves for New York. He has to fly out on a late afternoon flight. I'm not exactly sure what time yet."

"That's fine," I said. "I have a suite at the Casa Verde in Lauderdale by the Sea, but with the traffic and construction it takes an hour to get from there to Miami Beach."

"In that case, I'd better call you sometime in the afternoon. If you're out, I'll leave a message saying when I'll be free and where you can meet me. Until then. . . ."

The airport came into view over a small rise, and no one was in sight as the Lincoln sped down the access road to where the private aircraft were hangared. However, when we reached the Comanche, I spotted two men in the shadows who waved and stepped out to meet us upon recognizing the big car. I opened the door, but Françoise put her hand on my arm and I waited until Powell's guests got out. "Again, until tomorrow night."

By the time my bodyguard and I had helped the two men strap themselves into the rear seat of the Comanche, the Lincoln had disappeared. The panel clock indicated that fifteen hours had elapsed since I had first touched down on Bimini.

CHAPTER SIX NOTES:

1. Eladio del Valle was sometimes referred to as Oscar the Assassin, thus, the nickname. Another man who adopted this nickname was a man who trained a paramilitary force on No Name Key, for the assassination of Fidel Castro. This man, known as Colonel William C. Bishop, a rank that could never be verified and was probably self-bestowed, was identified in an FBI report (File # 105-78397-11, pg. 2–3) dated December 1960. Del Valle's brother was also known as Oscar.

2. Casa Verde was not the real name of the motel where the events portrayed in this book occurred. It is however, in Lauderdale by the Sea and easily identifiable by its description.

3. These funds were actually to be exchanged in Puerto Rico for British Pound notes. These notes were much easier to carry as they were worth $2.80 per Pound.

4. An actual copy of the list is shown in the Appendices.

5. The money was being laundered from the Carlos Marcello organization.

6. Powell's wife at that time.

7

JUNE 1961

I was glad to see Tracy Barnes. I could tell by his greeting that the feeling was mutual when he met me at the Miami International Airport. Having left the Comanche to be fueled, the two of us rushed through customs and immediately packed my Washingtonian passengers off to the Kenilworth Hotel. The Commanche was topped off with gas by the time we returned. We made a quick pre-flight check, buckled up and waited for clearance to begin the short trip back to Opa-Locka.

While waiting for the tower to give me clearance for take-off, Barnes explained his presence in Miami. He had been very concerned when I hadn't returned on schedule and when he told Richard Bissell, his boss, he was ordered to search for me.

I was flattered, though somewhat surprised, by Barnes' concern and Bissell's orders to find me. I suppose my expression registered my skepticism when I said, "I'm surprised the Deputy Director of Plans remembers me."

"As Chief of Covert Operations, he doesn't forget his people."

"It's reassuring to know he cares," I said without much conviction.

"Oh, he cares all right!" Barnes remarked with more seriousness than I would have anticipated. "We all care. We have to or we'd be six feet under by now. Besides, what the hell else can we trust?"

Barnes' remarks gave me pause for reflection throughout the remainder of our flight to Opa-Locka. In fact, I was still thinking about his comments and my own convictions during the hour it took us to service the Comanche in the expectation of the impending

Canada trip, and get to the hotel room where Kohly was awaiting our arrival. It was Kohly's voice that finally jolted me from my soul searching. As we opened the door of his room, he jumped out of his chair to greet me saying, "Thank God you're safe! Are you alright?"

Handing him the money belt, I replied, "It wasn't easy. At least it's all here."

Once again, the money had to be counted. He called del Valle and asked him to join us; we could use a helping hand. As the money was split between 100,000 U.S. dollars and the remainder in British pounds, our accounting task was more complicated than a simple bill count. Kohly didn't seem to mind this split in currency, and worked as determinedly as the rest of us. The last bill was counted as the clock struck midnight. Too tired to think about socializing, we quickly bid each other "good night" and retired.

Barnes, Kohly, del Valle and I met the next morning for breakfast. Barnes said that the trip to Canada was put on hold for a few days and, although not verbally stated, we all seemed to understand that this was a day for seeing to our personal agendas. I had decided that rest and relaxation were my top priorities, and looked forward to making the few calls I had to make to Baltimore and then simply idling away the rest of the day and evening.

Barnes provided a slight distraction when he handed me the keys to another souped-up Buick convertible. Although I didn't feel like road racing again, I left the table to take a look at the Buick and discovered that it was identical to the one I used to rescue Kohly from his pursuers the day he blew the whistle on Kennedy's refusal to acknowledge the presence of Soviet missiles in Cuba. The memory of that car chase from the Channel Five studio in Bethesda to Kohly's awaiting flight would remain with me for the rest of my life. Even to this day, I can't believe I lived through it all. It was like something straight out of a movie I didn't want to repeat.

I spent the remainder of my morning calling Baltimore. I wanted to let them know that I was fine. All my calls went well and it was certainly good to hear Amy's voice, but I knew that she did not believe that I was on a simple business trip. I had a very hard time trying to convince her and hung up the phone uncertain I had done so. One of the most difficult aspects of my work was its secrecy. I could never tell anyone, including those closest to me, about the nature of my real assignments or any aspect of the experiences I had in performing them.

Having completed all the items on my morning agenda, I decided that I needed to feel the sun's warmth for a bit and headed for the pool. I hadn't been there long when my relaxation was interrupted by a page announcing a phone call for me. Initially I thought it might be Kohly. Del Valle and he had rented a car to visit his son in Coral Gables. I thought perhaps something had happened, and my relaxation was really going to be cut short. When I got to the phone, I was surprised to hear Françoise's lovely voice. She invited me to join her in Powell's suite at the Fontainebleau. Apparently, Powell had left for New York that afternoon and she was free. I needed no further convincing. I left word of my destination for Barnes and headed out of there like a greyhound after a hare. The ride to the Fontainebleau was one of the shortest I had ever driven. I don't think it was the distance.

I hadn't been with Françoise very long when I realized that I was totally taken by her. I must confess, I felt as though we were honeymooning. We shopped for a while and then headed back to the room. Our shower was long and sensual, and after quickly drying off, we headed back to the bed to finish what we had started moments before. It was only after we were totally spent that we decided to regain our strength by having dinner, and dined in the hotel's lavish supper club.

The night seemed too young to waste and after dining we decided to go for a walk down Collins Avenue. It took only half an hour before I could stand it any longer, so I led her back to our suite where we continued where we'd left off only a few short hours before. At 3:00 A.M. I collapsed with exhaustion, having found my body incapable of keeping up with my desires. Slumber came easily and peacefully to both of us. I had not felt so relaxed and so eager to rest in weeks. But my serenity didn't last long. It seemed as though I had just closed my eyes when I was startled awake by intense light and a gruff voice yelling, "Wake up, you filthy Yankee pigs. I wish to have a little talk with you."

Instinctively, I reached under my pillow for the Walther, fumbling around trying to find it, cursing my sleep-induced clumsiness. As my eyes became more focused and accustomed to the light, I saw what my hand had already discovered—my gun was gone. A bearded Cuban, towering over me, was pointing it at point-blank range directly at my forehead.

Next to me, Françoise moaned groggily and rolled over to avoid the light. As she turned, I noticed a younger, clean-shaven Cuban on her side of the bed lecherously eyeing her nakedness.

Both of our visitors wore white hotel maintenance uniforms; their demeanor, so inconsistent with their dress, told me that our problems were much greater than what I had initially assumed. This certainly wasn't a matter of bad plumbing and, somehow, I didn't seem to think it was a routine hold-up. I was pissed but knew that I needed to try to find a way to dominate the situation, at least intellectually. I kept thinking that if only I could find out what they wanted, Françoise and I might have a chance. A forcefully demanding question seemed a good place to start. I shouted sternly: "Who in hell's name are you?"

They both stood up straighter, as if shocked by my language and needing to assert their position. "We ask the questions around here. Get out of bed!"

My shouts brought Françoise out of her semi-stupor and into reality. When she finally realized we were in serious trouble, she tried to scream. I cupped my hand over her mouth before she could utter a sound. Her eyes said all that needed to be said.

The man with my gun grabbed my arm and, shoving me, growled, "Porter, you come with me for a little talk." He turned to his clean-shaven compadre and said, "Watch her and keep her entertained."

"Nothing doing, punk," I exploded. "If either of you bastards touches her, I'll rip your heads off!"

The bearded one turned to his partner and laughed. "He talks big for a Yankee swine. Particularly a naked, unarmed one."

The bearded Cuban picked up the negligée Françoise had left on a chair and tossed it to her, saying, "Here, niña, put this on. My friend will not harm you if your amante tells us what we want to know."

For the first time she spoke. "Robert, don't let them . . ."

"That's enough out of you. Keep quiet. Come on, Roberto, you won't need your clothes."

He turned to the younger man and, addressing him in Spanish, told him to keep his hands off the girl. I couldn't make out all he said, but the intent was clear in his tone and the movement of his eyes. His subordinate's quick response left no doubt that he had been warned.

"Si, Capitan."

"Tie her to the bed and come help me."

The gun's muzzle between my vertebrae was all the convincing I needed to go over to an open-backed chair in the middle of the adjoining room.

"I really don't intend to kill either one of you, unless you force me to, of course," the bearded captain said as he paced in circles around the chair.

In what I thought to be a convincingly innocent voice, I asked, "What could I possibly know that could interest you?"

"Perhaps you'd like to tell us what that treasonous bastard Kohly intends to do with the $300,000 you brought back. Better yet, where is the traitor now? What was your CIA doing in Camaguey the night that the treasonous bastards were trying to invade our homeland? As you Americanos say, 'How is that for openers?'"

He spurted out questions as quickly as a machine gun, his voice crackling with a vile contempt equal in intensity to the rapidity of his questions. This Cuban knew a great deal. Clearly he was a major player and not some stringer sent on a search and seek intelligence mission. I quickly realized that I had to be very careful. My sense of danger increasing by the second, I knew that he probably wouldn't buy into my feigned innocence, but it was the only hope I seemed to have for the moment. I needed time, and a naive routine might just give me the extra minute I needed to clear my thoughts.

"I don't know why you think I have the answers," I said, hoping my moment to think had been bought. I should have anticipated his reaction. He didn't buy my routine, but I quickly realized how naive I really was in reading people. Il Capitano screamed out in a fit of real anger: "What do you take us for, Porter? Idiots? We know you work closely with Kohly. We know you're his link to the CIA. We know about EVERY flight you've made – YOU ARE TRYING MY PATIENCE! Now talk to me, you swine!"

His slap came from nowhere, but landed squarely on my face. He had hit me so hard, I quite literally saw stars. I shook myself back into consciousness, and felt him roughly tie my bare legs with a section of clothesline just below the knees. He jerked the rope up to bind my arms to the back of my seat, the movement causing the rope to bite more deeply into my legs. Blood spurted from my mouth in a salty red river. I could feel with my tongue that one of my front teeth was loose.

Having bound me securely to the chair, my captor yelled to his partner, "Hurry up in there, Callas. Porter needs to be persuaded to talk to us. I think this pig needs to be shown how we fix Americans."

I had visions of broken bones and plucked eyeballs swimming in my head while waiting for Callas to come over. I had figured out by now that these guys were the Cuban DGI (Directorate General of Intelligence), the equivalent of the Russian KGB. I knew I sure in hell wasn't going to have tea with them.

The Capitan propped my legs up with a coffee table and Callas went around to my back. I knew it was coming. I tensed. My inquisitor's palm suddenly smashed up into my nose . . . I couldn't breathe . . . the stars returned and I gasped. The moment my mouth opened, Callas whipped a twisted towel tightly between my teeth. I was gagging, trying to breathe . . . thinking I would choke to death. But the fear of choking was quickly interrupted by Callas' forearm pinning my head against his belly.

In terror, I watched his bearded superior pull a cigar lighter

lighter out of his pocket. Fingering it slowly, provocatively, he lit it and admired the flame. And then, ever so deliberately, almost gently, he increased the amount of fluid, feeding the flame, making it grow higher . . . and higher . . . and higher . . . I could see the steps of its wicked ballet in the blackness of his eyes.

I remember silently screaming, "Oh, God!" . . . Here it comes" . . . while holding my breath in anticipation of his next move. He held the lighter to my left shin and within seconds I jerked in agony. The fetid stink of my own burnt flesh filled my nostrils, making me want to vomit. I was gagging, choking and utterly helpless. I knew if I gave in to vanity I would choke to death. It took every bit of control I could muster to keep the vomit down. I couldn't do anything but pray for unconsciousness. It seemed to take forever, but my prayers were answered . . . at least temporarily.

I dreamt that I was drowning. It wasn't a dream; my captors had dumped a bucket of ice water over my head in an effort to revive me. I snorted, trying to clear my nose. The torture began again, the torch being run around my other leg. My vision was blurring, the tears streaming from my eyes. The voices of Callas and the Captain seemed to come from another dimension as they demanded that I talk.

"Had enough?" they growled.

I nodded, so they removed the gag. My left leg throbbed and sizzled as though it had been boiled in acid. I knew I couldn't placate them with trite data that wasn't classified, but as I was going to be dead meat in the end, whatever I said would make little difference. I'd had quite enough of the game, and decided that straightforward language was the best approach. So I told them to stick their heads up their asses. Callas immediately shoved the gag back between my aching jaws, and my right leg was subjected to the same treatment as my left. Mercifully, I faded to black again.

I had no idea how long I was unconscious, but I awoke to a room full of people, including Kohly and del Valle. I looked over to the room where Françoise had been. I saw my tormentor lying in a pool of blood and guts in the bedroom doorway. His belly was gaping open, his entrails hanging out touching the floor. I looked down at a doctor sticking needles into my blackened legs and wondered why I didn't feel any pain.

"You're full of Novacaine, my friend," comforted Kohly. 'We're taking you to a hospital now. You've also been given a shot to knock you out. It's time for you to have a siesta. I'll go over everything later."

"Where's Françoise?" I was very worried.

"Everything in due time," he dodged.

When I awoke the next day I was disoriented. My surroundings were unfamiliar and I couldn't recall how I had gotten to this place. Fortunately, my eyes focused on Barnes standing at my bedside. "What's going on?" I asked.

"You are being guarded by Kohly's own men in a private clinic here in Coral Gables."

"Where's Françoise?" I was determined to know.

"You're bound to find out sooner or later. Robert, she didn't make it." He was compassionate, but I was still in shock.

"Oh, my God. I did this to her. If she hadn't been with me, she'd still be alive today."

"Don't be a damned fool, Robert. They tailed her to find you in the first place."

"How did she die?"

Barnes sighed and shook his head. "It wasn't pretty. Robert, I must know what you told them. One of your interrogators got away with whatever you gave him."

"Believe me, Tracy. I didn't tell them anything. Not a damn thing. They already knew quite a bit. It took me by surprise. I couldn't stay conscious long enough. I've never felt that kind of pain before."

"Well, you may still have some pain when I need you to fly again in a few days." Then the nurse walked in with a needle in her hand. He left me to my sleep before telling me about Françoise. I found out eventually.

They had gagged her so she couldn't cry out. Then the young

creep took his superior's malevolent lighter and burned her nipples off completely. Since she had nothing of value to tell them, the vicious little bastard had raped her with a ten-inch knife—a horrific way to die. Del Valle avenged Françoise. He shot the Capitan, wounding him in the knee. Then, while the bastard was still alive and squirming to get away, del Valle removed the knife from Françoise's body and used it to slice open the Capitan's belly, disemboweling him.

It was a quirk of luck that sent Kohly and del Valle to my rescue that night. It seems the trouble had started back at my hotel in Fort Lauderdale. A night watchman was at a condo under construction close to our motel.

He noticed a small boat heading toward the beach that separated the complex from the motel. Brecken Security Service was immediately called and their night desk man responded. He filed the following report:

"Just as the gunmen slipped into the hall entrance of the hotel (where Kohly and I were staying), I pulled my car into the lot next door. Grabbing a flashlight, I got out of my car and walked about fifty feet toward the beach. Somewhere off to my left, I heard the noise of several automatic weapons. I knew my .38 police positive was no match for automatic weapons, so I ran back to the car and got my Colt .45 service automatic that I keep under the front seat. Then, I called in an emergency on the radio to the Sheriff's department.

I also tried reaching my headquarters, but got no response. I figured I'd better not wait any longer, so after cocking a round into the chamber of the .45, I ran toward the Casa Verde. I got to the building without incident and paused in the shadows. I couldn't believe what was happening. The rooms were being raked systematically by the Thompsons, while orders were shouted in Spanish.

I was about to make a run into the building when I spotted a man on one of the patios, reloading a submachine gun. Steadying myself, I fired directly into the small of the Cuban's back. He convulsed and fell. I discovered I had broken his spine.

Fortunately, the others failed to hear the shot over the racket they were making.

"I grabbed his Thompson, finished loading it and, hugging the wall, edged toward the door to the inner hallway and peered through its small glass panel. At that moment the firing stopped. In the center of the hall, less than fifteen feet from where I was standing, there were three men with submachine guns jabbering in Spanish.

"Now, I don't want to say I did the right thing or the wrong thing. But I knew I was thoroughly outnumbered. I did what they would have done. I flipped the door open with my foot, holding it against the automatic door closure, and opened fire at point blank range, emptying the clip of all fifteen rounds. I ditched the Thompson and pulled out the .45 and started cautiously down the hall. At the time, I didn't know how many there were.

"However, there was a fifth man, and he took off. He had been checking one of the rooms, and must have heard the men screaming as they got hit. The first I saw of him was the last. He was running toward the beach. When he reached the dinghy, he tossed in his weapon and as if the devil himself were chasing him, pushed the heavy boat through the surf and was off. I couldn't have gotten him if I tried. That's when I heard sirens racing toward me . . ."

Barnes continued to fill me in:

"While this chaos was occurring, Kohly and del Valle were just getting back to the hotel after visiting Kohly's son. The place was swarming with men from the police and sheriff's offices. Kohly rushed to call me and I immediately got in touch with several people in D.C. to insure there would be no compromising publicity for the CIA. I called back officially and talked to as many people as I could to keep the stories straight. When I realized you weren't around, I figured you were in danger. I told Kohly to find you at the Fontainebleau. He called you, but after ten rings he took del Valle with him straight to the Hotel in case you were in trouble."

"Damn. I'd stashed the phone in the nightstand's drawer so we wouldn't be bothered. That'll teach me."

"Who could know? When del Valle and Kohly started

knocking, Callas bolted out the bedroom door and eventually escaped in a laundry truck. We found the truck later in central Miami; the two drivers had been tied up and shot in the backs of their heads. So there you have it. I'm sure we'll get the bastard before he flees Miami." [1]

I spent two more days in the clinic nursing my wounded legs. Barnes apologetically pressed me to return to Washington as soon as possible. I learned how to doctor myself and was checked out. Then I said my goodbyes to Kohly and del Valle. With a bottle of aspirin and codeine pills in my pocket, I picked up the Comanche at Opa-Locka.

The weather was fine and I flew VFR to Savannah where I landed to refuel. I may not have needed it, but despite the clear skies I couldn't be sure about the changing climate in Baltimore. According to aviation weather, a line of thunderstorms was moving into the area from the west and it doesn't hurt to have a little margin for error. When I touched down, the tower turned me over to ground control and I was directed to Butler Aviation for refueling. I was also told to call the control tower for a message.

While the ground crew refueled the Comanche at the Butler ramp, I dialed the tower, wondering how Washington had tracked me down. To my surprise, the tower gave me a Miami call-back number. I found a pay phone, gave the operator my government credit card number, and placed the call. After two rings, I was talking to del Valle.

He was so excited he started talking in Spanish. "Roberto!" he exclaimed. "Madre de Dios! Oh, sorry, English. Yes, I am so glad that I found you. Are you all right?"

"Why? Shouldn't I be? What's the matter?"

"I have information that someone could have messed with your plane. You'd better check it out before it's too late."

"I always pre-flight, Eladio. I'll give it another once-over just for you, though, okay?"

"I mean it, Roberto. Something is definitely haywire."

I returned to the Comanche alert and worried. I wasn't prepared for another disaster. The last few days had taken their toll.

The ground crew had finished refueling the plane so I was free to begin a complete inspection of the Comanche. I figured I was looking for explosives.

It took me fifteen minutes to find the deadly charge, adroitly rigged with a fuse and barometric pressure switch. The insulated caulking around the engine cowl had been carefully removed and replaced with plastic explosive. The two substances are almost identical in color and texture, and I would never have found the device had it not been for the fuse buried in one end.

It was an ingenious rig. The pressure switch would activate when the plane had reached a specific altitude, directing electrical current into the fuse. But one thing made it clear that the person who did it was no amateur. He had connected the whole apparatus to the glide slope circuit. That, combined with the pressure switch, provided absolute insurance that the plane would be destroyed in the air and not on the ground. Even a preflight check wouldn't set off the charge. The pressure switch couldn't function until it reached several hundred feet. If conditions were minimal or I was making a night landing, I would normally turn on the glide slope on final approach, placing me several miles from the end of the runway when the explosive blew. The FAA would, in all probability, assume that something in the fuel system had malfunctioned, and write it off as a routine accident. Flying VFR, I had no need for the glide slope going into Savannah, but chances are I would have used it after dark at Friendship.[2] What I didn't discover until later was that the glide slope breaker had been temporarily deactivated.

Making sure the master switch was turned off, I gingerly removed the wires from the thermal fuse and gently worked it out with my fingers. Plastic explosive of this type is generally as harmless as clay, unless it is ignited electrically by this special type of fuse. Once the electrical circuitry was disconnected I began the tedious process of removing the explosive with a screwdriver and my fingernails.

This took me about forty-five minutes and, as expected, the attendants were obviously wondering what the hell I was doing. But

I couldn't worry about that. I bought some plastic caulking and refilled the channel where I had removed the plastique. I put the explosive in an empty coffee container and then took the thermal fuse, pressure sensor, and connecting wires and put them in a separate bag. I went into the men's room, molded the explosive into pellets, and flushed these down the john. Then, gently pulling the wires out of the fuse, I sent it down with another flush. A trash can took care of the rest.

By this time the ground crew was getting openly curious and I was glad to climb back into the Comanche and leave them with the mystery. The good weather held and I again flew VFR, staying close to the coast until I reached Chesapeake Bay, which I then followed all the way to Friendship Airport in Baltimore.

Approach control cleared me for a landing on runway 15. I taxied to Hinson Aviation at the south terminal, left instructions for refueling and called a cab. We made the trip through the new Baltimore Harbor Tunnel to my house in just under half an hour.

I was surprised to see my XK-150 in the back yard driveway with Barnes sitting in the driver's seat. As I paid the cab driver Tracy grabbed my suitcase and preceded me into the kitchen. "Everyone's out for the evening. I gave Cecily some money and told them to get dinner. It'll be an hour or so until they return. I have a car picking me up about then."

"Well, I've had another hell of an interesting day. I expected to have some peace and quiet tonight." Then, expressing what I really felt, I added, "Actually, Tracy, I'm glad you're here. I'd forgotten my car was in D.C. It would have been inconvenient as hell to get home and not have any transportation, to say nothing of having to pick the lock on my own door."

"Don't be too grateful," he replied. "I had to see you anyway. We've had a change in plans. How are your legs?"

"Hurting somewhat. I couldn't take any pain killers because I had to fly. I was afraid I might fall asleep and end up in the Atlantic."

"Any chance you'll be well enough to take a trip in a month?"

"Oh God, where to now?"

"We've postponed Mario's Canadian trip. Now that we don't have to get Kohly out of the country, he can operate freely. In fact he's scheduled to meet with Maxwell Taylor in the next few weeks. The President is using him as a military advisor. We received the information on the armaments. Everything we needed will be available in Europe from the Canadian company very shortly. I have the list with me.

"If you can do it, we want you to go to Europe in the next thirty to forty-five days. I'll give you the exact details just before the trip. We've determined it would be best if you make the transaction. Preliminary plans call for you to fly the Comanche into the Marine Terminal at LaGuardia. You'd leave it there, grab a cab to Idlewild,[3] and take TWA flight 900 into Madrid at 7:30 P.M."

"Well! Madrid sounds better than Peterboro. Now, how do I make peace with my family and friends in D.C.

He smiled and said, "Hell, you have a month or better to do it. When you get to Spain, you'll be checking into the Ritz Hotel; reservations will have been made." He took a large envelope from his pocket. "In the next week or so get a new personal passport, and an international drivers license. When I give you the money belt and credit cards, it should be all you will need, except for this." He handed me an envelope with $5,000 in cash. "The $300,000.00 is still intact," he said. "And speaking of money, from now on your paychecks will be held for you by the branch manager of the Suburban Trust Company.

"One of our people will contact you to show you around Madrid after you've caught a little sleep. You are then to phone the commercial attache at our Embassy. The Embassy is about fifteen blocks from your hotel up on the Serrano. Identify yourself. The commercial attache will let us know you arrived safely. Use the phrase, 'It seems extremely dry this year in Madrid.' If he's our man, he'll answer with, 'It's true, the rain does stay mainly in the plains.' If you don't use the phrase, he'll know you have a problem."

"Isn't that a bit corny? The phrase I mean."

"Perhaps, but any other code reply could be natural. With this one there'll be no mistake. After what you've gone through in the past week, you know what we're up against. I still find it hard to believe that Castro's boys could coordinate and pull off the operations they have."

"My God! I haven't told you what happened to me on the way back. Have you heard from Kohly or del Valle today?"

"I haven't had any reports from Miami. I've been waiting here for you most of the afternoon."

When I had filled him in, Barnes began pacing up and down the living room, "The Casa Verde—that I believe," he mused. "The Fontainebleau, I believe. What I can't believe is that your bomb was planted by Castro's boys." He suddenly stopped in mid-stride. "There may be another explanation. Did you use the ILS for your approach in either Bimini, Opa Locka or Miami?"

"No. But I didn't have to."

"Then it could have been installed earlier."

"Yes, because it wouldn't have exploded unless the pressure switch malfunctioned. . . ."

"Unless the switch had malfunctoned?" He mused, then asked abruptly, "when was the last time you used an instrument approach?"

"Now that you mention it, I haven't—not since I've been flying the Comanche."

"Then it could have been rigged anytime."

"I suppose so."

"That must be it. I'll bet the explosive was installed to be in reserve for future use. It probably could be activated with one simple adjustment whenever the need arose." Then, almost to himself, Barnes muttered, "Shaw and his group are damn fools. They're always playing with fire."

"Shaw? Who's he?"

"Clay Shaw. He's a contract consultant with the Agency and is associated with a number of firms we use as covers. Shaw heads the Trade Mart in New Orleans,[4] which is a perfect facade for the work he does for the Company."

"But why would they booby-trap the Comanche?"

"I'm not sure they did, and until I've done some checking I'm not prepared to talk about it. Now about the trip. Through an associate of Shaw's named Jack, Mario has agreed to buy some Schmeisser and Thompson machine guns.[5] Many of our purchases for the Bay of Pigs operation were arranged through him. Eladio del Valle will go to Canada as Kohly's representative. He will meet with Clay Shaw and arrange the buy. The weapons are being brokered through a Canadian firm, but the merchandise is in Greece.[5] You will go to Greece to make the payoff." Clay Shaw's right hand man is Dave Ferrie, the pilot with whom you flew into Cuba on the night of the invasion."

"How could I forget him. But seriously, why Greece?" I asked.

"Reasonable question, Robert. The arms are new, all packed in their original crates, complete with spare parts," Barnes explained. "The Germans left the Schmeissers behind when they evacuated Piraeus in 1944. The Thompsons were split off from our MAAG program by some Greek general who wanted a few thousand American dollars for his Swiss account."[7]

"Some deal. We have to buy back our own stuff?"

"Don't knock it, Robert. It's cheaper than buying used equipment in the States."

"I suppose it is, but it still galls me," I replied.

"I agree. At any rate Ferrie will arrange for Shaw to meet with del Valle in Montreal with one of our proprietarys called Permindex. It's a division of Central Mondiale Commercial, whose founder was a former O.S.S. Major named L.M. Bloomfield. With Shaw's personal authorization, Bloomfield will arrange to have the weapons waiting for you at a Permindex warehouse. The warehouse is in Piraeus, just outside of Athens."

"Ferrie will meet you in Greece. After you've made the buy and checked the merchandise, he will deliver the cash in Switzerland and complete the transfer of the weapons to Mario, in Guatemala. It will be transshipped through Liverpool. To make sure it gets there, I want you to go to England and make sure the papers are in order. Knowing Castro's DGI's ties to the KGB, they just might have it going elsewhere.[8] It's something in which we cannot involve our Embassy. Now, I'm going to get my tail out of here and let you get some sleep." Then with, "I guess I don't have to remind you that you better be watching your ass every second," he walked out the door.

I washed up and drove down to the Phil-Mar Grill, had an open pit hamburger and got home about 8:30 P.M. Aside from feeling tired and my legs smarting a little, I felt great. I was alive, although very tired. The next morning the pain in my legs had diminished to a dull throb, and I took several aspirins instead of my codeine pills. After a leisurely breakfast I went directly to my lab. It seemed strange after so long an absence. My partner Ross had everything under control, and one of our major commercial projects was well on its way to installation and testing. Pleased with the progress that had been made on the commercial scene, I worked for most of the day in the lab and prepared to return to Washington the following day.

The following morning I drove into Washington. I secured the documentation requested by Barnes for my European mission and arranged to look after some of my commercial enterprises in the Washington, D.C. area. I prepared to meet with Ross in Pittsburgh for the testing and installation of our biggest commercial venture together—the furnace.

Ross and I then met in Washington and travelled to Pittsburgh where we spent two days arranging the publicity and marketing for our furnace. When things seemed under control, I headed back to Washington. Once back in D.C. I had barely managed to open the door of my apartment when the telephone rang. It was Diggs. "Can you meet me later this afternoon in my office? I'll be with Mario. The next big project is about to start."

CHAPTER SEVEN NOTES:

1. The Cuban named Callas was later apprehended by Kohly's men. According to del Valle, he was later murdered by Carlos Rodrigues Quesada.
2. Today Friendship Airport is known as Baltimore/Washington International Airport (BWI).
3. Today Idlewild Airport is known as Kennedy Airport.
4. The New Orleans Trade Mart was affiliated with Centro Mondiale Commerciale, which was a CIA operation begun in Italy in the late 1950's. The organization, The World Trade Center, was initially formed in Montreal and was moved to Rome in 1961. Among its board of directors' members was Clay Shaw.
5. "Jack" was ultimately revealed to be Jack Ruby, the Dallas nightclub operator who killed Lee Harvey Oswald.
7. MAAG is the name for the U.S. Military Aid and Assistance Program for Foreign Countries. The author was, as late as the 1970's, a supplier to the Greek government for the M-60 machine gun.

8

JULY–SEPTEMBER 1961

It was a beautiful day in Washington, clear and pleasantly warm—not the hot humid days one expects at this time of year. I walked the seven blocks from my office/apartment to Diggs's law offices on Connecticut Avenue. I arrived at 5:00 P.M. Diggs and Carol were the only ones in, and she was preparing to leave for the day. Diggs politely waited for her to leave, bid her goodbye and a good weekend and, upon seeing her out of the office turned to me with a fresh look of intensity. "Kohly isn't here yet, which is just as well. It gives us an opportunity to speak privately. Kohly's wish to become the de facto president in exile has been granted. He wants to establish an Embassy here in Washington. I have told hm that you will be responsible for making the arrangements. We've attempted to assist you by funding a place suitable for his offices. There's a house on 32nd Street off Cleveland Avenue that's available for the summer and early fall. As Mario cannot sign a lease, I suggest that you and your wife Cecily act as his agents and sign the lease for him. Also, Cecily will be given an assignment for the Agency very shortly."

"Oh? And just what might that be? I sincerely doubt that she would accept any assignment, especially from the Agency."

"We want her to be the artist to replicate the ten and fifty peso Cuban notes, Robert."

"You're puttting me on." When I saw his look I knew he wasn't. "Well, I'll try."

123

"No, let Mario convince her. There will be sufficient money to justify it. Also the Agency will protect you."

"Well, I don't know about this. Go and convince her. Right now she wants nothing to do with what I'm doing. She's very concerned about our children and their safety. Frankly, given those circumstances, I don't blame her."

"Just let Mario try. That's all I ask."

"Obviously. I can't stop him. So be it; let him try."

"Politically we have two major problems. In addition to the Kennedy Administration's dislike of Kohly, our major source of information about the Kennedys' machinations in the White House is in danger of being investigated as the result of his unsavory personal associations. As you may or may not know, Lyndon Johnson is in our camp. Your friend, Frances Russell, who was with Wilbur Mills's Ways and Means Committee, is going to work for a reputed mob courier. He is a New Jersey attorney named Mickey Wiener. For a while, Senator Pete Williams lived in Wiener's apartment office complex in the LaSalle building right across the street.[1]

"Wiener is in some way connected to Johnson. It may be through Bobby Baker, although he also has other known connections.[2] Our esteemed new Vice President, however, has other legal and, consequently, political problems. He is intimately involved with a man in Texas named Billie Sol Estes. Three years ago, Estes commenced constructing grain warehouses. He simultaneously purchased federal cotton allotments, to cultivate cotton on land presently submerged by water. A rather unlikely investment wouldn't you say? At any rate, Estes received permission to trade his rights to cultivate cotton on his submerged lands for the right to grow cotton on fertile land. Cotton, by the way, is only permitted to be grown by allotment granted under the auspices of the Federal Department of Agriculture. Eventually, Estes's illicit trades were uncovered by investigators for the Department of Agriculture. Estes, who was in trouble with possible land fraud, and I now suspect murder, was let off the hook a month after the election by Johnson. He interceded with a Texas State

Committee which was calling upon Estes to testify about his activities."[3]

"Is Johnson that important to what we're doing?"

"Don't you remember the memorandum you read in Cabell's office? The one where LBJ wrote a memo to General Cabell which warned him that the Secretary of Defense had been secretly ordered to use any means at his disposal to control the activities of the CIA in order to render it powerless."

"Oh hell, yes. And the memorandum from JFK to his brother about the counterfeiting, and leaking it to the Cuban authorities. Of course. . . I remember."

"In view of what we've been discussing, does this answer your question about Johnson? LBJ is our inside man in the Kennedy Administration. Every morning he walks to his office through the White House. If his friend in the Secret Service has any information, he meets him on his morning walk and supplies him with all the latest inside dirt to come out of the Oval Office. If the Kennedys knew Johnson had an inside track on their dealings, particularly inside the White House, they would be on the warpath for revenge."[4]

"Say no more, Marshall."

At this point in our conversation, Mario finally arrived. The three of us wasted no time and immediately proceeded to discuss all necessary details and requirements pertinent to the establishment and maintenance of the counterfeiting operation. I informed Kohly, after he showed me the rather simple bills, that it would require approximately sixty days to produce the first counterfeit bills. After examining the rather worn bills he had shown me, I said it would also require two new samples of currency upon which to model our work. Kohly immediately reached into his wallet and produced two pristine ten and fifty peso notes. We then discussed the house on 32nd Street which had been selected by Diggs as an ideal location for the new unofficial embassy. I told Kohly that Cecily and I would have all necessary arrangements made with regard to the lease by the weekend. Kohly again reached into his wallet and brought out an envelope and handed it to me.

It contained the security deposit and the first month's rent on the house. A brief discussion on the possible timing of my trip to Europe followed. I left shortly thereafter and returned to my apartment in Washington.

The following morning I left for Baltimore. I had contacted my business partner, Ross, and informed him about the counterfeiting operation. He had successfully located all the necessary equipment we would need for printing the phony currency. Cecily possessed all the camera and darkroom equipment necessary for our operation. Her darkroom was ready and available to immediately commence our work. We had no space in the laboratory for the press Ross had secured and decided to use a portion of the living room that was out of sight. Once this arrangement had been made, we commenced with the initial preparation of the materials necessary for our currency.

As I had promised Kohly, Cecily and I returned to Washington over the weekend and met with the real estate broker handling the house on 32nd Street. We toured the house and realized that Diggs was correct; it was perfect for Mario's purposes. With Mario's money in hand, we signed the lease and received the keys. I phoned Kohly immediately thereafter and told him that he could move in on the first of July, a few days away. Mario was pleased and gave me a brief update on the preparations being made for my European trip. Del Valle was leaving for Canada the following week to meet with Major Bloomfield, a representative of Centro Mondiale Commercial and its European subsidiary, Permindex. I was well aware of the CIA's international ties; their extensiveness was a matter about which I would be made very familiar over the next two years. Having made all the necessary arrangements for Kohly's embassy, I spent the following two weeks setting up the press and engraving equipment necessary for our counterfeiting operation. Cecily completed her photographic enlargements of the ten and fifty peso notes and had commenced the artwork necessary to clean up the irregularities typical of the printing process we were to employ. Once Cecily's artwork was completed, the most labor intensive aspect of the operation was begun. To initiate the process we photographed Cecily's finished artwork and made the negatives for each of the three colors used on both of the peso notes. When this was completed, I assembled the negatives and burned in the plates; a process wherein the metal plates are etched with a hot lamp, resulting in the transference of the image onto the aluminum. With the plates burned, we were ready for a trial run; at least almost.

Our next step in the production was the perfection of both the registration process and the paper to be utilized. The registration caused us problems because of the extremely tight tolerance parameters of plus or minus 1/128 of an inch. With the paper, authenticity required that we achieve as close a match to the original as humanly possible. Fortunately, the paper was an easier issue than I thought. I selected a good high grade linen and made a plate with random specks and short wiggly lines which emulated the colored fibers contained throughout the original. Utilizing four of these random plates with different colored ink, the paper looked and felt identical to the original. Ross had secured the name of a company which manufactured reliable dyes and, following his advice, I contracted with them to create the ink hue needed. I was extremely gratified that none of the ink we required was green, as all customers ordering a hue of green similar to that used in the creation of U.S. currency were reported to the Secret Service. Our operation would have been immediately endangered, particularly with the politically antagonistic climate created by the Kennedys.

With the paper, registration and inks purchased and correctly prepared, we created our first run. By the third pass, Ross, Cecily and I had perfected our processes and, consequently, our resultant product. I contacted Mario with the news of our success and made arrangements to see him in Baltimore on the following day. Mario was scheduled to meet with Maxwell Taylor on the day following his trip to Baltimore. Although pleased with the success of our achievements in creating perfect phony pesos, I was concerned about Kohly's upcoming meeting with Maxwell Taylor. I remembered all too well Jack Kennedy's statements as presented in

Lyndon Johnson's memo to General Cabell. I suspected that Mario
might be betrayed and decided not to risk giving him samples of
our efforts until after the entire run was completed and his meeting
with Taylor over.

Mario arrived in Baltimore, reviewed our handiwork, and was
quite pleased with the results we had obtained. He, too, had
recognized the danger associated with revealing details about the
counterfeiting operation to Taylor. He agreed with my decision to
forestall giving him any large shipments of the currency but he
wanted a small sample to show to Marshall Diggs and Eladio del
Valle. Kohly and Diggs were scheduled to pick up del Valle early
the following morning at National Airport.[5] Del Valle was flying in
from New Orleans after having made arrangements to store the
equipment I was to purchase in Greece in a facility located near
New Orleans provided by Carlos Marcello.[6] To my surprise, Mario
requested that I come to Washington and accompany him and
Diggs to the airport. I agreed and left Baltimore that same evening.

Early the following morning, Diggs, Kohly and I met del Valle's
arriving Eastern Airlines flight from New Orleans at National
Airport. Both Diggs and Kohly seemed elated as they told del Valle
that a meeting had been arranged with President Kennedy's
military advisor, General Maxwell Taylor. In the cab, Diggs related
the chain of events which culminated in this meeting. "It appears,"
he said, turning to del Valle, "that the Kennedy brothers are
stymied in trying to free the Bay of Pigs prisoners. The President
has finally realized that Kohly still has absolute control of what
underground is left, and now wonders if you and he could also
unite the Cuban splinter groups here in the United States."

Eladio del Valle looked shocked. Kohly simply nodded and
looked out the window at the Jefferson Memorial as we crossed the
Fourteenth Street bridge into the city. The morning sunlight was
just beginning to highlight the magnificent monument. He seemed
to be collecting his thoughts before responding to del Valle's
quizzical look. After a few moments' pause, he said, "I will meet
with the General, of course. However, I will make no promises.

"When I could get no help for releasing the *Brigade* prisoners from the United States presently held in Cuba. I contacted President Quadros of Brazil. He is a close friend of Castro's, but not so close that he won't cooperate with me if there is enough money involved. You see, gentlemen, I have my own plan. If I can raise twenty-five million dollars, I will give it to Quadros. He will give Castro fifteen million dollars, keeping ten for himself, if Castro will agree to move all the prisoners to a remote Cuban port. Quadro will then send a Brazilian ship to deliver coffee, and the few guards assigned to the prisoners will allow them to escape to the Brazilian ship.

"Once the men are safely in the United Staes, preferably Miami, Quadros will break relations with Castro and recognize my de facto government in exile. You understand, of course, that only when all this is accomplished will the twenty-five million be released to Quadros. This plan will allow the *Brigade* to return to the United States as heroes who have escaped from Castro's prisons. It will also, as a fringe benefit, align Brazil with the United States."

Diggs responded. "I wondered how you were going to get the recognition as de facto Prsident. It sounds like a wild scheme, Mario, but you know the players better than I do. Taylor just might buy it, particularly if you can unite the Cubans here in the United States and provide the cooperation of your underground as well."

"We shall see," said Kohly. "By the way, have any of you heard any more reactions to the hard missile site being built in Cuba?"

"Nothing," Diggs replied, "and I wouldn't dare bring it up. I'm sure one of my sources would have let me know instantly if anything had been mentioned."

"I certainly haven't heard anything from Barnes," I said, shaking my head.

"Well. It should be an interesting meeting tomorrow," mused Kohly as the cab turned left onto H Street. As they looked across Lafayette Park, the light of the early morning sun brightly lit up the White House.

* * *

With Kohly's approval of our samples, we printed millions of pesos throughout the remaining summer months. Most of these were

delivered to Kohly who, in turn, filtered them to the members of
his underground in Cuba. By August, Kohly's infiltration process
had succeeded and the Cuban economy was seriously disrupted.
The only indication we received of this was an entry in the
Encyclopedia Brittanica's 1962 yearbook. In the calendar of events
for 1961, there is a reference for August 5 that states: "All entrance
into Cuba was barred pending replacement of Cuban currency."
Of course, at the time, Kohly was receiving reports steadily from
members of his underground regarding the extensive distribution
of the phony currency but the reports merely gave us a speculative
notion of the damage we were creating. Nonetheless, our counterfeiting operation was considered a success and, as the Kennedy
Administration monitored Cuba's deteriorating economy, Maxwell
Taylor instructed Kohly to establish his *United Organizations for
the Liberation of Cuba* (*UOLC*), and to contact Brazilian President
Quadros and proceed with his prisoner release scheme. However,
in the first week of September, Quadros was forced to resign amidst
criticism of his planning to establish a dictatorship.[7] As a result of
his resignation, Kohly's plan to secure the release of the *Brigade*
prisoners was aborted. The Kennedy Administration was,
according to a message Lyndon Johnson conveyed to Marshall
Diggs, singularly displeased with this turn of events. Kohly,
forewarned by Johnson's message of the Kennedys' anger over the
Brazilian president's plight, took immediate steps to guard against
a possible reversal of fortunes for the *UOLC* if the Kennedys were
to act upon their apparent frustration and anger with the foiled
scheme to release the prisoners. In order to facilitate this protection
for his organization, Kohly again turned to the Mafia.

I was not aware of Kohly's decision to solicit mob assistance
until the very beginning of October; my discovery was accidental and after the fact. I arrived at Mario's unofficial embassy on
32nd Street one evening for a scheduled appointment with Mario.
As I was early, I was met by Bill Grosh, Kohly's bodyguard.
Grosh brought me to the library which was located just beyond the
kitchen. From my position in the library I had an unobstructed
view of the living room. Two men whom I did not recognize

were present. Kohly, spotting me, waved me in to join them and introduced me to a Mr. Gold from Chicago, and a Mr. Rawlston from Las Vegas. He had apparently been discussing the success of our counerfeiting operation prior to my entrance. Both men seemed highly impressed and Rawlston asked me if I knew either Robert Mahcu, or Joe Shimon.[8] I told them I hadn't heard of Maheu, but my business associate had completed contract work for the International Police Academy which was run by Mr. Joe Shinon. Both the Messrs. Gold and Rawlston smiled at my reference to the International Police Academy and immediately prepared to leave. I perceived their movement as an indication that I was to make a discreet departure and indicated to Kohly that I would wait for him. Mario said he would join me momentarily, and I returned to my previous position in the library. Kohly's moment turned into an hour and I remained in the library until after the departure of both Messrs. Gold and Rawlston. When Kohly joined me in the library, he explained that all arrangements had been made for my European trip and suggested that I immediately make whatever personal arrangements I would require to facilitate a speedy departure to Spain. He also presented me with two newly minted Cuban pesos, a ten and a fifty peso note, and requested that I examine them closely. As Castro had changed the Cuban currency due to the massive infiltration of our counterfeit pesos into the Cuban economy, Kohly wanted us to alter our counterfeit notes to perfectly match the new Cuban currency. If possible, he wanted us to commence printing our new counterfeit notes prior to my departure from Europe.

After a few moments of study, I informed Mario that his request would be impossible to meet in such a short period of time, and suggested that we wait until my return before creating new notes. Kohly accepted my decision and agreed to place a hold on our counterfeiting operation until my return. With that agreement, I departed and returned to Baltimore.

The following morning I received a call from Marshall Diggs. I told Diggs about Kohly's desire to begin counterfeiting new Cuban notes immediately and our mutual decision to place the

operation on hold until my return. I also told him about my meeting
Messrs. Gold and Rawlston the previous evening. Diggs informed
me that Gold and Rawlston were actually Sam Giancanna of
Chicago and Johnny Rosselli of Las Vegas. I was surprised that
Kohly had not revealed the true identities of the two men to me
before our meeting, but assumed that there was a definite reason
for his discretion. In speaking with Diggs I further realized that
Mario's concern over the Kennedys' reaction to the Quadros resignation was far greater than I had first understood. Clearly Giancanna and Rosselli were the only *powerful* sources of protection
against the Kennedys to whom Kohly could turn. I would not learn
until much later how far their protection would eventually go.

Immediately following my conversation with Diggs I received
a call from Tracy Barnes. It had been months since I had last
spoken with Tracy. In fact, if I had not regularly received my
monthly fee at the Suburban Trust Company, I would have thought
that the Agency had forgotten about me. Barnes told me that as
a result of sweeping changes inside the Agency, events would
transpire over the coming months. I found his statement
inordinately vague and requested that he explain what he meant.
He responded that he had called to request a meeting with me
immediately upon my return from Europe and would discuss the
internal Agency changes and their subsequent results at that time.
In addition, he wanted to confirm that the weapons were in place
in the combined Centro Mondiale Commerciale/Permindex
warehouse and that I could depart for Europe immediately. I told
Barnes that I would contact him as soon as all my arrangements
and schedules for the trip were in order; in all likelihood, sometime
after the Thanksgiving holiday.

Within a few days afer my conversation with Barnes, I made
and confirmed my reservations on TWA's flight 900, scheduled
to leave on the Tuesday following Thanksgiving. As promised, I
contacted Barnes and was told that the Comanche would be
available at Friendship Airport on Tuesday morning for my flight
to LaGuardia. He reminded me that we were to meet upon my
return and advised that I was to expect contact after checking

in at the Ritz in Madrid.

Tuesday arrived more quickly than I had anticipated. I deliberately slept in on that morning as I knew I had a very long day ahead of me. After a leisurely brunch I headed for Friendship Airport. As promised, the Comanche was again waiting for me at the south terminal. I still had plenty of time. My flight for Madrid didn't leave until 7:30 P.M. and, once I'd tied the Comanche down at LaGuardia, it would take me less than thirty-five minutes to drive to Idlewild. I departed from Friendship at 3:00 P.M. and arrived at LaGuardia an hour later. I taxied the bird to the Old Marine Terminal, removed my luggage, checked in, and gave instructions for refueling. I scanned the area for possible pursuers and then took a cab to the TWA terminal at Idlewild.

My international flight was not due to depart for several hours, but I wanted to check through customs and immigration early. I needed plenty of time to study the crowds for potential enemies. After an hour and forty-five minutes in a corner of the temporary international bar, I was satisifed that no one had the slightest interest in me. Then, in the midst of the crowd mulling near the bar area I spotted my mother. I couldn't believe my eyes. She had mentioned while she was with us on Thanksgiving that she wanted to go to Spain with me, but I had thought her idea was impossible. Somehow between the time she left Baltimore on Sunday until today, she had managed to secure a passport and plane reservations, packed her luggage, and traveled to New York from Pittsburgh. The Agency could certainly use someone with her organizational talents.

I waved to catch her attention and she smiled when she saw me. I could tell from the determined look on her face that her arrival in New York had been no easy feat. She came over to join me and, after greeting me announced, just as our flight was called, that she had secured the seat next to mine. From that day forward I would never dispute my mother's word. When she announced her intentions they would become a reality . . . as was true when I was growing up. She did precisely what she intended to do.

* * *

The Ritz in Madrid is one of the most beautiful and exclusive hotels
in the world. When the head porter parted the heavy brocade
draperies in my room, I looked out of the full-length French
windows and found that I had a balcony overlooking a garden
courtyard with a magnificent marble fountain. Thank God, it was
two floors above my mother's suite.

It was already after 2:00 P.M., which meant that all of the
shops in town would be closed until five. Mother decided to take
a nap, so I took the opportunity to order a car. Our embassy also
closed between 1:00 P.M. and 5:00 P.M., so I had plenty of time
before I was to call for my appointment with the commercial
attache. I decided to follow Barnes's suggestion and my mother's
example and take a nap. I was awakened at 4:30 P.M. by the
telephone. I answered and was greeted by a husky female voice
asking if I was Robert Morrow. The voice startled me for a moment;
it hadn't occurred to me that my contact might be a woman. When
I said yes, she continued: "You don't know me, but my name is
Susan Cotts. I'm an American student studying under a Fulbright
scholarship at the University of Madrid. I was contacted by a
mutual friend who told my you might need an interpreter."[10]

Relieved, I replied, "Yes, I'm sure I will.

"Great. Welcome to Madrid."

"Thanks." Then, intrigued, I said, "Let me ask you something.
If you're a student, how old are you?"

She said, "Old enough to take care of myself. Why don't we
meet in the lounge for cocktails? It's located directly off the lobby.
I have red hair and I'm fairly tall with my shoes on. You won't be
able to miss me."

"Give me half an hour to shower and shave." Then I remembered. "Hold on. I must call the Embassy when it reopens."

"Don't bother," she said. "No one will be in until first thing in
the morning. Tonight I'll show you Madrid and make sure you stay
out of trouble. I understand you've had your share lately."

Thirty minutes later I stepped out of the elevator and spotted
a lovely young girl with a tousled head of strawberry blond hair.

As I crossed the room, she rose with a smile, extended a white gloved hand, and greeted me. "Robert Morrow, I presume."

By the time we had finished our second martini, I had learned that she was studying music and languages on her scholarship, and was intent on earning a master's degree. She was only twenty-two and, in her senior year at Wellsley, had allowed herself to be recruited as a student observer in Europe. She was, I was dismayed to learn, an avid admirer of John F. Kennedy. Her father was a well-known psychiatrist in the Washington area. I was just getting ready to call mother to jon us when she walked out of the elevator. I introduced the two of them, explaining Susan was going to be my interpreter. I don't think she believed it for a minute but refrained from comment, smiling sweetly instead. I asked if she wanted to join us for dinner, but she declined, claiming she was still too tired after the trip.

At Susan's suggestion, we dined at the Casa Botin. Afterward, while we were sipping our coffees, she looked at me thoughtfully, then asked abruptly: "It's time we got home. Tomorrow will be very busy. You can drop me at my apartment. It's over near the university. I'll meet you in the morning."

"Fine," I said, only mildly startled by her abruptness, and asked for the check.

Susan excused herself. "I'm going to powder my nose. I'll meet you downstairs in the bar."

Most of the drinkers downstairs appeared to be Americans. When I ordered a brandy grasshopper, the bartender grinned and said, "American officer club style?"

Surprised, I replied, "Si. But with four shots of cognac."

He replied in perfect English, "But, of course. I was chief bartender for the American officers' club for the past four years."

I said, "In that case, make it two; I'm expecting a friend."

"Ah, yes," he said, "the beautiful redhead you were dining with."

I gave him a searching look. "As a matter of fact, yes. You don't seem to miss much. Do you know her?"

"Si, senor. She comes here quite often. Usually with young

officers from the American air base outside Madrid."

"Oh," I replied.

"You are not one yourself, senor?"

"No, just an ordinary tourist." I was beginning to feel a little uneasy—and a bit jealous—when I spotted Susan coming down the stairs.

She sat down beside me, looked up dreamily, and asked, "Miss me?"

Before I could reply, she giggled and spoke to the bartender. "Bueno, Alfredo. I see you're fixing the senor a drink."

"Si, senorita, and one for you. We were just discussing the points of interest in Madrid."

"I'm sure you were. And, perhaps, all the men I've been here with?"

"Senorita," he waved his hands, starting to protest.

But she smiled sweetly and continued: "Don't worry, Alfredo. The gentleman is a friend from the States."

"Senorita, I didn't know." Then addressing me, he said, "Please call me Alfredo; the drinks are on me."

"Thank you, Alfredo."

As he moved down the bar, Susan said, "Alfredo bears watching. He's the only bartender in Madrid who can afford to drive a Pegaso. It's a handmade, completely customized Spanish sprots car and one of the most expensive in the world. Their price in Spain starts at twenty thousand dollars plus. You can imagine what they would cost in the States."

"What you are telling me is, he 'don't' make his money tending bar."

"Unfortunately, a lot of talk goes on here that shouldn't, particularly among Americans. Alfredo soaks it up and stores it until someone pays him to squeeze it back out."

"I'll watch myself," I said, and pulled our bar stools together so that our legs touched. Susan slipped her hand into mine and said, "We had better drink up. You should be at the embassy no later than 10:30 tomorrow morning, and we still have to swing by my place."

The following morning, she drove me back to the hotel and I thanked her profusely for the wonderful hospitality she had shown me. I phoned my mother's room and told her I wanted to take her out sightseeing for the day. This alleviated my guilt for having abandoned her the day before.

The next afternoon, Susan drove me to the air base where I was to meet with the U.S. commercial attache. After I had identified myself with Barnes's 'Rain in Spain' code exchange, the diplomat informed he had arranged my departure for Athens on a MATS flight at 1:30 P.M. I arrived at the U.S. air base in Athens at 4:30 P.M. and found an unobtrusive black 1961 Chevrolet with Greek license plates waiting for me. It was driven by a young American sporting an ill-fitting suit and crew cut. He said his name was "Mike" and that he was to drive me to a rendezvous with Dave Ferrie in Piraeus, about twelve miles east of the base.

In front of a waterfront rooftop cafe called the Vassilena, Mike opened the car door for me and said, "My instructions are to be at your disposal, Sir. So, if you don't mind, I'll park the car on a side street and make it a point to be seated a few tables from you. Now, if you will please go straight through to the stairs behind the shop, you will find there is a lovely rooftop view of the harbor."

I picked a secluded table and ordered gin on the rocks. The place was crowded, mostly with Greek patrons. Mike came in and took a table near the door. He sipped a bottle of "Fix" beer and appeared calm, although it was well beyond the scheduled meeting time. As I signaled the waiter for another drink, a tall Dave Ferrie arrived wearing a Panama hat and dark sunglasses.[11]

As he removed his hat and glasses and scanned the terrace, I saw his bald head and painted eyebrows. The identification was positive; it was Dave. Ferrie spotted Mike, crossed the room, and sat down next to him. After a few words together, they both got up and walked toward my table. Mike said, "Sir, this is Dave Ferrie." Dave gave no sign of recognition and I responded accordingly.

"I hope you'll excuse me for being late," Ferrie said. Before I could reply, he added, "You don't mind if I call you Bob, do you?"

I said, "Of course not. The way Mike's been ignoring me, I was beginning to need a friend."

He chuckled and turned to the driver whose face was turning red. "Would you mind bringing the car around while I pay the tab?"

"Right," Mike said, and disappeared down the stairs.

When he had gone Ferrie said, "Excuse the formality, but our young friend wasn't told that we know each other. Good to see you again. I'll be flying you back to Madrid as soon as we've finished our business here."

"You mean tonight?" I grinned and said, "I hope it isn't like our last one!"

Ferrie acted as if he hadn't heard me. "The warehouse is only a few blocks away, down on the docks." He lowered his voice. "You have the money, of course?"

I nodded. "Of course, but I'll have to see the merchandise first."

"Certainly." Then he leaned closer and added, "Incidentally, you'll only need two hundred and ten big ones. Between Jack and Clay, they struck a better deal than we had expected, so the rest of the money can be used for other gear."

Within two blocks we had left the brightness of the city and were driving between the darkened warehouses that lined the Piraeus waterfront. Mike stopped in front of a warehouse with a newly painted sign that read "Permindex S.A." Below it was an older sign with an arrow indicating that the other side of the building housed "Centro Mondiale Commerciale S.A."

We got out and Mike unlocked the warehouse door, locking it again behind us. Then he switched on a battery of lights. The place was filled with tier upon tier of crates reaching to the ceiling and marked "machine parts" and "machine tools." Most of them were new and stenciled in English with the names of firms from all over the world. Many were U.S. companies, such as Cincinnati Machine Tool, South Bend, and Caterpillar.

Mike took a clipboard from a hook beneath the light switches, examined some papers, and asked us to follow him. He led us to a stack of long boxes resting on pallets. Mounting an electric fork lift, he lowered the top box to the floor. It bore the name "Philips Globenfabriken," which I recognized as a large Dutch multinational firm.

With a crowbar, Mike pried off the top of the box. Inside were other boxes about four feet in length, eight inches wide, and twelve inches high. He pulled one out and opened it. Inside, embedded in cosmoline, was a German Schmeisser submachine gun in pristine condition along with a complete set of spare parts, including an extra barrel and cleaning equipment.

"There are two thousand of them here," Dave remarked. "We're also to get two hundred and fifty Thompsons."

Mike again boarded the forklift and proceeded down the line to another stack of crates marked Westinghouse Electric. The crate he opened contained boxes of brand new Thompson submachine guns, also with spare parts.

"O.K., Mike," Dave said. "Put everything back together." Then, turning to me, he added, "They'll be transshipped to Liverpool, then on to Guatemala. Now, if you'll just initial these papers and give me the cash, we'll have the stuff aboard the ship within three days."

It took us about forty-five minutes to count out the two hundred and ten thousand dollars in equivalent pound notes. I took what was left, distributed it evenly in the belt and put it back around my waist.

Dave Ferrie, flying a T-33 jet trainer placed at our disposal by the air force, dropped me off at the Madrid airport at 12:40 A.M. I caught up with Susan at the Casa Botin, and by the time we got back to the Ritz most of the night was gone. I was still exhausted when the phone jolted me awake at 8:30. It was on a table across the room, and I charged out of bed and caught it on the fifth ring. The hotel operator informed me that it was a call from Zurich for me.

I could barely hear Dave Ferrie's sleepy voice through the antiquated instrument. "Hi, stranger. I guess you know where I am."

"And I guess you know what time it is."

He ignored my snide comment. "I'm at the Permindex office," he continued, "and they just received a telex for you. Washington wants you to return to the States immediately, via Paris. We've already booked a flight for you."

"Is there anything else I have to do about the merchandise?" I asked.

"No. I'll handle it from this end. Tonight you'll be laying over in Paris at the Plaza Athenee on Avenue Montaigne. You'll be contacted there and given further instructions. You should use the same code words and reply as in Madrid."

"OK. Let me get this straight. I'm to head Stateside via Paris. Now, how do I get there?"

"Take Air France flight 510 out of Madrid at noon. You'll arrive in Paris at 1:00 P.M. Paris time. As I said, your reservations have been made. Good luck. I'll see you at home one of these days." The phone went dead. It was hard explaining to mother about the Paris detour. But she had a reservation on the same plane in minutes, and had the concierge arrange for an adjoining room at the Plaza Athenee. Again, I was astounded by her organizational expertise.

Mother and I had breakfast and spent the morning packing our things, checking out of the Ritz, and turning in the rental car. I confirmed our Air France reservations and was told that flight 510 was running about two hours late. I then contacted Susan and suggested that we have an early lunch at Horcher's on the Serrano. I told mother I would meet her at the airport. She didn't like it but agreed.

We were both half smashed when Susan deposited me at the immigration and customs hut at Madrid airport. During lunch, she asked if I could stay in Europe where we could travel together for the next couple of months. It was a hell of a temptation, so I didn't dare turn around as I trotted up the stair ramp to board the Air France Caravelle. By this time I was feeling I was the luckiest SOB in the world when it came to running into beautiful women.

* * *

Once in my room at the Plaza Athenee I quickly unpacked, took a shower and stretched out for a nap, leaving word with the desk to wake me at 6:00 P.M. I thought I had scarcely closed my eyes when the phone rang. I rose, shaved, and changed into fresh, lightweight clothes. It was now 7:00 P.M. As I did not expect my contact to reach me until early the following morning, I decided to go down to the English bar, have a few cocktails, and then take a stroll. Later, mother and I could have dinner at one of the sidewalk cafes along the Champs Elysees that I had so long wanted to visit.

I told the concierge where I would be and then went into the bar. As my eyes adjusted to the dim lighting, I saw that only one person, other than the bartender, was in the room; a heavy-set man of indeterminate nationality and age, sitting at a cocktail table near the entrance.

I ordered an extra-dry Gordon's martini on the rocks. As I quietly sat and nursed my drink I was startled by a midwestern American drawl behind me inquiring, "How was New York when you left it?"

It was the man who had been sitting at the table. "Well, it was still there when I left several days ago," I replied cautiously.

"You wouldn't perchance know what the climate's been like in Spain, would you?" he asked, sitting down beside me. "I heard you telling the bartender you had just arrived from Madrid."

"It seems extremely dry this year in Madrid," I said and swallowed hard, waiting for his reply.

He took a long sip from his highball. "Yes, the rain does stay mainly in the plains. . . I suppose."

I said nothing. My evening of sightseeing had just evaporated. "My name's Hamilton," he said lethargically, extending a puffy hand.[12]

He was so different from what I had expected that I began to wonder if his reply to the code might have been an accident.

"How about joining me at my table?" he asked. As I followed him to the table, I studied him, wondering if he might be ill. But once we were away from the scrutiny of the bartender, his eyes twinkled a bit and he said, "My wife and I have just come back from an extended tour of the Soviet Union."

"Really," I said, perturbed. "Where did you go?"

"All over, but one of our last stops was in Minsk." The notion that any American could travel through Russia in 1961 put me off again, and I had almost concluded that our verbal exchange had indeed been a coincidence when Hamilton continued: "You must come upstairs and meet my wife. She's a good friend of your mother's."

I just looked at him. The mention of my mother shocked me. It couldn't be a coincidence. I finally got enough composure to answer. "Really?" I said, "Then I'd love to meet your wife."

"Fine," he said, rising. Then he addressed the bartender. "Alfred, put this on my tab."

I watched Hamilton lay a new five franc note on the table and followed him into the lower lobby. When we were alone in the elevator, he asked, "What's your room number?"

"522."

"Fine. I'll call you there in a few minutes." He punched the buttons for the second and fifth floors. As the car came to a stop at the second floor, he smiled and stepped out. I watched him disappear down the hall.

The phone was ringing as I opened my door. It was Hamilton. "Meet me in 410 as soon as possible," he ordered.

Startled, I pulled the phone away from my ear, looked at it, then replied, "Be right there." I literally hadn't had time to get my key out of the lock. The exit stairs were a few doors away, so I walked down the flight rather than wait for the elevator. When I knocked on the door of 410, Hamilton opened it and invited me into the suite.

In the bright light of the foyer I observed that Hamilton was older than I had thought—at a guess, close to sixty-five. His wife appeared to be about ten to fifteen years younger and was beautifully dressed. They smelled of money.

He introduced his wife. She smiled radiantly and asked, "So

you're Rose Morrow's son. I don't believe we've ever met. Ed is a good friend of your uncle Ern Dietz. We now live in Pittsburgh."

Then Hamilton, looking annoyed for God knows what reason announced, "I have a package for you to deliver once you've returned to the States."

I watched as he took a large manila envelope from a suitcase, saying, "Just tell Barnes that this is the information he wanted from Harvey." Then he made me repeat the name: "Harvey." It took a long time for me to learn that "Harvey" was not a code name for one Lee Harvey Oswald, but rather it referred to CIA official William Harvey.[13]

I took the papers and asked, "Do you also have my itinerary?"

"You're booked on a BEA flight to London in the morning with a connecting TWA flight into Idlewild."

"Fine, although I might change them slightly. My mother is with me. I'm sure you want to see her." They both looked at each other. Ed Hamilton answered.

"It would be great, but we have a previous engagement. Perhaps tomorrow. Oh," he said, "I forgot you have a plane to catch. Give her our best and tell her that we'll catch up in Pittsburgh."

"I'll be sure to let her know. Nice meeting you finally." I then left. I told mother on the plane I had run into an old friend of hers. She was surprised that they hadn't even called her room. As our stay in Paris had been so abruptly cut short, mother suggested that we stay a few days in London, since we would be stopping over anyway. I was not in a hurry to return Stateside and readily agreed with her idea.

Our few days in London were enjoyable. Mother made reservations at Claridge's and the two of us occupied the suite opposite the King of Norway. It was amusing seeing him collect *The Times* in his bathrobe outside his door every morning. We exchanged civilized nods and morning greetings. Little did I know that, upon my return to the States, I was soon to enter a series of events far removed from the charm of royalty and the civilities of Claridge's high tea.

CHAPTER EIGHT NOTES:

1. Both Diggs's building and the LaSalle Building have been torn down to make room for modern buidings. Senator Harrison O. Williams was indicted and sent to prison during the ABSCAM affair for taking bribes.

2. I would discover later that some connections were through Baker's partner in the Serv-U Corporation, Fred Black, who bragged to me he was a good friend of Johnny Roselli and the last one to see him alive before he was found murdered. It occurred a few days before Roselli was to testify that he knew who murdered John F. Kennedy. See Appendices.

3. On January 31, 1961, Johnson wrote a letter to Secretary of Agriculture Orville Freeman, enclosing a letter of concern from one of his associates in Pecos, Texas named A. B. Foster. In late February, Freeman wrote back to Johnson about the "changes in regulations governing the transfer of cotton allotments from farms whose owners have been displaced by agencies having the right of eminent domain." Freeman pointed out that "there have been some abuses of the law in this regard." These "had the effect of an outright sale of the pooled allotment by the displaced owner under subterfuge practices. . ." which was not the simple transfer of the allotment to another farm actually owned by the displaced producer in accordance with the purpose of the law.

   However, Freeman continued, in view of the fraud, the department regulations had recently been changed. They now provided that before a county committee could act upon applications for such transfers—such as Estes'—the applicant shall personally appear before the county committee with all pertinent documents. This meant certificates of allotments, field notes, and deeds—and to answer all questions regarding same.

   Estes was in deep trouble. Then came the ringer. Freeman's letter to Johnson also spelled out that the State Committee could waive appearance if it unduly inconvenienced the applicant, or because of illness or other good cause. In conclusion, the Secretary felt sure that the State Committee would be reasonable in passing judgment should the applicant fail to appear under the condiions enumerated.

   On a note typed on a United States Senate memorandum slip and mailed to Estes, Johnson stated, "I hope the information contained in the attached letter will be of interest and helpful to you. If I can again assist you, let me know." It was signed "LBJ." For the moment Estes had an out. . . until a report surfaced from an investigator for the Agricultural Stabilization and Conservation office, named Henry Marshall.

   On June 3, 1961, Marshall was found dead from five bullets. Five days later he was declared a victim of suicide and buried without an autopsy.

4. This story was confirmed by Brooks Keller, head of Secret Service security
   for Jacqueline Kennedy, during a social gathering with some friends of his
   and myself in 1965. Keller said: "Every morning Johnson would have his
   limo drop him off at the White House. The Vice President would then
   proceed through the grounds and enter the White House; he would walk
   down the halls passing the Oval Office. Then, he would exit out the back
   door and, after talking to a Secret Service man, walk a block to the office
   building where he really worked.

5. Confirmation of Ferrie's trip to Montreal with Shaw to arrange for the
   guns—and the trip back to New Orleans with del Valle—was supplied by
   a Garrison investigation witness named Jules Rico Kimble. Kimble, a
   member of far-right groups like the Minutemen and the Ku Klux Klan, was
   a youngster in his teens in late 1960 or early 1961. Kimble was drinking
   at one of the bistros located in the French Quarter when Dave Ferrie
   introduced him to Clay Shaw. After that, recalled Kimble, he saw Shaw on
   various occasions. One day in late 1961 or early 1962, he received a
   phone call from Ferrie, who asked if he would like to take an overnight
   plane trip with him. Kimble was agreeable; he met Ferrie at the airport and
   at that time learned that Shaw was also coming along. They were going to
   fly to Canada to pick someone up.

   Kimble remembered Shaw as seated in the back of the airplane during
   the trip and either sleeping or thumbing through a book. He also recalled
   that Shaw carried a brown briefcase with him.

   Ferrie landed the plane in Nashville, Tennessee, Louisville, Kentucky,
   and Toronto, Canada, to gas up. The final stop was Montreal. Kimble and
   Ferrie stayed overnight in a hotel in Dorvall right outside of Montreal. Shaw
   disappeared after they landed, and they did not see him until the next
   morning at about eight o'clock, the agreed-upon time for departure to
   New Orleans.

   When Shaw arrived back at the plane, as Kimble recalled, he had a
   "Mexican or Cuban" with him. He described the man as heavy-set, dark-
   skinned, balding in the front, and in his early or middle thirties. Shaw and
   the Latin man sat in the back of the airplane together, and the latter spoke
   to Shaw only in broken English. Kimble described the plane as a Cessna
   172, which he thought belonged to a friend of Ferrie's. When they arrived
   back at the New Orleans Lakefront Airport, Kimble said, they all climbed
   into his automobile and he drove them into town. About a month or so later,
   he got another phone call from Ferrie asking if he wanted to make a similar
   trip back to Canada, but this time he declined.

   There were a couple of interesting aspects to this tale. First, Shaw was
   known to have a fear of flying. Yet here he was in a small Cessna on a long
   journey. This might well have indicated a more than routine mission for

which Shaw felt personally responsible. Second, Ferrie never filed flight plans, so conveniently for Shaw, there was no record of this trip or any other he may have made with Ferrie.

6. The arms which I was told by Ferrie in Greece were to be shipped to Guatemala were actually sent to a home in the Lake Ponchatrain area. This house was rented by William and Mike McLarey, the former owners of the National Casino in Havana. Jack Ruby visited William McLarey in the Tropicana hotel in 1959. The two brothers were directly associated with the Marcello organization in New Orleans, as noted by the Senate Permanent Subcommittee on Investigations in 1973, chaired by Senator Henry M. Jackson. In July 1963 the FBI made a raid on the house, seizing some of the arms and a member of the anti-Castro exiles training there for the next invasion, set for December by Kohly. The story of this raid was carried in the *Washington Post* on July 31st, 1963.

7. Stung by this mounting criticism and possibly suffering from overwork, Quadros, on August 25th, addressed a letter of resignation to the Brazilian Congress in which he said that he was the victim of forces both inside and outside Brazil that were working against him. In a separate message to the Brazilian people, he declared that his "efforts to conduct the country on a course of political freedom and liberation" had failed "in face of corruption, lies, and cowardliness."

8. Shimon was a former detective in the New York Police Department.

9. An organization to train CIA guerilla terrorists.

10. His name was Mark Sandground, a prominent Washington, D.C. attorney.

11. Ferrie in 1961 still had some semblance of hair and eyebrows. With the hat and sunglasses he looked fairly normal. By late 1962 he would lose all of his body hair due to some type of dermatological disease.

12. Edward Hamilton was from Pittsburgh, Pennsylvania. His wife's name was Lydia.

13. William Harvey was an ex-FBI agent who would become, within a few days of my returning home, the new coordinator for the CIA plans for assassinating Fidel Castro. Harvey would meet regularly with John Roselli, Santos Trafficante, Sam Giancana, Robert Maheu, and Eladio del Valle, through whom I originally met him.

9

SEPTEMBER–DECEMBER 1961

Prior to departing Claridge's for Heathrow Airport Terminal 3, I attempted to contact Tracy Barnes. Unable to reach him, I left a message stating my time of arrival in New York. Mother made arrangements to fly directly to Pittsburgh on an Allegheny flight, and I booked a flight from LaGuardia to Baltimore for appearances' sake. Upon our arrival in New York, and as I was in the process of clearing customs, I received a page. It was Barnes calling. He told me to take the airport bus around the international complex to the executive terminal. He and the Comanche would be waiting for me. I wondered why he had bothered to meet me, but was pleased to avoid the cab ride to LaGuardia, where I'd left the Comanche a few days before departing for Spain.

When I joined Tracy he brusquely greeted me and then busied himself with filing an instrument clearance for the flight back to Friendship Airport. The weather was getting murky and he wanted to beat a line of thunderstorms moving in from the west.

There was lightning in the western sky when we rolled up to the south terminal at Friendship a little over an hour later. We had to rush to get everything unloaded and the Comanche hangered before the rain began.

We were dodging the first drops of rain on our walk to the car when Tracy resumed the conversation we had had the last time I had seen him, several months prior to my departure for Europe. "I was right about the explosive in the Comanche," he said.

"It was installed by Shaw's people and rigged into the glide slope so it couldn't go off until someone reset the breaker to complete the circuit. I've learned that Shaw knows about the call you got from del Valle in Savannah. He's been told that you found nothing on the plane. So as far as Shaw knows, the Comanche is still rigged."

"Damn," I said. "I'd almost rather it had been Castro than one of our own people. Do you have any idea why he'd have something like that done?"

"Oh I have an idea, but I'm not going to comment on it now." I looked at him questioningly but he made no further comment on the subject other than to say, "There's one consolation. We're now checking every piece of equipment going in and out of Miami and New Orleans. While you were away, we found two of our southern-based cars with homing devices on them. The irony is that Shaw's using the very same equipment on us that we gave him to check on his own people."

"It sounds like you have an out-of-control, wild-eyed bunch of rightwingers on your hands."

"Listen, Robert, some of those bastards are to the right of Genghis Khan. If Shaw had his way, the brothers Kennedy would already be dead and buried."

"They're bugging us with Agency devices in our own vehicles?" That amused me immensely. "In effect, we're spying on each other?"

"Everyone in this business spies on each other. Christ, we have almost as many FBI men on our payroll as J. Edgar Hoover."

We climbed into a new Ford Galaxy Tracy had parked on the lot. On the way into town he asked, "By the way, where are the papers you picked up in Paris?"

"Good thing you asked. I'd forgotten all about them. I was told to tell you they came from 'Harvey.' They're in my briefcase. I've got them sandwiched among some magazines I picked up at the Paris airport."

"Good enough. I'll get them when we get to your place."

As we plunged into the Baltimore Harbor Tunnel another thought occurred to me. "What was the big rush about getting me back to the States?"

"Mario is back in Washington. He has what he needs to manufacture the plates for the new currency and he's ready to turn the
project over to you."

"Turn it over to me? Damn it, Tracy, I'm loaded with work as
it is. What's going on?"

"It's very simple. Mario made a direct request that you handle
this phase of his operation. He's got everything you'll need. He's
also relying on you or Ross to handle the communication purchases. In fact, at the moment your group is the only one that he
trusts. Besides, I suspect that your legs aren't in the best of shape
and you probably should stay put somewhere for a while."

"They could be worse," I replied.

"Well, I think you need some rest. This will keep you out of
the limelight and away from the attention of that vindictive SOB,
the Attorney General."

"My, how you talk about the heir apparent to the throne."

"That's nothing compared to some of the adjectives the boss
has used lately. If our President sits on the missile information to
serve his political ends, it's my opinion that he won't live through
his first term. In fact, he's following in the same traitorous footsteps
as his father."

* * *

I didn't have to ask Barnes what he meant. On many occasions just
prior to the Second World War, my father made the feelings of the
intelligence community about the Ambassador to the Court of St.
James, Joseph P. Kennedy, excruciatingly clear. My father had
worked for the Justice Department during World War I, and in
1923, when the Army set up a formal Military Intelligence section
of its own, he joined as a reserve officer.

All during the period preceding World War II, my father was
very active both commercially and in keeping abreast of events in
Europe. His commercial and political interests in the European
theater stemmed from his close associaton with his brother-in-law,
Wenman A. Hicks—a short, rotund man—who I knew as Uncle
Nappy. Nappy was an extremely wealthy industrialist who owned

a major interest in the Allegheny Steel Company—later to become Allegheny Ludlum Steel—and the Hicks Coal Company. As a result, he had a lot of business interests in Europe, especially Germany, and frequently held long discussions with my father.

I vividly remember the night when the newsboys were shouting an extra edition in March of 1939 . . . *Czechs Mobilize* . . . Father said the following day that this was the beginning of the end. As events in Europe began to escalate in intensity and ferociousness, Father's long discussions with Uncle Nappy increased. Most of these discussions revolved around Nappy's business interests in Germany and why Father considered our Ambassador to the Court of St. James, Joseph P. Kennedy, to be a traitor. Father maintained that since his appointment as Ambassador in 1937, Kennedy had kept up a constant litany of pro-German, anti-British propaganda. He had embraced select members of the pro-Nazi British aristocracy, and championed Neville Chamberlin's "Peace in Our Time" position at Munich. He even went so far as to arrogantly state that it was his influence—Kennedy's—that caused the British Prime Minister to trust Hitler and accept the "official diplomatic German position." After listening to the German broadcasts on the short-wave regarding statements made by Ambassador Kennedy that ". . . Hitler would win the war, and the United States should stay neutral . . . on the basis that a conflict with Germany involved no moral issues" my father was infuriated. His anger was caused not by Kennedy's statements but, as he told Uncle Nappy, by Germany's deliberate perpetration of flagrantly genocidal policies. As an intelligence officer Father was advised of the staggering reports issued by our embassy in Switzerland of Hitler's policies on racial purity and their horrifying consequences. Uncle Nappy tried to argue Kennedy's point and maintained that U.S. business interests would suffer if the United States were to become involved in the current European conflict. I remembered his statement seven long years later when I ran a 16mm projector while my father reviewed captured evidence of Nazi concentration camp experiments for the international tribunal at Nuremberg. My recollections of my father's discussions seemed to be particularly relevant with respect to Barnes's remark. I sensed that John Kennedy was following in his father's footsteps; the stakes were much higher than the loss of an ambassadorship, however.

I queried Tracy after his remark about Joe Kennedy and said, "I take it things are heating up?"

"Yes, dangerously so. Characters like Shaw add a volatile and unpredictable element to an already rapidly deteriorating situation. He's a wild card and a loose cannon; anything can happen. The Agency is in the middle of a full-scale war with McNamara at DOD, and the President's trying to put pressure on Senator Chavez to curtail our unvouchered funds. To make matters worse, Bobby wants to instigate a complete investigation of the Agency's activities. Something absolutely must give and I know it will not be the Director."

"You know, Tracy, I think you're right. I would be more comfortable working in Baltimore. I'm not a political animal at heart."

"Then you should be pleased to know that Mario has apparently been given tacit approval by Maxwell Taylor to carry out this specific counterfeiting operation. Officially, of course, we won't know anything about it."

"That's reassuring. What kind of time frame are we talking about?"

"I'm not sure, but I would guess quite a while. I've seen the bills. They are going to be difficult. . . very difficult."

Barnes swung the car from the Harbor Tunnel Thruway on to the Pulaski Highway exit, and within a few minutes we were turning left on Moravia Road to the Cedonia apartment complex at the top of the hill. He pulled into the parking spot next to Amy's front door; her Lincoln was parked in front of the apartment. After I gave him the envelope from Harvey he helped me deposit my luggage at the doorstep. Reminding me to be ready to go by 10:00 A.M. the following morning, Tracy departed.

Amy and I had just finished our breakfast when there was a knock on the door. It was Barnes. He said, "We better get going, Robert. Mario should be arriving at your house any minute."

My house in Baltimore was located at 6324 Hazelwood

Avenue. It was an expansive bungalow set apart from a small group of houses and situated at least one hundred feet from a winding country road. A long gravel driveway led to a parking lot at the rear. To reach the house, you had to cross over the beginnings of a large road building project that was part of the extension of the Baltimore Harbor Tunnel. The surrounding farmland was being developed at a surprisingly rapid rate and the area would soon be heavily populated. At this time, however, the house was isolated. There were houses on either side, but we were sheltered by dense trees and shrubbery. Tracy must have realized how close we actually were to Baltimore because as we drove into the driveway he asked, "We're actually not that far from the city, are we?"

"About ten miles," I answered, just as Cecily opened the front door.

"Hi," she said. "Come on in. I'm just making fresh coffee." Then she looked at me and said, "I was expecting you home last night. Mario hasn't arrived yet. He called and said he was going to be a little late. He's picking up a Commander Pons."

Tracy interjected, "Pons used to be the Cuban naval attache in Washington."

Cecily closed and locked the door behind us and said, "Let's go down to the lab. Ross is waiting."

We followed her through the kitchen and down the back stairs. Passing through the heavy fire-proof door, we entered my facility. It was one that would make some of the better commercial laboratories look ill-equipped. There was a complete precision model shop, an environmental test laboratory with humidity, temperature, and acoustical test chambers, and an assemblage of other instrumentation that was overwhelming. The main laboratory contained everything from Cambridge galvanometers to several of the most modern 545 Tektronix oscilloscopes, complete with all the available plug-in units.

In addition, the facility was emergency powered. Sitting on one side of the large two-car garage was a twenty-five kilowatt gasoline powered generator. On the telephone and power pole at the front of the drive as you came in, were independent loops isolating the local power company from any possible carrier current taps. In addition, all the phone lines had been looped and checked for taps. When I built this facility, it was used by the Martin Company for developing a commercial speaker and transducer line.

There was also a complete photographic darkroom. We waited outside the darkroom until a warning light extinguished and a grinning Ross emerged from the door.

"Hell, we figured you were never coming back." I smiled, thinking of Susan, and thought how right he almost was.

Cecily said, "We'll have to make room for the printing press in the living room again." Then, turning to Ross and myself she asked, "What type of equipment are you planning to use?"

Ross said, "I assume the same A. B. Dick machine we used earlier. It should do just fine. What about it, Robert?"

"I couldn't agree more, except registry is going to be a lot more difficult. I've seen the bills. It'll take four different plates for the front, but the rear's the same, one plate."

"Your funding will be taken care of by commercial sub-contracts," Barnes said. "You will supply the necessary out-of-pocket cash."

"Which reminds me," I said, "I still have a chunk of it."

"That's what I mean."

It was well past noon when Cecily asked, "Does anyone want some lunch? I made some sandwiches earlier. There's plenty of room in the kitchen. I would like to eat before the kids get back from Sunday school."

I declined the sandwiches, remarking, "Had a big breakfast, but I could sure use some coffee."

As we took seats around the table, a car pulled in and parked. At a nod from Tracy, I got up and looked out the window. It looked like the Buick convertible I had driven in Florida, still carrying Dade County plates. In a moment, Mario, Commander Pons, and Bill Grosh, Mario's chauffeur and bodyguard, appeared at the door. After introducing Pons, Tracy brought the group to order.

"We're going to make this Mario's secondary headquarters. You're well equipped and well staffed, and the operational plan is as follows: ostensibly, you'll be working on commercial developments, the primary one being your video tape recorder. It's the cover, but you'll actually be working on one. Are there any questions on that point?"

Cecily asked, "What you're saying is, in effect, we'll be working on two projects simultaneously. One covert and one overt."

"Affirmative. Perhaps more. Granted, it makes it tough, but with the way the Administration's been acting, we do not want the Kennedy whistle blown on us again."

"Who's going to know about this operation?"

"We've got several key senators like Goldwater from Arizona and Chavez from New Mexico, and a few reliable congressmen. Mario can give you their names.

Upon occasion, Bob will have to go to Washington to explain the operation and give a status report to some people, but Mario will carry the main load on that score. In a word, you'll be carrying the load here from this point forward. You have your telephone code number if you need us. It's imperative that you keep as low a profile as possible."

Ross spoke up, asking, "What about the Agency project, the anti-jamming device for Comcor, Inc.?"

"I'm afraid it will have to stay in the works, at least temporarily," Barnes said.

"OK," I replied. "Except for emergencies I'm to contact no one at the Agency?"

"Yes, that's correct. Until further notice, the Agency is to be contacted only in emergency situations." Then Tracy turned to Ross. "You are in charge of our other project. Robert will fund you for the purchase of surplus equipment for re-outfitting Mario's new underground army in the Escambray. They're lacking adequate communications equipment and other warning gear to keep out of reach of the Castroites. You can coordinate this activity with Mario."

Tracy turned to me and said, "There's one other item concerning logistics. Ross and Mario will possibly be needing a few runs into Cuba with some of the supplies, especially the medical gear. Could we count on you in the event we become shorthanded?"

All of a sudden I saw everyone staring at me. I remembered that damn trip the night of the Bay of Pigs. After a moment of complete silence I finally said, "I suppose so." There was an almost audible sigh of relief from everyone. . . except me.

After securing my agreement to assist in making runs to Cuba, Barnes said that he had to return to Washington. I didn't see him again for fourteen months. When I spoke with Diggs late in the fall, I was told that Tracy now had a new position with the Agency, although he did not know Barnes's new title. He also informed me that Cabell, Dulles, and Bissell were to be replaced by the Administration within 60 days. Diggs had no further information.

On several occasions Amy and I went into Washington to visit Fran Russell. She was working for Mickey Wiener and not very happy about it. Fran had one-half of a townhouse on Queen Annes Lane, near Foggy Bottom. The other half was shared by a decorator named Bob Waldron, a friend of Lyndon Johnson's aide Walter Jenkins. Although he lived there, Bob kept the unit primarily for Lyndon's use. Lyndon's favorite mistress in Washington was Mary Margret Wiley—his secretary—and on many an evening, when Amy and I were at Fran's, they arrived and went upstairs. Bob was then seen going out, if he was at home. It was no secret among the Vice President's associates, or inside the Beltway for that matter, that Mary Margret suddenly married Lyndon's sidekick, Jack Valenti, after she discovered she was pregnant. Valenti, now president of the Academy of Motion Picture Arts & Sciences, would rise rapidly during the Johnson Administration. One would not have need to speculate why.

I would also see Marshall Diggs on at least one occasion a month. They were primarily social visits, with the exception of the last one. It was two weeks before Christmas, and late in the afternoon. I had gone into Washington to have lunch with George Pierce. He had called the day before and told me he had some information that might be useful. We arranged to meet at his office and from there went out to lunch. What he told me curled my hair. He said that he had confirmed what Mario's underground had reported on there being IRBM missiles being shipped to Cuba. It had come up when he queried a friend of his from the Office of Naval Intelligence. After leaving Pierce I called Marshall and said I would like to meet with him. He then informed me that he and Barnes had been trying to reach me all afternoon.

When we were secluded in his office, Diggs, with a frown on his face said, "You are to put a hold on the counterfeiting operation."

I almost fell out of my chair. "What the hell?" It was all I could say, I was so shocked.

"The operation was to support a new invasion scheduled to take place next spring. All of Castro's top men were to be paid millions to defect to Kohly once the new force hit the beach. However, Castro got wind of the intended invasion. To the best of our knowledge he is still unaware of the counterfeiting operation. At any rate, to prevent an invasion, Castro has made it known that all prisoners captured at the Bay of Pigs will be publicly executed if another invasion attempt is made."

"In that event, I can understand the concern. Now what?"

"Just continue with your operations as usual. I'll be in touch. With the changes at the Agency, who knows what will fall out."

10

DECEMBER 1961–OCTOBER 1962

By the end of 1961, the onset of the CIA's darkest period was initiated by the Kennedy Administration. John McCone, a former defense contractor and head of the Atomic Energy Commission was appointed the Agency's director, as a replacement for Allen Dulles. Dulles, prior to his enforced retirement, recommended Richard Helms as Richard Bissell's replacement. Helms placed Tracy Barnes as the new head of the super-secret Domestic Operations Division, or as some would call it the division of dirty tricks. Tracy then appointed E. Howard Hunt as the Domestic Operation Division's Chief of Covert Activities.

When the shock of Marshall's demand to place our counterfeiting operation on hold wore off, I began to see and understand why a fall invasion of Cuba would be an exercise in sheer madness. Castro's threat of public execution for the imprisoned *Brigade* prisoners would have been sufficient cause to delay the invasion. President Kennedy appeared to be helpless and floundering during the 1962 Soviet buildup and utilization of Cuba as a Soviet military base. The progression of events was staggering both in the destructive magnitude they represented and in the apparent incompetency with which they were met by the Kennedy Administration. On February 3, he ordered an embargo on United States trade with Cuba. Then, at a March 21st news conference, he maintained that no evidence was present of a Soviet-sponsored buildup in Cuban military strength around our Guantanamo Navy base, stating, "We are always concerned about the defense of American territory wherever it may be, and we take whatever proper steps are necessary."

On August 22, 1962, however, Kennedy confirmed that during the months of July and August, the Soviets had begun shipping to Cuba substantial quantities of modern war equipment and military technicians. "What we are talking about are supplies and technicians of rather intensive quantity in recent weeks," he observed. On August 24th, government intelligence sources reported that Soviet arrivals included the following: 3,000 to 5,000 specialists, of which at least half were military technicians; guided missiles similar in structure and potential to the United States Nike anti-aircraft missiles; and assorted transportation, communications, and electronic equipment. This data was then conveyed to the State Department, which then leaked the information to the media. Several days later, on August 28th, Kennedy countered the media onslaught with a watered down version, stating at a press conference: "I don't know who at the State Department told you that they are going to operate Nike missiles, because we do not have that information at this time. . . . But on the question of troops, as it is generally understood, we do not have evidence that there are Russian troops there."

In spite of Kennedy's attempts to counteract the State Department's leak to the media, Republican Senator Keating of New York announced the "real" facts to the American public on September 5, 1962. Keating stated that Soviet ships had landed at least 1,200 troops wearing "Soviet fatigue uniforms" in Cuba. Kennedy then countered Keating's statement and "officially" acknowledged that the Soviets had brought in anti-aircraft guided missiles "similar to early models of our Nike," along with motor-torpedo boats carrying "ship-to-ship guided missiles having a range of 15 miles." He then went on to declare, however, that "there is no evidence of any organized combat force in Cuba from any Soviet bloc country, or the presence of offensive ground-to-ground missiles, or of other significant offensive capability, either in Cuban hands hands or under Soviet direction or guidance. Were it to be otherwise, the gravest issues would arise."

Kennedy followed up his September 5 statement with an additional one on September 13 where he stated that "If the United States ever should find it necessary to take military action against communism in Cuba, all of Castro's communist-supplied weapons and technicians will not change the result or significantly extend the time required to achieve those results."

Two days after this rather ambiguous "position" was taken by the President, Washington correspondent Charles Keely reported to the *San Diego Union* (September 15th) that should Castro provide the pretext, the United States would take military action against Cuba. "This," wrote Keely, "Mr. Kennedy would like very much to do before the [1962] congressional elections on November 6."

* * *

Mario Kohly agreed with Keely's observation. The election campaign was clearly not going well for the Democrats. Poll soundings taken on his behalf convinced the President that Cuba had emerged as a foremost issue. On September 18th his former rival, Richard Nixon, seeking the governorship of California, called for a "quarantine" of Cuba, possibly taken unilaterlly. Nixon suggested this would involve use of a naval blockade.[1]

While all this media hype was going on during the summer of 1962, I was gathering communications gear for Mario Kohly's underground, whose reports had become more and more alarming. According to Kohly, the Russians were preparing to erect secondary IRBM (intermediate range ballistic missiles) sites in addition to the hard sites already in place. He reported this information to Diggs and me in a meeting we had in early October. After this meeting, I relayed the information to Tracy Barnes. The CIA presented Kohly's data to the White House, where it was received with the same indifference that had typified the Kennedy Administration's handling of all matters pertaining to

Cuba. I would find out the reason for both the Administration's indifference and its inactivity soon enough.

Wednesday, October 9, 1962, had been just another dreary work day until Tracy Barnes called and asked if I could meet with him at 7:30 P.M. that evening. The pace at which we had worked for the past year had strained relations between all the members of our team to the limit. After placing the counterfeiting operation on hold, we had concentrated on commercial and other CIA contract projects, in addition to Mario's needs.

Although Barnes's call was a welcome relief from the drudgery, the urgency in his voice prompted a flood of speculation. When I pulled into the parking slot at the apartment building where we were to meet, the yellow convertible was already parked two cars away. I hurried up the stairs and, for the first time in nearly more than a year, was face to face with Tracy. We shook hands and he invited me to sit beside him on the divan. After moving the ashtray and magazines off the coffee table, he unzipped his briefcase, and pulled out an audio tape recorder, a magnifying glass, and a large set of 11 x 14 photos.

Pointing to the top one, he said, "This photograph of a new ballistic missile site, being prepared in San Cristobal, Cuba, was taken yesterday. On the morning of the 7th, to be precise. This morning we took one of another site in Guanajay, which is almost finished."

"My God," I said, "more of them. But they don't look like the one installed last year in the Camaguey."

"That's because the Camaguey site is the master control center. These new installations are temporary satellites of that master site, and are controlled by the computer in the Camaguey just as our systems are from Omaha."

"Jesus Christ!"

"I'm afraid he can't help," Tracy retorted. "The installation that you surveyed last year was ready for firing at that time. That installation is now complete with nuclear warheads and everything else necessary to effectively launch a nuclear strike. These new ones are backup sites, and from what Kohly's underground has relayed to us we're sure they have a hell of a lot of permanent sites installed. We're still trying to find out just how many. At any rate, the Soviet arms build-up in Cuba over the past year has been massive. It's beginning to look as though they are setting up a major strike force."

"Why did the Administration wait this long? I assumed something had already been done. Other than Mario's reports, I haven't heard anything except media hoopla in the last year."

"You've been stuck in that basement too long, Robert. If nothing else, the President and his brother are smart politicians. They knew they'd be in trouble this year. Have you read the latest Gallop polls? Right now it appears that the Republicans are going to take a majority in both the House and the Senate. If that happens, the Kennedy clan will be powerless to control a large enough block for their intended succession."

"Succession?" I asked.

Barnes interrupted. "Of course. Robert takes over after John abdicates the throne, as it were. . . . then young Ted . . . But back to business."

"The Camaguey control site you found is now guarded by at least eight independent SAM missile installations and a MIG-21 fighter force. The Soviets obviously feel that any attack will be coming from the air, and therefore do not have a large ground force installation.

"In the Agency's opinion, it would be almost impossible to destroy this installation with bombers. On the island, there are known to be at least sixteen more SAM-2 sites, not including the eight I just mentioned. Over and above these units are five surface-to-surface missile installations that could be used against any attempted operations by our Navy.

"As for the ballistic locations, San Cristobal, near the northwest Cuban coast, has four temporary MRBM (medium range ballistic missile) sites under construction, and the Guanajay, which is closest to the States, has two temporary IRBM (intermediate range ballistic missile) sites being built; the latter is backed up with another MIG defense force and a bomber strike force of IL-28's. Approximately

ten miles west of where you landed in the Camaguey during the
Bay of Pigs invasion, there are two more MRBM sites under
construction at Sagua la Grande. That's a total of six. Five miles
east and a few miles inland, at Remedios, a third solitary IRBM
installation is being prepared."

I was nearly dumbfounded by this data, but had the presence
of mind to at least attempt a response. "It's totally baffling that all
these temporary installations should be openly under construction
when the Soviets already have all the hidden hard sites reported
by the underground. The Russians must be so confident that they
can knock us out or intimidate us that they haven't even bothered
to camouflage these new installations."[2]

"I agree with your observation, Robert. Something is terribly
wrong."

"I take it we've resumed the U-2 flights?" I asked.

"That's affirmative. In fact, the President ordered in low range
Air Force FR-101's and Navy F-84 recon aircraft, now that the
situation has gotten out of control."

"So, what's going to happen?"

Tracy looked at me hard. "We want Mario to send in an
underground team to knock out the computer center—and we need
you to convince him. If we can destroy it, the Russians will have
to back off."

"What does the President think of that plan?" I asked.

"He refuses to make any comment," Tracy answered angrily.
"He's got his own private little group working on the problem. He
calls it the Executive Committee, or as the Attorney General refers
to it, the Ex Com. I know some of the "types" that have been called
to serve on it, including our illustrious new Director. They'll sit on
it. Actually, there's no reason for the Russians to back down. The
little traitor we call a President waited too long. We need action
now! We want Mario's underground to try to take out that control
center tomorrow night."

"Tomorrow night! Jesus, Tracy, you don't give me much time.
That's going to be a hard sell to Kohly, and a tough job to do. Del
Valle's pictures showed that their control apparatus was buried

in bunkers fifteen to twenty feet underground."

"That's true, Robert, but its' only protection on the ground are two dozen guards and a cyclone-type charged fence around the perimeter. If they can get inside the compound, Mario's boys can drop explosive charges down the ventilator shafts. We have mapped their locations from del Valle's pictures. In addition, they will be able to set a heavy mine-charge to destroy the underground communications cable that connects the computer to the microwave relay transmitter. If time permits, they can also try to knock out the transmitter. Simultaneously, another group will attack the radio communications building. If we can manage to detonate all the charges within a few minutes, the Cubans won't know what hit them until it's all over. Now," he continued, "let's get to the other business at hand. Mario's men have discovered that Jack spent several weeks in Cuba in both April and July of this year."

"Jack?" I interrupted.

"He's the arms dealer associated with Carlos Prio Socarras, who helped arrange the arms buy you made in Greece."

I thought for a moment and then remembered. "Oh, right, Ruby. He's the man you told me was connected with Clay Shaw, isn't he?"

"That's right. He manages to get into Cuba via Mexico City. The Agency has known for quite some time that he has been playing both ends against the middle, but looked the other way until it became obvious that Red China was trading cocaine for sugar. It appears that Jack, knowing of this trade agreement, may have seen a golden opportunity to make a buck. While he was dealing in guns for Kohly's underground, he may have been running narcotics out of Cuba from Castro for either Carlos Marcello or himself."

"Do you think that's even a remote possibility?"

"I don't know anymore. But let me tell you a story. One that must never be divulged, under any circumstances. Even though you signed a secrecy agreement, you may someday be tempted. . . . Will you agree to that?"

"You know I will. Damn, haven't I come this far?"

"I just had to make sure Robert. I know you think they can't torture it out of you; however, for your own sake, you will, at some point, after this discussion, be outfitted with a special front tooth. If for some reason you find yourself in a position where you have no choice, well. . .It only takes a few seconds!"

I know that I paled perceptively. "Maybe I don't want to know."

Tracy smiled rather grimly. "Just after the last of Mario's guerilla army was evacuated in March of 1961, prior to the Bay of Pigs, my boss in the agency, Richard Bissell, instructed our Technical Services Section to form an Executive Action Program capable of performing specialized assassination projects. This operation was founded by a man known to you as Harvey. You may recall that you picked up a package from Harvey which you received from Hamilton in Paris[3] and delivered to me upon your return from Europe. As the information was sensitive and dealt with problems connected with Centro Mondiale Commerciale, I thought it best to have you hand-carry the package directly to me. Harvey is now running the Castro assassination operations as part of a program known as *ZR/RIFLE*.

"As is true of Kohly's *Operation Forty*, *ZR/RIFLE* is licensed to kill. Its targets, however, are infinitely more specific and powerful: *ZR/RIFLE* is licensed to kill heads of state. It consists of several people whose primary function is to recruit and oversee a pool of assassins from foreign countries. One of these assassins is a man who has been involved with Jack Ruby in gunrunning operations since 1959. His name is Thomas Davis.[4]

"Davis is also tied up with the training of anti-Castro exiles for assassination operations, and works with several organizations such as the illegal French OAS—a right wing militant group determined to keep French President DeGualle from freeing French North Africa. At present, we understand he is working with Clay Shaw and his group in New Orleans. He is also involved with Carlos Marcello, a man determined to get rid of both Robert and John Kennedy. . .since the Attorney General had him kidnapped and deported illegally to Guatemala.

"If our suspicions are correct, we have a New Orleans-based

assassination team, operated with Agency sanction, under the direction of Clay Shaw and his organization. . . along with Mob boss Carlos Marcello."

"Oh my God." I just sat there on the couch, looking at the troubled face of Tracy Barnes. The man was terribly worried. Now I could see why. Then I asked him, "That's the territory under the control of Kohly's United Organizations, isn't it?"

"For most of the Cubans, yes. However, some of the Cuban extremists now run with Shaw in New Orleans."

"I must say, things have changed in the last year."

"That's an understatement," Tracy said, a grim look crossing his face. "Now, about Jack Ruby's activities in Dallas. What I'm getting at is this: we suspect that Jack is running an open narcotics business under the protection of the Agency. If in fact he is, he knows we can't stop it without blowing our ZR/RIFLE operation. To make matters worse, Dave Ferrie, who's supposed to be under our direct control, is also operating with Marcello and Shaw."

"Does Shaw know what's going on?"

He thought for a moment, then said, "Hell, Robert. I honestly do not think that Shaw is aware of the narcotics. Interestingly enough, most of Shaw's Dallas and New Orleans personnel were recruited from the Minutemen. Consequently, one would think that such personnel recruitment policies would automatically preclude any narcotics activity. Nevertheless, we really cannot afford to take chances. Actually, this is the second reason why I'm meeting with you today. I must make sure that Kohly isn't involved in any of this. You're the closest to him."

"Yes," I said, suddenly feeling uneasy. "Who else could be implicated?"

"It could be Shaw's right arm and Ferrie's superior, a man in his forties named Guy Banister, a contract employee about whom I know very little. He's an ex-FBI man, the former Special-Agent-in-Charge of the Chicago office. In fact, he was Robert Maheu's boss. Maheu, as I'm sure you remember, was the man who helped set up the Agency's Castro assassination attempts with the Mafia.

You met his two contacts at Mario's place after the Bay of Pigs—Messrs. Rawlston and Gold—or I should say Mr. Johnny Roselli and Mr. Sam Giancana."

I blanched; they were the ones with whom Mario was dealing at the time I was doing the original counterfeiting operation which resulted in Castro's enforced change of Cuban currency, a little over a year ago. "Yeah, I remember. I don't remember Maheu, however. Or, I should say, I wasn't introduced to anyone else."*

"That's not surprising; Maheu may not have been present at that time. At any rate, let's continue. Getting back to Banister, today, he is reported to be an active member of the Minutemen and head of the anti-Communist League of the Caribbean. We suspect that this latter group may be part of a Miami-based organization called the *anti-Communist Brigade*. Banister also founded an organization called the *Friends of Democratic Cuba (FDC)* in January of last year. The *FDC* was originally an arm of the *Cuban Revolutionary Front*, which Kohly opposed as being full of former Castro people with the exception of Carlos Prio Socarras and New Orleans based Sergio Arcacha Smith. This was the group that attempted to take control of the Bay of Pigs invasion, afterwards becoming known as the *Cuban Revolutionary Council*."

"I remember it well. They were the ones that were to be 'terminated with extreme prejudice' (murdered), with the sanction of Vice President Nixon, by the *Operation 40* group."

"The very same," Tracy agreed. "And what worries me is that a lot of people we used to count on are getting out of hand because of this new regime. We don't know whom we can trust. Shaw could be operating alone with the right-wingers who operate Centro Mondiale Commercial and Permindex. We even set up a direct contact inside Banister's organization, but now we suspect that he's gone to the far right."

"May I ask who it is?"

Barnes paused, "I don't think so. It's not that I don't feel you

---

*Actually, there were two other men with Kohly at that meeting.

shouldn't know. It just might affect your judgment if you find out anything and he's a part of it."

"Then may I ask, who controls Jack. . . .?"

"Until now we had assumed that Banister was coordinating Jack's activities. Today, it could also be Marcello and Shaw. We're just not sure."

"Obviously I didn't know any of this, Tracy, but I'll try to find out if Mario does."

"I'd appreciate it, Robert. Until now there was no need to involve you, but it could become a serious situation. We need to know that Kohly isn't getting away from us either."

"That I understand. Banister must have quite a crew."

"To be precise, several dozen; although only a few are in the inner circle. He uses Ferrie now more and more as a personal aide and pilot. There is also a young man named Hugh Ward who is used as both a hatchet and research man, and a pilot by the name of Maurice Gatlin, Sr., who is supposed to be another of the Agency's inside men. Perhaps the most dangerous of all Bannister's men is Carlos Rigal, a hit man of French origin, whose Agency code name is QJ/WIN. He was spawned from ZR/RIFLE. I won't tell you his real name.

"Did Shaw solicit Banister's service through the Agency in Washington?"

"No, he was introduced originally through a lawyer in New Orleans, Guy Johnson, a former officer in the Office of Naval Intelligence and now Shaw's personal attorney. What really has me worried is something more sinister. Gatlin claims he spotted another of our fringe operators with Dave Ferrie and Banister several times last week. He's a man who recently finished an assignment for us inside the U.S.S.R. He's an ex-Marine with a Russian wife."

"Well, at any rate, when President Kennedy reveals that the missiles are in Cuba, all hell will break loose. Every radical element from the John Birch Society to the Ku Klux Klan will be after his ass."

After he made this statement I knew what Barnes was going

to answer, but had to ask anyway. Given the data he had provided to me, there was no doubt in my mind how the characters and the numbers were adding up.

"Tracy, in light of everything that you've told me and the organization you've described, what do you really think will happen when Kennedy announces this Cuban Missile situation?"

Barnes held his hands together and very quietly said, "I think someone may try to assassinate the President."

"That's what I thought you were going to say. But, you wouldn't let it happen? Would you?" I waited almost five seconds, then exploded. "Good God, Tracy, answer me!"

"Hell no, Robert. . . . But the Agency can't stop someone we don't know about."

I knew he was referring to the situation in New Orleans, when he continued with, "We must, of course, know what's going on, if for no other reason than to protect our image, and of course, prevent any attempt on the President's life from happening. We must gather as much information as possible on any potential plot, particularly if any of our people are involved and nip it in the bud."

"What if we find out too late?"

Tracy looked at me steadily. "There is always that chance. But we can't spread our suspicions around and at the same time maintain an effective organization; however, we must try to cover all the bases. Shaw's already training several paramilitary teams, possibly with some of our own and Kohly's men, for God knows what operation. We've got to know precisely what Kohly knows about New Orleans, their plans and operations."

"Can you give me another run-down on these people so I know whom and what I'll be looking for?"

"Sure, commit them to memory. Then I'll give you your tentative assignment."

Tracy reached into a briefcase next to his chair and pulled out a number of folders. "To recapitulate, here's a rundown on Shaw's inside group. The first one is Shaw himself, who sometimes uses the aliases Clyde Bertrum and Alton Bernard. He is currently, and has been for some time, president of the New Orleans International

Trade Mart. He is also on the Board of CMC and the Permindex Corporation, both CIA-funded companies with which you are familiar. His official relationship with the Agency is as a consultant. Second in command in both the Dallas and New Orleans areas, is Guy Banister. Up until 1955, Banister was in charge of the FBI field office in Chicago. He then went to New Orleans to become deputy superintendent of police, a position he held for several years.

"After leaving that post, he became violently anti-Castro and started his own highly specialized detective agency, just like his old employee Robert Maheu, formerly our Mafia assassination coordinator. Banister located his offices at 544 Camp Street, which also houses the Free Cuba Movement, which is part of the United Organizations. It's possible that this group is part of Kohly's new outfit—the Cuban Christian Democratic Movement or CDM for short. We need to find out. In addition, Banister publishes an anticommunist rag called *The Louisiana Intelligence Digest*. He first met Clay Shaw through a mutual friend, Guy Johnson, who was formerly with the Office of Naval Intelligence. Johnson's still in the naval reserve and is also Shaw's attorney.

"Ostensibly, Banister's top aid is still Dave Ferrie, who, as you know, worked for Banister in the past as an investigator and transporter. Currently, he is also Carlos Marcello's pilot. Recently, Dave had some unfortunate publicity that labeled him a homosexual, which he is, and he was dismissed as a pilot for Eastern Air Lines. Ferrie now appears to be the most important and versatile man under Banister and Shaw's command. We are told that he has set up the paramilitary training facility at Lake Pontchatrain, Louisiana. It may also be for Kohly."

This information was flowing so quickly, I was struggling to fix the names and roles in my memory.

"In addition, he has trained several of his compatriots to fly and has personally run several missions into Cuba, similar to the one you went on.

"Under Shaw's direction, Ferrie and Banister are also known to have compiled the largest collection of anti- and pro-communist

intelligence dossiers in Louisiana. It has to be a massive file, considering all the Cubans located in that area. In fact, being an old
FBI man, Banister modeled his system after theirs, and the information file consists of both friends and enemies. If our sources are
correct, the 10-23 classification deals with Cuban matters, the 23-5
category deals with the *Cuban Democratic Revolutionary Front,* and
the 10-209 classification is simply the Cuban file. Category 23-14,
we are told, is Shaw's personal file."

"I'd love to see that," I said, and then added, "I gather that
you want me to find out what Mario's role is in New Orleans, if
any?"

"Frankly, yes," Tracy said. "That's the idea. Shaw, if he controls Kohly's forces, may go wild now that Bissell has been replaced
and Cabell has been officially removed as Deputy Director. After
all, just consider what Shaw did earlier, on his own, to our vehicles
and aircraft. You frequently see Kohly here in Baltimore; you may
be able to learn something we haven't."

I nodded and he continued.

"Now, let's get back to Banister's people. There is Hugh Ward,
whom we've already discussed and who is one of Ferrie's more
adept pilot trainees. You know about Carlos Rigal. Then, of course,
there is Jack. Jack's most important working partners are Davis and
Loren Eugene Hall, about whom we don't know much, except that
he was part of the old Cuban Mafia.[6]

"Do they operate out of Dallas?" I asked.

"Dallas, Miami and New Orleans." Then, almost as an afterthought, he said, "There is one other. The young man who served
in the Marine Corps who now has the young Russian wife. His
name is Lee Oswald. After being trained as both a radar operator
and cryptographer, he was assigned to our base in Atsugi, Japan.
While working there he learned Russian. Atsugi, as you probably
know, is the base that launches most of the covert U-2 overflies of
China and the U.S.S.R. From there they go into Turkey."

"Just like Gary Powers," I interjected.

"Yes." Tracy looked annoyed at being interrupted. "Anyway,
that's where he was trained. He served a covert stint in the Philip-

pines with his MAAG group and, in September of 1959, at our request, he applied for and received a hardship discharge within three days. For obvious reasons, when we sent him to Russia posing as a defector, it was changed to a dishonorable discharge. From the marines, he went home to New Orleans. After spending a few days with his mother, he was reimbursed $2,000 dollars from our local New Orleans office located across from 544 Camp Street, in the federal office building. He had a top secret clearance, as well as a crypto clearance, and was on a sensitive mission."[7]

"What do you mean by sensitive?" I asked.

"Oswald's assignment was to get into Russia, state that he was revoking his citizenship, and defect to the other side with all our top secret codes, radar data, frequencies and whatever else he had memorized. He would be used for an internal security operation in Russia. Hence, the establishment of the anti-American, pro-Commie identification. His job was to make contact with a girl in Moscow who's the niece of a KGB colonel and get her out of Russia so her uncle could defect. Although the uncle was married, the girl was his only blood relation.

"It was a complex mission. He went to England by ship and then was passed on to Helsinki by land. The boys in London felt he should make the trip overland instead of by plane. They figured it would make his defection look more authentic. Using ground transport, it took him almost two weeks to get to Moscow. When he arrived there, acting on his instructions, he charged into the American Embassy and denounced his American citizenship.

"Next, again as instructed, he contacted certain Russian officials and gave them detailed information on our radar, intelligence frequencies and codes. It had been prearranged, of course, to discontinue sensitive transmissions as soon as he arrived in Moscow, and to change every frequency and code he passed to the Russians within a day or two after he appeared at our Moscow embassy. This gave the Russians time to verify the accuracy of what he told them, but also kept them from learning anything really important.

"The operation worked perfectly in the opening stages, but he was then exiled to Minsk for two years. He did manage, however, to marry and bring the KGB colonel's niece with him. It wasn't easy. He had to slash his wrists and act like a maniac to get the girl and their baby out."

"Baby?" I said.

"He married her and they had a baby. Apparently, he fell in love with her." We pulled them out on a prearranged plan where he would ask our Embassy to loan him some money and issue him a passport. Our man at the Embassy provided him with over $400.00 to pay for their transport.

"On the night of his arrival back in the U.S. one of our people debriefed him and immediately reported into headquarters in D.C. He was told to send Oswald directly down south to await further contact. He finally hooked up with Jack in Dallas, and we think the FBI is also using him.

"Now we're waiting for her uncle to come over. At any rate, as you can see, we've got an army of people on the payroll down there, and we want to double-check what the hell is going on."

"OK," I said. "Anybody else?"

Tracy looked at me quizzically and said, "No."

"I'm overwhelmed," I replied.

After Barnes left, I reached Mario by phone and learned that he already had a group poised and ready for a strike at the Cuban control center. Despite his disenchantment with the Administration, he had agreed to order his team in the next night, not only to help the United States but, more importantly, to save his countrymen from a potential holocaust, if the U.S. decided to attack Cuba with a nuclear strike force.

CHAPTER TEN NOTES:

1. Not all blockade advocates were Republicans seeking political advantage. Democratic leaders were becoming increasingly apprehensive over the seeming helplessness of the Kennedy Administration toward Castro's Cuba. They feared such "do-nothingism" would cost the Democrats votes at the polls. The "do-something" demands snowballed. Wherever Kennedy went on his campaign tours, political signs taunted his Administration about Cuba. "More profile than courage" was again raised against him. "Castro loves Democrats" was another slogan. These signs greatly irritated President Kennedy.

2. Administrative spokesmen claimed that a heavy cloud cover prevented getting any photographs of the missile build-up in Cuba until October 14, 1962. It was flatly announced by several high Administration sources that photos were not taken several days prior to that date because "the weather intervened. Hurricane Ella delayed flights for a week and then a cloud cover blocked high-level surveillance." This was a total fabrication, because Ella did not become a hurricane until October 16 — well after the period referred to in the statement. Official Weather Bureau maps show clear weather over Western Cuba most of the time between October 5th and 9th, and good photographic weather in the morning from October 10 to 14.

3. In 1975, the Senate Intelligence Committee started looking into the operations of the CIA's Executive Action Program. The committee was especially concerned with the program because it was established for the purpose of committing assassinations of political leaders and heads of state. It was part of the operational arm of the Technical Services Division, code-named ZR/RIFLE.

4. Among the major questions no one asked of Ruby, the day the Warren Commission met with him, were about his connection with a mystery-man named Davis. Hubert and Griffin had alerted Warren, Ford and the rest of the Commission members about the existence of Davis more than two months earlier, in a memorandum dated March 19, 1964. Not only did the Commission fail to let Hubert or Griffin ask Ruby anything, but their question about Davis was ignored. Their March 19 memorandum said, in part:

> Ruby has acknowledged independently that, prior to the time that Castro fell into disfavor in the United States, he had been interested in selling jeeps to Cuba. Ruby states that he contacted a man in Beaumont, Texas, whose name, he recalled, was Davis. The FBI has been unable to identify anyone engaged in the sale of arms to Cuba who might be identical with the person named Davis.

The FBI could never even find a first name for Davis. But the CIA knew all about him and still does in a closed file, under the name of Thomas Eli Davis III; born: Aug. 27, 1937; died: Sept. 6, 1973.

Not long after Ruby was jailed for the murder of Oswald, his first lawyer, Tom Howard of Dallas, asked him if there were any names of people the prosecution could produce who could be damaging to Ruby's defense. Unhesitatingly, Ruby came up with Davis. Ruby told Tom Howard he had been involved with Davis, who was a gun-runner entangled in anti-Castro efforts. Ruby also told Howard he intended to go into the gun-running business on a regular basis with Davis.

While still serving his federal prison term on probation, Davis obtained a passport, No. D236764, issued January 31, 1963, through the State Department, which could not be done by a convict without some extra-ordinary help. By then Davis had become involved in activities familiar to the CIA.

Sometimes Davis freelanced on his passport. At the time of President Kennedy's assassination, for instance, Davis was in jail in Algiers, charged with running guns to the secret army terrorist movement then attempting to assassinate French President Charles de Gaulle. Davis was quietly released from the Algerian jail and returned to the United States. Evidence shows Davis was freed from jail through the efforts of QJ/WIN, the code name given by the CIA to an unsavory foreign agent with a network of Mafia contacts. He specialized in recruiting and directing other criminals to handle CIA assignments. QJ/WIN worked on African and European projects.

5. After the assassination, QJ/WIN was later identified to me by Barnes as Victor Michael Mertz, who was also known as Michel Roux and Jean Soutre, a noted international heroin dealer. The FBI found out that a John Marty, Sara Marty, and Irma Rio Mertz flew from Houston to Mexico City on November 23, 1963, the morning David Ferrie was reported in Dallas, then later that day in Galveston and Houston.

6. Loran Eugene Hall was expelled from Cuba in 1959 after fighting alongside Castro during the overthrow of the Batista regime. Hall became involved in anti-Castro activity in the U.S. and by 1975, at least one former CIA operative and several researchers had named Hall as one of the gunmen firing at President Kennedy in Dealey Plaza. Reportedly, on July 11, 1975, he fled the United States—first to Mexico, then Rhodesia—after becoming alarmed at reports linking him to the actual shooting of JFK. Hall was also a member of the Free Cuba Committee, and was known to have engaged in drug trafficking.

7. To substantiate this claim, there were at least two disclosures in 1976 that indicated the CIA may have recruited Oswald at one time for some unknown purpose. On October 1, 1976, the Associated Press disclosed a previously

classified memorandum which noted that several agency officials showed intelligence interest in Lee Oswald sometime in 1960, and discussed setting up interviews with him. The November 25, 1963 CIA document further noted that the Agency had considered using Oswald for several purposes, including one to "help develop [foreign] personality dossiers." This startling CIA revelation directly contradicts the sworn testimony of Richard Helms, who in his May 1964 Warren Commission testimony, claimed, "There's no material in the Central Intelligence Agency, either in the records or in the minds of any of the individuals that there was never any actual contact, or any contemplated, with Lee Harvey Oswald.

8. Lee Harvey Oswald's first contact was made by George de Mohrenschildt, a deep-cover CIA Operative, whose name was in de Mohrenschildt's personal phone book. Also in the same phone book was was intelligence Colonel Howard Burris, a personal friend of Lyndon Johnson, and former associate of Mafia courier Mickey Wiener. Oswald was sent to New Orleans, where he was taken under the wings of David Ferrie and Guy Banister.

Tracy Barnes, Robert D. Morrow's case officer and deputy to the CIA's Deputy Director of Plans, Richard Bissell. Barnes was later made Director of Covert Domestic Operations.

President Kennedy, Attorney General Kennedy, and F.B.I. Director J. Edgar Hoover, together in a rare White House meeting.

Above: Robert Morrow, bottom row, second from right, as a cadet at the Pennsylvania Military College, 1946.

Left: Author's mother, father and grandmother with author in 1937.

Above: 6324 Hazelwood Avenue, Baltimore, Maryland. Author's house where lab and counterfeiting operation took place. *Below:* Cecily H. Morrow, author's wife and artist for the counterfeit currency. Photo taken November 22, the night JFK was killed.

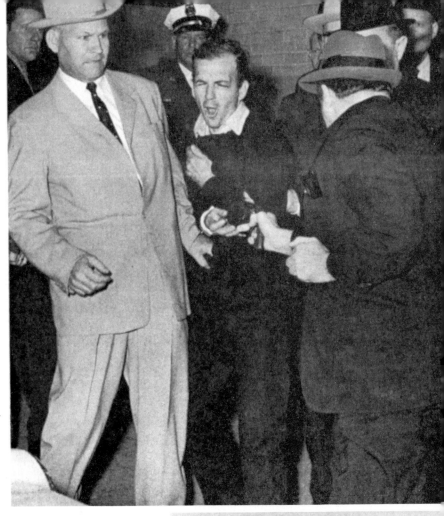

Lee Harvey Oswald's fatal shooting
by Dallas nightclub operator
Jack Ruby, November 24, 1963.

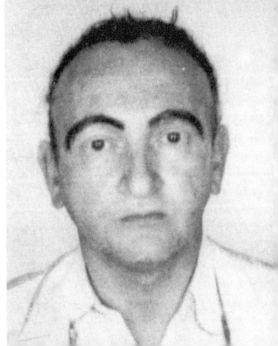

David Ferrie, New Orleans Mafia
boss Carlos Marcello's private pilot,
active participant in the Cuban
anti-Castro resistance movement,
and the master planner of
JFK's assassination.

Mario Garcia Kohly describing the details of the missiles in Cuba in 1961.

Left: David Atlee Philips, 1978, the CIA official in charge of Bay o Pigs propaganda activities and the man most knowledgeable research believe was depicted by Antonio Veciana in the sketch on the next page.

Below: Picture of man arrested on the day of the assassination. H bears an uncanny resemblance to David Atlee Philips. A sketch was distributed to the media by the H Select Committee on Assassinatior

Right: Sketch of "Maurice Bishop" as described to the House Select Committee on Assassinations by Antonio Veciana, head of the Cuban militant Alpha/66 group. Closely resembling David Atlee Philips, this is the sketch that was nationally distributed by the media on behalf of the HSCA.

Left: John O'Hare, CIA mercenary and assassin responsible for murder of Manuel Rodriguez Quesada and Gilberto Rodriguez Hernandez in 1964.

Left: Guy W. Bannister—former FBI agent, associate of Carlos Marcello and David Ferrie.

Right: E. Howard Hunt, a CIA official under the direction of Tracy Barnes for the Bay of Pigs operation, and later a key figure in the Watergate break-in.

Right: General Charles P. Cabell, Deputy Director of the CIA.

Below: New Orleans mob associate Jack Ruby in his Dallas nightclub.

Left: Mob boss Sam Giancana, who operated from Chicago, was found shot to death prior to giving testimony before the House Select Committee on Assassinations.

Right: Mob boss Santos Trafficante, who operated from Tampa, took part in the Castro assassinaton plots.

Left: Mob boss Carlos Marcello, who operated from New Orleans, was the key Mafia don instrumental in putting out the contract on President Kennedy.

Eugene Braden, a Mafia associate who was arrested in Dealey Plaza at the time of the assassination.

Mob boss Johnny Roselli, who operated from Las Vegas, was found dead and dismembered in an oil drum in Miami's Biscayne Bay, after divulging information on the JFK assassination.

In New Orleans on September 8, 1970, Carlos Marcello (left) testifies before a Louisiana legislative committee investigating charges of Mafia influence in the state government. One of Marcello's attorneys, Dean Andrews (behind Marcello, with dark glasses), also represented Clay Shaw. *(AP/Wide World Photos)*

Carlos Marcello and associates dining at La Stella Restaurant in Forest Hills, New York. Clockwise: Joseph Marcello, Jr. (back to camera), attorney Jack Wasserman, Carlos Marcello, Santos Trafficante, attorney Frank Ragano, Anthony Carolla, and Frank Gagliano. *(AP/Wide World Photos)*

F.B.I. Director
J. Edgar Hoover

The author with President Nixon, at the time he was running for the newly gerrymandered Baltimore third district Congressional seat, 1971.

Top: Sunny's Surplus in Towson, M.D., where assassination rifles were purchased by author . . modified 7.35 mm Mannlicher rifle used in assassination of JFK . . . close-up of modified stock created by author . . . Mannlicher 7.35 mm prior to author's modification.

David Ferrie, on the far right, in Civil Air Patrol uniform, 1955.

Lee Harvey Oswald, good friend of David Ferrie, protests his innocence at a press conference in Dallas Police Headquarters after being accused of assassinating President Kennedy. "I'm just a patsy," Oswald shouted to reporters, 1963.

President John F. Kennedy and Attorney General Robert Kennedy in the
White House during the Cuban Missile Crisis.

11

OCTOBER 1962–MAY 1963

I returned to work in my lab after my last discussion with Barnes in Amy's apartment. The next day and a half were filled with feverish activity and concentrated work as I was attempting to complete several commercial projects initiated earlier in the year. Although my days were hectic and demanding, I was often preoccupied with the mission undertaken by Kohly's men: the destruction of the Cuban missile control center. By Friday, October 10, my anxiety had grown nearly unbearable. I hadn't received any news, either from Kohly or Tracy Barnes, about the Cuban mission. I was just thinking of Kohly when I was called to the phone by my wife, Cecily. Barnes was on the other end of the line. His emotionless voice tipped me off immediately. I knew that something had gone terribly wrong with the mission. Barnes was brief:

"Can you meet me at the Colony Seven on the Baltimore–Washington Parkway in two hours?"

Knowing my worst fears were to be realized, I responded that I could but would be a few minutes late; I was in the middle of completing a project.

I finished my work and met Barnes at 2:00 P.M. as scheduled. We quickly found an isolated table in the restaurant; Barnes wasted no time in introducing what had been troubling both of us over the last couple of days.

"Mario's group failed. They succeeded in causing a great deal of damage but did not manage to destroy the missile control center. The director has re-briefed the President."

"Oh, Christ!" I said, at a loss for words. This latest development appeared to decimate any chances we might have of rectifying a situation growing increasingly more perilous by the moment. Barnes continued, "The only survivor out of the twelve men sent in was tortured to death last night in Havana."

"Poor bastard. . . So what do we do now?" I asked, pessimistically. Barnes's response was immediate. "Right now, we're helpless, but Kohly's people have thoroughly briefed Senator Keating on the reliable evidence they've secured, depicting the construction of nuclear missile bases in Cuba. The Senator received no comment from the White House when he confronted the President with the disturbing news."

Barnes's last statement seemed to weigh on him even more heavily than the failure of Kohly's mission. He appeared quite despondent. I wanted to try and understand the implications of his last remarks and queried him, hoping to shake him from his obvious hopelessness.

"What's going on, Tracy? What's the matter with this Administration? Why do you suppose they're refusing to acknowledge what's right before their eyes?" Barnes took little time for reflection before saying, "It's got to be a political power play. If the preliminary polls are correct, the Democrats will lose control of both the House and Senate. The President and the Attorney General are going into the ring against Khruschev themselves. They've allowed this crisis to reach its present proportion. If they can publicly force the Kremlin to retreat by removing the warheads from Cuban soil, the public will gladly give the credit to the Kennedys and the Democrats for solving the crisis. In supporting the President, the public will flip its present electoral preference, turning the tide away from the Republicans and toward a resounding Democratic victory. It seems to me that this is the real coup d'etat and the Kennedys have orchestrated it brilliantly."

"Are you suggesting that the President and the Attorney General of the United States are placing this country under a threat of nuclear war in order to keep a Democratic majority in Congress?" I was completely appalled and disgusted. To risk a global confrontation was beyond senselessness; it was absurd. The United States stood an excellent chance of overthrowing the Castro regime if we would only intelligently and expeditiously employ our Cuban subversives and the resources so readily at our disposal.

"Exactly, Robert. The news gets worse, however. The most recent polls indicated that Americans—by a factor of two to one—were in favor of a large scale intervention in Asia if the Communist threat continues; the opposite position of that espoused by the Kennedy Administration. The Kennedys are in big political trouble and they know it. No one knows how far they will go to assure themselves of a Democratic victory. Scary, isn't it?"

I said nothing and continued to be dumbstruck by what I was hearing.

Barnes continued, "The Agency has resolved to take whatever steps are necessary to stop this insanity. This afternoon, we leaked the information to Paul Scott, the Washington reporter responsible for the 'Scott Report.' Would you believe, Robert Kennedy threatened to throw that poor reporter in prison if he published the story? Scott did it anyway."[1]

"Will it do any good?" At this point I felt completely skeptical of any course of action we might undertake.

"Time will tell, but in the interim, get ready to build Kohly some specialized gear; he may decide to brave another attempt."

"Do I have to accompany the merchandise into Cuba?"

"I rather doubt it, but I'll keep you posted."

To ignore circumstances which, if activated, could decimate everything from Canada to Peru was suicidal. The Kennedys knew this. Finally, with photographic evidence from a U-2 in Robert Kennedy's hands, the President officially acknowledged the existence of the Cuban Missile Crisis. He admitted what Keating had been saying for months; what Kohly's underground, the British and the CIA had known for nearly two years: the Soviet Union had installed both hard and portable missile sites throughout Cuba and the nuclear warheads atop those missiles were aimed directly at the United States of America.

As a nation, we were living on the eve of our destruction.

Kennedy's stategy was incisive and quick. After his announcement to the nation, two weeks prior to the Congressional elections, he implemented Nixon's advice of several months' previous and ordered a naval blockade of Cuba. Throughout the entirety of the Congressional campaigns, he negiotated with the Soviets, keeping the nation in a state of enthralled suspense and fear until the conclusion of the campaigns.

Then, in yet another brilliant stroke of timing and political manipulation, the President announced that negotiations with the Soviets had been successful: Khruschev had agreed to withdraw his deadly missiles and Soviet technical advisors from Cuban soil. The response of the American people was overwhelming. With an unprecedented popularity and an overwhelming vote of confidence from the American public, JFK was able to fortify the Democratic leadership of Congress. He was also able to influence the defeat of Richard Nixon in the California governor's race (Pat Brown won the election). The President had single-handedly revitalized the failing Democratic Party — a feat much admired by his aging and sickly father, Joseph.[2]

Kennedy's newly found serenity was short-lived. Castro and Cuban communism were incurable diseases; our nation's morale and, ultimately, Kennedy's life blood were infected and disastrously altered. In Kennedy's case, this final alteration would lead to his death. The Missile Crisis was simply in a momentary state of remission. Its cure was complete only in the blind words of a coerced media and a duped public, seeking comfort and relief from their fear and terror.

As a gesture of good will toward the Kennedy Administration and in honor of the December 23rd release of the *Brigade* prisoners from Cuba, Mario Kohly, on December 30, presented Robert Kennedy with irrefutable proof that Khruschev's promises had been fulfilled in word only: many IRBM missiles were still in position in Cuba, threatening the false security into which the United States had been lulled.[3] The Attorney General's reaction was incomprehensible. He flew into one of his predictable rages, accused Kohly of malicious fabrication, and none-too-gently showed him to the door of his office.

Kohly, however, was not dissuaded by the dismissive and rough treatment he had received at Robert Kennedy's hands. He and his supporters in the CIA and the United States military were incensed by the manner in which the Administration had not only steadfastly refused to acknowledge the continuing threat, but had duplicitously negotiated with Khruschev. The Kennedys had agreed to trade a reduction of our Turkey-based missiles for the Soviet removal of IRBMs in Cuba.[4] Further, they had agreed to a "hands-off" Cuban policy, thus rendering a Cuban invasion sanctioned by the United States, its allies, or any American-supported group impossible. The CIA, tired of the Administration's self-serving manipulation and compromise of national security interests, finally decided to take matters into its own hands. With knowledge of Soviet missiles only ninety miles away from our shores, and American missiles now removed—by presidential order—from our bases in Turkey, the CIA planned another Cuban invasion, this time to be launched from Costa Rica.

* * *

To insure the success of this second invasion, Mario Kohly, in January of 1963, requested that I resume my counterfeiting operation. He would use the counterfeit bills to bribe Castro's military, extorting their support of an exile landing. I contacted Tracy Barnes and was given his approval to resume the counterfeiting operation. Kohly provided me with the initial start-up capital and I commenced the operation immediately. As we began our preparation, I was under the impression that our activities were tacitly supported by the Kennedy Administration; this, in spite of the accords reached with the Soviets. I soon learned that my assumption was premature. It was Barnes's hesitancy that provoked my suspicions.

Barnes told me, shortly after having given his approval to resume the counterfeiting operation, that the CIA was being pres-sured from the Kennedy Administration to suppress the Cuban exiles and their proposed activities. The Kennedys wanted their "hands-off Cuba" policy implemented to the very letter of the accord. Barnes's brief explanation clarified the hesitancy I had heard in his voice when granting permission to resume the operation. Clearly, the CIA was operating outside of the aegis of the Kennedy Administration's dictates. They were not alone, however, in bypassing the efforts of the Administration to suppress and frustrate any attempt to depose the Cuban regime. The Cuban exiles were also acutely aware of the Administration's attempts to frustrate their activities. In response, they decided to bring their evidence to the media. If they could make their evidence of the remaining IRBM's presence in Cuba publicly known, they might be able to back the Kennedys into a corner, forcing them to take action. As was to be expected, the Cubans were unable to attract the media's attention.

The Kennedy Administration, sensing their vulnerability after the near disaster of October 1962, launched an even more aggressive program of media censorship than that previously undertaken in the autumn preceding the 1962 Missile Crisis. Although the present situation was gravely influencing American security and the lives of millions of American citizens, it was very clear that the Kennedys' chief aim in the maintenance of this rigorous censorship was the sustenance and stabilization of their political interests. The utilization of "news management" and censorship by the Kennedy Administration commenced with JFK's steadfast refusal to acknowledge the Soviet military build-up and presence of IRBM missiles, with accompanying technicians in Cuba, nearly two years prior to the 1962 October Missile Crisis. Senator Keating's revelation of the missile information to the public forced Kennedy's hand and resulted in the President's public recognition of the Cuban situation. The Administration's manipulation of news continued without remark from the media until shortly after the October crisis. At that time, a crisis of confidence in Kennedy's credibility led to disclosures of the Administration's censorship tactics and, in some instances, justification for the methodology employed at the time.

After the events in October, the Assistant Secretary of Defense for Public Affairs, Arthur Sylvester, admitted that news was deliberately manipulated by the Kennedy Administration. It was basic knowledge that the government would legitimately provide misinformation in the face of a nuclear disaster. Sylvester added, ". . .if any of us are virtuous 51% of the time, that's a good record."

As shocking as the remarks made by Sylvester were at the time, it was the April 1963 *Atlantic Monthly* article written by Hanson W. Baldwin, military analyst for *The New York Times*, which thoroughly exposed the tactics and news suppression practiced by the Kennedy Administration. Baldwin stated that the manner in which the Administration blatantly tampered with the news deserved significantly more criticism and discussion than it was receiving. He then proceeded to present, with illustrative examples, the four major tactics employed by the Kennedy Administration in its censorship and manipulation of the news. The first method discussed JFK's utilization of both the CIA and the FBI as a means by which to seek out and isolate sources of news "leaks" to the media. He accused both agencies of enshrining secrecy as an abstract good, and supported his accusation with examples of numerous Washington reporters who were the unfortunate recipients of the FBI's "treatment": surveillance by agents, phone taps, home visits and interrogation of friends and family members. Intimidation was, according to Baldwin, an established priority of the Kennedy Administration; neither the media, its constituents, the Pentagon, State Department nor other executive branches of the government were exempt from his watchful eye. In fact, JFK was the first president to commission an FBI investigation of the Pentagon, even though the Pentagon had its own internal security department.

Baldwin soon discovered that he, too, was not exempt from the Administration's ever-watchful gaze. Not long after his article was published, he was visited by agents who were obviously displeased with his very accurate revelations of the manipulative, yet decidedly effective methods employed by the Kennedys. Baldwin's second illustration of the Kennedy Administration's manipulation entailed use of compliment, personal reprimand and "official blacklisting"

as alternative means by which to maintain effective control over
the media. A case in point was the personal reprimand and de-
nouncement by JFK of the honorable Charles J.V. Murphy, the
author of a *Fortune* magazine article, who provided a detailed
presentation and analysis of the Bay of Pigs fiasco. Murphy, an Air
Force Reserve colonel, was demoted by the White House and
found all Washington's doors subsequently closed to him, because
the facts he published in his *Fortune* article were not complimentary
to JFK or his Administration.

Both the calculated leak and the withholding of information
were the final two methods of manipulation consistently employed
by the Kennedy Administration. Of the former, Baldwin cited the
example of the Stewart Alsop and Charles Bartlett article on Adlai
Stevenson in the *Saturday Evening Post*. The article's source was
thought to have been someone close to JFK's inner circle. The
information obtained – Stevenson's purported softness during the
1962 Cuban Missile Crisis – reflected the Kennedys' disenchantment with both Stevenson and his performance as United States
Ambassador to the United Nations. Interestingly, it was this article
which added to our present day political parlance the terms
"hawks" and "doves."

The latter method of influence cited by Baldwin was typified
by JFK's adroit handling of the Cuban crisis. The Administration's
effective blackout of news pertaining to the Soviet build-up of IRBM
missiles, technicians and military advisors in Cuba, effectively
deceived the American public throughout the two years immediately preceding the 1962 October Missile Crisis. In his article,
Baldwin further advised that the Kennedy Administration was
continuing to withhold information from the American public. As
evidence, he cited the presence of missiles in Cuba, which were
to have been removed after the accord reached by the Soviets and
the President – a fact established by Kohly's Cuban exiles, but
effectively "squelched" by both the President and the Attorney
General.

Whether using "calculated leaks" or simply keeping information quiet, the Kennedy Administration was proficient in

deceiving the American public with a false sense of security. The public had no idea how much military strength Cuba had, or how many long-range missiles were still in place on Cuban soil and aimed at the United States, in post-October 1962. The Cuban exile communities of New Orleans and Miami, however, were acutely aware of the remaining threat to the United States. They were not duped by the Administration's media censorship. They were, however, momentarily fooled by both JFK's and Robert Kennedy's duplicitous policies.

The Cubans in New Orleans were the second largest Cuban population in the United States. They reacted strongly to the Kennedys' passivity about their homeland's situation. Like their Miami counterparts, they felt betrayed when the initial missile challenge wasn't met with force by the President and were embittered by Kennedy's negotiations with the Soviets. The accords reached between Khruschev and JFK, which resulted in the Administration's "hands-off Cuba" pledge, further exacerbated the Cuban exiles' disgust and disappointment. The final blow to both Cuban communities came with the CIA's abandonment, in response to JFK's "hands-off Cuba" and "no invasion" directives, of all training camps and guerilla bases that were previously established to assist the exiles in their fight to depose Castro.[5]

Nonetheless, the CIA's withdrawal did not deter the anti-Castro Cubans. Without American aid, the anti-communist raiders, led by Antonio Veciana, continued their fight.[6] On March 17, the militant SNFE/ALPHA 66 group attacked a Soviet military post and two Soviet freighters in the Cuban port d'Caribbean. While the Soviet Union protested vehemently to the President, Veciana—encouraged by the covert insistence of the CIA—held a special press conference in Washington, its obvious intent the embarrassment of the Kennedy Administration and the flagrantly rebellious dismissal of its announced Cuban policies. The President, who was in Costa Rica at the time soliciting support from other Latin American countries for his "hands-off Cuba" policy, was both embarrassed and infuriated.

On March 30, Kennedy directed both the State and Justice

Departments to disavow any American knowledge of, or complicity with, the perpetrators of the raid, and to issue statements revealing that the United States "would take every step necessary to ensure that such raids were not launched, manned or equipped from U.S. territory."

Undaunted by the Administration's clear warning, del Valle made a determined effort to sabotage another Soviet ship on March 18. To this end, he ordered a group of Rolando Massferrer's anti-Castro mercenaries to repeat Veciana's earlier exploit and destroy a Soviet ship. The British were tipped off by an American informant of his plan and, at the conclusion of the successful mission, detained the exiles' boat in the Bahamas. On the same evening, another exile boat was seized in Miami Harbor.

On April 3, the Soviet Union formally charged the United States with complicity in the anti-Castro commandos' two most recent attacks on Soviet ships harbored in Cuban ports. Again, the Kennedy Administration responded with a denial of responsibility and reasserted the official response given to the Soviets after the first attack of March 17.[7] To further appease the Soviet Union, the President directed the Coast Guard, on April 5, to substantially increase the number of planes, armaments and men currently policing the Florida Straits. This increase, coupled with Robert Kennedy's assignment of six hundred federal agents to the Miami area, was envisioned by JFK as a deterrent to further anti-Castro activities staged by the exile community from United States territory. The Cuban exile community did not share the President's vision.

The months of April and May hosted increased activity by the Cuban rebels: an oil refinery in suburban Havana was bombed by a group identified as the *Cuban Freedom Fighters* and a nearby militia camp was raided by anti-Castro rebels. In late May, Kohly established a military junta in Cuba to serve as the country's "provisional government in arms." Shortly thereafter, exiles returning to the United States claimed to have destroyed a Cuban refinery, gunboat and many of Castro's soldiers. Although the number has been debated, Antonio Veciana, the leader of the infamous March

17 raid which initiated the anti-Castro exiles' revenge against the Kennedy Administration's policies, claimed that at least eleven raids on Cuba took place after the October Missile Crisis and were known by the U.S. Government.

The Cuban exiles found additional support for their activities among constituents of American conservative and right-wing groups. Even the left-leaning constituency of the Cuban exile community was in support of the raids. Their reaction caused Miro Cardona to angrily resign as the head of the former CIA-supported *Cuban Revolutionary Council (CRC)*. At the time of his resignation, Cardona accused the United States and the Kennedy administration of reneging on its promise to support a new invasion of Cuba, and postulated that Kennedy was "the victim of a master Russian plan."

A personal friend of Robert Kennedy and former leader of the Bay of Pigs invasion, Enrique Williams, tried to unite Miami's anti-Castro leaders by promising a December invasion of Cuba, to be launched from Costa Rica. Williams claimed that the Attorney General had promised both CIA assistance, arms and money for this invasion. As a United States-basd coup such as that authorized by the President in 1962 was not politically feasible, guerilla warfare, sabotage and infiltration of Castro's armed forces would be the means by which the Cuban exiles would prepare for the scheduled December operation.

Williams was not the only Cuban exile who promulgated the feasibility and inevitability of a December invasion. Kohly had previously explained to me his role in staging this invasion at the time he had requested my assistance in resuming the counterfeiting operation. Tracy Barnes had further verified Kohly's statement, intimating in our discussion that the Kennedy Administration both knew and approved of our counterfeiting activities and Kohly's preparation for the December invasion of Cuba from Costa Rican shores. I would discover much later that, as was true of our second counterfeiting operation, this December 1963 invasion of Cuba was funded not by the Kennedy Administration or the CIA, but by the Mafia. In fact, time and the Kennedy Administration's deliberate undermining of all anti-Castro activities would prove the Administration's "supposed" approval and support of both the invasion and the counterfeiting activities preceding it, to be an elaborately orchestrated lie.

It did not take the more militant members of the Cuban community very long to recognize the Kennedys' statements for what they were: false promises meant to momentarily appease the exiles. The militant Cuban community had run out of patience. They decided to pursue a different game plan, one designed to terminate not Castro's regime, but the life of the President of the United States. Towards this end, militant Cuban exiles joined forces with the Mafia.

Mob boss Carlos Marcello had initiated a contract on JFK in April of 1963. Having been kidnapped at the direction of Robert Kennedy by Justice Department agents and subsequently deported to Guatemala, Marcello had now publicly manifested a festering hatred of both the President and his brother.[9] The Cuban exiles were aware of both Marcello's contract and his serious willingness to enlist the services of anyone capable of fulfilling the job.

Members of the exile community also reasoned that the only remedy for the Kennedy Administration's continued interference with their plans to liberate Cuba was the extermination of the President. Therefore, they intended to assist the Mafia by fulfilling the contract. Their assistance would, of course, provide the Cuban resistance with much needed funds to continue their rebellion against the Castro regime.

The Cuban-Mafia consortium planned to rely on Santos Trafficante's assets: Cuban Mafia mercenaries, Kohly's anti-Castro exiles, inside men on the Dallas police force and an assassination expert who worked on the CIA's official hit squad—John Michael Mertz.

Rolando Masferrer would be the financial conduit for Kohly's Miami exile groups and Cuban Mafia mercenaries. Carlos Marcello would utilize Guy Bannister and David Ferrie for Kohly's exile groups at Lake Pontchatrain, Louisiana. Eladio del Valle was the coordinator and liaison between the two groups. This network had been established at the time of the Bay of Pigs invasion and had remained intact, as Kohly had continued to rely upon Mafia monies to finance his anti-Castro activities.

Protected inside his 6,000-acre Churchill Farms estate, Marcello relied upon Ferrie and Bannister to design and implement a plan to eliminate the Kennedys. Ferrie was one of the principal architects and organizers of the plan. The brilliant pilot worked closely with Clay Shaw and Sergio Arcacha Smith in New Orleans, and with del Valle in Miami. He was well aware of the CIA-Castro hit teams that Masferrer recruited for Santos Trafficante. In addition, as I was later to find out in a conversation with Guy Bannister during a meeting held in Miami with Kohly, Bannister and myself, Dave Ferrie was the "brains" behind both Clay Shaw's and Marcello's operations. His organizational genius and ability to plan extraordinarily complex operations was unparalleled within the Mob, and certainly within the New Orleans Cuban exile community.

Ferrie's plan to assassinate the President evolved quickly. Its key ingredients were the desperation of the Cuban exiles and the careful manipulation of Fidel Castro. It was common knowledge that the exiles had lost all patience with the Kennedy Administration and continued to seek the extermination of Castro and his regime and the return of democracy to Cuba. Although the exile community continued to plan and prepare for a December 1963 invasion of Cuba, this event's occurrence was becoming increasingly more improbable with the Kennedy Administration's advancement of its current anti-exile policies — policies which would ultimately culminate in the arrest of Kohly and the destruction of his second counterfeiting operation and the assassination of JFK.

Ferrie realized that if an attempt on Castro's life was made and failed, the Cuban dictator would likely seek revenge against the United States government. It would therefore be very easy to make the assassination of JFK look like the handiwork of the enraged, revenge-seeking Cuban dictator. A highly incensed American population would demand an all-out invasion of Cuba and the ousting of its dictator as retribution for the assassination of their beloved president. The Mafia contract and the Cuban exiles' agenda would simultaneously be fulfilled.

The execution of John F. Kennedy would be performed by a series of teams selected from CIA-sponsored exile and mercenary groups in Miami and New Orleans. The modus operandi to be employed would be very simple. The murder of the President of the United States could not resemble a standard syndicate killing. It should, ideally, be made to look as if it were the work of a lone gunman. As a sure kill could not be guaranteed by the work of only one gunman, two additional firing sites would be necessary.

The next item to pursue was the involvement of Fidel Castro. Trafficante planned the scenario. He would act as a double agent and, through an intermediary, warn Castro that the CIA, under presidential directive, would execute another assassination attempt on the Cuban dictator. Trafficante would then select two expendable subordinates who would be set up to murder Castro. The hitmen, under the impression they were actually working for the CIA, would be caught by Castro and reveal, after having been tortured, the identity of their supposed employer. As further evidence of their CIA affiliation, they would be equipped with assassination items readily identifiable with the clandestine agency. With both this evidence and the confessions of the hitmen, Fidel Castro would undoubtedly make a statement indicating his desire for revenge against the United States government. After the death of JFK, Castro's statement would be viewed as evidence of his complicity in the President's assassination.

Now that the actual plan for the assassination of JFK had been completed, it was time to find the players to fit the designated roles. To this end, Trafficante sent out word to the Mafia families and clearly detailed his requirements for personnel, armaments, communications and management of the two-phased operation.

David Ferrie received word of Trafficante's requirements and suggested Lee Harvey Oswald for the role of lone gunman in the assassination scenario. Oswald was the perfect patsy and fit all the requirements established to render the assassination a non-syndicate hit: he was supposedly a liberal political activist with no traceable mob connections and presently residing in New

Orleans—Marcello's home territory. Trafficante chose Rolando Masferrer, a Cuban mercenary closely associated with Kohly and del Valle, to assist in the implementation of the JFK assassination scheme. Masferrer would both coordinate and finance the assigned Kennedy hit teams, one of which would include John Michael Mertz. The staged Castro assassination attempt was coordinated by Tony Verona, "Prio" Socarras' former prime minister. To legitimize the Castro assassination attempt as a CIA operation, Trafficante had John Roselli report Verona's dispatch of a Castro assassination team to the CIA. The team's existence was leaked to Castro via Trafficante's use of a Cuban attorney named Carlos Garcia Bongo.[11]

Trafficante's plan worked. On September 7, 1963, Fidel Castro told Associated Press reporter Dan Harker that the United States was assisting terrorist plans to eliminate Cuban leaders. He added a warning to his statement, maintaining that, if this continued, U.S. leaders could find their own lives in jeopardy.

Although Trafficante and Ferrie maintained vigilant security precautions while both planning and staffing the JFK operation, their secrecy was breached. J. Edgar Hoover learned of both the contract on JFK and the ensuing plot to assassinate him. His method of securing the information was through FBI surveillance of the Trafficante organization and paid FBI informants. A Cuban Mafia member told a wealthy Cuban exile, José Alemán of Miami, that Trafficante felt indebted to Alemán's cousin, and wanted to reciprocate by helping Alemán solve the cash problems he was having trying to build a new motel. Trafficante said Jimmy Hoffa had already cleared a loan for Alemán from the Teamster's Pension Fund.

Trafficante met with Alemán to offer him the $1.5 million loan, and together they spent most of the evening philosophizing poetically about democracy and civil liberties. Unfortunately, in the course of their relaxed discussion, Trafficante unleashed his blunt feelings about the Kennedys: their dishonesty, acceptance of graft, inability to maintain a bargain, etc. Eventually, he revealed that JFK was to be assassinated. According to Alemán, Trafficante wasn't guessing. He knew Kennedy was a dead man. Alemán did not suspect Trafficante's involvement in the planned assassination. As a result of remarks made during the course of their conversation (Trafficante spoke at length about the Jimmmy Hoffa–Robert Kennedy showdown), he mentioned that Hoffa would play a principal role in the planned hit.

Trafficante did not realize that Alemán was an FBI informant. Alemán promptly reported the plan as detailed by Trafficante to his FBI contacts, George Davis and Paul Scranton. The information quickly passed up the FBI chain of command until it reached Hoover's desk. The contract Hoover learned about called for the assassination of the President prior to November 4, 1964, and was clearly the directive of New Orleans crime boss Carlos Marcello.

J. Edgar Hoover was one of the few people with access to all intelligence gathered on various Mafia leaders. Logically, those closely associated with Trafficante and with a motive to kill the President were prime suspects. The information at Hoover's disposal revealed that Marcello had contacted Trafficante recently and was also known to be close to Hoffa.

Marcello was in a powerful position. He did not require approval from the national crime families to carry out his plan. He was not only the one Mafia leader who had been personally humiliated and almost exterminated by the Kennedys, but was the head of the oldest Mafia family in the United States; as such, his position and his decisions were sacrosanct. Hoover's analysis of the vast amount of intelligence at his disposal predictably suggested that Marcello was the prime suspect.

Hoover's decision not to act on this crucial information and advance knowledge of JFK's impending assassination was motivated by his hatred for the Kennedys and his desire to maintain his powerful position. Hoover's political situation was almost as desperate as Marcello's. Word had spread that his days as head of the FBI were numbered.

Hoover did have a trump card up his sleeve. He had previously established a dossier of information on Vice President Johnson. LBJ had participated in the cover-up of the Billy Sol Estes case with the Department of Agriculture, and the Bobby Baker case was beginning to take on ominous proportions. Hoover's information about these transactions, coupled with his long-time friendship with LBJ, provided him with an inside track to a favorable job situation if Johnson were to become President. Hoover was well aware of LBJ's dislike of the Kennedys. His only risk in passively disregarding the information he had gleaned was whether or not, in the event of JFK's assassination, the Texan Vice President would vehemently push an investigation into the matter. Hoover gambled that LBJ would not pursue an investigation of Kennedy's death aggressively.

Hoover had exhausted all means available to him in negotiating his position with the Kennedys. His carefully gathered intelligence on JFK's sexual improprieties had yielded failed blackmail attempts, and to publicly reveal the President's sexual misconduct would ensure his swift replacement as Director of the FBI. As Hoover's impending retirement by Federal statute had already been approved by the Congress and blessed by JFK, nothing remained to save his position except the removal of JFK from office. Marcello's contract on JFK was Hoover's only opportunity to save himself. He took that opportunity, gambled on Johnson's non-aggressive pursuit of JFK's assassins, and chose to ignore the information at his disposal.

History has shown that J. Edgar Hoover's gamble paid off. It has also shown that Hoover kept his end of the bargain. In fact, as we will see later, Hoover became a key member of the assassination cover-up immediately following the death of John F. Kennedy.[12]

I had watched this maelstrom gather its dark clouds of conspiracy and death. It had touched the CIA, FBI, Mafia and the Cuban underground. It would now touch me. I would be called upon to do that which, at that time, I thought to be my duty. I would be called upon to commit treason.

CHAPTER ELEVEN NOTES:

1. Scott confirmed this inside story of the attempted cover-up during an impromptu interview with him in August 1976, just prior to the formation of the House Select Committee on Assassinations. He said he published the story in spite of threats of imprisonment by Robert Kennedy.

2. Three days after the 1962 election, Joseph Alsop wrote, "Until only a fortnight ago, the atmosphere of the Democratic campaign was donwright dank, to put it mildly. The President's barnstorming on domestic issues had lighted no bonfires among the voters. There was no enthusiasm, no spark to ignite the faithful with excitement.

    "Then came the Cuban crisis. The President. . . took the kind of action most Americans wanted to see taken. . . Cuba was the spark that had been lacking before. In some states, the way the resulting fire singed the Republicans was easy to see."

3. After 1976 I talked to several other knowledgeable sources who had agreed to testify that the missiles of October 1962 were not all removed from Cuban soil. One of them provided me with a taped interview. His name is Dr. Herminio Portell-Vila, a former Guggenheim Fellow in the 1930s and Chubb Fellow at Yale University in 1957. Dr. Portell-Vila revealed that medium-range ballistic missiles were in Cuba as late as 1966 — four years after the so-called October 1962 missile crisis, and three years after President Kennedy's death.

    Dr. Portell-Villa's credentials are unimpeachable. He was a grantee of the Rockefeller Foundation from 1960 through 1961 and is considered the elder statesman of Cuban history. He has lectured and taught at the National War College, the United States War College, the United States Defense Intelligence School, and the Inter-American Defense College.

4. An admission made by presidential advisor Arthur M. Schlesinger in his book, "Robert Kennedy and His Times," Houghton Mifflin [paperback], pp. 562–565.

5. As noted by Paul Bethel: "There is no doubt that President Kennedy and his brother, the Attorney General, consciously set about the business of stopping all efforts to unhorse Fidel Castro — from outside exile attacks, and from Cuba's internal resistance movement.

6. Antonio Veciana was the head of the militant SNFE/ALPHA 66 group.

7. The United States Government officially maintained that the U.S. was "taking every step necessary to insure that such attacks are not launched, manned or equipped from U.S. territory."

8. House Select Committee on Assassinations, Vol. 10, p. 58.

9. It should be noted that even though Marcello was out of the United States for a period of only twenty-four hours, his fury against the Kennedy brothers knew no bounds.

10. House Select Committee on Assassinations, Vol. 10, p. 177.

11. House Select Committee on Assassinations, Vol. 10, p. 184.

12. It was from his good friend Hoover that Richard Nixon learned of the pending assassination. Interestingly, on the eve of the assassination, Hoover and Nixon attended a meeting together at the Dallas home of oil-baron Clint Murchinson. Among the subjects discussed at this meeting were the political futures of Hoover and Nixon in the event President Kennedy was assassinated.

12

JANUARY–SEPTEMBER 1963

By the end of May, I had completed the requisite preparations for Kohly's second counterfeiting operation despite the political turbulence which characterized the months preceding January, 1963. The preparation for this second operation required significantly more work than that undertaken in the first counterfeiting venture. The new Cuban currency minted by Castro in late 1961 was comprised of remarkably complex notes, with both denominations containing as many as four colors on each face. Consequently, our reproduction process was infinitely more complicated and demanding than the first one. In addition, Kohly required a production run of fifty million pesos. The sheer volume of currency made an already complex production process even more time-consuming and difficult.

The second invasion attempt had been scheduled to take place during the first week of December; Kohly set the date and Barnes confirmed it. The counterfeit currency, which would be used to bribe select members of Castro's armed forces in preparation for the December invasion, was needed for distribution in Cuba no later than the end of October. In reviewing the staggering amount of work still left to be accomplished by the end of October—the printing, cutting and binding of the fifty million pesos—I quickly realized was beyond our capability and that an outside printer was necessary. I contacted Diggs and explained our quandary, requesting that he to find a reliable printer for us through his many contacts. Diggs complied and secured the services of a New York printer by the name of Harris through one of his associates, an Annapolis, Maryland attorney named Shultz. Mr. Harris, whose resume included the printing of large amounts of currency for other South and Central American governments. With the plates made and a printer waiting in the wings, the counterfeiting operation was secure and on schedule. I could now turn my attention to both my own commercial projects and any additional assignments I might receive from Kohly.

Throughout the summer months, I turned my attention to my video tape recorder project which was advancing smoothly. A second project I had undertaken at the request of Comcor, Inc. was nearing completion and I was quickly getting restless and somewhat bored. The only excitement I experienced was from two additional covert missions I made into Cuba. At Kohly's request, I delivered medical supplies to his newly recruited underground army, strategically repositioned in the Escambray mountains. His first army in the Escambray had, of course, been decimated during the Bay of Pigs invasion.

The plans for Kohly's second invasion of Cuba were a re-enactment of his first invasion attempt, with amphibious landings scheduled to take place in Trinidad. As selected officers in Castro's Air Force, Navy and Army would have received our counterfeit currency by the time the invasion was scheduled, Kohly's invading guerillas were not expected to encounter any significant resistance.

Kohly's invasion plan was a logistically and strategically intelligent operation. With all the preparations completed and the guerilla forces in position, its execution should have been a simple and straightforward undertaking. With the precautions we were then taking to complete our preparations for the invasion, nothing should have interfered. As it happened, something did—the Kennedy Administration. This interference was so complete and so devastating that Kohly's second invasion of Cuba never took place.

*   *   *

The political scheming and chicanery which had characterized Kennedy Administration policies continued into the early months of 1963. Although neither Kohly nor his colleagues were directly involved with these events, the resulting aftermath not only paved the way to the JFK assassination, but enabled both the Mafia and their Cuban co-conspirators to execute their grisly task with what amounted to near political, legal and governmental immunity.

With the commencement of 1963, the President and the Attorney General made several fateful decisions. It was rumored that the first of these was the removal of Lyndon Johnson as the Democratic Vice Presidential candidate on the 1964 Democratic ticket. The second was the attempt to force the resignation of FBI Director J. Edgar Hoover on his seventieth birthday. Both Johnson and Hoover had become enormous liabilities to the Kennedy Administration, the former as a result of his numerous Mafia associates and friends, the latter because of his detailed intelligence files on the Kennedys' sexual misconduct and malfeasance.

Lyndon Johnson's position as Vice President at that time shielded him from possible criminal indictments on charges ranging from the acceptance of political graft to conspiracy to commit murder. His association with Bobby Baker had exposed his Mafia connnections and ongoing friendships with those individuals targeted by the Attorney General as key criminal figures in his war on organized crime.

Bobby Baker, known facetiously on Capital Hill as the "101st Senator," prior to his 1967 conviction on seven counts of tax evasion and larceny, had numerous ties to Mafia and Teamster enterprises in Texas, Nevada and the Caribbean. LBJ had long-standing relationships with Mafia members prior to his association with Baker. As Senate Majority Leader, he had appeared as one of Cleveland mobster Moe Dalitz's guests of honor at the opening of his Stardust Hotel Casino in Las Vegas. Throughout his Vice Presidency, LBJ's Mafia associations substantially increased as a result of his friendship with Baker. By the fall of 1963, their friendship would involve Johnson in lucrative financial ventures in the Caribbean and financial deals with the oil-rich Murchinsons, life-long friends of both J. Edgar Hoover and LBJ.

The Baker/Levinson scandal which exploded in September

1963 revealed Johnson's ties with Las Vegas casino mafiosi whose casino construction financing was supplied by Jimmy Hoffa, and whose comptrollers were Meyer Lansky and Levinson. Hoffa's close association with the Vice President would become highly visible when a number of conservative Democratic House members denounced Robert Kennedy on the floor of the House of Representatives for his prosecution of the Teamsters' president when he was locked in battle with the Justice Department.

It was, however, LBJ's intimate association with Billie Sol Estes—and the legal vulnerability which resulted from his association—that most concerned the Kennedys. In early fall, 1963, an investigation had been launched into Estes' real estate activities and the growing rash of mysterious deaths which surrounded his activities. Johnson's association was scrutinized and the possibility of his complicity with Estes's activities, and the unexplainable deaths which seemed to result from these activities, did not escape the attention of the Kennedys or of J. Edgar Hoover.[1] As Director of the FBI, Hoover was investigating the Estes case. No stranger to the power of the Lone Star State, Hoover shared with Johnson a close mutual friend, Texas oil man Clint Murchinson. In the Kennedys' eyes, Johnson's legal vulnerability caused by his Mafia connections and his involvement with Estes, coupled with his close personal friendship with Hoover's best friend, Murchinson, rendered him a prime candidate for a powerful and highly uncomfortable political deal involving their second target for dismissal, J. Edgar Hoover. However, if Johnson were to become Hoover's man in the White House, both Kennedys would find their attempts to solidify their power severely threatened. Hoover's potential disclosure of the Kennedys' sexual exploits, political malfeasance and legal improprieties could, conceivably, destroy their political careers and, certainly, JFK's chances for re-election in the 1964 Presidential election.

J. Edgar Hoover had no intention of accepting the Kennedys' decision to force him to retire at the age of seventy. The Kennedys, however, were determined to dismiss the ageing Director whose power and intelligence-gathering had, throughout the decades of his tenure, claimed many victims. Once their decision had been made, Robert Kennedy commenced a campaign of humiliation, intimidation and misinformation[2] against the aging Director. The tactics employed were in keeping with those typically used by the Kennedy Administration: sudden unannounced appearances in the Director's office, summons for appearances at the Justice Department, selected leaks and rumours about Hoover's management of the FBI and his impending retirement by federal statute.[3]

Hoover was incensed but refused to be intimidated by the Kennedys' tactics. He had survived every presidential administration since 1924 by maintaining accurate and consistently updated intelligence information on noted Washington personages, their families, friends and associates. Hoover's now-infamous files were one weapon he sought to use against both JFK and Robert Kennedy.

In Hoover's eyes, the Kennedy's were notoriously immoral and amoral individuals. Robert's intimate association with Marilyn Monroe and JFK's involvement with the girlfriend of Chicago Mafia don Sam Giancana were only two examples of their personal and sexual malfeasance. Their abuses of power in Washington and the number of victims they had both left in their wake were mounting daily. Hoover had already confronted Robert Kennedy about JFK's mounting sexual exploits. He was also acutely aware of the means by which Robert Kennedy had obtained evidence against members of mob families in his fight against the Mafia. His confrontations with Robert had been of little avail. Hoover's position was as vulnerable as Vice President Johnson's.

By the summer of 1963, the Kennedys were high on Hoover's black list. The conflict could be resolved only as an either/or proposition: either the Kennedy Administration went or Hoover went, and Hoover had no intention of losing.

It was Hoover's belief that the FBI was charged with the responsibility of maintaining the internal security of the United States. As its Director, Hoover believed he was above the common law of the land. Aligned with his powerful Texas friends, of which Murchinson was the most prominent, Hoover could command a political force powerful enough to maintain his position as Director until the day of his death. His strategy, of course, required the removal of the Kennedys from political office. Allowing Carlos Marcello's contract on JFK's life to proceed as planned would achieve this end.

With the removal of the Kennedys, Hoover would be free to recapture for the FBI its Domestic Intelligcne Division which at one time in the FBI's early development enabled them to conduct domestic intelligence investigations. These responsibilities were carried out through the FBI's Division Five. Eventually this power over domestic intelligence was surrendered to the CIA. The establishment of Division Five had been one of Hoover's first acts as the new FBI Director in 1924. It had been organized for espionage and counter-espionage work; its existence was rendered official in 1936 by Franklin Roosevelt.[4] With the restoration of Division Five, Hoover would be master of all intelligence activities in the United States. At present his mastery was hampered by both the Kennedys and a member of his own department whose activities had been concealed from his ubiquitous gaze.[5]

Hoover was aware of the covert operations conducted by the CIA within the United States. These operations, although illegal, were supposedly "related" to the CIA's ongoing foreign operations. Hoover was powerless to interfere with the operations because the delineation of authority between foreign and domestic operations was vague and confused. As a result of this ill-defined distinction, constant bureaucratic friction existed between the FBI and the CIA.

In theory, the FBI and the CIA had made compromises and working arrangements which granted the CIA a certain operational latitude within the United States. A reciprocal operational latitude had been granted to the FBI internationally. In reality, the situation experienced by both the Agency and the Bureau was a stand-off; the odds favored Hoover. The advantage was obtained as a result of Hoover's uncanny intelligence-gathering capabilities. He was privy to numerous CIA secrets, one of the most significant of which was the Mafia-CIA assassination attempt against Fidel Castro. Not even the President knew about this operation. As a matter of fact, neither did CIA Director John McCone. Hoover unearthed the attempts in May of 1962. He was also cognizant of other illegal domestic activities in which the CIA was involved, such as the secret postal surveillance program, in which the CIA would open the mail of anyone they had an interest in.

The postal surveillance (mail-opening) program had been initially implemented as a means of gathering intelligence on Soviet intentions and activities by monitoring the mail of a number of former agents, suspected agents, defectors and suspicious foreigners. The suspect list gradually increased to include American citizens with no known connections to foreign powers.

The program was a clear violation of American law and, as such, required a feasible cover in case of discovery. To this end, the CIA circulated a memo, which I saw in 1962, detailing how the program's possible discovery by any domestic governmental agency or the Administration should be handled. It advised the following:

> Since no good can be served by an official admission of the violation, and existing federal statutes preclude the concoction of any legal excuse for the violation . . . it is important that all federal law enforcement and U.S. intelligence agencies vigorously deny any association, direct or indirect, with any such activity if charged.[6]

In the event a leak disclosed the program's existence, the CIA created a number of cover stories to facilitate the legitimacy of their official line on the matter.

Ironically, the operation was uncovered by the FBI at the time officials of the Bureau solicited postal authorities to initiate their own FBI mail surveillance operation. The discovery of the CIA's illicit domestic program in February of 1963 provided Hoover with the necessary leverage to forge a forced and uneasy alliance with Richard Helms. Each agreed to ignore, absolve and cover up the misdeeds of the other, Helms being particularly concerned that the secrecy of both the mail surveillance and Castro assassination operations remain impenetrable.[7]

The tenuous alliance between the CIA and the FBI was of

tremendous import for those desiring the termination of John and Robert Kennedy. By April of 1963, the spirit of the exiled Cuban community had reached its nadir. This was initially caused by the Kennedy Administration's revocation of all financial support to the anti-Castro Cubans' activities. It was finalized with the announcement of more stringent State and Justice Department policies against Cuban exiles conducting guerilla raids against both Cuban and Soviet targets from United States territory. This action of the Kennedys was viewed by the exiled community as a betrayal of both the trust and the support they had given to JFK during his 1960 presidential campaign. The Kennedys, in exchange for this support, had agreed to openly support and subsidize the left-leaning CRC and activities sponsored by the committee and other members of the exile community. In the eyes of the exiles, the Kennedys had "hung them out to dry."

Thus, a dramatic shuffling of alliances between various Cuban exile groups and the Mafia occurred as a result of the Kennedys' double-handedness. Suddenly, Rolando Masferrer commanded a sizeable portion of the Miami and South Florida Cuban exile communities whose more militant members were willing to terminate   the   life of John F. Kennedy. Among the population of Cuban exiles at Masferrer's command were groups of highly trained mercenaries, a portion of whose members were former employees of the Cuban organized crime syndicate.[8] The influential Clay Shaw of New Orleans, formerly an operative for the CIA, had become a loose cannon in New Orleans. As history later revealed, Shaw, with the cooperation of Carlos Marcello, marshalled his assets and ultimately supplied the men and material to assassinate JFK. In addition, both Santos Trafficante and Sam Giancana cooperated with Carlos Marcello and thus also became involved in the assassination of the President in Dallas.

* * *

My involvement with the plans to assassinate John F. Kennedy commenced at the end of June, 1963. On July 1, I was contacted by Tracy Barnes. He requested that I purchase four Mannlicher 7.35 mm surplus rifles. According to Barnes, the rifles were available in the Baltimore area from Sunny's Supply stores. Upon my agreement to make the purchase, Barnes requested that I alter the forepiece of each rifle so that the rifles could be dismantled, hidden and reassembled quickly. I thought this last request odd until I was informed that the rifles were to be used for a clandestine operation.

One day later I received a second phone call. It was del Valle calling from, I assumed, Miami. He asked me to supply him with four transceivers which were not detectable by any communications equipment then available on the market. Although his request seemed impossible, I told him that I had an idea which might fulfill his requirement. I could provide him with sub-miniaturized units whose operation would be confined to a range of fifty or one hundred kilohertz. To operate any sizeable distance, the units would require an antenna at least several feet in length. A wire taped to the user's leg would easily suffice for this purpose. The set-up would not be pretty, but I could assure him that no one would be monitoring these low frequencies.

Del Valle then requested that I deliver the transceivers and the rifles to David Ferrie. I was surprised by Ferrie's involvement in this transaction. Barnes, in our previous conversation, had neither informed me that the rifles were being made for Clay Shaw in New Orleans nor that David Ferrie would be the person responsible for picking them up once I had completed the required alterations. Del Valle explained to me that the rifles and communications equipment were for his Free Cuba Committee,[9] and that Clay and Ferrie were assisting him in the operation. I assured him that the equipment would be ready on time as I would immediately order the Motorola-made special transceiver units. Motorola was manufacturing the units for railroad communications equipment; they were relatively easy to secure. Del Valle thanked me and said I'd hear from him later.

I had purchased and altered all four rifles to Barnes's specifications by July 15. By the time my alterations were complete, the rifles could be quickly disassembled by removing only three screws. Tracy contacted me shortly thereafter. Prior to his call, I discovered

that a screw on one of the rifles had been stripped. I informed
Barnes of this fact during our second conversation, suggesting that
I replace the screw. Barnes replied that three rifles would suffice.
He told me that someone I knew would pick up the rifles in a few
weeks. He did not reveal the identity of the individual to whom I
was to deliver the rifles. But from my conversation with del Valle,
I assumed that the person to whom I would consign both the rifles
and communications equipment would be David Ferrie.

The radio transceivers for del Valle were more difficult to
create than I had originally thought they'd be. An unusual amount
of power was required for them to transmit over any significant
distance. To solve this dilemma, I included an extra pack of
four "D" type battery cells to be used for transmitting purposes only. The pack was plugged into the transceiver unit and
could easily be carried in the user's pocket. Ironically, I later
learned from del Valle that the transmission time was to be limited
to five minutes, which meant my additional adjustments had been
unnecessary.

The transceivers were completed by August 1. In that first
week of August, David Ferrie contacted me by telephone and told
me that he was in Baltimore. He asked that I bring the equipment
to him as soon as possible; he wanted to leave the city as soon as
possible. Approximately one hour after receiving his call, I met
Ferrie at a private airstrip run by the Campbell Company, a local
brick manufacturer.[10] He was clearly in a hurry, but I did ask
him about the intended use of the Mannlicher rifles. Ferrie
responded curtly and informed me that the rifles were to be used
for the assassination of a "head of state." He then immediately
qualified his remark by identifying the probable target as Juan Bosh
of the Dominican Republic.[11] Having given me this brief
explanation, he promptly said goodbye, claiming that he did not
want to arouse the curiosity of the man who had allowed him to
use the phone at the airstrip. After a quick handshake, he immediately jumped into the cockpit and piloted the small plane down
the grass air-strip, taking off over what would be called, upon its
completion much later, the John F. Kennedy Highway.

Although I was unaware of it at the time, preparations were being readied for the assassination of John F. Kennedy. In handing over the equipment to David Ferrie, I had just supplied the very weapons responsible for the death of the President of the United States.

Meanwhile, during the weeks in which I had been busily preparing the rifles and transceivers to be used in the assassination of JFK, the Miami-based Castro hit squad created by Santos Trafficante was being prepared for its mission. As had been planned by Trafficante, Tony Verona delivered the CIA poison pills to the unsuspecting team which would be forced to identify themselves as CIA operatives after their capture. The team was dispatched to Cuba with firm orders to assassinate Castro. Castro had, of course, been tipped off, and the team was promptly taken into custody by Castro's men once they reached Cuban shores. With the CIA-issued pills and high-powered rifles found in their possession, Castro, as planned, formed the conclusion that the United States Government was again involved in an attempt to assassinate him. Trafficante had brilliantly staged the creation of a key suspect in the murder of the president.

The implementation of David Ferrie's plot to assassinate JFK commenced with the dispatch and capture of Trafficante's team in Cuba. The time had now come to set the wheels in motion for the JFK hit. The first item on the assassination agenda was the activation of the patsy selected to take the fall for JFK's assassination, Lee Harvey Oswald. Ferrie had selected and recommended Oswald. Ferrie, with the assistance of many others, known and unknown, had masterfully staged the set-up.

The story of Oswald's association with Ferrie begins in 1955. Oswald lived in New Orleans with his mother at this time. A shy and retiring youth, he became a cadet in the New Orleans Civil Air Patrol. Dave Ferrie, whose reputation as a pilot was growing substantially at the time, was the brilliant captain of the squadron which Oswald joined. The exact relationship between Oswald and Ferrie during this period has never been determined. Investigations subsequent to the assassination have verified Ferrie's homosexuality, and his illicit activities with the boys in his squadron are rumored to have cost him his command. It is largely undetermined whether Oswald took part in any of Ferrie's other nefarious activities. Their contact with one another as squadron leader and cadet during this period has, however, been verified by the testimony of over six different witnesses.[12] Ferrie, however, denied meeting or even seeing Oswald during 1955, or for that matter at any time.

Oswald, after returning home from his overseas assignment in Russia had been contacted upon his arrival in New Orleans by Ferrie. Through Dave Ferrie, Oswald was introduced to Guy Banister. Banister, through Clay Shaw's CIA affiliations, was told that Oswald was an Agency affiliate. Banister's source for this information was my case officer, Tracy Barnes. Marshall Diggs confirmed Barnes's substantiation of Oswald's affiliation with the CIA to Bannister in a conversation we had after the assassination of John Kennedy. Officially, the CIA categorically denied allegations of Oswald's involvement with the Agency, maintaining that his obvious ineptitude precluded the possiblity of his employment as either an operative or contract consultant.[13]

A former Agency employee, James Wilcott, however, also claimed that he was advised by fellow employees at a CIA post abroad that Oswald was a CIA agent who had received financial disbursements under an assigned cryptonym.[14] Needless to say, any files that could prove Oswald had any formal association with the Agency suddenly became non-existent after the assassination.

The House Select Committee on Assassinations stated in their Final Report that a formal association between Oswald and any government agency could neither be proved nor refuted. Evidence contrary to the CIA's assertions, however, surfaced outside of any committee investigations. These commenced with Oswald's initial attempt to join the anti-Castro exile movement. A No Name Key mercenary, Gerry Patrick Hemming, told Florida reporter Bob Martin that in 1959, Oswald, after leaving the Marine Corps, was denied membership to Rolando Masferrer's anti-Castro group in Los Angeles. At that time, the group was known as the Second

National Front of the Escambre. By late 1962, it had combined with Antonio Veciana's Alpha 66 and was called SNFE/Alpha 66. It was Mario Kohly's CDM group out of New Orleans which directed the Cuban operations of SNFE/Alpha 66 in Dallas under the leadership of Manuel Rodriges Quesada.

Oswald, or a deliberately planted twin, had been spotted in Los Angeles in late 1962 or early 1963. (The Oswald twin concept is a real possibility and would have facilitated the trail that was created on Oswald's behalf prior to the assassination.) I found out about this Oswald incident on March 27, 1978, during a telephone interview with the well-known *Los Angeles Times* photographer Boris Yaro, who told me this interesting story: "In Monterey Park, either the early part of 1963 or the latter part of 1962, there was a big knock-down drag out brawl in a house, where shots were fired. There were a lot of pictures made of the holes in the wall and the furniture, and of everybody that was arrested. They were lined up, because nobody would point fingers at one another. Ostensibly, aside from the bunch of Cubans that were in this group, there was one gentleman by the name of Lee Harvey Oswald. I went back there in 1967 and tried to find the negatives. The Monterey Park Police Department was nice as could be and confirmed the incident, the date, everything. But when they went for the negatives they were gone, with no sign-out form."

Lee Harvey Oswald didn't surface again publicly until August 9, 1963, when he was arrested during a scuffle while standing on the streets of New Orleans, handing out not anti-Castro, but pro-Castro, literature. The leaflets proclaimed the attributes of the Fair Play for Cuba Committee and gave the address of the same office building housing Carlos Marcello's aide, Guy Banister, and the mobster's personal pilot, David Ferrie.[15]

Just down the hall was another office used by a mobster associate of Santos Trafficante and Carlos Marcello named Eugene Hale Brading (a.k.a. Jim Braden), who would be arrested in Dealey Plaza minutes after the President's assassination.

Oswald's arrest was the result of a confrontation with Carlos Bringuier, the violent anti-Kennedy leader of the New Orleans branch of the Student Revolutionary Directorate [DRE]. Bringuier and two of his associates, Miguel Cruz and Celso Hernandez, saw Oswald handing out pro-Castro leaflets and approached him. When Hernandez tried to take the leaflets from Oswald, a shouting match began, and the New Orleans police intervened, arresting all of them. As he had done in 1959, trying to join the SNFE in Los Angeles, Oswald had a few weeks earlier approached Bringuier, offering to help train his anti-Castro Cubans in paramilitary operations. Oswald's offer—directly conflicting with his pro-Castro activities during that same period—has never been explained. The only possible explanation for this discrepancy is what appears to me to be the most obvious one: Oswald was working as an agent for the CIA through someone local and was assigned to work with the anti-Castro Cuban exile community and their supporters in New Orleans.

Oswald was apparently instructed to pretend to be pro-Castro and, by getting arrested, a convenient record was established that portrayed hm as a supporter of the Castro government. This would later serve those attempting to create his "patsy" image. I would confirm this in 1964 at the time the Warren Commission was winding up its activities. It was knowledge I would have preferred never to have known. Oswald had begun playing his role; the emergence of an Oswald double would enhance it.

Six weeks prior to the assassination date, Oswald sightings began once again, when—judging from the number of reports contained in the twenty-six volumes of the Warren Commission Report—it became apparent that one or more persons started to impersonate Lee Harvey Oswald. During the post-assassination investigation by the FBI, a number of individuals came forward to tell of their encounters with the man who was eventually to be charged with the assassination of President Kennedy. Most of the stories could not have involved the real Oswald, but were certainly most incriminating to him. The man or men claiming to be Oswald were clearly trying to attract attention, repeating the name Oswald several times as if he or they wanted it to be indelibly remembered. In addition, several of the incidents clearly indicated that someone was trying to create the image of a man who could and did plan to kill the President.

The Oswald impersonators did their job well. They left a public image of a man who was loud and arrogant, supported Castro, had defected to the Soviet Union, would soon come into a large sum of money, and displayed expert marksmanship while practicing at local rifle ranges.

The move that would tie Oswald irrevocably into the anti-Castro Cubans was an incident where a man — strongly resembling Oswald — was seen in Sulfur, Oklahoma, five days before the assassination. With him was one of Kohly's most trusted men, Manuel Rodriguez Quesada, the violently anti-Kennedy, anti-Castro exile who was the head of a Dallas-based activist group.

On the evening of November 22, Dallas Deputy Sheriff Buddy Walthers submitted a report stating that Oswald had attended meetings at the group's 3126 Harlandale Street address.[17] According to Walthers, the Cubans staying there evacuated the premises sometime between November 15 and November 23, 1963.

After the assassination, Dave Ferrie, aside from his denials, could not escape some damning facts with regard to his association with Oswald. Oswald's former landlady in New Orleans, Mrs. Jesse Garner, told the House Select Committee on Assassinations (HSCA) that David Ferrie visited her home on the night of the assassination and asked about Oswald's library card. Because of his manner, she refused to talk to him. A former neighbor of Oswald's, Mrs. Doris Eames, makes the same claim. She told New Orleans' district attorney investigators in 1968 that Ferrie had come by her house after the assassination, inquiring if Mrs. Eames had any information regarding Oswald's library card. Eames told Ferrie she had seen Oswald in the public library but had no other information about the library card Oswald used.[19] This may all seem like closing the barn door after losing the horse, but Oswald was still alive when he was supposed to be dead.

Ferrie also talked with several former members of the Civil Air Patrol in an attempt to find out if any former cadet members recalled Lee Harvey Oswald being in Ferrie's squadron. Among

those contacted was former cadet Roy McCoy, who told the FBI
that Ferrie had come by looking for photographs of the cadets to
see if Oswald was pictured in any photos of Ferrie's squadron.[20]

It appeared that Ferrie was suddenly quite concerned with this
past affiliation, for he had been seen in the company of Oswald just
a few months prior to the assassination. As the HSCA would report,
in August or September of 1963, Dave Ferrie and Clay Shaw were
seen together with Oswald in Clinton, Louisiana. There were six
witnesses in Clinton who verified this story. Among them were a
state representative, a deputy sheriff and a registrar of voters. By
synthesizing the testimony of all of them, since they each
contributed to the overall account, the HSCA was able to piece
together the following sequence of events:

Clinton, Louisiana, is about 130 miles from New Orleans, and
the county seat of East Feliciana Parish. In the late summer of
1963 it was targeted by the Congress of Racial Equality for a voting
rights campaign. Oswald first showed up in nearby Jackson,
Louisiana, seeking employment at the East Louisiana State
Hospital, a mental institution. Apparently on advice that his job
would depend on his becoming a registered voter, Oswald went to
Clinton for that purpose. The HSCA could find no record that he
was successful in getting registered. In addition to the physical
descriptions they gave that matched that of Oswald, other obser-
vations of the witnesses tended to substantiate their belief that he
was, in fact, the man they saw. For example, he referred to himself
as Oswald, and he produced his Marine Corps discharge papers
as identification. Some of the witnesses said that Oswald was
accompanied by two older men, who they identified as David
Ferrie and Clay Shaw. If the witnesses were not only truthful but
accurate as well in their accounts, they established an association
of an undetermined nature between Ferrie, Shaw and Oswald less
than three months before the assassination. The Committee found
that the Clinton witnesses were credible and significant. While there
were points that could be raised to call into question their
credibility, it was the judgment of the Committee that they were
telling the truth as they knew it.[21]

Oswald was not sighted again until his arrest in New Orleans on August 9, 1963. The three Cubans arrested with him were set free. Oswald was detained. He obtained his release only after supposedly speaking with FBI agent John L. Quigley. The truth, however, is a somewhat different story. It was Carlos Marcello's top lieutenant, Nofio Pecora, who provided bail for Oswald's release.[22]

If in fact Oswald was a pro-Castro sympathizer, why would the Mafia chieftain want to bail him out of jail? Based on the Clinton sighting, the above event, and several other incidents that would later be attributed to Oswald, the only logical conclusion one can arrive at is: Oswald was unknowingly being set up as a patsy while playing a part in a carefully prepared scenario, orchestrated by David Ferrie, Guy Banister, and the CIA.

According to del Valle, Oswald was being set-up. He stated this to me in the course of a meeting held in New York in 1964. The meeting was held secretly because Kohly, on the advice of Richard Nixon, had jumped bail for the counterfeiting charges against him. About this time two unsettling things occurred, within a day of each other. Both incidents made me believe we were headed for dire trouble.

First, Mario Kohly asked me to come to New York and talk to Mr. Harris, the man who was to print the currency. I told him it would be another few weeks before we could deliver, however he implored me to meet him and give an assessment of the project. I finally concurred and that evening drove to New York, taking Amy with me, We checked into the Gotham and the next morning I left her asleep and walked the few blocks up Fifth Avenue to meet Kohly at the Plaza. We caught a cab at 10:30 A.M. and as we headed downtown Mario briefed me on what was going on in Cuba.

Although it was already late August, the temperature had soared and I was soaked with perspiration when we pulled up in front of Churchill's Restaurant twenty minutes later. I was surprised to see Manuel Rodriguez Quesada standing on the hot sidewalk outside the restaurant. He was with a heavy-set, florid-faced man who wore a nondescript suit with only one distinguishing feature—

an obvious bulge under the jacket. Mario paid the driver while
Manuel introduced me to William Harris. A sixth sense told me
that somehow Harris didn't look like a printer, and the fact that he
was carrying a gun made me doubly apprehensive. It was Kohly's
show, however, and in the face of his confidence, I had nothing
really substantive with which to challenge his judgment. In the air-
conditioned comfort of the Churchill I began to feel better and after
we had ordered a round of drinks, I asked Harris if he had done
work of this type before. He replied that his firm printed large
quantities of currency for several South American countries under
legitimate contracts. "That's reassuring," I said. "Could you be
specific as to the countries?"

"Several," he replied evasively. My comfort index dropped
another notch when I asked if his equipment was designed to do
multiple color gradations from a single plate. Instead of providing
information on the type of equipment available, he simply said,
"Why, sure."

His answers to a number of other technical questions were
equally evasive. Harris then changed the subject by asking me
when the plates would be ready and, without thinking, I replied,
"Within the next sixty to ninety days."

He seemed disappointed. "That long?"

For the first time, Mario looked at him suspiciously. Harris
seemed to realize that he might have made a mistake. "No offense,"
he said hastily. "I was just curious about the timing because I have
to work the job into our production schedule. This is our light
season, and I'd like to get started as soon as possible."

I found him increasingly annoying and said rather testily, "I'm
sure you realize that many lives are going to depend on the quality
of this currency. We've got to do our best on the plates, and we've
got to be certain that you'll do a quality job on the printing."

"Oh, sure, sure," he said apologetically. "Don't worry. We've
had a great deal of experience, and we'll do everything right."

I tried again to ask him specifics about paper, ink, and printing
techniques, but his answers were again vague and I soon realized
that it was pointless to press him further. Mario finally broke up

the meeting by telling Harris that he would be back in touch. I could hardly wait to voice my concern as Mario, Manuel and I headed uptown. "He's the damnedest printer I ever saw," I said. "I suppose you noticed that he was packing a weapon?"

Mario gave me a startled look and said he hadn't noticed. "Well, he was," I said. "And from the answers I received to my questions, I'd say he knows less about printing than my eight-year-old son Sandy."

Mario looked perturbed for a moment but shook it off. "I admit he sounded strange," he said, "but I have confidence that he is all right. He was recommended by a very reliable person."

I said, "Nobody in our group, I hope?"

"As a matter of fact, no," Mario replied, "but someone just as good — a reputable attorney and a friend of Cuba in Annapolis, Walter Schultz."

"Well," I said, "he may be a friend of Cuba, but I hope you know who his friends are in the U.S.; I smell a rat."

Manuel spoke up. "I am concerned, too, compadre."

Mario shook his head. "I don't agree but even if I did, we're committed. Besides, I don't know anyone else who would do the job on speculation."

"You mean no money up front?" I asked.

"That's right. At first he said he wanted fifty thousand dollars in advance, but when I protested he finally agreed to accept some of the pesos he prints as collateral."

Although the arrangement was not credible, I felt powerless to change it. I asked Mario if he'd mind dropping me off at Fifty-fifth Street. I didn't relish the thought of walking back down the blistering sidewalks from the Plaza to the Gotham.

"I'd hoped you'd stay long enough to meet some more of our people here in New York," Mario protested.

"I will another time," I assured him, "but the less exposure I have now the better, and I have a hell of a lot to do back in Baltimore."

"Okay," he acquiesced. "I'll be in Washington next week. Meanwhile, thanks for coming."

When the cab pulled to the corner in front of the Fifth Avenue Presbyterian Church, I got out. As the light changed, the Cubans continued up Fifth Avenue and I walked across Fifty-fifth Street into the refreshingly cool Gotham lobby. The Terrace Bar was almost deserted, and instead of going directly to my room to check out, I went to the bar and ordered a Campari on the rocks. I sat there nursing my drink and worrying about Mario's unlikely printer. I called up, and Amy was already dressed and ready to go. She also hadn't had anything to eat so we went into the dining room where she had lunch and I had dessert and a cup of coffee. We set out for Baltimore immediately after completing our meal.

The second incident occurred when we returned home. I made excellent time on the trip back to Baltimore, and after dropping Amy off at the apartment, I drove to my Hazelwood Avenue house. Ross appeared at the breezeway door looking distraught. As we walked into the kitchen, he pointed to the phone and said, "Pick it up and tell me what you think."

I put the receiver to my ear and through the dial tone could hear the distinct click of an automatic switch being activated. Sophisticated as it might be, the tap was very noticeable because of the special isolation circuits I had placed on my telephone lines. I slipped the receiver down on the hook, looked at Ross, and asked, "Who do you think it is?"

"I don't know, but you'd better tell Barnes immediately."

"You're right. I'll call when I get back to the apartment. No, better yet, I'll call from a booth."

"Damn!" said Ross. "Do you think the Kennedys are on to us? What the hell happened at your meeting in New York?"

I told Ross the story of our meeting with Harris and finished with the warning I had given to Mario. I told Mario I smelled a rat. I'd better call him when he gets back to Virginia.

Ross asked, "Where's he living?"

"At the River House. His lines are probably tapped, too. If he calls and I'm not here, suggest a face-to-face meeting." Then I asked, "Where's Cecily?"

"She's working in the lab."

"Fine. Tell her I'll see her first thing in the morning. I'll stay at the apartment tonight."

"Got ya. Meanwhile, let's keep off the phone. If I need you, I'll drive over."

Twenty minutes later, when I entered Amy's apartment, I told her what Ross had uncovered. Then I picked up her phone and listened intently. Although there was a great deal of background noise, I could still detect the double click of an activating switch. I replaced the receiver in the cradle, warned Amy about saying anything that could be incriminating in her conversations and walked over to the shopping center.

I called Barnes from the Woodshed bar. When I told Barnes what had happened in New York, he asked if I could be in Florida for a meeting with del Valle and a person representing the New Orleans segment of the Free Cuba Committee (*Cuba Libre*). I agreed and hoped the meeting would be soon. Barnes surprised me by instructing me to book a morning flight to Miami the following day. Del Valle would be expecting me and would meet me at the airport. I was to contact Tracy once I had booked my flight and give him my flight number and arrival time. He would be responsible for contacting del Valle and relaying the information to him. Barnes reminded me that since New Orleans was funding our operation, it would be best to talk to them directly.

I arrived in Miami on the early morning Eastern flight and was met by del Valle and a heavyset man who was introduced to me as Dave Ferrie's associate. The man's name was Harry. Initially, I thought him to be a Mafia type. My impression was quickly disproved when he informed me of his past position with the United States Department of Justice.

Del Valle, Harry and I went to a cafeteria style restaurant in order to have our meeting. Once we had selected our meal and were seated at a table somewhat removed from the other customers, I explained to them what had transpired at our meeting in New York with Harris, the printer.

Harry seemed very nervous and became progressively more so as my story unfolded. Del Valle was equally upset. In an attempt to calm both of them, I explained that Mario had been introduced to Harris by a man named Schultz who, in turn, had been introduced to Mario by Marshall Diggs. At the mention of Marshall Diggs's name, both men grew perceptibly calmer. Nonetheless, my opinion of Harris was not in the least altered and I expressed this to both of them. Harry and del Valle told me not to worry about it and Harry said that he would check Harris out immediately.

Harry then changed the subject and engaged me in a conversation about Dave Ferrie. He apparently knew that Ferrie and I had flown together on several occasions in connection with my work for Mario. After I told him of my impression of Ferrie's brilliance, both he and del Valle said that all the planning done in New Orleans for their major operations and those of certain other organizations were primarily Ferrie's. In fact, Ferrie was the driving force behind the operations now being carried out in New Orleans against the Castro regime. Somehow I felt relieved to know that Dave was the brains behind the muscle. In fact, it was probably the only good thing I felt about my hurried trip to Florida.

When our meeting was concluded, Harry and del Valle drove me to the airport to catch my return flight to Baltimore. Harry left del Valle and I for a moment to go to the men's room. Del Valle took the opportunity to tell me that Harry had once been a senior FBI agent in Chicago during the war and the boss of the present field coordinator for the Agency's ongoing assassination attempts against Fidel Castro. I didn't put two and two together right then, but a short time later realized that Harry was Guy Banister and the field coordinator del Valle mentioned was Robert Maheu.

I returned to Baltimore within a few hours of my meeting with del Valle and Bannister. Little did I know that I had just met with the two men who would be instrumental in the assassination of John F. Kennedy, and that we had been speaking pleasantly about the one man whose genius was responsible for creating the plan that would end the President's life.

CHAPTER TWELVE NOTES:

1. The followng four people were killed under questionable circumstances:
    1. Henry Marshall, shot to death while investigating Estes' acquisition of extensive cotton allotments.
    2. George Krutilek, CPA, found dead of carbon monoxide poisoning after undergoing secret interrogation by FBI agents investigating Estes' affairs.
    3. Harold Eugene Orr, president of an Amarillo, Texas company, found dead of carbon monoxide poisoning; played a key role in Estes' finance frauds.
    4. Howard Pratt, Chicago office manager, Estes' fertilizer supplier, found dead of carbon monoxide poisoning.
2. As an example, the Attorney General would go barging into Hoover's office unannounced, or summon him to the Justice Department like a clerk, something no other Attorney General had ever done. Then, to add insult to injury, Bobby Kennedy, either directly or through the men around him, started leaking derogatory stories about Hoover and the Bureau to the Washington press corps. It created a mythology that lasts to this day: Hoover had no interest in combating the Mafia; there were no black FBI agents; there was no interest in enforcing civil rights statutes; and last but not least, that all agents assigned to the South were southerners.
3. As William Hundley, head of the Justice Department's organized crime section in 1963 recalled: "I am convinced that the thing that finally destroyed their relationship [Hoover and JFK's] was that Bobby mentioned to too many people, who complained to him about Hoover that, 'Look, just wait,' and we all got the message that they were going to retire him after Jack got re-elected and Hoover hit seventy. And it got back to him.
4. Actually, Division Five had unofficially been in existence as the General Intelligence Division of the Justice Department since 1919. After World War II, when the CIA took over all foreign espionage work, Division Five was limited to domestic activities.
5. What Hoover didn't know was that William C. Sullivan, who was in charge of Division Five at the time of the President's assassination, and in command of the original FBI investigation for the Warren Commission, was also a CIA informant. Sullivan's strange death just prior to testifying before the HSCA will be discussed later.
6. Final Report of the Select Committee to Study Governmental Relations with Respect to Intelligence Activities, United States Senate, Supplementary Detailed Staff Reports on Intelligence Activities and the Rights of Americans,

Book III: "Domestic CIA and FBI Mail Opening," p. 609 [Washington, D.C.: U.S. Government Printing Office, 1976]

7. House Select Committee on Assassinations Final Report, p. 135.

8. Since his original summons from Santos Trafficante to provide the Mafia chief with a cadre of hit men, Rolando Masferrer had amassed a wealth of Cuban exiles who would gladly see the President dead, including a number of groups in Miami and south Florida, such as the one on No Name Key, which CIA man James O'Connell had once recommended to Colonel Sheffield Edwards.

9. The Free Cuba Committee, one of Kohly's UOLC groups, #8, was headed by Eladio del Valle—the same man who paid David Ferrie and died the same day he did.

    Citizens for a Free Cuba was founded by Guy Bannister. He was closely associated with Sergio Arcacha Smith who had been a member of the Cuban Revolutionary Front and Council which were both closely linked to E. Howard Hunt.

    The Citizens Committee for a Free Cuba, the Cuban Freedom Committee and The Free Cuba Committee, all located in Washington, D.C., were really one organization. In *Undercover*, Hunt said a Washington-based public relations firm named Mullen & Co. "established and managed a Free Cuba Committee for the CIA." In Watergate Exhibit 142 it is apparent that Mullen & Co. was also involved in setting up the Cuban Freedom Committee, which is the same thing. When Dallas District Attorney Henry Wade stated that Oswald was a member of the Free Cuba Committee at a late night press conference on November 22, 1963, none other than Jack Ruby "interrupted Wade when he made that statement and pointed out that Oswald was a member of the Fair Play for Cuba Committee and there was a great difference" betwen the two.

10. Radio investigator Lou Creiger of WLPL, in Baltimore, Maryland in 1977, did a thorough research job on my actions in Baltimore as described in my first book *Betrayal*. He even talked to the man who flew in from the deep south in a Tri-Pacer to pick up some equpiment, and wanted to use a phone. It was Ferrie!

11. Juan Bosch took office on February 27, 1963, and was overthrown on September 25th by elements of the Dominican armed forces and police. They alleged that Bosch's government was chaotic and had allowed free reign to communist and pro-Castro forces. It was therefore unnecessary for the Mannlichers to be used against him. They would be used against another head of state in Dallas.

12. House Select Committee on Assassinations, Vol. IX, pp. 103–115.

13

SEPTEMBER, 1963–
NOVEMBER 22, 1963

Two ironic twists of fate occurred in the tumultuous atmosphere of Fall, 1963. After the deliberate abortive attack on Castro, engineered by Rolando Masferrer and Tony Verona for Santos Trafficante, the CIA—this time without the aid of their Mafia allies— again decided to renew their efforts to assassinate Fidel Castro. The operation involved a high Castro official named Dr. Rolando Cubelo (code name AM/LASH) and Bay of Pigs Brigade leader, Manuel Artime.[1]

In a meeting with case officers of the CIA in Brazil in 1961, Cubelo expressed his growing disapproval of his former friend, Fidel Castro, and offered to defect to the United States. In the interim, he offered to provide intelligence information on Castro's activities and Soviet movements in Cuba to the Agency. The case officers convinced Cubelo of the importance of his remaining in Cuba to provide the Agency with the intelligence he had access to. Cubelo agreed. After providing information for more than two years, he offered to up the ante by assassinating the Cuban premier himself.

On September 7, 1963 the information was immediately conveyed to Desmond Fitzgerald's Special Affairs Staff (SAS) at CIA headquarters in Langley, Virginia. Langley delayed any action on the information as the result of Chief of Counterintelligence

James Angleton's suspicions about Cubelo. Angleton thought Cubelo a double agent who might well be attempting to entrap the CIA in an overt assassination attempt.

Consequently, the operation was not discussed until September 12, at a meeting attended by Robert Kennedy, General Maxwell Taylor, John McCone (CIA Director), Lyman Lemnitzer of the Joint Chiefs, McGeorge Bundy (National Security Advisor to the President), and Roswell Gilpatric (Undersecretary of Defense).

At this meeting Attorney General Robert Kennedy supposedly vetoed the AM/LASH assassination attempt on Castro. He also set the wheels in motion to prevent the Cuban exiles from engaging in their last effort to regain their homeland: a December invasion of Cuba from Costa Rica.

* * *

By the end of September 1963, all of our preparatory work over the last year on our counterfeiting project had finally come to fruition. October 1 was greeted with a mixture of relief and satisfaction as everyone on the team was pleased with the counterfeit peso plates. All the minute flaws had been corrected and the registration was perfect. I was confident that the currency printed from the plates would be absolutely undetectable as counterfeit, even with sophisticated electronic scanners. All that now remained was to await the pickup man who was to meet us at my house and then deliver the plates to Kohly in New York.

Meanwhile, I couldn't shake my doubts about Kohly's "printer." In fact, I was so dubious about William Harris that while we waited in the laboratory, I suggested to Ross that we hide the proofs, the ink drawings, and other paraphernalia used to make the actual plates. Ross agreed and the two of us went to the kitchen and removed the refrigerator door, unscrewing the fifty-four fasteners that held in its plasic lining, and stored the material by taping it in place to the inside of the door. We then reaffixed the plastic lining and rehung the door. Before closing it, Ross grabbed a cold beer and commented, "No one will ever find that stuff in there."

Before either Ross or I had an opportunity to say another word, a car pulled into the rear lot. Mario's courier had arrived. It was

Bill Grosh, his bodyguard. During the next few minutes, we gave him detailed instructions on how to handle the plates so they would not be damaged in transit. Within twenty minutes of his arrival, he was out the door and heading north.

Ross and I spent the rest of the day in the lab cleaning up the chaos created during the last final push to complete the plates. I was interrupted at approximately 5:15 P.M. by a telephone call from New York. Cecily answered the phone and called me to take it upstairs. She held her hand over the mouthpiece as she handed it to me, saying "It's New York. I think there's a problem."

Mario was very brief, "Roberto, I'm with Harris, the printer. He wants to know if it would be possible for you to catch a plane to New York this evening and meet with us. He's evidently encountering some problems with colors."

Something felt very wrong to me and a cold chill went up my spine. "Encountering problems with colors? Padre, how?"

"He said he needs advice on blending the colors that go on the front of the document."

"That's nonsense, Mario," I said. "He has the original sample we provided him. There shouldn't be a problem duplicating that. Anyway, there's no way I can come up. Maybe tomorrow, padre, but there's no conceivable way I could get to New York tonight."

"O.K., chico. He wanted me to ask. I'll tell him what you said."

"O.K., Mario. But watch your ass. I have a damn funny feeling about this whole thing. As I said before, I think your printer stinks."

"Right, chico," he said and hung up.

Ross, who in the interim had come up from the lab, was sitting at the kitchen table, beer in hand. I told him about Mario's call and suggested that, rather than go out, we have dinner at home and stay near the phone.

Ross, realizing I was referring to the phone tap, and sensing how worried I was, cheerfully agreed. "How would you like some spaghetti?" he asked. "I'll have a hamburger." It was a great concession, because Ross loved spaghetti but was allergic to tomatoes.

By nine o'clock, it had been dark for nearly two hours. I still hadn't heard anything back from Mario and was growing more concerned by the minute. Around 9:30, the spaghetti was almost ready. Cecily had fed the children and sent them to bed. The three of us were finishing cocktails, and Ross had just started to fry his hamburger when we were startled by a loud knock on the breeze-way door.

I looked at Ross who said, "I didn't hear a car come up the drive, did you?"

"Hell, no," I replied.

Cecily went over, flipped on the spotlight covering the rear lot, and reported that there were no cars in sight.

The banging resumed, even louder, and I said, "It doesn't sound like a neighbor. Well, there's not a damn thing to do but answer it. With all the lights on, they know we're here."

When I opened the door, two men were standing in the breezeway, one slightly to the rear of the other in the shadows.

The one in front identified himself and said, "We're with the Secret Service. We're looking for Mr. Robert Morrow, a woman by the name of Cecily Morrow, and a Mr. Ross Schoyer."

"Come in, gentlemen," I said politely. "I'm Robert Morrow."

As the first man stepped into the kitchen, the second one appeared out of the shadows, carrying a Thompson submachine gun. I stared at it, and he dropped the muzzle slightly so that it wouldn't point directly at my stomach. Two more men stepped out of the darkness and followed him through the door. Obviously, the house was surrounded.

I closed the door, and the first man to enter produced his credentials and handed them to me. "I'm William Holmes, U.S. Treasury Department from the Secret Service office here in Baltimore."[2]

Ross steadfastly cooked his hamburger, and when Holmes looked at him he casually flipped it over as you would a pancake. Ross and I both grinned, and I asked, "Well, Mr. Holmes, what can I do for you?"

He looked absolutely nonplused by our attitude. "We have warrants to arrest all of you and orders to search these premises.

I'd also like to ask you a few questions."

I said, "Go right ahead. You don't mind if I finish my dinner, do you?" and sat down.

He gave me a puzzled look, then he said, "You know damn well why we're here."

As I put a fork full of spaghetti in my mouth, I replied, "Why don't you get a beer out of the refrigerator and tell me about it."

He was losing his patience, and after glaring at me he turned to the two men standing behind him and snapped, "Well, don't just stand there, get the hell on with it."

They convulsed into motion, but I stopped them by saying, "Be careful searching this floor. There are two young children living here and we don't want them scared out of their wits."

Holmes looked as if he didn't believe what was happening to him, but he backed me up by telling his men, "Well, you heard him. Move!"

"Yes, Sir," they answered in unison, heading quickly out of the room.

"About the beer?" I remarked, turning to Holmes.

He said, exasperated, "Damn it, Morrow. I don't drink on duty," and sat down in the adjoining chair.

I turned around to Ross who was still cooking and flipping his incinerated hamburger. "I think you'd better take it off, Ross."

"You're right, I don't think I'm really hungry." He turned off the flame. "I'll just have a beer." He looked at the Secret Service man for approval.

Holmes nodded and Ross walked over to the refrigerator, opened the door, grabbed a beer, then slammed it shut. He opened the bottle and sat down at the table opposite Holmes and myself.

Cecily, with Holmes's permission, went to our daughter's room to tell her not to worry about the men searching the house.

Holmes turned to me in frustration and asked, "Can I see you privately . . . somewhere?"

"Sure. Let's go down to the electronics lab. You haven't checked there yet." I left my spaghetti and we descended to the basement, leaving Ross, Cecily, and the other agents upstairs.

As we walked through the library I said to Holmes, "I think you'd better have this," and reached up to the top shelf of one of the bookcases to take down my Walther.

Out of the corner of my eye, I saw Holmes make a move toward his gun and quickly exclaimed, "Don't worry." As I handed it to him I said, "Be careful, it's loaded."

He relaxed. "Sorry. You understand, we've got to be extremely careful. Sometimes those things go off!"

"I understand completely," I said. "What I can't understand is why in the hell this whole thing is happening. It's obvious that the government's right hand doesn't know what the hell the left one's doing."

Looking slightly embarrassed, he commented, "We're under direct orders to deliver you into the custody of the United States District Court in New York as of tomorrow."

At that I got upset for the first time and repeated, "New York?"

"Yes, Sir." Then he spoke quietly. "Off the record, we picked up your associate Kohly late this afternoon trying to pass your counterfeit plates to one of our agents."

I said, "Are you telling me that little shit Harris is really a Secret Service agent?"

"That's right," he replied. "By the name of William Martin. We have Kohly, we have you, and we have the plates. Now we want the original negatives and artwork. We know they're here, damn it, so you might as well give them up."

I hesitated and then, acting upon impulse, I said, "I believe all that material was delivered."

"To whom?" he shouted.

At that moment the phone started to ring, so I looked at Holmes and asked, "You don't mind if I answer it, do you? It's obvious your agency is the one that had it tapped."

He looked at me blankly and said, "Go ahead. I'll listen in on an extension."

"There's one on the next lab bench," I said, pointing.

He nodded and I walked into my office to pick up the phone. It was Bill Grosh, sounding worried. "I haven't heard from

the old man. I think something is wrong. I called a friend at the
Waldorf when I got back to D.C., and he said someone matching
Mario's description had been picked up by federal agents in the
lobby."

I said, "I've heard the same thing. I understand they're looking
for all of us. I would recommend that you give yourself up."

He said, "What the hell happened? What are you talking
about?"

"I've been told that Mario's in custody and I assume it won't
be long before we are, too. In which case, since we really haven't
done anything illegal, I would recommend that you go to your
attorney and place yourself in his custody until the authorities pick
you up. That way you'll be thoroughly protected."

He sensed that something was wrong at my end and his voice
became guarded. "Thanks," he said, "I'll take it under advisement," and hung up.

Holmes and I returned to the kitchen, where Cecily and Ross
were calmly cleaning up the dinner dishes, and sat down at the
kitchen table. Holmes sent one of his agents to search the huge
basement, and the man soon came back up the stairs.

"My God, Bill!" he said. "It'd take us a year to go through all
that stuff, and then we'd probably never find what we're looking
for."

I said, "I have to agree. If the stuff you are looking for was
here, that is."

Holmes turned to me and said, "Mr. Morrow, I think you'd all
better come downtown with us."

I decided to try a little cooperation. "Agent Holmes, these two
people really had nothing at all to do with this operation. I'm
prepared to make a full statement. My wife must stay here with her
children, and Mr. Schoyer is just an employee of mine working on
electronics projects."

Grudgingly, he said, "All right. I'll accept that for now, but I'm
going to leave an agent in the house. Meanwhile, you come
downtown and make your statement."

Half an hour later I was in the Secret Service office in

downtown Baltimore, being fingerprinted and photographed. After another thirty minutes of conversation with Holmes, it was clear that there was no longer any point in concealing the location of the additional plates, negatives, and artwork. Someone had informed the Secret Service about our operations, and we had been under surveillance for months. I told Holmes I would surrender the material and, less than an hour and a half after we had left, we were back at the house, once again taking apart the refrigerator door.

When the agents pulled out the cache, Holmes said, "Well, I'll be damned. And you offered me a bottle of beer, knowing the stuff was right there."

I said, "Well, there's nothing like keeping hot currency on ice."

Even the agents laughed, and things became relaxed. Holmes said, "Cecily can stay here tonight with the children. We'll pick her up and take her downtown in the morning after they leave for school. We'll also take your word for Mr. Schoyer, but I'm afraid we're going to have to take you downtown tonight. Is there anything you want?"

Since it was now about two o'clock in the morning, I said, "Well, you did interrupt my dinner. . . . I'm still hungry."

On the way back downtown we stopped at the White Coffee Pot at North and Charles, where we had sandwiches while we talked unofficially about the operation. I was sorry I hadn't had an opportunity to tell Barnes what had happened, but I was sure that Ross would, so I wasn't too perturbed. I found myself, in the wee hours of the morning of October 2, a VIP prisoner in the Baltimore City Jail. For four hours I had a cell to myself.

At 8:30 the next morning Holmes picked me up and drove me out to the Eastern Office of the First National Bank. It was located on Route 40 and was where I had stashed the old, out-of-date pesos in safety deposit boxes. By 9:30, we had stopped by Hazelwood Avenue to pick up Cecily, and she and I were in the federal courthouse waiting to be arraigned. I was thankful that Ross had already called a good friend of mind, Fred E. Weisgal, who was, at the time, considered the best criminal attorney in Baltimore.[3] Fred appeared at the Federal Marshal's office around ten o'clock, just prior to our hearing, and Cecily and I were both grateful and relieved.

Upon seeing us he said, "Don't worry. I have instructions to take care of everything." Within an hour we had both been arraigned and charged with the making of counterfeit plates, conspiracy to counterfeit, and a host of other miscellaneous charges that New York District Attorney Robert Morgenthau, Jr., and the Attorney General hoped to make stick. Fred arranged to have Cecily released on her own recognizance and for a $25,000 bond to be posted for me. When we walked out of the Federal Building, we were besieged by reporters and photographers. Fred whispered in my ear, "Just act normally and say nothing."

I nodded, and we walked up Fayette Street toward his office. Once he had disposed of the press he said, "I'll take care of all official statements. If you get cornered by the media, refer them to me."

"O.K. Any other instructions?"

"No," he replied. We turned into a building at the corner of Charles and took the elevator to his office. He asked Cecily to sit in the waiting room, explaining, "I've got something to discuss with Robert." Inside, he closed the door and said, "You'd better get in touch with Washington right away."

"Will do. First, let me ask you a question. In your honest opinion, what's the upshot of this going to be?"

"I would assume Morgenthau will want to try you in New York, and we'll stop him if we can. Maybe your friends in D.C. can place some pressure on his office there. Now, Kohly is another matter. If what you say about the Kennedys and the missile crisis is true, Morgenthau probably has instructions to give him the chair."

"That's not a goddamn bit funny," I said.

"I didn't say it was funny," he replied. "Just understand that the next few months are going to be one hell of a rat race. The only sure chance you've got of staying out of jail and, for that matter, alive, is if the president contracts an incurable case of the plague."

"Thanks a lot," I said.

"Keep in touch," he urged while turning around to his dictating machine. In the outer office, I grabbed Cecily's arm and we took off. Ross was waiting in the car just outside the entrance. After we had started up Charles Street, he said, "Thanks for getting me off the hook, ol' buddy."

"Don't mention it. They probably know you're as guilty as sin, but they can't prove it and I had to have someone out operating."

"Like I said, thanks a lot," he retorted. "Anyway, as you might have guessed, I got hold of Diggs who said he'd get in touch with Barnes. He's also alerted Kohly's people in Miami and New Orleans; unfortunately, however, not until after they had read about Mario's arrest in the morning papers."

*   *   *

With our arrest, the Kennedy brothers had once again thwarted Kohly's conservatives from taking over Cuba. With Kohly's arrest and the destruction of the counterfeiting operation, their last chance of having a successful invasion was destroyed.

Then, a short time after our arrest, in mid-October of 1963, Richard Helms, without the knowledge of the President, Attorney General, or the Director of the CIA, finally gave the go ahead for Cubelo's assassination attempt on Castro.[4] Unfortunately, a snag occurred. At the end of October, Cubelo made a demand of the CIA. Before he would go ahead with the plan to eliminate Castro, he wanted some sort of personal assurance or signal from the Attorney General that the administration would actively support him. Once again, objections by the CIA's Chief of Counterintelligence, James Angleton, were unofficially overruled by our team within the Agency and, with this having been accomplished, CIA/SAS chief Desmond Fitzgerald had full clearance to deliberately perpetrate a fraud. Fitzgerald would meet with Cubelo as Robert Kennedy's personal representative.

Fitzgerald knew his scheme would work. Although he would not use his real name, he was a well-known figure in Washington and readily identifiable. The meeting took place on October 29, 1963, with Fitzgerald assuring Cubelo that, once the coup had succeeded, the Kennedy administration would be fully prepared to aid and support a new government friendly to the U.S.

Cubelo, totally deceived, asked for a delivery of specific weapons—a rifle with telescopic sight and a means to deliver poison without detection. At this meeting, however, Fitzgerald claimed that he refused to discuss such specifics. He wanted Cubelo to be assured that the President himself was involved in, and approved of, the assassination of Fidel Castro. Fitzgerald didn't want Cubelo to back out once he had started, in the event he heard from other exiles that, in reality, just the opposite was the case as far as the President was concerned.

Fitzgerald's testimony before the Senate Select Committee of that meeting is in total conflict with the statements made by Cubelo's case officer. The case officer, who was also the interpreter for Fitzgerald, testified that: Fitzgerald gave assurances that the U.S. not only would support the government which emerged after a successful coup, but also gave assurances that the U.S. would help in bringing about this coup. The case officer recalled no discussion which stated that the U.S. would have no part in the assassination.[5]

So, without JFK's knowledge, Fitzgerald would involve the President in the AM/LASH plot. He told Cubelo he was arranging a further administrative signal, specifically for Cubelo and his followers in Cuba. Cubelo was told by Fitzgerald that he had personally written a section of the speech President Kennedy was to deliver in Miami on November 18. It described the Castro government as a "small band of conspirators" that, "once removed," would ensure United States' assistance to the Cuban nation. This passage was to be the "signal to proceed."

According to Arthur M. Schlesinger, Jr., the speech was mainly written by Richard Goodwin.[6] How Fitzgerald or the CIA secured a copy of Kennedy's speech beforehand remains a mystery; however, according to Diggs, in a conversation I had with him after JFK's assassination, he secured a copy of the speech from Lyndon Johnson, and then turned it over to Tracy Barnes.

The day after the President delivered his speech, Fitzgerald ordered Cubelo's case officer to arrange another meeting with Cubelo—a meeting in which specifics would be discussed. Cubelo agreed to postpone his return to Cuba if the meeting could be held three days later in Paris. The date agreed upon was November 22, 1963.

* * *

It was Sunday morning, November 10th. I had not heard from del Valle since he had called and thanked me for the transceiver units, several weeks earlier. In fact, during all the trauma of the arrest and the subsequent destruction of the invasion plans, I'd forgotten completely about both the transceiver units and the rifles. Hearing del Valle's voice brought them to mind again, but I did not bring them up, waiting first to hear what he had to say to me. After amenities, del Valle and I discussed Mario's state of affairs. Then, without warning, he asked if I would return a call to him at the Miami number he was about to give me later that afternoon. I agreed. Clearly what he wanted was a call from a clean phone. He undoubtedly assumed that my phone and possibly his were all still being tapped by either the Secret Service or the Attorney General's office. We said our goodbyes and arranged to speak again at 5:00 P.M. At 4:30 that afternoon, I checked into a motel on Pulaski Highway, near my home, and placed the 5:00 P.M. call to del Valle.

Initially, de Valle queried me about the operation of the transceivers. His people had been experimenting with them and not getting clear reception. I explained how to tune them once they had been attached to the individual. Because of the low frequency, body capacitance had a tendency to detune them; this was particularly the case when the antennas were taped to the leg.

Then he dropped the bomb. Del Valle exclaimed, "They had better be perfect, compadre. They are for Texas!"

"Texas?" I replied.

"For the big one. Along with the rifles. In Dallas. A head of state, remember?"

For a moment I was confused, then I remembered what Ferrie had said about a hit on Juan Bosch.

"I don't understand, del Valle," was all I could manage to say in my confusion.

"You will, compadre. I found out about it last night.[7] Kennedy's going to get it in Dallas."

After this last statement, del Valle signed off.

I was not terribly alarmed by del Valle's remark. Frankly, I'd heard so much crap about revenge against the President from the Cuban exile community that I generally took such remarks with a grain of salt. However, given all that I knew from discussions with Tracy Barnes, particularly our discussion about the New Orleans group operating under Marcello, Bannister and Shaw, I decided to call Tracy and report what I had just learned from del Valle. Barnes was not available, so I contacted Marshall Diggs. Diggs listened attentively but his reaction to my conversation with del Valle was very reserved. He told me that he would relay the information to Tracy, but, in all likelihood, this was probably another example of exile frustration. I hung up with Diggs, checked out of the motel and returned to my home. By the following morning, I had completely forgotten about the incident. I did think about what the Kennedys had done to Kohly. I remembered speaking with Diggs shortly after our arrest. I recalled Diggs informing me at that time that the President and the Attorney General had gone back on their promise to the exiles to help mount another invasion from outside the U.S. Given the missile situation in Cuba, their decision made sense. Since the Kennedys knew that most of the Cuban missiles were still nestled safely in the hard sites built for them by the Soviets, they could not let an exile invasion expose them to be liars.

Further, the Kennedy's ploy to rid themselves of Kohly was brilliant. It eliminated a man the Attorney General hated, and yes, even feared. Kohly knew too much about the missiles in Cuba and had steadfastly refused to remain silent. Given his status in both the international banking business and diplomatic communities, he was both listened to and admired. He could not be attacked professionally. Therefore the only means available were through his activities to destabilize the Cuban economy—his Cuban counterfeiting operation. The only way the Kennedys could discredit Kohly was to render his patriotic activities to restore democracy to Cuba criminal: Kohly was to be marked and branded a common criminal. With his political demise, the Kennedy administration fulfilled their ultimate desire in dealing with the Cuban exile community; to completely destroy and render impotent all of the anti-Castro organizations from the militant to the extreme right-wing groups.

By November 22, 1963, there was no further hope that exiles—supporting the 1940 Cuban constitution—could ever again regain control of their homeland; nor was there any hope that the CIA would be able to expose the continuing presence of Cuban missiles armed with nuclear warheads and pointing toward the United States. This remained the case until November 22, 1963 at 12:30 P.M. (CST)... until the assassination of John F. Kennedy in Dallas, Texas.

CHAPTER THIRTEEN NOTES:

1. Senate Intelligence Committee Report on Foreign Assassinations, pp. 89–90.
2. In 1977 William Holmes was stationed in Washington, D.C. as head of Presidential Security.
3. Fred E. Weisgal, the year following our arraignment, immigrated to Israel. Within a few years he was made Deputy Minister of Justice. In the late 1980's he and his family returned to the U.S. He passed away in June of 1991, in Baltimore. The author has maintained contact with his wife Jean.
4. Senate Select Committee, Final Report: The Investigation of the Assassination of the President of the United States, p. 17n.
5. Ibid, p. 18
6. *Bobby Kennedy and His Times*, Ballantine, p. 598 fn.
7. The timing was evidently concise, and where del Valle got the information is to me unknown. The only logical source, however, would be Dave Ferrie. Advance preparations for President Kennedy's visit to Dallas were primarily the responsibility of two Secret Service agents: Special Agent Winston G. Lawson, a member of the White House detail who acted as the advance agent, and Forrest V. Sorrels, special agent in charge of the Dallas office. Both agents were advised of the trip on November 4. Lawson received a tentative schedule of the Texas trip on November 8 from Roy H. Kellerman, assistant special agent in charge of the White House detail, who was the Secret Service official responsible for the entire Texas journey. As advance agent working closely with Sorrels, Lawson had responsibility for arranging the timetable for the President's visit to Dallas and coordinating local activities with the White House staff, the organizations directly concerned with the visit, and local law enforcement officials. Lawson's most important responsibilities were to take preventive action against anyone in Dallas considered a threat to the President, to select the luncheon site and motorcade route, and to plan security measures for the luncheon and the motorcade.

14

NOVEMBER 22–24, 1963

I woke up Saturday morning in a state of shock and consumed with total fear. Del Valle's statement about the rifles during our conversation of two weeks earlier had haunted me. Then, to have seen a rifle similar to the four I had altered on television and presented as the instrument responsible for the assassination of JFK had shaken me to the core. My state became increasingly more agitated when it was announced that the man who had shot the President was an anti-Castro sympathizer. Later in the evening, Dallas District Attorney Henry Wade's proclamation that Oswald was a member of Eladio del Valle's "Free Cuba Committee," almost caused me to have a cardiac arrest. My state did not improve until Jack Ruby publicly contradicted Wade by saying that Oswald was a member of *The Fair Play For Cuba Committee* which was an entirely different organization.

By Saturday afternoon, I realized how very much information about the assassination had been given to me over the course of my extensive dealings with Mario Kohly, Tracy Barnes and del Valle. The name of Lee Harvey Oswald had sounded very familiar to me. In fact, when his name and his past were disclosed on television—that he was from New Orleans, had defected to the Soviet Union and had married a Russian girl—an unholy pattern started to emerge. Tracy Barnes had revealed this man's story to me and his association with the Agency during a conversation held on October 9, 1963 in which we discussed the renegade, Mafia-

237

connected, anti-Castro New Orleans group comprised of Dave
Ferrie, Guy Bannister, Clay Shaw and Jack Ruby. I also realized
that del Valle had told me the complete truth in our conversation
two weeks prior to JFK's death. Del Valle's statements were not,
as Marshall Diggs had stated, simply typical of the vented
frustration from the Cuban exile community over the Kennedy
Administration's Cuban policies.

I was afraid to mention my fears to Ross when he appeared.
When I did, he tried to alleviate my concerns by saying that what
I had been told and asked to do was probably coincident to the
assassination. It was a very kind try on Ross's behalf but he knew
as well as I that the President's assassination and the rifles,
transceivers and conversations I had had were not coincidental.
The rifles and transceivers were real; the transceivers easily
traceable to me. If the transceivers could be traced, so also could
the rifles. I was panicked and desperate and wondering if, just
perhaps, I had been deliberately framed.

My fear led me to immediately contact Tracy Barnes. I needed
assurances and needed them quickly. Barnes answered but said
he would get back to me. He instructed me to go to a bar called
the Woodshed located in a shopping center near my home. He said
that he would contact me at the pay phone there at 7:00 P.M. that
evening. We said rushed goodbyes and I spent the day anxiously
waiting for 7:00 P.M. By 6:30 P.M., I could stand it no longer and,
unable to deal with my anxiety went to the Woodshed to have a
drink. I was just beginning my second martini when Barnes's call,
which was several minutes late, came through. The minute the pay
phone rang I rushed to pick it up. After saying hello, Tracy spoke.
"Just wanted to make sure it was you. From the way you sounded
this morning, I sensed you were upset. What's the problem?"

"You're right I'm upset. Did Marshall mention my conversation
with del Valle a couple of weeks ago?"

"Yes he did, and I'm telling you not to worry. It's all taken care
of. You're as clean as a whistle. Now, if that's all, I've got to get
back. This place is a madhouse. If you need anything more, call
Marshall. We'd better keep our distance for the time being. With

that, he hung up. I felt I'd just been slapped in the face; however, I was also relieved. I knew that I must be safe or Barnes would never have talked to me.

I finished my drink and went to Amy's apartment. Together we spent the evening watching television's depiction of the grim proceedings in Washington just as most Americans did that evening in the safety and security of their own home. Unfortunately, in spite of Barnes's assurances to the contrary, I did not feel like most Americans. I did feel a sense of relief, but I certainly did not feel secure. I felt scared and disconcerted by the manner in which Barnes had dealt with me during our last conversation. Something felt terribly wrong, and I knew that the slight edge of panic in his voice, and his suggestion that we keep our distance were responsible for my forboding.

* * *

The incredible story of the panic that rocked Langley immediately after JFK's assassination was told to me by Marshall Diggs almost a year later. Diggs explained that, In order to cover up some monumental errors, a massive governmental conspiracy was instituted almost immediately. This resulted in one of the greatest smokescreens in history; one that would prevent anyone from discovering the President's real assassins. It would be a story of continuing intrigue and murder.

After Kohly and I were arrested, Eladio del Valle spent six weeks investigating how the Kennedy Administration had discovered our new counterfeiting operation. The tangible results of his investigation were two additional assassinations: Gilberto Rodriguez Hernandez and Manuel Rodriguez Quesada.

In statements made to Diggs by del Valle, the exposure of our operation, and a number of Mario's other projects, had been the handiwork of Kohly's former *Cuban Government in Exile* military coordinator, Gilberto Rodriguez Hernandez. Hernandez apparently reported his information on Kohly's operations, and particularly the second counterfeiting operation, to the leftist Cardona faction of the Cuban exile community whose leaders were members of the CRC and the intended victims of *Operation Forty*. The Cardona faction, in turn, informed the Kennedy Administration.

Quesada was assassinated as the result of del Valle's fear that he was preparing to expose the identities of the individuals responsible for the assassination of President Kennedy. The assassinations of Quesada and Hernandez were graphically described to me by John O'Hare, a well-known CIA mercenary and the man who performed the deeds. I taped the interview with O'Hare in 1983 and deposited copies in several hands.

"I killed Hernandez in exactly the same manner as I killed Quesada (Manuel Rodriguez Quesada, Rolando Masferrer's bodyguard). I borrowed one of Tony Veciana's boats on the pretext of going fishing and shot Hernandez in the back of the head as he was trolling from the stern."

According to several Cuban exile sources, Quesada was killed by O'Hare in order to prevent him from profiting from his knowledge of the JFK assassination. O'Hare's description of the Quesada assassination is equally as graphic as his termination of Hernandez. The exact conversation on the tape, which I still have in my possession, went as follows:

MORROW: O.K. This is the assassination of Quesada. You're the one that killed him?

O'HARE: Yes. We'd been fishing for several hours. Couldn't get any bites, and I said, 'Let's churn the water and fish for sharks . . . put some sport in it.' Which of course was planned. We churned the water and four, five . . . six sharks, I suppose . . . a small school . . . and he was sitting on the stern . . . and I hit him.

MORROW: What did you hit him with?

O'HARE: A pistol. . . . I shot him, and he tumbled backwards into the water. We were trolling at the time.

MORROW: The sharks got him, uh?

O'HARE: Yes.

MORROW: In the Gulf of Mexico?

O'HARE: He fell overboard.

MORROW: This is the fall of '64?

O'HARE: Yes. It had to be September. . . October 1964.

John O'Hare recently died of natural causes in Cleburne, Texas in mid-1992 with O'Hare's permission, I had also videotaped him describing his activities on No Name Key where he trained groups of Cuban anti-Castro assassins.

With the assassination of the President and those of Cuban anti-Castro exiles surrounding me, I was understandably frightened. I would have been terrified had I known the real circumstances behind our arrest and how the exiles, the CIA, and the Mafia, in a final act of desperation, expected to use the President's death to trigger an invasion of Cuba by the United States.

One of the most frightening of these circumstances revolved around a rabidly active Cuban exile leader named Antonio Veciana. Veciana claimed he had seen his CIA case officer, a man known to him as Maurice Bishop, in the presence of Lee Harvey Oswald, several weeks prior to the President's assassination in Dallas. In view of this, the following sequence immediately following the events in Dealey Plaza take on a ominous connotation.

At 1:40 P.M. in Dallas, Texas, the time Walter Cronkite was going on the air to announce that the President had been shot, Lee Harvey Oswald was reported looking for a telephone. Of course, in the few blocks surrounding the Texas Book Depository on that hectic day, a pay phone was not readily accessible; the ones that were in the Depository were also crowded with people waiting to use them—among them the Secret Service.[1]

Unable to use the telephone, Oswald boarded a bus that he had spotted in an effort to find a telephone and go home. If there was a man waiting for his call in Ft. Worth, he would have to wait a while longer. Oswald had the slip of paper with the number written on it in his pocket at the time of his arrest.[2]

Oswald was supposedly taken into custody before he could make the call. The slip of paper with the telephone number of a public phone located in the lobby of a Ft. Worth building would be part of the personal effects found on the accused presidential assassin. It would, like the name of Bishop next to the number for the American Guild of Variety Artists (AGVA) in O'Hare's telephone directory, be deemed unimportant by the Warren Commission. With what we now know about Oswald's involvement with the anti-Castro Cubans, the Commission's oversite would be a dreadful mistake.

According to Diggs and, much later, Tracy Barnes, the man waiting for the call in Ft. Worth coordinated the activities of Rolando Masferrer's and Antonio Veciana's Cubans who were in the safe house on Harlandale Street. This individual could only be David Atlee Phillips, a CIA man who, according to O'Hare and Col. L. Fletcher Prouty, had once used the name of Bishop in Guatemala in 1953. Phillips denied ever using that name.[4] There is a photograph, however, of a man picked up in Ft. Worth that afternoon who is the spitting image of the individual described by Veciana as Maurice Bishop. Furthermore, there is a police composite of this same suspect nationally published in the newspapers during the House Select Committee on Assassination hearings in 1978, which looks very much like CIA man David Atlee Phillips.

In his large fifth floor office in the Justice Department, J. Edgar Hoover, Director of the FBI, received the same information Walter Cronkite had flashed over the CBS television network moments before. It had come over the Bureau teletype machine.

Now that the threat of his removal as Director of the FBI had been terminated, this immensely powerful information broker was free to make his political move. The information he had had for the past year regarding JFK's assassination would be delicately impressed upon the new president, Lyndon B. Johhnson.

At CIA headquarters in Langley, Virginia, John McCone, after hanging up from his call with the Attorney General, immediately called for his car. He then contacted the critic of Dr. Rolando Cubelo, CIA Chief of SAS/Counterintelligence, James Angleton and requested all available Agency material on one Lee Harvey Oswald—a man who had just been identified as the president's assassin. He had, just moment's before, been given Oswald's name and address.

Within minutes of the President's death, Secret Service agents,

Emory Roberts and Rufus Youngblood, spoke to Vice President Lyndon Johnson in Trauma Room 13 of Parkland Memorial Hospital. Roberts suggested, after having seen the President's wounds, that Kennedy's chances were slim. He recommended that Vice President Johnson leave Dallas immediately.

By 2:30 P.M. Eastern Standard Time, exactly one hour after his brother had been shot, Robert Kennedy finished a conversation with Lyndon Johnson, who was now on board Air Force One at Dallas' Love Field. Due to overloaded circuits, the call to the Attorney General had been maddeningly difficult to place. Robert Kennedy had been reached only after numerously repeated attempts had failed. The discussion which finally ensued was equally as difficult as the placement of the call. Lyndon Baines Johnson, the man Robert Kennedy detested with as much vehemence as he detested J. Edgar Hoover, was seeking the legal answer to a ticklish query: should he be sworn in as President in Dallas or wait until he returned to Washington with the slain President's body.

Robert Kennedy did not answer Johnson's query immediately, apparently requesting time to consider the matter under advisement. Lyndon Johnson, sensing that the Attorney General's eventual response would be negative, did not wait for a return call. He decided to be sworn in immediately. Thus, at 2:38 P.M. EST, in the central compartment of Air Force One, Lyndon B. Johnson was sworn in as the thirty-sixth President of the United States by Federal District Judge Sarah T. Hughes. Moments later, Lyndon Johnson, now the new President of the United States, was lifted off Texas soil in Air Force One and headed for Washington, D.C. In addition to his own entourage, was the casket of the fallen President and his bereaved widow.

Later that afternoon, J. Edgar Hoover completed his discussions with the FBI's Dallas Field Office and was satisfied with the information he had received about Oswald. Unfortunately, his handling of this information set the wheels in motion which, within a few years, would totally undermine the credibility of the Bureau.

Hoover instructed his top aide and close friend, Assistant

Director of the FBI, Clyde Tolson, to "exert pressure on all the senior Bureau officials to complete an investigation of the assassination and issue a factual report that would support a conclusion that Lee Harvey Oswald was the lone gunman."[6] What prompted Hoover to issue such a directive had long puzzled investigators of the Kennedy assassination. The answer to the puzzle, however, can be found within an examination of the strange yet cooperative marriage between the FBI and the CIA; perhaps more specifically, between J. Edgar Hoover and Richard Helms.

* * *

Hoover's directive to hide the truth about Lee Harvey Oswald, and thereby facilitate the image of the assassin as a lone deranged gunman, was a decision that would plague Hoover throughout the entirety the Warren Commission investigation. It was a decision that would nearly destroy the Bureau thirteen years later during the Senate Select Committee's investigation. The reason for this near devastation was simple. Hoover's directive carried an addendum: in his zealousness, Hoover had also directed Tolson to relay special instructions for the Dallas and New Orleans field officers. Although the instructions given were not unprecedented in the Bureau's protocol, the consequences were devastating in this instance. Hoover demanded that his New Orleans and Dallas field officers were to "destroy anything that could be embarrassing to the Bureau."

Unfortunately, the FBI Director did not know that his Assistant Director and Chief of Domestic Intelligence Operations, William Sullivan, was a good friend of the CIA and one who regularly provided information to the CIA's support chief, Col. Sheffield Edwards.[7]

This information did not surprise me. I reported to the staff of the Senate Select Committee in 1975, my conversations with various CIA personnel during the 1960–1963 period wherein I was told that key Bureau people, including those in close proximity to the FBI Director, were actually working for the CIA. I also reported this information in my testimony to the House Select Committee on Assassinations.

(In 1971, an incident involving operational jurisdiction over the handling of an informant/agent in Denver, Colorado, arose between the CIA and the FBI. Sam Papich, the FBI's officer in charge of liaison with the CIA and a member of J. Edgar Hoover's immediate staff, turned Bureau information over to the CIA. For this indiscretion, Papich was dismissed by the Bureau chief. A few weeks later in 1971, William Sullivan, then head of the FBI's Division of Internal Security and the Bureau's representative on the U.S. Intelligence Board, was locked out of his office and also mysteriously fired by Hoover.)

So, in 1963, when the news was received of Oswald being picked up as the President's assassin, Sullivan was panicked. He had issued the directive which had removed Lee Harvey Oswald from any security risk lists. Sullivan had issued this directive to delete Oswald's name at the insistence of my case officer, Tracy Barnes.[8]

The security list deletion remained undetected until December 10, 1963, three weeks after the assassination. It was found by another FBI assistant director, H. H. Gale, who had been ordered by Hoover to investigate the deficiencies in the Oswald case. Gale reported that Oswald should have been on the Security Index; his wife should have been interviewed before the assassination; and, most certainly, the investigation should have been intensified after Oswald was reported to have contacted the Soviet Embassy in Mexico.

Sullivan knew that the Director would be livid, and would be forced to cover up Oswald's deletion from the Security Index. Sullivan had performed his job for the CIA well. It would be unfortunate that he would also have to die a strange and violent death before he could personally reveal the identity of the individual at the CIA responsible for the directive which resulted in Oswald's deletion from the Security Index.

After receiving his call from Clyde Tolson, Ken Maynard, Special-agent-in-charge of the New Orleans FBI office, was faced with two problems completely different from those of his Dallas

counterpart. The first was with Warren deBrueys, the agent he had
assigned to report on the various political groups in the New
Orleans area (primarily the anti-Castro exiles). DeBrueys had an
informant named Orest Pena.[9] Pena, who was active in the anti-
Castro exile community in New Orleans,[10] had worked closely
with New Orleans exile leader Sergio Arcacha Smith[11]—former
New Orleans director of the *Cuban Revolutionary Council* (CRC)
during the Bay of Pigs invasion. Maynard knew from Warren
deBruey's report that Pena could claim that agent deBrueys had
been involved with Lee Harvey Oswald.

The second problem also involved Pena. Pena was a known
associate of Dave Ferrie's, and, indirectly, Guy Banister. He was
the owner of the Habana Bar, where Ferrie, Bannister and Shaw
had been seen frequently prior to the Kennedy assassination. Pena
could also be directly associated with underworld kingpin, Carlos
Marcello. Marcello, as everyone in the Bureau knew, had not only
threatened to have the President killed, but had placed a contract
on his head. Maynard also knew that for the past year New Orleans
Special Agent Regis Kennedy, who was responsible for the direct
submission of reports on organized crime to Bureau Headquarters
in Washington, had said there was no organized crime in New
Orleans.[12] As far as the FBI's Regis Kennedy was concerned,
Marcello was a simple tomato and real estate salesman.[13]

In effect, Maynard's office had been generating too many inane
reports on the New Orleans Mafia don. Consequently, Pena was
told to keep silent about Ferrie, Oswald, private investigator Guy
Banister, and Marcello.

Orest Pena did finally talk, however, thirteen years later, when
he charged agent deBrueys with threatening his life and thus
forcing him to lie to the Warren Commission. In a CBS interview
broadcast on November 26, 1975 ("The Assassins"), Pena claimed
that about ten days before he went to testify before the Warren
Commission, deBrueys came over, called him from behind the bar
and said he wanted to talk to him. DeBrueys told Pena he was very,
very nervous, and said, "If you ever say anything about me, I will
get rid of your ass." Just in those words.

* * *

Diggs's incredible explanation of the aftermath of the assassination clarified many additional points about what really went on behind the scenes in Washington. Apparently, when LBJ arrived at the White House, the new President told his personal advisor, Walter Jenkins, and Ted Reardon, JFK's liaison to the cabinet, to set up a meeting for the following morning. By 7:10 P.M., he had talked to ex-Presidents Harry Truman and Dwight Eisenhower, requesting that they be in Washington on the following day. Then, for reasons known only to himself, placed a call that would start a decade and a half of controversy, and preclude Robert Kennedy from conducting a Justice Department search for his brother's assassin(s). Johnson purposely bypassed the Attorney General's office and called J. Edgar Hoover. After reaching him at home, the new President told the FBI Director to initiate a complete in-depth investigation of the assassination. His rationale in making this request was obvious. If there was something that would eventually surface and require an efficient cover-up, J. Edgar Hoover was the man to ferret out all the weak spots and eliminate them.

Hoover knew then that he was back in the driver's seat, and assured the President that the Bureau was already on the case. He cautiously suggested that the President stop any Texas investigation into the assassination before evidence was uncovered that both would regret. He added that, with Oswald's possible connection to Castro's Cubans exposed, the situation could have serious inter-national complications. Johnson concurred with Hoover's assess-ment, and agreed that his suggestion would probably be best. Then, after a few more minutes of conversation not recorded for posterity, they said good-by. Johnson, following Hoover's instruction to stop the investigation in Texas, placed the call the following morning.

J. Edgar Hoover had already set the Bureau wheels in motion to find and pronounce Lee Harvey Oswald as the lone deranged presidential assassin. In fact, within two days of the assassination, once Jack Ruby had conveniently killed Oswald, Hoover knew the FBI could generate all the evidence it needed to prove that

Oswald had acted alone.

At 8:00 P.M., the official autopsy of the dead President was begun at the National Naval Medical Center in Bethesda and would be performed by Commander James J. Humes. What he discovered halfway through his gruesome task would cause him to burn his notes and medical report. Humes discovered a missile, i.e., a bullet, in the President's body. It was a discovery that would never be reported to the Warren Commission.

In all probability, the bullet was from the first shot from the grassy knoll that entered the President's neck, was deflected off his spine, and ended up in his chest cavity. According to a resident in the trauma room at the time, this entry wound was opened up at Parkland Hospital in order to insert a tracheotomy tube; the tracheotomy, consequently, altered all evidence of the entry wound.

Also altered would be the Parkland Hospital doctors' reports. The reason was simple. It would mean that at least four bullets had been fired in Dealey Plaza, and four bullets indicated a conspiracy.

Instead, the bullet was handed over to FBI special agents Francis X. O'Neill, Jr., and James W. Sibert, who were rushed to Bethesda from the Baltimore, Maryland field office with Dr. Russell Morgan, head of radiology at Johns Hopkins. Morgan would be the one to supervise all the X-Ray photos of JFK's wounds.[14]

Dr. Morgan was ever reluctant to discuss the actual events that took place in the operating theatre that night, but in one conversation he had with me, he told me that O'Neill and Sibert, his escorts, took the shell, signed a receipt for it, and gave it to Humes. Humes in turn, gave the signed receipt to the Secret Service, where it remained secreted until it was uncovered in 1977, through a Freedom of Information Act suit filed by Washington attorney Mark Lane.[15]

It would be ironic that one year after that signed receipt surfaced, the House Select Committee on Assassinations would determine that a gunman did, in all probability, fire from the grassy knoll, as well as from the Texas School Book Depository.

In Dallas, Jack Ruby would be quite busy on that fateful day in November, but his activities and associations would be deemed unimportant by the Warren Commission. The mob's man in Dallas, the man former Vice President Richard Nixon excused from testifying before a Congressional committee, the man identified by CIA personnel as a gunrunner to Cuba, the man who was identified in 1956 by an informant for the Federal Narcotics Bureau and the Los Angeles Police Department as a key figure in a major narcotics operation between Mexico, Texas and the East, the man the Warren Commission would dismiss as a simple night club operator with no involvement in organized crime . . . would kill Lee Harvey Oswald.

* * *

Diggs also explained to me what was going on inside the CIA. At 8:30 A.M., on Saturday, the 24th of November, 1963, the limousine carrying CIA Director John McCone pulled into the White House grounds. McCone was there to brief the President and the slain President's former aide, McGeorge Bundy, on some disturbing information the Agency's headquarters had received from their Mexican station chief. He was also there to transact one piece of business prior to becoming involved in all the details entailed in a presidential transition—the signing of National Security Memorandum 278, a classified document which immediately reversed John Kennedy's decision to de-escalate the war in Vietnam. The effect of Memorandum 278 would give the Central Intelligence Agency carte blanche to proceed with a full-scale war in the Far East, a war that would eventually involve over half a million Americans in a life and death struggle without the necessity of Congressional approval.

In effect, as of November 23, 1963, the Far East would replace Cuba as the thorn in America's side. It would also create a whole new source of narcotics for the Mafia's worldwide markets. (As mentioned earlier, Victor Marchetti, the former Deputy Director to Richard Helms, claimed in his book, *The CIA and the Cult of Intelligence,* that Air America, the CIA's proprietary airline, was used as a carrier for opium.[16])

At this point, the CIA began a program designed to create the perception that Oswald was a pro-Castro contract killer. This suited the anti-Castro Cubans' plans beautifully. To guarantee this image and trigger another invasion of Cuba, they implemented their own plan to blame the assassination of JFK on Castro. To accomplish the task, Rolando Masferrer used the talents of a delegate of Mario Kohly's *Junta del Gobierno de Cuba en el Exilio (JGCE)* and close associate of Prio's, Salvador Diaz Verson. Verson had been Prio's former military intelligence chief during his reign as president of Cuba. Diaz was also head of one of Kohly's groups in his former *UOLC,* which eventually became the *JGCE.*[17]

Masferrer had figured Mexico to be the place to initiate the campaign. Mexico, of course, was an ideal choice. Lee Harvey Oswald had supposedly been in Mexico less than six weeks prior to the assassination, and reports would indicate he had tried to obtain an entry visa to Cuba. Masferrer knew Diaz was in Mexico to attend the International Federation of Journalists convention in Mexico City. He didn't relish having Diaz there, as he knew Diaz could be indirectly linked to Oswald through his association in New Orleans with Carlos Bringuier, head of the militant exile *DRE* organization, based in New Orleans. Bringuier was a member of the New Orleans branch of the *Cuban Revolutionary Front (CRF),* at the time it was led by Sergio Arcacha Smith, a close friend of David Ferrie and associate of Carlos Marcello.[18]

Masferrer knew that Oswald's direct ties to Ferrie in New Orleans and the *SNFE/Alpha 66/30th of November Movement*— who had manned the safe house on Harlandale Street in Dallas— now all working as part of Kohly's *(JGCE)* group, could also lead to Marcello.

By early evening, Diaz had every journalist in Mexico City touting the rumor that Fidel Castro had engineered the assassination of John F. Kennedy, and that Oswald had been to the home of Cuban Embassy employee, Sylvia Duran. This story would be finally investigated eighteen years later by the House Select Committee on Assassinations, after they discovered another source had claimed the same story—Elena Garro de Paz, a famous Mexican playwright.[19]

Diaz also spread the story that Oswald had met with the Cuban ambassador at a Mexico City restaurant called Caballo Bayo in the company of Miss Duran, and that afterwards the Cuban ambassador and Oswald went for a car ride. Diaz's disinformation would be a complete success. The story would even be picked up by the federal police in Mexico City.

About the time CIA Director McCone's meeting with President Johnson was breaking up, a CIA case officer was being cabled from Langley to break off any more contact with potential CIA Castro assassin, Dr. Rolando Cubelo (code name AM/LASH).

After the meeting, the President, pursuant to Hoover's request, gave instructions to his political aide to terminate any local investigation of the assassination by Dallas officials. By afternoon, however, his concern had become so pressing that LBJ personally contacted Dallas Police Chief, Will Fritz.

(Years later, Fritz would remember when the President had requested that he halt his investigation of the assassination and, most particularly, the possibility of an association between Oswald and any foreign government.)

The information McCone had related to the President was about Sylvia Duran and the Cuban ambassador. The story had spread through the media and press agencies like wild fire and had sent the Mexican federal police scurrying to the U.S. embassy. When Mexican CIA station chief Winston Scott heard it, he immediately transmitted the story to Langley. McCone, in turn, at their 8:30 A.M. White House meeting related the story to the President and McGeorge Bundy. McCone's closing remark could easily have been left unsaid. It was that Oswald's Mexico City contacts with Soviet officials might have sinister implications.[20]

Diggs pointed out to me that the CIA Director's remark was right on the money, especially considering the fact that it was not actually Oswald in Mexico City, but rather an Oswald impersonator.

Two hours later, James Angleton's counter-intelligence staff prepared a memorandum for the FBI based on Scott's information. It was transmitted by telephone to the FBI via the CIA liaison at 10:30 A.M. Then that afternoon, CIA Deputy Director of Plans Richard Helms called a meeting to tell his Deputy, Thomas

Karamessines, and Angleton, that the man who would be responsible for the CIA's part in the investigation of the President's assassination was to be a desk officer in the Western Hemisphere Division—a desk officer would have sufficient expertise to conduct counterintelligence investigations for the Agency. This way Helms knew that Karamessines and Angleton would receive only what he wanted them to receive—which, as noted earlier, would be absolutely nothing. Accordingly, he instructed the two of them to provide the yet to be named desk officer with their full cooperation and access to any information the desk officer might request.[21]

Diggs explained that Hoover's next step was to absolutely convince the President and the media, that the FBI had the answer, i.e., Oswald acted alone. Oswald had been a lone deranged gunman. At 10:00 A.M. Hoover called Johnson at the Executive Offices. Their conversation was confined to Hoover's five-page report on the assassination prepared for Johnson. The Director informed him he would like to issue a report projecting this image of Oswald. Hoover's memo to Johnson then attempted to substantiate this analysis. That morning Hoover also ordered the conflicting teletypes of the previous day rescinded and instructed Bureau officials to cease communication with the Justice Department's Organized Crime section.

Hoover's motivation was twofold. Obviously he could not allow his prior knowledge of the Marcello contract on JFK to become known. Further, he could not allow Johnson to be directly implicated (and very probably impeached) over the Baker/Levinson scandal. Hoover, from this point forward, communicated directly with Johnson. The five-page report to Johnson is a point-by-point summation of the case against Oswald, and little else. Fortunately for the Bureau Director, the new President, at that point, knew nothing of Oswald or Ruby's background, or of any formal Mafia/CIA relationship.

Meanwhile, in Langley, Virginia, Richard Helms was having a problem that could put the Agency in a worse position than it was in after the Bay of Pigs. One of the Agency's peripheral operations had returned to haunt Helms.

Early that morning, the Mexican station had cabled their response to a Langley request for the names of all Oswald's known Soviet contacts in Mexico City.[22] Thus, on the morning of November 24th, CIA officials investigating the President's assassination had routinely come across a name that could once again open up the Pandora's box that would finally do what John Fitzgerald Kennedy and his brother could not achieve—destroy the CIA. The name was Rolando Cubalo.

When the case officers in the SAS division were notified that Angleton's staff had put out a trace on Cubelo only days after Kennedy was killed, there was immediate alarm: they knew that only a few weeks before the assassination, Cubelo had received the infamous signal from their chief, Desmond Fitzgerald, that Kennedy would back a plot to eliminate Castro. Now, counter-intelligence wanted to know about this man. Should they provide the operational file on Cubelo which listed his contacts with the CIA and his involvement in the plan to remove Castro from power (as well as the allegation that he might be a security risk, or even a double agent)? Such operational files were always kept separately by the division handling the agent.

Fitzgerald took the problem to Richard Helms. After some consideration and consultation, Fitzgerald was ordered by Helms not to provide the operational file on Cubelo to Angleton or his staff. (The '201' dossier, which contained only overt biographical data on Cubelo, was all that was available to Angleton—without his operational file.) In addition, Fitzgerald ordered the case officer who had met with Cubelo on November 22, to omit from his report any mention of the poison to be used to kill Castro. Since this information was not turned over to Angleton's staff, which was to serve as the liaison between the CIA and the Warren Commission, none of this would be known to the investigators of the Kennedy assassination.

In effect, Helms acted quickly and personally, pulling the cable and all the references to the assassination plots against Castro from both Cubelo's 201 and AM/LASH files.[23] It was obvious that Helms never replaced the cable and assassination references, for none of the documents left in the AM/LASH file made any reference to assassinations or poison pills. As a matter of historical interest, the text of the 11/24/63 cables never surfaced until 1975, when it was quoted in the Senate Select Committee Final Report.[24]

Had routine Agency procedure been followed, Cubelo's file would normally have disclosed operational information such as the details of the CIA plots with AM/LASH to assassinate Castro and Cubelo's connections with Manuel Artime, former brigade leader of the ill-fated Bay of Pigs' troops.

The cover-up would deepen, and the Cubelo–AM/LASH assassination data would be buried along with the information about the involvement of anti-Castro Cubans with organized crime. As a result, Masferrer and his Mafia associates would be protected from discovery by the CIA Deputy Director of Plans, and the Warren Commission's CIA files would contain no evidence that any such information ever existed.

In keeping with the CIA's cover-up strategy, Raymond Rocca would be appointed by CIA Deputy Director of Plans, Richard Helms, as the desk officer who would coordinate the CIA investigation of the presidential assassination. Rocca testified before the Senate Select Committee in 1975 that he was never aware of the AM/LASH plots.[25] He was not alone!

CHAPTER FOURTEEN NOTES:

1. Another person who reportedly wanted to use the phone across the street from the School Book Depository was mobster Eugene Hale Brading, whose association with Jack Ruby and the syndicate would be well documented over the years.
2. Secret Service File #C0234030.
3. Ibid.
4. O'Hare also claims he was in Guatemala in 1963, and several sources have told me that O'Hare was a feared assassin.
5. See photograph of unknown man detained in Ft. Worth by police. According to JFK researcher, J. Gary Shaw of Ft. Worth, the negatives of this picture disappeared almost immediately from newspaper files, never to be seen again.
6. Senate Select Committee to Study Governmental Operations with Respect to Intelligence Activities, Vol. V, p. 33.
7. Victor Marchetti, former Deputy to Richard Helms. The CIA and the Cult of Intelligence, p. 222.
8. I was originally told the story by Washington attorney Marshall Diggs and I asked my former case officer Tracy Barnes, about it in February 1964, when I was asked to meet Mario Kohly by the Secret Service. Barnes would not admit it, but his smile after I asked the question was confirmation enough.
9. WCV, pp. 353-362; CBS Reports, "The Assassins," Part II.
10. Warren Commission, Volume 2, pp. 23787 –86 358.
11. Ibid.
12. House Select Committee on Assassinations, Final Report, Volume IV, p. 70.
13. Ibid., p. 71.
14. I met Morgan when he and Dr. John Howard Seipel were doing research on the electromagnetic detection of neuron activity in the brain, in conjunction with Georgetown University. Later, he became a friend and neighbor in Baltimore during the 1980's. He had retired and was professor emeritus at Johns Hopkins at the time of his death in 1986.
15. In 1977, Assistant Special Agent in Charge of the Baltimore FBI field office, James Dolan, confirmed that O'Neill and Sibert were both assigned to the Baltimore office in 1963.
16. While the CIA has never trafficked in narcotics as a matter of official policy, its clandestine personnel have used this trade extensively. In Laos, for example, the CIA hoped to defeat the Pathet Lao and North Vietnamese. For that purpose, the Agency was willing to supply guns, money, and

training to the Meo tribe. The CIA was willing to overlook the fact that the Meos' primary cash crop was opium; a narcotic they continued to sell during the years they acted as our cutting edge against the anti-communist force in Laos. While Air America was used on occasion, the agency could still claim that it did not officially sanction these activities. However, it was not until the heroin traffic from Southeast Asia was perceived as a major American problem a few years ago that the CIA made any serious effort to curb its flow.

17. Verson headed the Anti-Communist League of Cuba, organization number 88. See Appendices.
18. HSCA, Vol. X, p. 112.
19. HSCA, Vol. III, pp. 290–307.
20. Senate Select Committee to Study Governmental Operations with Respect to Intelligence Activities, Book V, p. 26.
21. His name was Raymond Rocca.
22. Final Report of Senate Select Committee to Study Governmental Operations with Respect to Intelligence Activities, Bk. V, p. 27.
23. Ibid.
24. Ibid.
25. Ibid.

15

NOVEMBER 24, 1963

Sunday, November 24, 1963 was one of the most unbelievable days in this century. At 10:00 A.M., CIA Director John McCone was once again in the White House briefing Lyndon Johnson about the Agency's operational plans against Cuba. He did not brief the President about Rolando Cubelo (AM/LASH) or any of the CIA/Mafia's abortive attempts to assassinate Fidel Castro. McCone was neither duplicitous nor dissembling in this instance. In sworn testimony before the Senate Select Committee, in 1976, McCone claimed that in 1963 he was not aware of the AM/LASH plot. The reason for his ignorance was simple: Richard Helms, Deputy Director of Plans for the CIA, deliberately withheld critical information from his superior and, most importantly, from the President of the United States. His was an act that could be considered tantamount to treason.

* * *

When I awoke Sunday morning, November 24, 1963, the events of the preceding two days almost caused me to forget my mother's arrival from Pittsburgh. She was scheduled to arrive on a United Airlines flight at nearby Friendship Airport to spend the Thanksgiving holiday with me.

By the time I had gotten her bags, put them in the car, and was headed back toward Baltimore, it was nearly noon. Neither of us had had anything to eat, so I suggested that we stop at a

of us had had anything to eat, so I suggested that we stop at a
Howard Johnson's just off the freeway. At 12:15, as mother and
I waited for our brunch to be served, I could hear a television set
in the bar next to us loudly announcing the transfer of Oswald to
other quarters in Dallas. He was scheduled to appear on camera
within a few minutes. I excused myself and walked toward the bar,
positioning myself where I could see the set.

I reached it just in time to see the corridor doors open with Lee
Harvey Oswald walking out manacled between two deputies wearing white Stetsons. Within seconds, I was among twenty million
television viewers who saw a dark shadow push out of the crowd
and shoot Oswald in the stomach at point blank range. I would
always vividly remember the surprise, then agony, that registered
on Oswald's face. It was a scene that has been recorded for history
in a dozen different photographs taken during those few seconds.

The shock was especially horrible to me when I realized what
that muffled gunshot could mean if Ruby was even remotely
connected to any of our Cuban exile groups. Unfortunately,
remembering Tracy's remarks about Jack's assistance in setting up
the arms deal for Kohly in Athens, I instinctively knew it was
probably Jack Ruby. As I stood transfixed, watching the
pandemonium unfold on the screen, I suddenly realized my mother
was beside me announcing that our breakfast was getting cold. I
was literally so shaken, that I couldn't explain to her what had just
happened. It was a visual experience I will take to my grave.

Ironically, David Ferrie was reported seen in Dallas that fateful
Sunday morning. In an FBI interview of NBC cameraman Gene
Barnes by Agents Eugene P. Pittman and John C. Oakes, Barnes
recalled that Robert Muholland of NBC News, Chicago:

> . . . talked in Dallas to one Ferrie or a man named Ferrie,
> a narcotics addict now reported out on bail on a sodomy
> charge in that city. Ferrie allegedly said to Muholland that
> Oswald had been under hypnosis from a man doing a
> mind reading act at Ruby's Carousel Night Club. Ferrie
> was said to be a private detective and the owner of an

airplane who took young boys on flights just for kicks. Muholland may be located in room 1537 of the Statler Hotel in Dallas or through his Chicago Headquarters.[1]

Ferrie was not in New Orleans on Sunday, but was reportedly in Galveston and Houston at least through Saturday. His presence in Dallas is conceivable, however it is highly unlikely that he would have told an NBC news man he was a narcotics addict out on bail on a sodomy charge in Dallas. It is also unlikely that he would have made references to Jack Ruby's Carousel Club. His direct ties to Ruby and Oswald would have been revealed as the result of such an action; a risk he would not have taken. It is infinitely more probable that an attempt was made to set Ferrie up as a potential conspirator in the presidential assassination.

On the evening of November 22, Jack Martin, an associate of Guy Banister and Ferrie, told New Orleans police that Ferrie may have been involved in the Kennedy assassination. Martin maintained that Ferrie was in Texas on the day of the assassination because he was to have been the assassin(s)' getaway pilot. Further, he asserted that Ferrie had known Oswald as a result of their days together in the Civil Air Patrol. Martin claimed that Ferrie had given Oswald instructions in the use of a rifle.[2] Martin's accusation was damning. It required the immediate attention of those individuals directly involved in the assassination's planning and implementation, even if such action resulted in the sacrifice of Dave Ferrie, the "brain" behind both the Kennedy assassination and many of Marcello's operations. When Ferrie later headed back to New Orleans in a car with two homosexual companions, he was unaware that District Attorney Jim Garrison's men anxiously awaited his return. Jack Martin, after speaking with the New Orleans police department on the previous day, made additional allegations concerning Dave Ferrie to the FBI. He told the FBI that he recalled having seen a photograph of Oswald and other Civil Air Patrol members when he last visited Ferrie's home. He also stated that Ferrie may have assisted Oswald in purchasing a foreign firearm. Martin told the FBI that Ferrie had a history of arrests, and that he was an amateur hypnotist who was possibly capable of hypnotizing Oswald. It was virtually the same story Mohulland told the FBI in Dallas.[3]

By 1967, New Orleans' District Attorney Jim Garrison knew Ferrie well. He was keenly aware that the homosexual pilot was a trusted and valued aide to Carlos Marcello. What role Garrison would play by charging Ferrie in the President's murder can only be guessed. Garrison's own ties to the New Orleans Mafia don would come to light in September of 1967, when *Life* magazine printed a series of sensational charges against Garrison, charges which included Garrison's involvement with Marcello and his involvement with both Jimmy Hoffa and the Teamsters Union.

* * *

As was evidenced by his actions on the day of the assassination, Lee Harvey Oswald's death on the morning of the 25th didn't surprise J. Edgar Hoover. From the directive he had issued earlier, requesting that the case be wrapped up with Oswald as the lone guilty perpetrator, he had obviously been relieved to discover it. In fact, he was relieved of a serious potential problem. The sudden demise of the accused presidential assassin solved the possibility of Oswald disclosing the existence of a conspiracy.

From the reports coming in from Dallas and New Orleans, it wouldn't take long for someone to discover that the young ex-marine had a family background associated with organized crime. That could have people starting to ask a whole lot of embarrassing questions.

Oswald's uncle, Charles "Dutz" Murret, with whom he had spent a significant part of his young life, had been closely associated with Carlos Marcello's operations. Murret, according to Aaron Kohn, former head of the New Orleans Crime Commission, was associated with Sam Saia. For years Saia had been identified by various federal and state authorities as an organized crime leader and effectively Carlos Marcello's top bookmaker.[4] It was no secret that Saia's gambling and betting operations were also operated through Marcello's wire service.

To Hoover, these minor links to the Mob could be overlooked.

The big thing was to keep the lid on any talk of conspiracy, particularly any thought of it having to do with leading organized crime figures. Richard Helms would appreciate that. It had been over a year since the CIA Deputy Director of Plans had lied to Bobby Kennedy by claiming that the Agency had stopped its plans for assassinating Fidel Castro. The FBI Director, however, sensed it was still going on.[4]

Hoover waited until the official report on Oswald's death was issued from Parkland Hospital, then picked up his phone and called the White House. After a conversation with presidential aide Walter Jenkins which would reach the President within the hour, the Bureau Director (as was his practice) spent the next few minutes writing a short memorandum to himself. He noted that in his conversation with Jenkins, he had neglected to do anything other than to push the lone deranged gunman theory. Anything else would open up a bag of worms that could involve both Johnson and expose himself. He told Jenkins:

> The thing he and the Deputy Attorney General, Nicholas Katzenback were concerned about was having something issued so they could convince the public that Oswald was the real assassin.[5]

When Jenkins agreed, Hoover started increasing internal Bureau pressure to issue a report that would conclusively establish Oswald as the lone assassin. Any mention of a potential con-spiracy — known to several of his agents — would mean banishment to FBI Siberia, or worse. This pressure was reflected in an internal Bureau memorandum, on 24 November 1963, when Assistant FBI Director Alan Belmont informed Associate FBI Director Clyde Tolson that he was sending two headquarters supervisors to Dallas. The purpose was to review:

> the written interview and investigative findings of our agents on the Oswald matter, so that we can prepare a memorandum to the Attorney General. . . [setting] out the evidence showing that Oswald [alone] is responsible for the shooting that killed the President.[6]

Hoover would hand the memorandum to Associate FBI Director Clyde Tolson or Assistant Director Cartha DeLoach in the morning.

Another thing Hoover didn't tell Jenkins was that he was also coordinating certain of his actions with CIA Deputy Director of Plans, Richard Helms. Their cooperation would be intensified as a result of a cable that had arrived from the Bureau's legal attache in our Mexico City Embassy. It read:

> [The] Ambassador. . . is greatly concerned that Cubans behind subject's assassination of President. He feels that both we and CIA not doing everything possible there to establish or refute Cuban connection.[7]

The Director's problems would then begin to compound themselves, when later that afternoon, another cable from the FBI legal attache in Mexico City arrived. It said, quote:

> Ambassador here feels Soviets much too sophisticated to participate in direction of assassination of President by subject [meaning Oswald], but thinks Cubans stupid enough to have participated in such direction even to extent of hiring subject. If this should be case, it would appear likely that the contract would have been made with subject in U.S. and purpose of his trip to Mexico was to set up getaway route. Bureau may desire to give consideration to polling all Cuban sources in U.S. in effort to confirm or refute this theory.[8]

With all this cable traffic, a cover-up was going to be extremely difficult, particularly in view of the fact that the Ambassador was asking for a confirmation or refutation of his suspicions. So, Hoover acted and issued a direct order:

> The effort to confirm or deny our Mexican Ambassador's suspicions should be discouraged. No investigation should be undertaken or attempted.

Then, the Director wrote a note to himself referencing the cable and put it aside for filing. Thirteen years later it would be found with a handwritten notation on it, stating: "Not desirable. Would serve to promote rumors."[9]

With this FBI turnoff, urgent messages from our ambassador to Mexico were then relayed to CIA headquarters from Mexico. However, Richard Helms had another fire to put out. An additional disturbing piece of information was received from overseas as a result of Helms' cable request of the previous day. It was a second cable, this time from Europe, stating that information from yet another sensitive and reliable source indicated that AM/LASH was "involved" in the President's assassination. Once more Rolando Cubelo's name had surfaced. All in the space of four days.

This was, of course, just what Helms needed . . . another reference to an undercover CIA assassin who nobody knew existed, specifically the President, CIA Director John McCone, and, of course, the Attorney General. And, as was noted earlier, Robert Kennedy would have had the leverage to destroy the Company. Between that and the fact that the Agency could be blackmailed at any time by members of the Mafia, the Deputy Director was sitting on a keg of dynamite. That could only mean one thing, of course. Execute anyone who might possibly talk. And, as with all the other controversial material before it, any reference to AM/LASH's cable would also disappear via the Deputy Director of Plans. For Richard Helms, Hoover couldn't act fast enough to prove Oswald was the lone deranged gunman.

During my own attempt at trying to justify the murder of John Kennedy, I would try and find a rational explanation for the Deputy Director of Plans' actions. Richard Helms was, after all, a dedicated, respected intelligence officer who had to know the potential ramifications of his actions. It seems very clear that Helms knew that someone in the Agency was involved, either directly or indirectly, in the act itself—someone who would be in a high and sensitive position. Of course, it would be more kind to think that the future CIA Director and Ambassador to Iran knew nothing about such a Company involvement or about Oswald, anti-Castro

Cubans, Marcello, Trafficante, and a host of others.

Of course, in 1972, Helms would admit to lying under oath to the U.S. Congress. At any rate, Helms did cover-up any CIA involvement in the presidential assassination.

Meanwhile, back at the FBI, Alan Belmont, under Hoover's direction, was discussing with Assistant Attorney General Nicholas Katzenback the timing for the delivery of the sanitized FBI report on the President's assassination. Belmont told Katzenback that the report would be completed by November 29. Unbelievably, that would be just one week from the day the President was shot. Then Belmont dropped the bomb, not knowing anything of Hoover's real reasons for pinning the death solely on Oswald. Belmont told Katzenback that the FBI investigation would continue even after the report was issued, because the Bureau was receiving hundreds of allegations regarding both Oswald and Ruby.

The Belmont bomb was disclosed later that afternoon when he wrote an internal memorandum to Clyde Tolson. . . a memorandum that couldn't be changed. It was as follows:

> Relative to the Director's question as to how long we estimate the investigation in this matter will take, we plan to have the report on this matter, and on the Jack Ruby matter, this Friday, 11/29/63.
>
> The investigation in both cases will, however, continue, because we are receiving literally hundreds of allegations regarding the activities of Oswald and Ruby, and these, of course, are being run out as received. I think this will continue and in the absence of being able to prove Oswald's motive and complete activities, we must check out and continue to investigate to resolve as far as possible any allegations or possibility that he [Oswald] was associated with others in this assassination. Likewise, we have to continue to prove the possibility that Jack Ruby was associated with someone else in connection with his killing of Oswald.
>
> [Edited for clarity.][10]

Belmont's admission to Katzenbach was a massive mistake. Up
until then, only Hoover and certain Bureau personnel knew the true
magnitude of the information regarding the assassination that was
being received by the FBI. Hoover would now have to convince
Johnson not to initiate a separate investigation. What he wouldn't
know for two more days was that Katzenbach, already alarmed by
Belmont's mistake, was insisting to the President that a separate
and independent governmental investigation should be conducted.

Johnson was no fool, however; and, as noted earlier in the text,
the new President knew Hoover could be a formidable ally or
enemy, depending on how it was played. To back Katzenbach all
the way would be foolish in the face of Hoover's having his report
ready in just two more days. . . . He would solve the problem
another way and keep both Katzenbach and Hoover pacified.

Moreover, the problems at the FBI were rapidly starting to
compound. For, later that day, another cable arrived at Bureau
headquarters from our embassy in Mexico City. This time it had
been sent by the embassy's legal attache, referring to Castro's
speech of September 7, 1963.[11] It was the speech Castro made
in response to the capture of the hapless duo set up by Trafficante
to prove to Castro that the Kennedy Administration was out to kill
him. In the cable, the legal attache quoted a former Cuban
diplomat: "They [the U.S. Ambassador and his staff] did not have
the slightest doubt that the assassination of President Kennedy and
subsequent elimination of his assassin was the work of communist
direction."[12]

What the legal attache in Mexico City didn't know was that,
because of assurances supplied by the FBI Director, the State
Department in Washington had independently concluded that
Oswald was a lone deranged gunman. And, more specifically, that
there was no foreign conspiracy involved in the President's
assassination. This information was provided to Secretary of State
Dean Rusk the day after the assassination.[13]

The State Department couldn't have been more right. There
was no foreign conspiracy. It was strictly home-grown.

The legal attache's cable was also discounted by Hoover. Then a new development appeared which the FBI Director just couldn't shove aside. Ambassador Mann must have been convinced that some hanky panky was occurring in Washington, for he literally demanded that an FBI Bureau supervisor be immediately sent to Mexico City. The ambassador was concerned that the FBI was doing nothing. He, of course, was right. It had been five days since the assassination, and with all the talk and different incidents occurring in Mexico City which were dutifully being reported to Washington, there was no apparent reaction, much less action.

It would be sixteen years before the CIA cables sent during that period of several days were made public. They would reflect the ambassador's belief that he was not being fully informed from Washington of all developments in the FBI investigation of the President's murder.[14] How surprising!

Sensing the ambassador could no longer be ignored, Hoover briefed and sent an FBI supervisor to Mexico City the following day. The supervisor's stay, however, would be short lived. In fact, it would be over almost before it started.

Considering what actions they were taking and information they were withholding, Hoover and Helms' silence amounted to a criminal conspiracy. There was no question of national security involved. Even Fidel Castro knew the CIA was still trying to kill him. It's too bad the President of the United States and the CIA Director didn't.

In Mexico City, on Thanksgiving morning the 28th, the supervisor, the legal attache, and the CIA station chief, Winston Scott, met with Ambassador Mann to discuss his fears. It was a tough meeting in which the ambassador didn't pull any punches. He said, in no uncertain terms, that he felt the assassination was definitely a conspiracy and he wanted to know if there was a Cuban participation in it. It fell on deaf ears. The FBI man told the ambassador that every bit of information that the Bureau had in its possession indicated that the assassination was the job of a lone deranged gunman, i.e., Lee Harvey Oswald, and that was that.

As was to be expected, and as per arrangement, the FBI supervisor's assurances given to Ambassador Mann coincided directly with Richard Helms' sentiments. For Helms took the time on Thanksgiving Day to privately cable CIA station chief Winston Scott the following message:

> For your private information, their distinct feeling here in all three agencies (CIA, FBI, State) that Ambassador is pushing this case too hard . . . and that we could well create flap with Cubans which could have serious repercussions.

In effect, Helms was telling Scott to call off the Ambassador. After all, like J. Edgar Hoover, who would know better than Richard Helms if Cubans, anti-Castro or otherwise, might be involved? The important thing was to keep any information on the subject from the Attorney General.[15]

From that point on, "the legal attache's time would be limited to establishing Oswald's movement in Mexico."[16] Those were Hoover's direct orders.

It wouldn't be until 1976 that the Senate Select Committee discovered that the FBI never instructed its field agents to contact any of their informants or sources to determine whether they may have had any information concerning Cuban involvement in the President's assassination. Any Cuban issues which the FBI explored were related solely to Oswald and Oswald's contacts.

At no time did the Bureau attempt to determine whether subversive activities of the Cuban government or Cuban exile community were relevant to the assassination. In addition, no counterintelligence program, operation or investigation was ever initiated or discussed, to pursue this question. Again, it was no surprise.

With this goal obtained, by the only two agencies that could tell the real story of the assassination of John F. Kennedy and its participants, the Warren Commission started its investigation. Even they would have a hard time rationalizing the false, and non-data, into a plausible story.

CHAPTER FIFTEEN NOTES:

1. WCV 24, Exhibit 2038.
2. HSCA, Vol. X, p. 113.
3. HSCA, Final Report, p. 172.
4. HSCA, Vol. IX, p. 97.
5. Second memorandum to the Files, by Walter Jenkins, 11/24/63, 4 p.m.; Senate Select Committee to Study Governmental Operations with Respect to Intelligence Activities, Vol. V, p. 33.
6. Ibid., Memorandum from Belmont to Tolson, 11/24/63, p. 33.
7. Ibid., Mexico Legate to Headquarters, 11/23/63, p. 40.
8. Ibid., FBI cable, Mexico Legate to Headquarters, 11/24/63, p. 40.
9. Ibid., p. 41.
10. Memorandum from Belmont to Tolson, 11/27/63; Final Report of the Senate Select Committee to Study Governmental Operations with Respect to Intelligence Activities, Book V, p. 33.
11. The legal attache (Legat) is the FBI counterpart to the CIA Station Chief (normally, the military attache) in U.S. embassies. In Mexico, the Legat is the highest ranking civilian official.
12. Op. Cit., p. 41.
13. Dean Rusk testimony, 6/10/64, WCV V, pp. 367-368. Final Report of the Senate Select Committee to Study Governmental Operations with Respect to Intelligence Activities, Book V, p. 33.
14. Ibid., p. 41.
15. Ibid., p. 41.
16. Ibid., p. 44.

16

JANUARY 1964–OCTOBER 1964

On November 29, 1963 Lyndon Johnson issued Executive Order 1130, establishing what would be called the Warren Commission. Although J. Edgar Hoover was initially adamant in his opposition to its formation, he saw the political practicality of its establishment. He and Helms were in a position to effectively control any data the commission might receive. In addition, the committee was weighted with members who were totally committed to seeing that the CIA and FBI were protected regardless of the cost to truth and justice.

So, by January all the pieces were in place, and the committee and staff selected and ready to go.

Unfortunately, for Helms and Hoover the worst was yet to come. The committee staff, not knowing that it was not to find anything, proceeded to take in reports, sift out details from information sources, and generally do what was expected of them. By the middle of January it was obvious—that the Commission was performing its task thoroughly and, in the process thereof, creating a difficult situation for Helms and Hoover to control. The Warren Commission was beginning to have serious doubts about both the FBI's motive in wanting to terminate the assassination investigation and the CIA's reluctance to provide information. This is perhaps best illustrated with the testimony of Texas Attorney General Waggoner Carr. Carr maintained that he knew of Lee Harvey Oswald's recruitment as an FBI informant. Also, according to

Carr, Oswald was assigned informer number S-179 in September
of 1962 and was being paid $200 a month.

This allegation which came just three days after Earl Warren
told the Commission that "President Johnson's fear of wild rumors
was the reason why he accepted the Commission chairmanship."
The top-secret transcript of the January 27, 1964, meeting
(declassified in late 1974) reveals how Commission General
Counsel J. Lee Rankin informed Warren about the Carr allegation.

> I called the Chief Justice immediately and went over and
> told him the story. . . . and it was the consensus of the
> meeting that we should try to get those people up here,
> including District Attorney Wade, the Texas Attorney
> General, Waggoner Carr, Special Counsels to the Attorney
> General Leon Jaworski and Bob Storey, and Mr.
> Alexander, the Assistant District Attorney in Dallas.
>
> We asked them to all come up, and they did on
> Friday. At that time they were—they said the rumors were
> constant there [in Dallas] that Oswald was an undercover
> agent, but they extended it also to the CIA saying that they
> [the CIA] had a number assigned to him connecting
> [Oswald] with the CIA, and gave that to him, and none of
> them had any original information of their own.[1]

The Commission's choice was: having the public reject Hoover's
word that Oswald was not an informer, or incurring the Director's
wrath if they tried to conduct an independent investigation. Rankin,
knowing the ramifications, told the Commission members at the
same January 27, 1964, session:

> It is going to be very difficult for us to be able to establish
> the facts in it. I am confident that the FBI would never
> admit it, and I presume the [FBI] records will never show
> it, or if the records do show anything, I would think their
> records would show some kind of a number that could be
> assigned to a dozen different people according to how they

want to describe them. So that it seemed to me if it's really happened, he [Oswald] did use postal boxes practically every place that he went, and that would be an ideal way to get money to anyone that you wanted as an undercover agent, or anybody else that you wanted to do business that way without having [known about] any particular transaction.[2]

The transcript of the January 27, 1964, Warren Commission session leaves one with the impression that the Commission members seemed terrified of the FBI Director. For two hours they discussed possible ways of asking Hoover about the informant rumor without upsetting him. Then they spent four months debating on how to approach Hoover for a disclaimer, one that would convince the public. They decided that a formal denial from the Bureau would not suffice, after being told by former CIA Director and Commission member Allen Dulles that Hoover would probably lie under oath, if Oswald was in fact an informer.

Dulles confided that, during his tenure as CIA Director, he would have also lied under oath to anyone except the President if, in his opinion, he thought it was in the interest of the nation or the Agency. It was a policy that Richard Helms was also implementing with the notable exception that he would refrain from conveying information to the President as well.

The members of the Commission voted unanimously to allow General Counsel Lee Rankin to approach Hoover in whatever manner he thought best. As expected, the Director flatly denied the allegation. The matter, at least as far as the Commission was concerned, was dropped. It was understandable, especially since each Commission member had been made aware of the embarrassing dossier created by the Director on each of them.

* * *

During this period of time, the U.S. District Attorney for the Southern District of New York continued his attempts to transfer the counterfeiting case to New York where it would be under the control of Robert Kennedy. Fred Weisgal had been successful in getting a plea of nolo contendere accepted by the local District Court in Baltimore and the case removed from New York under the provisions of their Rule 20. By the end of February, they were still attempting to change the venue when the court accepted our plea in Baltimore and gave us probation before a verdict.

A few weeks later, on March 23rd, Cecily and I were subpoenaed to appear and testify as adversarial government witnesses at Mario Kohly's trial on April 6th, in New York. I had been told by Diggs, Tracy Barnes, and ironically Bill Holmes of the Secret Service, to tell Kohly he would be vindicated, if he told the court he would cease his anti-Castro activities. Kohly would not agree, and I knew that he would be incarcerated as a result of his stubborn refusal. In the course of testifying on Kohly's behalf, I was again faced with the possibility of imprisonment. When asked by the Federal Prosecutor if I was employed by the CIA, I refused to answer. The query was posed several times; the language changed for each additional question. Finally, I was ordered to respond by the judge, or be held in contempt of court. I requested that the prosecutor rephrase his query, emphasizing acceptance of monetary compensation instead of employment. The prosecutor finally understood my "hints" and asked if I had ever received any money for services from the CIA. I replied that I had, and proceeded to tell the court that Kohly's sole intent in the creation and use of the counterfeit pesos was the demise of Castro and the return of democracy to Cuba. I then explained to the court that the amount of capital required to establish and sustain a counterfeiting operation far exceeded the actual worth of the finished product. In point of fact, the counterfeit pesos were worthless, save their potential use as an alternative energy source—namely, fire. The prosecutor was infuriated by my responses and sent an extraordinarily zealous young assistant prosecuting attorney to alert me to his wrath. Before I left the courthouse, the young assistant threatened me with incarceration unless I admitted that the counterfeit pesos were created for the perpetration of international criminal acts. He also called me a convicted felon. I called my attorney, Fred Weisgal, immediately upon leaving the courthouse.

Fred attended to the matter promptly and no further statements or remarks of their nature were ever again issued from the New York prosecuting attorney's office.

*   *   *

By the first of March, another problem confronted Warren Commission General Counsel Lee Rankin. Staff counsel William Coleman, in charge of potential conspiratorial relationships for the Commission, saw the possibility of an anti-Castro/Cuban involvement in Kennedy's assassination and stated such in his and staff attorney David Slawson's famous memorandum.

> The evidence here could lead to an anti-Castro involvement in the assassination on some sort of basis as this: Oswald could have become known to the Cubans as being strongly pro-Castro. He made no secret of his sympathies, and so the anti-Castro Cubans must have realized that law enforcement authorities were also aware of Oswald's feelings and that, therefore, if he got into trouble, the public would also learn of them. The anti-Castro group may have even believed the fiction Oswald tried to create that he had organized some sort of large, active Fair Play for Cuba group in New Orleans. Second, someone in the anti-Castro organization might have been keen enough to sense that Oswald had a penchant for violence that might easily be aroused. . . . On these facts, it is possible that some sort of deception was used to encourage Oswald to kill the President when he came to Dallas. Perhaps "double agents" were even used to persuade Oswald that pro-Castro Cubans would help in the assassination or in the getaway afterwards. The motive of this would of course be the expectation that after the President was killed Oswald would be caught or at least his identity ascertained, the law enforcement authorities and the public would then blame the assassination on the Castro government, and the call for its forceful overthrow would be irresistible. A "second Bay of Pigs invasion" would

begin, this time, hopefully, to end successfully.

This memorandum described exactly what the Cuban exiles had attempted to accomplish. Declassified in 1975, it was a damning indictment of the Warren Commission in that the information uncovered was never investigated in a manner indicative of thoroughness or comprehensiveness. In fact, the only attempt to investigate any information on anti-Castro Cuban involvement came on March 26, 1964, when, as an afterthought, Rankin requested that the FBI respond to fifty-two questions regarding its handling of the presidential assassination investigation and submit to the Commission any information pertaining to certain pro-Castro and anti-Castro organizations.

Hoover showed the request to Helms. In response to the request, both Hoover and Helms testified to the Commission. Both avowed that the Kennedy assassination case, as far as they were concerned, would always be open. It was an effort on their part to assure the Commission of their compliance with its requests and to divert attention from the anti-Castro Cuban involvement in the assassinatin—an involvement which would definitely disclose CIA-Mafia complicity in JFK's death.

Neither Hoover nor Helms were able to stop the Commission's Cuban investigation. On May 26, 1964 the Commission responded to their testimony by making its second request to the FBI for information on the anti-Castro Cuban exiles; this time, however, the parameters of the request were very specific. The Commission wanted information on specific anti-Castro groups: *MRP, SNFE/Alpha 66/30th of November Movement,* and the *DRE.** For some reason, known only to them, they were getting very close to uncovering the whole truth.

Hoover, as chief of the Commission's investigating arm knew that if the Commission came up with the Oswald/anti-Castro Cuban link, they would be led directly to the Mafia, the Agency, and the

*All these groups at this point were operating under the umbrella of Mario Kohly's UOLC or de facto government in exile.

Bureau's complicity in the assassination. Therefore, on June 11, 1964, Hoover, through a letter of transmittal (covering a supposed summary from all field offices) informed the Warren Commission that either the CIA or Department of the Army would have the information they requested concerning the Cuban organizations. The response implied that the FBI had none.

On September 25, 1964, when the final copy of the Commission's report was delivered to the Bureau, it would be sans any questionable information regarding Cuban exiles, the Mafia, or the CIA. Hoover was pleased, Helms relieved, Kohly upset that Castro was not blamed, Masferrer and the Mafia dons delighted, and a host of other U.S. citizens—such as myself—puzzled. This was a condition that would not, however, last much longer for me.

Seventeen days after Hoover received the Warren Commission Report on September 25, 1964, I found out just how deeply I was involved in the Kennedy assassination. The unexplained October 12, 1964 murder of Mary Meyer, former wife of Richard Helms' number-two man, and James Angleton's deputy, Cord Meyer, on the towpath of the C & O Canal in Georgetown would confirm my revelation.

Mary Meyer, aside from being a good friend of Angleton and Robert Kennedy, had been the favorite mistress of John F. Kennedy. Unfortunately for Angleton, Mary was also the sister of Tony Bradlee, wife of *Washington Post* editor, Ben Bradlee. According to Tony, the friendship between Mary and Ben Bradlee ceased six months prior to her murder. It was due to an article Bradlee had published in *Newsweek* Magazine alluding to her affair with the President.

After her murder, Bradlee claimed he discovered Angleton breaking into Mary's studio with a pick lock in an attempt to find her personal diary. Tony Bradlee, now divorced from Ben, says she found the diary among Mary's personal papers and turned it over to Angleton. Angleton maintained that he burned it along with other personal correspondence of the dead woman.

Angleton would be forced into retirement in late 1974 as a result of his involvement in the CIA's illegal "Operation Chaos," a secret domestic spy program that had been greatly enlarged under the Nixon administration.

Shortly prior to Mary Meyer's murder and after the release of the Warren Commission Report to the American public, I was contacted by Marshall Diggs who requested an urgent meeting. I had not heard from Diggs for nearly nine months and was alarmed by the urgency of his request. He suggested that we meet for lunch at Paul Young's Restaurant in Washington.[3] I arrived promptly.

Diggs looked much older than I had remembered him. What we discussed during the course of the next hour also aged me. After the waiter had taken our order and served our drinks, he discreetly retired. Then Diggs, without any preamble, informed me there could be a possible attempt on my life. My attention was immediate, focused and complete.

"There is a very prominent lady here in Washington who knows too much about the Company, its Cuban operations, and more specifically about the President's assassination."

Cautiously, I remarked, "So?"

"What my friend claims to know could frankly mean a lot of trouble for Kohly's people, myself, the former Vice President and especially you. If you remember, the President was killed shortly after Robert closed down your counterfeiting operation. . . ."

"I remember, but . . . Cuban involvement? We all thought that was a dead issue. Seriously, we never heard anything about such a possibility from the Warren Commission."

"Forget that," he said, shaking his hand at me impatiently, "and listen carefully. The Commission was suspicious, and had they been allowed to pursue certain leads. . . . well, it's probable you and I wouldn't be sitting here."

"Damn it, Marshall, if you're trying to frighten me, you are. It's over. . . and not one mention of Cubans, any Cubans, or the CIA. There isn't a hint of anything, other than that Oswald got up one morning and decided he didn't like the President."

"I wish his brother thought that," Diggs said, shifting his sad gaze from his plate to my eyes.

"You mean RFK?"

"Yes, RFK. Now damn it, listen. As I said, there's a certain lady in town who has an inside track to Langley, and most importantly, to Bobby. Fortunately, an intimate friend of mine is one of her best friends. . . ."

I interrupted, "Marshall, who the hell are you talking about?"

I had caught him off-guard. He stopped for a moment, pondering. Then he replied, "The woman in question is Cord Meyers' ex-wife, Mary."

"Mary Meyer. . . ." At first it didn't ring a bell, then it struck me. "You mean Cord Meyer of the CIA?"

"The same," he replied. "Except Mary divorced Cord in 1956. Then, after Jack Kennedy was elected, she started spending nights in the White House."

"Well, well, well," was all I could say.

"To get to the point, Meyer claimed to my friend that she positively knew that Agency-affiliated Cuban exiles and the Mafia were responsible for killing John Kennedy. Knowing of my association with Kohly, my friend immediately called me."

Trying to curb the fear that started my stomach churning, I tentatively asked, "Well, Marshall. . . . did Mario have anything to do with it?"

Soberly, he answered, "I don't know about Mario directly. If I were to hazard a guess I'd say del Valle, possibly Prio, because of Jack Ruby. I do know Mario had a lot to do with trying to pin the blame on Castro."

"Un huh, de Valle, and are you trying to tell me Jack Ruby is the gun runner we dealt with in buying Kohly's arms in Greece?"

"The same."

At that point I could only expect the worse. I was starting to get that old feeling of total anxiety that gripped me last fall and winter. In almost a daze I said, "well, it doesn't surprise me. So, why don't you warn him about Meyer?"

"That's the whole point. I don't know where he is and don't want to know. He's been told he's going to lose his appeal; so, he's preparing to jump bail and disappear."

Remembering my experience with the U.S. District Attorney

in New York, I exclaimed. "What? Christ! If he's caught, they'll put him away forever."

"Not necessarily. I have a friend working on it."

I just looked at him, wondering if his friend was the ex-Vice President of the United States. However, I didn't pursue it. The waiter had appeared with our meal. After he left, Diggs continued.

"Now, getting back to the subject at hand. When they find out Kohly's disappeared, I can't place myself in a position of actually knowing where Kohly is, and chance perjuring myself with either the Attorney General or a Federal Marshal."

"I see your point. So, why this meeting?"

"Because Mario told me before he left he was going to contact you. He needs a favor."

Now, I didn't want to know where Kohly was anymore than Diggs, and my stomach had actually started to ache; but, I still asked, "what kind of favor?"

"Mario wants you to call a Judge Murphy in New York, tell him what kind of person he is, explain how you worked for the CIA and that you were saved from going to jail by them, that. . . ."

I quickly interjected, "Damn it, Marshall, you know I can't do that! I told Mario how he could save himself back in February. He wouldn't listen. . . ."

Diggs threw up his hands and said, "I know, I know. But that's not important now. Someone's got to tell him about Meyer, and I'm sure he'll call you before he calls me."

"Hell, I don't want to talk to him either. Like you, I don't want to get any more involved."

The expression I got from Diggs could have frosted a bonfire. "Obviously you have forgotten about the Mannlicher rifles you bought. . . . The electronic gear you provided del Valle . . . the pick up by Ferrie."

I know I paled, as he continued, "and of course, Mr. Brown, Mr. Gold and Mr. Rawlston."

Diggs was referring to New York Mafia don, Thomas Lucchese, Sam Giancana, and John Roselli, the latter of the two who would later be identified as working for the CIA.

Sitting across from Diggs, it all seemed so long ago. Reluctantly, I asked. "So, what do I tell Kohly?"

"Tell him what I told you—that as soon as the Meyer woman has the whole story, Robert Kennedy is going to be told that CIA-affiliated Cuban exiles and the Mafia killed his brother. Tell him, for God's sake, to make sure he has us covered, or Miami and New Orleans will be down the drain, and maybe us with them."

"My God, Marshall, you're serious?"

He signaled the waiter for our check and said grimly. "Believe it. Even Tracy is concerned. Even though he could sanction it, he wouldn't dare put a hit on her. At least not now."

After we parted, I was in a quandry. How far should I go about telling the authorities what I knew? If I did, could I be setting myself up? However, what if I didn't and the authorities found out? The Warren Commission said that the President was killed by that poor bastard, Lee Harvey Oswald. But, I had to admit I knew it was wrong, based on my association with the Cuban exiles and the Agency.

Diggs was neither paranoid, nor completely off his rocker. I remembered that a few months before the assassination, a number of people—including Diggs and Barnes—had expressed concern about something being planned in New Orleans. Then, with del Valle's request and subsequent statement, after receiving the equipment, along with Tracy's literal admission they had been used in the Dallas hit, I felt like the proverbial trapped rat. I don't think anyone could have hated himself more than I hated myself for being so stupid as I made my way back to Baltimore.

A few days later, when I had almost given up hearing from Kohly, I received a call from a Spanish-speaking voice. It asked if I could meet a mutual friend in New York the following day. When I said, "Yes," I was given an address on the Upper West Side and told to be there by 3:00 P.M.

The following day, in a state of depression, I drove to New York and met with Kohly. After I told him the story of Mary Meyer, he looked very concerned and didn't bring up or even mention my calling Judge Murphy.[6] He said, "Just tell Diggs I'll take care of the matter."

Then he told me to stay away from him and not tell anyone I had seen him or where he could be found. I don't know why, but I urged him to give himself up. Smiling sadly, he just shook his head and offered me his hand. That evening I drove back to Baltimore and tried to forget the matter.

A week later, Mary Meyer was dead and her personal diary given to another friend of Robert Kennedy, James Angleton. The diary's contents, according to those who claim to have read it, contained cryptic memories of Mary's relationship with JFK. If Diggs was right, it possibly contained a lot more. It wouldn't be until the 1976 Senate Select Committee hearings that Angleton would admit knowing that the CIA had been dealing with the anti-Castro Cubans and Mafia in 1963 and 1964.[4] Unfortunately, like my testimony to the Senate Select Committee's staff, Angleton's additional remarks, if indeed he made any, would never be known.

* * *

Kohly's fate after his conviction in April of 1964 dumbfounded me. I found out Richard Nixon, after unsuccessfully trying to influence Judge Henry Wienfeld to acquit him, advised Kohly to first go into hiding and if his appeal failed, jump bail.[5]

In retrospect, the only reason for such a move was to preclude the possibility of having Kohly available to testify before the Warren Commission, or any subsequent inquiry. This would effectively prevent Kohly from divulging any information about the exile/CIA/Mafia assassination plots or the deal he made with Nixon prior to the Bay of Pigs involving *Operation 40*. Kohly, the once proud Cuban leader who would have been the next president of Cuba, was close to a broken man. A fugitive, hiding from a vindictive New York prosecuter, he would never give up fighting for Cuba's freedom from Fidel Castro.

Confirmation of Nixon's participation in Kohly's decision to go underground was confirmed by Kohly, shortly before his death in 1975. It was also confirmed by a man who used to work in Marshall Diggs' office, journalist Edward von Rothkirch.

In a taped interview on August 26, 1976, with me, my future

wife and research associate, Tiny Hutton, and other staff members of the first chairman of the House Select Committee on Assassinations, Congressman Thomas N. Downing, Rothkirch stated:

HUTTON:[7]   Do you think it was on the basis of that meeting with Nixon?

ROTHKIRCH: Nixon advised Kohly, that if he could stay clear for a while that they [the Nixon law firm] could do something. But, of course, he couldn't stay clear as long as they wanted him to stay.

HUTTON: All right. On what do you base this?

ROTHKIRCH: Well, Kohly came to me on the Thursday or Friday before he disappeared and told me he was going underground; and I pointed out the dangers of going underground unless he was absolutely sure.

MORROW: So. . .jumping bail. Right?

ROTHKIRCH: Right. And I pointed out the dangers unless he was absolutely certain he could be hidden; and he claimed that he could be hidden. [Kohly also said] . . . as a result of his trips to New York and his meetings with Nixon, that this was [the] advisable situation if he could stay underground for a certain period of time [that] everything would be all right and he would be vindicated. Now, Kohly believed, up to the time he was brought into custody, that he was going to be vindicated — that mysteriously that [something] was going to occur and that would wipe the slate clean and that he wouldn't have to go [to prison].

Slightly later in the same interview Hutton asked:

HUTTON: Well, basically, is it after his [Kohly's] trips to New York and his visits with Nixon that he was convinced that going underground was the thing to do and that [he, Kohly] would eventually be vindicated?

ROTHKIRCH: Yes.

HUTTON: Did he ever indicate actually that Nixon himself had
            advised him to do this?
ROTHKIRCH: He indicated that Nixon himself had counseled him
            on the course of action he was taking. Whether that
            was the only specific action or the counseling included
            a group of collateral actions, this I do not know.

Unfortunately, Nixon's advice resulted in sending Kohly to
Allenwood Prison. As mentioned above, during Kohly's original
trial, I was told by government people to tell Kohly he could get
off with a simple slap of the wrists if he would promise to stop his
anti-Castro activities. Kohly refused and was convicted and
sentenced to two one-year concurrent terms in federal prison.
When he finally gave himself up in 1965, he was then given two
years to run consecutively. As a result, Nixon's law firm again tried
to intercede with the court, asking for a reduction insentence.[8]

Kohly told me, after he was finally taken into custody by
Federal Marshals, that Nixon assured him he would handle his case
and pay all legal fees,[9] if he would not divulge any of their past
relationships or deals regarding the Bay of Pigs. Nixon told Kohly
that he was going to be the next president of the United States.
According to Kohly, after a long conversation with his Cuban
advisors, he agreed to go along with the former Vice President.[10]

Richard Nixon went on to become the GOP presidential
candidate in 1968. Kohly made a mistake. He relied on the
assurances of his advisors who mistakenly called Nixon Cuba's
greatest friend.

Nixon's continuing ties to the Cubans and Mafia, wouldn't start
surfacing until the Watergate investigation, with the discovery that
a Miami-based business having underworld connections, Keyes
Realty Co.,[11] had helped both Nixon and his best friend Bebe
Rebozo, owner of the Key Biscayne Bank, to transact various land
deals. One included the securing of land for the future president's
winter White House. Keyes Realty was reported to have collaborated in the transfer of southern Key Biscayne to a Cuban
investment group known as the Ansan Corporation.

As early as 1948, an Internal Revenue Service investigator reported that he suspected Ansan of having a fund belonging "to Luciano or other underworld characters."[12] Ansan's visible partners were Kohly's friend, Carlos Prio Socarras, and the ex-Cuban president's former Education Minister, Jose Manuel Aleman, father of Jose Aleman, the FBI informant to whom Santos Trafficante revealed the plot to assassinate John F. Kennedy.

* * *

By the end of 1964, as the Warren Commission submitted its report, the Vietnam war was rapidly escalating. In 1966, Richard Helms, critic of the volatile Cuban exiles, was appointed Director of the CIA by President Johnson. After his appointment, Helms immediately chose to replace the capricious Cubans as domestic bad guys with specially trained elite members of the Iranian secret police.[13] These members of the Shah of Iran's torture squads, were highly disciplined operatives known as SAVAK.

Their allegiance to Richard Helms, the man who engineered the coup d'etat for the Shah in 1953, was unquestioned. Helms, who had also been a boyhood friend of the Shah, would control the monarch through his position as director of the CIA. Suddenly, Helms would have at his beck and call a worldwide, covert strike-force of dedicated, trained professional agents and assassins. The Cubans had outlived their usefulness to the CIA.

CHAPTER THREE NOTES:

1. Warren Commission Transcript, January 27, 1964.
2. Ibid.
3. Paul Young's, which was located directly across Connecticut Avenue from the Mayflower Hotel, and is no longer in business.
4. Robert Kennedy was adamant about Kohly going to prison. It is the author's opinion he knew members of Kohly's JGCE participated in the assassination of his brother.
5. Senate Select Committee to Study Governmental Operations with Respect to Intelligence Activities, Vol. V, p. 69.
6. Letter from Richard Nixon to Judge Henry Wienfeld, dated March 6, 1965, on Nixon, Mudge, Rose, Guthrie & Alexander stationary. See Appendices.
7. Hutton was Deputy Director of the House Select Committee on Assassinations up until 6/30/78.
8. See Appendices.
9. Letter to Mrs. M. G. Kohly from the law firm of Nixon, Mudge, Rose, Guthrie & Alexander, dated April 29, 1966. See Appendices.
10. Doris Kohly, informal interview, August 1975.
11. Kefauver Crime Hearings, Part I, p. 716.
12. IRS Report, February 20, 1948.
13. Jack Anderson, 1/19/75, 1/20/75, 11/4/76, 5/3/77, 6/11/77, 9/20/77.

EPILOGUE

In 1967, Jim Garrison, the District Attorney for New Orleans, re-opened the entire Kennedy assassination bag of worms. He had held the key in 1963, but neglected to pursue it.

The whole scenario, as it unfolded, placed me in the middle of a quandary. Garrison was aggressively pursuing the people who had been actively involved in the assassination: Dave Ferrie, Guy Banister, Eladio del Valle, and Clay Shaw. The notable exception to this list was Carlos Marcello. Although he did not name any of the actual killers, he certainly knew who they were. My position in Garrison's roundup was relatively safe, or I would have been called to testify in New Orleans. As it turned out, Dave Ferrie was killed the day he was to be picked up by Garrison's men.

On February 22, 1967, less than a week after newspapers broke the story of Garrison's investigation, Ferrie—his chief suspect—was found dead in his cluttered New Orleans apartment. His nude body had been discovered lying on a living-room sofa surrounded by prescription medicine bottles, several completely empty. One typed suicide note was found on a nearby table while a second was discovered on an upright piano. Three days later the New Orleans coroner ruled that Ferrie had died from natural causes, specifically a ruptured blood vessel in the brain.

Ferrie's death should not have been unexpected by Garrison. The first day the newspaper story ran, Ferrie telephoned Garrison aide Lou Ivon to say: "You know what this news story does to me, don't you. I'm a dead man."

Unconvinced, Garrison checked the empty medicine bottles and discovered one that had contained a drug designed to greatly increase a person's metabolism.

It is known that Ferrie suffered from hypertension. A physician friend confirmed to Garrison that if someone suffering from hypertension took a whole bottle of this specific drug, it would cause death very quickly. Garrison later wrote: "I phoned immediately but was told that no blood samples or spinal fluid from Ferrie's autopsy had been retained. I was left with an empty bottle and a number of unanswered questions."

Eladio del Valle was also killed the same day in Miami. For three days Garrison's men had been looking for him. He was eventually found. He had been tortured, bludgeoned, shot, and left in his car in a parking lot. Because Guy Banister had succumbed to a heart attack in 1964, that left only one person to indite, Clay Shaw. Shaw would be the most difficult of the New Orleans group to convict. He was receiving help from CIA Director, Richard Helms.

Damning proof of Helms's concern about Shaw surfaced in 1975. It was in an interview of a former, high ranking CIA staff officer, Victor Marchetti. Marchetti disclosed in *True* magazine: "I was then told, 'Well. . . Shaw, a long time ago, had been a contact of the Agency. . . . He was in the export-import business. . . he knew people coming and going from certain areas – the Domestic Contact Service[1] – he used to deal with them . . . and it's been cut off a long time ago'. . . and then I was told, 'well of course the Agency doesn't want this to come out now because Garrision will distort it, the public would misconstrue it.' "

In the interview, Marchetti added: "At that time or shortly thereafter this guy Ferrie came up. . . and I was given a similar kind of explanation, that he's been involved in the Bay of Pigs and been a contract agent or contact at the time."

After a disastrous trial, Shaw received a verdict of not guilty within hours of the judge's instructions to the jury.

The events surrounding Shaw's death were, according to Garrison,[2] also mysterious. On August 14, 1974, a neighbor saw some men carrying a body on a stretcher in the front door of Shaw's carriage house. The entire body, including the head, was covered with a sheet. The neighbor, finding this unusual, called the coroner's office, which promptly sent its investigators to Shaw's residence. By the time they arrived, the place was empty. After a day of inquiry, the Orleans Parish coroner's investigators learned that Shaw had just been buried in Kentwood, in Tangipahoa Parish where he was born.

The New Orleans coroner, Dr. Frank Minyard, concerned about the circumstances and the speed of the burial, decided to exhume Shaw's body so that he could assure himself that Shaw had not died a victim of foul play. Before he could obtain the court order, however, word of the proposed exhumation reached the media. This caused the local New Orleans papers to publish scathing editorials protesting the callous desecration of Shaw's remains. With the heated publicity, the coroner reconsidered. There was no exhumation.

Although I was concerned about Garrison's investigation and the deaths of Clay Shaw and Dave Ferrie, I was particularly worried by Helms's admission that Shaw had worked as a contract man for Tracy Barnes's Domestic Contact Division (known facetiously as the Domestic Dirty Tricks Operation Division).

In a 1979 trial, Helms was asked if he knew Clay Shaw. He responded, under oath:

> The only recollection I have of Clay Shaw and the Agency is that I believe that at one time as a businessman he was one of the part-time contacts of the Domestic Contact Division (Tracy Barnes operation), the people that talked to businessmen, professors, and so forth, and who traveled in and out of the country.

In a subsequent trial, in 1984, this answer was repeated to Helms, and he was asked, "Do you recall making that statement under oath on May 17, 1979?" He responded, "If it says here I did make it under oath, I guess I did." Helms also conceded then

that he had publicly denied this fact when he was the Director of
the Agency.

In 1970, two years after Robert Kennedy's demise, I was
asked by a prominent surgeon in Baltimore, who was running for
Mayor on the Republican ticket, if I would join his campaign as
a candidate for President of the Baltimore City Council.

I agreed to do so but warned him about the controversy which
would result, reminding him that I had been arrested eight years
earlier due to my participation in Kohly's counterfeiting operation.
At the time, my admission did not seem to disturb my running
mate. *The Baltimore Sun*, however, created a major issue out of
my felony arrest and plea of nolo contendere. The fact that I had
been working to overthrow Fidel Castro, at the express desire of
the United States government, had no bearing on the case
presented by the newspaper to the public. The resulting publicity
was devastating and its outcome, disastrous.[3]

My running mate requested that I remove my name from the
race. I refused, and, made an attempt to vindicate myself in the
eyes of the public, I called upon Mario Kohly to join me in a press
conference. Our joint explanation of the events surrouding my
arrest and plea did little to bolster my standings in the electoral
polls. Kohly's support did, however, greatly bolster my sense of
confidence.

In 1971, I was urged by friends to run for a congressional seat
in the newly gerrymandered, Baltimore third district. As a result
of this, I wound up in the strange position of being on the same
side as Richard Nixon in the 1972 campaign. Then as luck would
have it, I got involved in the Watergate fiasco.

I had kept in touch with Mario after the city council race. He
was still trying to get U.S. recognition for his Cuban Government
in Exile and, as would be expected, was interested in my election
to a congressional seat. I didn't think twice when he contacted me
two weeks prior to the election with an urgent message.

We met at my office in Baltimore as planned. Kohly then
proceeded to tell me an incredible story. He said he had been
approached by two men who identified themselves as working for

the Committee to Re-elect the President [CREEP]. They told him that the National Democratic Committee had some damaging information about Nixon and the Bay of Pigs, which they were going to release just prior to the election. I immediately thought of *Operation Forty*. Kohly went on to say that he was asked if he could arrange for some of his people to recover this data from the National Democratic Committee. If he succeeded in doing so, he would earn the undying gratitude of Mr. Nixon. Although the two representatives refused to identify the specific content of the information they wanted recovered, Kohly, putting two and two together, figured it had to be data dealing with *Operation Forty*.

Smelling a set-up, Kohly said he declined the offer, and shortly after discovered that the men who had approached him were working for the Democratic party. By this time, the Watergate break-in had occurred. After thinking about it, Kohly decided to come to me in order that I might be able to make some use of his story.

Stunned by what he had told me, I called Senator Charles "Mac" Mathias. Mac said wait, don't do anything until you are contacted. The following day, I received a phone call asking if I could attend a meeting in Washington with Paul O'Brien, the attorney for CREEP. I said yes, and the meeting was set for Saturday, one week before the election.

Then, less than one hour after our conversation, I received a phone call from a man representing Resorts International. (The predecessor of Resorts International was a company known as the Mary Carter Paint Company of Florida. Carter Paint was originally an active corporation set up by Thomas Dewey and Allen Dulles as a CIA front. In 1958, Dewey and some friends purchased a controlling interest in the Crosby Miller Corporation for $2,000,000. The financing for the purchase was provided by the CIA and authorized by Allen Dulles. Then, in 1959, the Crosby Miller Corporation was merged with the CIA-owned paint company. As an example of one of its early activities, Mary Carter Paint had provided laundered CIA money for the *2506 Brigade* and the Cuban exile invasion force which stormed the beaches at the

Bay of Pigs. In 1963, after a Florida land scandal, Mary Carter
Paint spun off its paint division, and became Resorts International.)

The representative from Resorts International claimed, during
our phone conversation, that his company was interested in making
a campaign contribution. I agreed to meet with him and scheduled
an appointment for the following day. We met at my office but were
not able to arrive at an agreement after a lengthy discussion. The
contribution offered was, in actuality, a substantial loan which I
refused to accept. My refusal was fortuitous; I discovered shortly
thereafter that Nixon, the Mafia and the CIA were associated with
Resorts International as early as 1961.

Resorts International spearheaded organized crime's beach-
head in the Bahamas, following their large losses after the Castro
revolution. By 1966, the Syndicate had control of three casinos
through a front company known as the Bahamas Amusement
Company, for which two of Meyer Lansky's associates, Lou Chesler
and Wallace Groves, were, ostensibly, partners and majority share-
holders. Meyer Lansky was the silent partner and spokesman for
the Syndicate.

Two of the casinos involved with the Mary Carter Paint
Company agreed, in conjunction with Bahamas Amusement, to
purchase the highly desirable Paradise Island casinos just off the
coast of Nassau. A Justice Department memo of January 1966,
stated that the "Mary Carter Paint Company will be in control of
Paradise Island casinos with the exception of the one which Groves
will control. The atmosphere seems ripe for a Lansky skim." The
details of the purchase were handled by a consultant named
Seymor Alter, a man who had known his way around the Bahamas
for a long time. Alter had been the man responsible for hosting
Richard Nixon on the first of his many visits to the islands.

He was also investigated for allegedly skimming funds from
the Paradise Island Casino — through Nixon's friend Bebe Rebozo's
Key Biscayne Bank.

As late as 1970, there was solid evidence of Lansky's presence
in the Bahamas, and specifically the Paradise Island Casino. A
June 1972 federal indictment in Miami of Lansky and an associate,

Dino Cellini, alleged that in 1968 Lansky maintained some control over running junkets to the island casino.

In 1969 the Mary Carter Paint Company—by then known as Resorts International—released Dino Cellini's brother, Eddie, from his post at the casino. After his dismissal, the Dade County sheriff's office placed both Cellinis in the Miami office of Resorts, checking credits and booking junkets. As late as 1970, newspapers were quoting government investigators as believing that Lansky is still managing to get his cut out of the Bahamas.

Although Nixon's connection to Resorts International was suspicious, the most damning evidence of his affiliations with the company is Resort's CEO, James Crosby's, donation of $100,000 to Nixon's 1968 campaign and fundraising efforts which resulted in yet another $100,000 from Crosby's friends.

While much more can be added to support Nixon's connection to the syndicate network, such as Lou Chesler's $14,000 contribution to his 1960 campaign, we will never know the complete story or the extent of Nixon's involvement with Resorts International. All avenues to his murky past were closed with his pardon by Gerald Ford. My refusal to accept Resort's offer allowed me to disassociate myself from any unsavory connections potentially injurious to my political campaign.

On Saturday, one week before the election, I met with CREEP representative Paul O'Brian as planned. We met at the Columbia Country Club in Chevy Chase, Maryland at eleven o'clock. I took my campaign manager, Mr. Brent Kansler with me. Paul O'Brien listened to my story without comment. When I asked him if I should hold a press conference regarding the story, he replied, "Let me see what kind of statement you'll be making. I'll let you know then."

The following Tuesday, I sent O'Brien, via my then administrative assistant, now my wife, Hap Morrow, a copy of the proposed statement.[4]

When we talked later, O'Brien told me, "Do what you think best"—the underlying message being that CREEP had no objections.

I held the press conference that Friday. Only one TV station, an ABC affiliate, showed up. Evidently, by not accepting a substantial loan from Resorts, I was persona-non-grata with the powers that be. I lost the election.

In 1981, I decided to write *Betrayal*. It was a lightly fictionalized account of my involvement with the Cuban anti-Castro movement and the events culminating in the assassination of John Kennedy. In spite of my sworn secrecy agreement with the CIA, I was able to reconstruct my involvement in and arrest while participating in Kohly's counterfeiting operation.

After the book was released, I became very much aware of the hornets nest I had created. I was asked by friends to meet with Tom Downing, the Congressman spearheading a bill to reopen the Kennedy assassination. As noted earlier, I then met Bernard (Bud) Fensterwald. Because of the necessity to prove the very real allegations in *Betrayal* that were not fictionalized, I decided to give Tom Downing enough information to at least prove to the House Rules Committee, that what I alleged against Nixon and *Operation 40* were real. To validate the statements, I also supplied him with a sworn affidavit of mine, and one from Mario Kohly, Jr., attesting to their authenticity.[5] The information prompted Representative Downing to hold a press conference on August 2, 1976. The reaction to this press conference moved the House Rules Committee to send HR 1540 — the directive to reopen the investigation into the assassination of President John F. Kennedy — on to the full House for a vote.

The following is an excerpt from the statement made at that August 2, 1976, press conference by Congressman Thomas N. Downing prior to his becoming the first chairman of the House Select Committee on Assassinations.

> I would like to know what was behind the intense interest shown by President Nixon and his staff in the Bay of Pigs. Reportedly, in a memo to H. R. Haldeman, July 2, 1971, concerning Howard Hunt, Charles Colson wrote, "... that he [Hunt] was the CIA mastermind on the Bay of Pigs. He told me a long time ago that if the truth were ever known Kennedy would be destroyed."[6]

A note made by John Ehrlichman after a meeting with President Nixon, September 18, 1971, reads "Bay of Pigs—order to CIA—President is to have the full file or else. Nothing withheld. President was involved in Bay of Pigs. President must have full file—deeply involved—must know all the facts."

I find it most interesting that, according to transcripts of the conversations between President Nixon and H. R. Haldeman on July 23, 1972, five weeks after the Watergate break-in, great concern was expressed about what an investigation might divulge concerning the Bay of Pigs which took place 11 years earlier.

Downing then read quotes from the Nixon White House Tapes and concluded his statement on Nixon with:

> The association between Nixon and Kohly apparently went back at least to 1960 when Vice President Nixon had a direct role in our government's Cuban policy, particularly as it involved the training of Cuban exiles in the United States. There have been far too many allegations concerning connections between the Bay of Pigs, Cuban exiles, attempts to overthrow the Castro government, attempts to assassinate Castro, the assassination of John F. Kennedy, and an alleged conspiracy which connects some, if not all, of them. I want to see the possibility of such a conspiracy investigated fully.

I decided to provide the Committee with substantiating evidence for all of the allegations set forth in *Betrayal* (those that were not fictionalized). I felt I would be part of the Committee Staff, and therefore felt capable of providing specific parameters for an investigation of the exiles' involvement in the assassination. By adopting this approach, I was able to remain unscathed by the political bloodbath which occurred subsequent to Downing's retirement.

After the House Select Committee on Assassinations (HSCA) established the existence of a conspiracy but was unable to delineate its potential prospective members—individual, group, government, or government agency—I felt cheated. Again, the CIA had pulled off another cover-up. For, as I suspected, the CIA, in a brilliant ploy, had taken control of the HSCA in early 1977.

It happened in the fall of 1976 when, with Tom Downing as chairman, the HSCA selected Richard A. Sprague, from the Philadelphia District Attorney's office, to be chief counsel. Sprague hired four professional independent investigators and criminal lawyers from New York, persons who had no affiliations with the Federal government, i.e. the CIA or FBI. With this team, headed by Bob Tanenbaum as chief attorney, and Cliff Fenton as chief detective, Sprague was committed to pursuing the real assassins and their bosses, no matter where the trail lead. Upon joining the committee, Sprague, who was politically irascible, unwisely publicized his intent to investigate both the CIA and FBI, and, in the process thereof, to subpoena CIA and FBI records, documents — both classified or unclassified — and people.

Sprague immediately contacted Jim Garrison in New Orleans and informed him of his intention to follow up on all of the data Garrison felt had been pertinent in his investigation. Sprague and Tanenbaum were cognizant that individuals from New Orleans and Florida with CIA connections were, in all probability, involved in the JFK assassination. They had, in November 1976, shown photographs to the entire HSCA staff of some of these people in Dealey Plaza at the time of the assassination, and in other compromising contexts.

They then initiated searches for the real assassins. To accomplish this in the most efficient and propitious manner, Cliff Fenton had been appointed head of a team of investigators to follow up on the New Orleans part of the conspiracy, which he felt included CIA agents and people such as Clay Shaw, David Ferrie, Guy Bannister, Sergio Arcacha Smith and others; ironically, all people with whom I had worked. They were also going to contact others they felt had attended assassination planning meetings in New Orleans.

From the photographic evidence surrounding the sixth floor window, as well as the grassy knoll, Sprague, Tanenbaum and most of the staff suspected Oswald had not fired any shots.[7]

Using common sense, they concluded that the single bullet

theory was not feasible, and that there had been a crossfire in Dealey Plaza. In effect, they were not planning to waste time covering the same old ground reviewing the Dealey Plaza evidence, unless it might give them a lead to the real assassins. Accordingly, they set up a Florida investigation, especially looking at the No Name Key group, from evidence and leads developed by Garrison in 1967. Gaeton Fonzi, who I had consulted with, prior to his joining the committee, was in charge of that team. They were going to check out the CIA people who had been running and funding the No Name Key, and other anti-Castro groups: Jerry Patrick Hemming, Loren Hall, Lawrence Howard, Rolando Masferrer and Carlos Prio Socarras were finally all to be found and interrogated. In addition, Antonio Veciano's allegations about Maurice Bishop were to also be examined and investigated. Tanenbaum and his research team had seen the photo collection of Dick Billings, from *Life* magazine, which by 1976, was part of the JFK assassination collection in the Georgetown University Library. No Name Key personnel, along with others from the Garrison investigation, appeared in those photos along with high level CIA agents.

Then came the disaster. In 1976, Tom Downing did not run for re-election and was retiring. At that point, Henry Gonzalez, a Representative from the state of New Mexico took over the chairmanship. Fortunately, Gonzalez and Sprague could work together, and both believed that if challenged by the CIA, they could expose the Agency's involvement, at least in the cover-up.

With this very real potential threat, the CIA knew it was up against a much more serious opponent than it had ever faced before. With the HSCA's present posture the CIA could not control the investigation, or for that matter even continue to cover it up.

They had easily discredited the Garrison investigation through a number of moves, which as the reader saw earlier, were acknowledged by Richard Helms and Victor Marchette. Thirteen years earlier, the clandestine Agency had been able to masterfully control the Warren Commission. It was a much simpler job because they had several members beholden to them, the most prominent of whom were Gerald Ford and Allen Dulles.

But with Sprague, backed by Congressman Gonzalez, the Agency now faced a crisis. They had to get rid of them. It was relatively easy. Both men had outstanding egos and violent tempers. Over a course of several months, the ensuing battle created by congressional members in the CIA pocket, coupled with a vociferous, disbelieving media, caused both Sprague and Gonzalez to resign in disgust. In the wake of their departure, the door was again open to suppress any and all evidence of CIA involvement. The CIA managed to suppress such evidence quite successfully.

By March of 1977, Lewis Stokes, a champion of Martin Luther King, was installed as chairman. He was a good political if not practical choice. The next step was to replace Sprague. The man selected was Law Professor Robert Blakey, a scientifically-oriented, academic person, with a respected background of work against organized crime. At the time, he was on leave from Cornell University's Institute for Organized Crime. To clear the decks of all the previous in-fighting, he asked for, and got, Bob Tanenbaum, Bob Lehner, and Donovan Gay's resignations. Blakey, unfamiliar with the involvement of the CIA and FBI in the JFK assassination and not wanting to perpetuate the bad scene previously created by the committee's press, accepted the bad advice of George Bush, a man selected by Gerald Ford and one with definite proprietary interests in the Agency.

Prior to his death in 1972, James Angleton, a man I once met in General Cabell's office, confided to me that Nixon had arranged a deal with Gerald Ford. If Ford fulfilled two conditions after Nixon's resignation, Nixon would make Ford president. The conditions were a pardon for Nixon and a promise that he make sure any information held by the CIA concerning Nixon's involvement with the CIA/anti-Castro operations—specifically *Operation Forty*—would be actively concealed. Ford honored his end of the deal and appointed a man well acquainted with the CIA. George Bush made sure the Senate Select Committee uncovered no damaging information from the CIA and immediately demanded information on any and all persons capable of exposing the Agency's complicity in the Kennedy assassination and subsequent cover-up. In 1989,

I discovered that Frank Sturgis, who was a friend of Mario Kohly, a hired hand in *Operation Forty* and one of the Watergate burglars, was the second person on the list. I was the first.

Then, when Jimmy Carter became president in 1977, he appointed Admiral Stansfield Turner as Director. With Turner at the helm of the CIA, he inherited the monkey of knowing about the complicity the Agency had allowed itself to get involved in and what it could mean to national security if the CIA was exposed to yet another scandal that could destroy it. For this they had a champion. He came in the form of Robert Blakey, who for whatever reason instituted a personal "Nondisclosure Agreement."[8] This agreement was to be signed by the committee's members, staffers, consultants and independent researchers. Signing this agreement was a condition for employment on the committee staff, or as a contract consultant.

When Tiny Hutton, the newly appointed Deputy Director of the committee, showed me a copy, I blanched. If I was to be able to continue my own probe, I would never be able to independently publish anything on the assassination. I declined to sign the nondisclosure agreement, but still provided pertinent information to Tiny to pass on.

The particular non-disclosure agreement adopted by the committee was insidious.

First, it bound outside contractors to silence. Second, it prevented for perpetuity the signer from revealing or using any information garnered as a result of working for the committee [see Appendices for extract of non-disclosure agreement, paragraphs 2 and 12]. Third, it gave the committee, and the House, once the committee terminated, the power to take legal action against the signer, in any court designated by the committee or the House, in the event either body had reason to believe the signer violated the agreement. Fourth, the signer had to agree to pay the court costs for such a suit in the event he lost [see paragraphs 14 and 15].

As if these four parts were not bad enough—to silence any potential malcontent—paragraphs 2, 3, and 7 gave the CIA control over what the committee could and could not do with any information they considered "classified."

The director of the CIA was given the authority to determine what information should remain classified to everyone. In effect, the signer, including congressional members, had to agree not to reveal or discuss any information that the CIA decided should remain unavailable. Because of the past disarray during the Gonzales era, Lewis Stokes did not attempt any final decisions. The net result was that Blakey, in a sense of harmony, elected to keep nearly all of the CIA sensitive information, evidence, and witnesses away from the committee members. Stokes never had anything to argue about with the CIA because the House Committee's investigation did not provide any substantive CIA-related material.

In effect the CIA's guiding hand indirectly controlled the House Select Committee on Assassinations. Typical of what then happened, is the manner in which the newly developed New Orleans information was handled. As mentioned earlier, an investigating team headed by Cliff Fenton, had already been hard at work tracking down leads to conspirators generated by D.A. Jim Garrison's investigation in New Orleans.

This team also included four professional investigators, and their work led them to believe that CIA people, affiliated with the mob in New Orleans, and a splinter group from No Name Key in Florida, had been involved in a conspiracy to assassinate JFK.[9]

Tiny Hutton eventually told me, after reading *Behind Betrayal,* which would eventually become the first draft of this book, that Fenton's team had found a CIA man who attended the New Orleans assassination meetings, a man who was willing to testify before the committee.

According to Tiny, this evidence, along with my evidence, was far more convincing than any of the testimony Garrison presented at the Clay Shaw trial. Shaw, David Ferrie, and others were all clearly implicated.

Fenton's team evidently uncovered a lot of other facts about how the CIA people planned and carried out the assassination. It was, Tiny exclaimed, almost a replay of my book *Betrayal.*

Their report was clearly solid and convincing. Yet Robert

Blakey inexplicably buried the Fenton report. Committee members were never informed about the CIA involvement. The consequence of this deprivation of crucial information was that the evidence was not included in the HSCA report, nor was it even alluded to in the ten supplementary volumes. The witnesses in New Orleans were never called to testify, including the CIA man who had attended the meetings and was willing to talk. To this day, Fenton and his team refuse to discuss any aspect of their investigation with anyone. Of course, they are well aware of the myriad of peripheral assassinations that occurred prior to their testifying before the committee. These assassinations included: William Sullivan, the FBI deputy, who headed Division V; George deMorenschildt, Oswald's alluded-to CIA contact in Dallas; John Roselli, the Mafia man involved in the CIA plots to assassinate Castro; Regis Kennedy, the FBI agent who referred to Carlos Marcello as just "a tomato salesman," knew a lot about Clay Shaw, and was said to be one of Lee Harvey Oswald's FBI contacts in New Orleans; Rolando Masferrer and Eladio del Valle, murdered in Miami; and Carlos Prio Socarras, who supposedly committed suicide by shooting himself twice through the heart with a .45 in his Miami garage.

When the committee finally wound down to its inevitable end, all avenues to the real truth about the CIA involvement had been covered.

After the Ricky White story surfaced in Dallas in 1990, I was asked by one of the alternative newspapers, called *East Side Weekend*, to write a story on why John F. Kennedy was really killed.[10]

The story came out on August 16, 1990, entitled "Did The CIA Kill Kennedy," and with a few minor editorial errors shook most of the midwestern community who read it. It also shook the CIA. Within days, I was under surveillance. Their surveillance was so blatant, and I had enough proof of my charges, that *East Side* followed up the August 16th story in another article on October 18th, with an update called, "The CIA is Watching."[11] The CIA even approached one of my friends, an ex-homicide detective, identified themselves as ex-CIA agents and queried him with regard to my activities. I was shocked by the stupidity with which the

Agency handled my surveillance.[12] I couldn't believe they were
that naive. Legally, the CIA cannot conduct any domestic surveillance activities except in the interest of national security. However, this did not prevent the CIA from continuing their physical
surveillance of me nor of their tappng my phones — another illegal act.

   Meanwhile, I got a call from an avid researcher of the Kennedy
assassination, Gus Russo. Russo, originally from Baltimore, was
working on a PBS-Frontline television series about the JFK
assassination. Gus told me he had been in Florida interviewing a
man whom I had indentified as a possible CIA bag-man in the
conspiracy. This man, also a former Air Force Colonel, was a good
friend and former busiess assiciate of Col. Howard Burris, the man
I had met years earlier through mob courier Micky Weiner.

   Gus Russo felt the man was ready to talk about the assas-
sination and, based on this assessment, the head of the JFK
Assassination Archives in Washington, D.C., attorney Bud
Fensterwald was ready to head to Florida and interview him. When
I heard of Bud's intention, I told Russo in no uncertain terms that
Bud would never be allowed to approach the man and, if Bud
attempted to go through with the interview, he would be killed.
Russo believed me, but, unfortunately, Bud did not. He laughed
it off when I repeated to him the same warning. Bud asked me to
set-up a luncheon date with the Colonel for the first or second week
in April of 1991. I said I would, but told Bud that, as my phone
was tapped, the CIA was well aware of his trip and would, undoubtedly, be aware of his luncheon appointment. Again he laughed and
asked if I wanted a bodyguard. I told him it wouldn't help.

   I set up the luncheon date for the 11th of April, 1991, with
the Colonel, and told Bud. He said he would send me the money
for the tickets and meet me at the Palm Beach airport just before
noon. Worried, I called Gus again. Gus responded by saying that
Bud was convinced that if the man was involved, he would get it
out of him. I then reported all this to Doug Sandhage, the publisher
of *East Side Weekend.* Just days before I was to meet Bud, I
received a call from Bud's secretary that he had died the previous

night. Before I could do anything, Bud's body was cremated and an autopsy had not been performed. I was shaken and immediately called Russo, who was equally shaken. I then called, Doug Sandhage and gave him the news. The result was the third article, entitled "The Kennedy Cover Up," published on April 25, 1991, detailing the Fensterwald story.

Shortly after this incident, Oliver Stone, the Hollywood producer, was in the process of making a movie called *JFK*. The announcement brought a huge amount of publicity. Again, I received a call from Sandhage who asked me if I would mind if they did another story on me, and incidentally in the process if I would mind taking a polygraph test. I had already said I would at the time the first article was published and it was arranged for in January. Also as part of the article, Doug went to the trouble of verifying some of my data himself. The article speaks for itself.[13]

In some ways this book is a result of my chagrin over what has been perpetrated on the American public for over four decades. There is no question that we need a CIA, and that it will still continue doing what it has always done—whether right or wrong. However, one has to say sometimes . . . wait a minute . . .

The people have a right to finally know the truth. This book is the result.

EPILOGUE NOTES:

1. The CIA division headed by Tracy Barnes, my case officer.
2. *On the Trail of the Assassins*; Garrison, Sheridan Square Press, p. 274.
3. See Appendices.
4. See Appendices.
5. See Appendices.
6. Nixon was referring, no doubt, to the fact that missiles were in Cuba long before the October 1962 missile crisis, and were not taken out after it, as President Kennedy had claimed.
7. The author made this same contention based on information he had garnered during his association with the CIA and anti-Castro Cubans.
8. See Appendices.
9. A belief that Garrison also reiterated to me in our phone interviews.
10. *East Side Weekend Newsmagazine*, Vol. 3, No. 5, February 20–26, 1990.
11. *East Side Weekend Newsmagazine*, Vol. 1, No. 30, October 18–24, 1990.
12. See sworn affidavit of Paul Choma in the Appendices.
13. *East Side Weekend Newsmagazine*, Vol. 3, No. 5, February 20–26, 1992.

CHRONOLOGY

1956

April: Morrow leaves Pittsburgh to go to work for
               Martin Company as a senior engineer in
               Baltimore, Maryland.

1958

January: Morrow leaves Martin to do consulting work
               in Washington, D.C., and set up independent
               laboratory at Hazelwood Avenue home.

               Morrow starts to work with Stan Clark on
               Doomsday Project.

July: Morrow finishes work on Doomsday Project.
               Starts work on Neurology Project with Dr. John
               Seipel of Georgetown University.

September: Morrow introduced to attorney Darwin Brown.

1959

January: Fidel Castro takes over the Cuban government.
               Batista and his personal aides leave Cuba.

February: Mario Kohly escapes Cuban prison, flees to U.S.,
               starts to organize exile groups into a unified
               cohesive group.

May: Kohly goes to Washington, D.C., meets Marshall
               Diggs.

December: Dulles approves "thorough consideration be given to the elimination of Fidel Castro."

1960

January: British discover construction of installations in Cuba.

February: Morrow introduced to attorney Marshall Diggs.

March: British reach conclusion IRBM missile sites being built.

President Eisenhower authorizes NSC directive 5412/2, allowing CIA to conduct a program of covert action against the Castro regime, and formation of 5412 Committee.

Marshall Diggs recruits Morrow into working for Kohly.

April: British inform U.S. State Department of missile site construction.

U.S. Press attache to Havana Embassy, Paul Bethel, informed of missile site construction by friend.

Morrow sets of office/apartment on 19th St. in Washington, meets Amy Klingaman.

May: Mario Kohly agrees to accept help from CIA, and starts consolidating Cuban splinter groups.

CIA forms Cuban Revolutionary Front (CRF), asks Kohly to join. Kohly refuses on basis it is predominately made up of former Castroites. State Department starts campaign against Kohly.

June: Morrow meets New York, Mafia don, Thomas Luchesse, at Diggs home. Two days later Morrow introduced to Tracy Barnes of CIA at Diggs office.

Morrow meets whole of Kohly's top people at Diggs home and Tracy Barnes of CIA. One week later Morrow is recruited to be contact man for CIA.

Kohly turns over to CIA, his plans for new provisional Cuban government and invasion plans by exiles.

July: CIA sets up Cuban Revolutionary Council (CRC), to replace CRF. CRC is totally made up of former high ranking Casto officials. State Department starts working actively against Kohly.

Members of the newly formed CRC, inform Jack Kennedy of CIA plans to invade Cuba at Democratic National Convention. This gives Kennedy advantage over Nixon in upcoming TV debates.

August: Kohly's provisional government plan reviewed by National Security Council and meets with favor.

September: Kohly's provisional government plan given to Nixon, and meeting is arranged between Nixon, Kohly, and CIA.

Kohly's underground reports construction sites in Cuba are definitely for offensive missiles.

Bissell and Edwards brief Dulles and Cabell about operations against Castro.

Initial meeting between Rosselli, Maheu and CIA Support Chief. A subsequent meeting takes place in Florida.

October: Kohly meets Vice President Nixon and CIA; makes deal on invasion and provisional government. As outgrowth of this deal Nixon forms Operation 40.

Morrow informed by Kohly of deal with Nixon, and Operation 40.

November: Nixon loses election to John F. Kennedy.

Kennedy briefed for first time on training program for Cuban exiles.

Kennedy not briefed on agreement between Kohly, Nixon, and CIA or of Operation 40.

1961
January 20: President Kennedy succeeds President Eisenhower.

March: President Kennedy raises subject of assassination with Senator Smathers, indicating his disapproval.

Kennedy does not let CIA move on invasion plans.

Kohly's 300 man guerrilla army in the Escambray Mountains is decimated by Castro forces with failure to move on invasion.

Kennedy warned by Allen Dulles it could be too late for a successful invasion.

April: Rosselli passes poison pills to a Cuban in Miami.

Bay of Pigs invasion goes forward.

CIA honors Nixon deal, orders leftist Cuban exile leaders held prisoner at Opa Locka Air Base.

Kennedy witholds air cover for invasion.

Kohly orders underground not to act as last remnants of his guerilla army in Escambray Mountains are killed.

Hard proof of missile site construction provided by Kohly's underground and confirmed by secret mission into Cuba by Ferrie and Morrow.

Bay of Pigs ends in Brigade being captured by Castro, and underground leaders being killed after their identity is disclosed by CRC members.

May: Morrow picks up cash for Kohly in Puerto Rico to rebuild Cuban underground, also starts first counterfeiting operation to undermine Cuban economy.

June: Kennedy rebriefed on increasing danger of Cuban missile capability.

July: Kennedy warns Fidel Castro of first counterfeiting operation.

Start of crackdown on exile groups by Kennedy administration, while tacitly giving them support.

August: Castro changes currency, after economic chaos is caused by counterfeiting operation.

September: Administration suppression of exile activities increases at rapid rate.

October: Morrow makes trip to Europe to buy arms for Kohly's new army and underground. In process picks up package in Paris from man called Harvey. Delivers to Tracy Barnes.

November: Hoover memorandum to Attorney General Robert Kennedy noting CIA has used Giancana in "clandestine efforts" against Castro.

President gives speech mentioning opposition to assassination attempts.

John McCone succeeds Allen Dulles as Director of CIA.

Operation MONGOOSE is created.

December: FBI meets with Lansdale re: MONGOOSE.

1962

February: Helms succeeds Bissell as CIA, Deputy Director
                of Plans. Barnes made head of super secret
                Domestic Operations Division.

April: Harvey establishes contact with Rosselli.

Late April: Harvey passes poison pills to Rosselli in Miami.

May: Houston and Edwards brief Attorney General on
                pre-Bay of Pigs underworld assassination plot.

September: Rosselli tells Harvey the pills are still in Cuba.

October   Kennedy forced to admit IRBM missiles are in
22–28:   Cuba, and creates Cuban missile crisis. Institutes
                Nixon idea of blockade as own policy. Kennedy
                pledges no interference and no invasion pledge
                to Castro. Missiles never removed from Cuba,
                relocated in caves instead.

1963

Early 1963:   William Harvey tells underworld figures the CIA
                is no longer interested in assassinating Castro.

March: Attack on a Soviet vessel off the northern coast of
                Cuba by members of Alpha 66, assisted by
                members of the Second National Front of
                Escambray reportedly occurs.

                Attack on a Soviet vessel by members of
                Commandos L-66, another anti-Castro group,
                reportedly occurs.

April: Special Group discusses the contingency of
                Castro's death.

May: Series of meetings among major leaders of the
                anti-Castro movement.

June: Special Group decides to step up covert
                operations against Cuba.

July: Ten Cuban exiles arrive in New Orleans from
                   Miami and join the "training camp" north of New
                   Orleans. This "training camp" is directed by the
                   same individuals who were previously involved in
                   procuring dynamite. "A", a life-long friend of
                   AMLASH, had helped procure the the dynamite.

                   Carlos Bringuier is requested to assist exiles at the
                   "training camp" in returning to Miami.

                   FBI seizes more than a ton of dynamite, 20 bomb
                   easings, napalm material and other devices at a
                   home in the New Orleans area. Articles appear in
                   the New Orleans "Time Picayune" on August 1,
                   2, and 4th.

August 16:   *Chicago Sun Times* carries an article that reports
                   CIA had dealings with the underworld figure Sam
                   Giancana.

                   Helms informs McCone of the CIA operation
                   involving Giancana, and tells him it involved
                   assassination.

                   According to FBI report, a Latin American
                   military officer attends a Cuban exile group
                   meeting and talks of assassination.

                   Morrow delivers rifles and transceivers to Ferrie.

September: Talks between the Cuban delegate to the United
                   Nations, La Chuga, and a U.S. delegate, William
                   Atwood, are proposed by the Cubans.

                   CIA case officers, after their first meeting with
                   AMLASH since prior to the October 1962 missile
                   crisis, cable headquarters that AMLASH is
                   interested in attempting an "inside job" against
                   Castro and is awaiting a U.S. plan of action.

Castro gives an impromptu, three-hour interview with AP reporter Daniel Harker. He warns that U.S. leaders aiding terrorist plans to eliminate Cuban leaders will themselves not be safe.

Cuban Coordinating Committee meets to conduct a broad review of the U.S. Government's Cuban contingency plans. They agree there is a strong likelihood that Castro would retaliate in some way against the rash of covert activity in Cuba; however, an attack on U.S. officials within the U.S. is considered unlikely.

The coordinator of Cuban Affairs circulates a memorandum listing assignments for contingency papers relating to possible retaliatory actions by the Castro regime. No responsibility is assigned for attacks on U.S. officials within the U.S.

October 6:   FBI Headquarters learns of Oswald contacts in Mexico City.

FBI is told by an informant that CIA is meeting with AM/LASH.

Jean Daniel, the French reporter, conducts a brief interview with President Kennedy before setting off on an assignment in Cuba. President Kennedy expresses his feeling that Castro had betrayed the revolution.

October 29:   Desmond Fitzgerald, a senior CIA officer, meets AM/LASH. Fitzgerald tells AMLASH that a coup would receive U.S. support.

November 22: President John F. Kennedy is assassinated in Dallas, Texas.

APPENDICES

United States Patent Office

3,097,686

Patented July 16, 1963

1

3,097,686
FURNACE SYSTEM
Robert D. Morrow, Baltimore, Md., assignor to Product
Development Associates, Ltd., Baltimore, Md.
Filed May 12, 1960, Ser. No. 28,588
14 Claims. (Cl. 158—1)

This invention relates to a furnace system for heating water or another suitable fluid medium and more particularly to a heating system wherein the hotter portions of the flue gases are fed back into the input of a combustion chamber.

Various systems are known wherein portions of the exhaust products or flue gases are fed back to the input of a combustion chamber to improve the overall efficiency of a heating system. However, these systems suffer from the serious disadvantage in that there is little or no selectivity exercised with respect to which portions of the flue gas are recirculated through the system. In most instances the feed back gases are selected on a quantity basis with a certain percentage passing through a ratio valve or other type of valving system so that a certain portion of the entire exhaust gas composition is recirculated to the combustion chamber.

The present invention provides a heating system having substantially increased efficiency which incorporates a selective feed back of flue gases from the exhaust system of a combustion chamber to the input wherein the fed back exhaust gases are mixed with fuel and air entering the combustion chamber. The selectivity is exercised through a vortex tube which separates the exhaust gases into relatively warm and cold components. The cold component is permitted to exhaust to the atmosphere and only the warm component is fed back to the input of the heating system. In this way it is possible to reduce the temperature of the exiting gases from the system and consequently substantially increase the thermal efficiency of the furnace. It is theoretically possible by actually cooling the exhaust gases below atmospheric temperature to obtain a thermal efficiency for the heating system of the present invention of over 100%.

It is therefore, a primary object of the present invention to provide a novel heating system having increased efficiency.

Another object of the present invention is to provide a heating system having selective feed back of portions of the flue gas exhaust to the system input.

Another object of the present invention is to provide a heating system with flue gas feed back and incorporating means for separating the exhaust gas into distinct components and feeding back only the hotter component to the system input.

These and other objects and advantages of the invention will be more apparent upon reference to the following specification, claims and appended drawings wherein:

FIGURE 1 is schematic diagram showing in simplified form the basic heating system of the invention and,

FIGURE 2 is a schematic diagram of a modified embodiment of the heating system of the present invention.

Referring to the drawings and particularly to FIGURE 1, the heating system of the present invention generally indicated at 10 comprises a gas inlet conduit 12 which supplies either ambient or super charged air to the input of an air blower 14. Fuel is supplied from any suitable source to the system through a supply pipe 16 connected to a restricted portion 18 in the output line 20 of the blower which restricted portion defines a venturi connection so that the pressurized air flowing from outlet 20 through the restriction 18 draws fuel from pipe 16. The pressurized air-fuel mixture passes through a check valve 22 in the direction of the arrow to a combustion chamber

2

24 forming the major heating chamber of the furnace system.

Combustion products from chamber 24 pass outwardly in the direction of the arrow through a second check valve 26 to a conventional uniflow vortex tube 28. Vortex tube 28 is the type sometimes referred to as a Ranque-Hilsch tube first described by G. Ranque in U.S. Patent 1,952,281. In the system illustrated the vortex tube is of the uniflow type with the relatively hot and cold gas outlets positioned at the same end of the tube.

It is well known that in operation a vortex tube divides a compressed gas into two moving streams each with a different temperature. The outer stream is substantially hotter than the inner one. The exact mode of operation is not fully understood and several theories have been advanced for explaining the operation of these tubes. One of the most widely accepted theories presumes that the gas is broken up into separate helical gyrating layers with the inner layer compressing the outer layer through centrifugal force and giving up some of its energy to the outer layer. The energy given up is represented by an increase in temperature of the outer layer and a decrease in temperature of the inner layer each of which may be separately removed from the same end of a uniflow tube by means of suitably positioned and throttled concentric apertures. It has been found that a maximum temperature differential between the exiting relatively hot and cool gas streams is obtained by a division of 30% of cold gas and 70% hot gas. Temperature differentials of as much as 100° F. are not unusual.

As shown the vortex tube 28 comprises a generator chamber 30 and a vortex generator 32 having a tangential inlet 34 through which the high pressure gases gain access to the central tubular channel 36 of the vortex tube. The gases are caused to spiral through the tube so the cooler portions of the gas collect in a central stream and the warmer portions collect in an outer annular stream surrounding the cooler gas. The central cooler stream is extracted through a central restriction 38 and passes to atmosphere through outlet conduit 40. Hotter portions of the flue gas pass outwardly through the outer restriction 42 to a hot gas feed back line 44.

Feed back line 44 supplies the hotter portion of the exhaust or flue gases to the inlet conduit 12 where these hotter portions are mixed with the incoming air supplied to a blower 14 and tend to preheat this air. In operation, the air-fuel mixture feed to the combustion chamber is controlled so that it contains approximately 200% excess air. This excess air serves to sustain complete combustion and further lowers the temperature in the combustion chamber to an acceptable value.

The combustion chamber and vortex tube are surrounded by an insulating jacket 46 containing a heat exchange fluid such as water as indicated at 48 which takes heat produced in the combustion chamber from the outer surface of the vortex tube 36 and from the hot gas feed back line 44. Cold water may be supplied to the water jacket through inlet 50 from a suitable supply and the hot water is drawn off through outlet conduit 52.

In operation, as the air fuel mixture burns in the combustion chamber the pressure in the chamber rises forcing the flue gases into the vortex generator of the vortex tube. Water is circulated over the chamber and tube extracting heat to be used for any suitable hot water heating system application such as tap water or for use in a hot water type radiant heating system. The products of combustion are removed from the center or colder section of the vortex tube through outlet conduit 40. The excess air tends to be retained in the outer air stream of the vortex tube and is returned to the high pressure side of the combustion chamber.

FIGURE 2 shows a schematic diagram of a modified

1.1, 1.2 United States Patent Office document (first page) followed by schematic detailing furnace created by author based upon the Ranque Hilsch Effect.

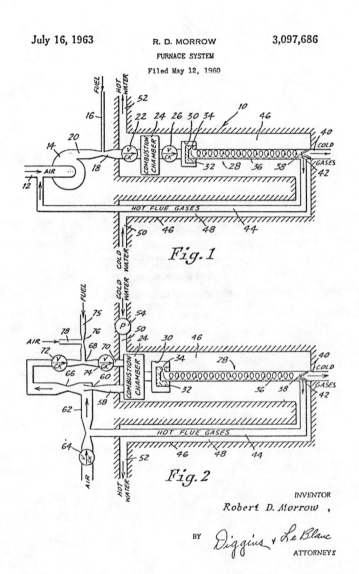

July 16, 1963   R. D. MORROW   3,097,686

FURNACE SYSTEM

Filed May 12, 1960

Fig.1

Fig.2

INVENTOR

Robert D. Morrow ,

BY   Diggins & Le Blanc

ATTORNEYS

CONFIDENTIAL

MEMORANDUM

Prepared by:

MARSHALL R. DIGGS, ESQUIRE,
Attorney and Counsellor at Law
1025 Connecticut Avenue, N. W.
Washington 6, D. C.;

WILLIAM JACKSON POWELL, ESQUIRE,
Attorney and Counsellor at Law
1741 K Street, N. W.
Washington 6, D. C.;

ROBERT C. MATHIS, ESQUIRE,
1000 Vermont Avenue, N. W.
Washington, D. C.;

and

AMERICAN FOUNDATION FOR WORLD TRADE STUDIES,
INCORPORATED

CONFIDENTIAL

1.3 Confidential Memorandum prepared by Marshall R. Diggs, Esquire, dated February 27, 1961, summarizing Mario Garcia Kohly's "Plan for Cuba" and "Report on the Unification of Cuban Factions in Exile."

MEMORANDUM

Date: February 27, 1961

Subject: Synopsis of the program for CUBA of MARIO GARCIA KOHLY

Reference: "A Report on the Unification of Cuban Factions in Exile and the Plan for Cuba of Mario Garcia Kohly," of December 12, 1960.

Purpose: To make recommendations to the President of the United States concerning the establishment of foreign policy with regard to Cuba specifically and Latin America generally.

I. THE FACTS

1. Cuba is a Russian Satellite and headquarters for the subjection of all Latin American Nations to Communism. This Communist plan of subjection is succeeding at present.

2. Because of the O.A.S. Treaty and the fact that many Latin American Nations still recognize the Castro Government of Cuba, the United States must consider whether its actions would violate the precept of "non-intervention" into the internal affairs of a treaty nation.

3. Yet, if action is not taken to stop the Communist subjection of Latin America to the dictates of Moscow, the security of the United States itself will be greatly imperilled.

4. The security of the United States is in jeopardy at the present time due to the advances made by both Chinese and Russian Communism in Cuba and the rest of Latin America.

II. THE PROBLEMS

1. The first problem is Communism, not Latin America. With this in mind, what action can the United States take in the very near future without violating the precept of "non-intervention" into the internal affairs of Cuba, such action to set a precedent for action with regard to other Latin American Nations?

2. The second problem is Latin America, not Communism. How can the United States best help Cuba and the other Latin American Nations toward economic and political stability and prosperity, thus making the United States more secure against Communism?

III. RECOMMENDATIONS

1. Follow through the partial break of diplomatic relations with the Castro Dictatorship by announcing a complete break of relations with Castro basing this action on the simultaneous declaration of policy that, after having observed and evaluated the actions of the Castro Government for over one year, the following conclusions are adopted by the United States Government:

    (a) That the Castro Government is not a Cuban govern-

ment but the agent of a foreign power which is not located in
the Western Hemisphere - the U.S.S.R.

(b) That as such agent of such foreign government,
the Castro Dictatorship constitutes a violation of the Monroe
Doctrine which the United States has pledged itself to support,
which pledge the United States now reaffirms.

(c) That not only has such foreign power, through
its agent, violated the Monroe Doctrine in Cuba, but in other
Western Hemisphere Nations, and the United States pledges itself
to support appropriate action to stop these violations wherever
and whenever they are found.

2. Instruct a high-placed United States Government
official in the foreign policy field to give unofficial approval
of contributions to the Initial Organizational and Operational
Budget for the Provisional Government of Mario Garcia Kohly, such
contributions to be made by United States industrialists through
properly covered channels. See Appendix C of the referenced report
for the details of this budget. The purpose of this budget is to
create the proper climate for the following recommendation.

3. When Senor Kohly's declaration is made on Cuban soil
that his government is the legitimate government of the Cuban People,
the President of the United States should forthwith issue official
recognition of that government as such. Such a declaration might
be made by the followers of Senor Kohly now in the Escambray Mountains by means of an air-dropped broadcast station, while Senor
Kohly himself is in another part of the Caribbean preparing an
invasion force of Cubans.

4. Support the invasion force of Cubans with the necessary
arms and supplies and advice, the materials being furnished to a
European intermediary from whom the provisional government of Senor
Kohly would then purchase them. This plan has been investigated
and can be arranged. When the invasion force of Cubans strikes, the
United States Armed Forces should be standing by in case the provisional government, now recognized, should request aid. If this
plan is followed the military aspect will be strictly Cuban in
nature, and a nation cannot be invaded by its own people.

5. The Reconstruction Program as outlined in the referenced
report at $1,500,000,000 consists of short, medium, and long range
projects for Cuba, and all should be eventually put into effect so
as to make Cuba a model for the rest of Latin America, but this
budget can be divided into phases and financed by the treaty agreement of the provisional government to put up the income from the
two cents per pound premium on a reinstituted sugar quota as a funding of either a bond issue or an issue of currency, the latter being
the more desirable due to greater flexibility of handling. This
sugar premium income amounts to $150,000,000 per year. By accepted
standards, the studies we have made indicate that the reinstituted
free enterprise economy of Cuba will support from $5 billion to
$8 billion of additional debt, based on pre-Castro conditions and
the pre-Castro governmental capital structure.

0000000

- 2 -

II. U.S. AFFILIATES OR SUBSIDIARIES EXPROPRIATED BY LAW 851 of July 6, 1960

Resolution 1
   Compania Cubana de Electricidad (Cuban Electric Co., American Foreign Power).
   Compania Cubana de Telefonos (Cuban Telephone Co., ITT).
   Equipos Telefonicos Standard de Cuba, S.A. (ITT subsidiary manufacturing assembler telephone components).
   Sinclair Cuba Oil Co., S.A. petroleum storage facilities, distribution system.
   Esso Standard Oil, S.A. (Standard Oil of New Jersey), petroleum refinery storage facilities, distribution system.
   Texas Co. (West Indies) Ltd., petroleum refinery, storage facilities, distribution system.
   Sugar companies (excludes lands nationalized by agrarian reform law):
   Atlantica del Golfo, S.A.
   Baragua Industrial Corp.
   Central Curagua S.A. (American Sugar Refining)
   Central Ermita, S.A.
   Cia. Agricola San Sebastian (Cuban-American Sugar Co.).
   Cia. Azucarera Cespedes.
   Cia. Azucarera Soledad.
   Cia. Central Altagracia of West Indies
   Cia. Cubana S.A.
   Cia. Azucarera Vertientes-Camaguey.
   Cuba American Sugar Co.
   Cuban Trading Co.
   Florida Industrial Corp. of New York
   Francisco Sugar Co.
   General Sugar Estates.
   Guantanamo Sugar Co.
   Macareno Industrial Corp. of New York
   Manati Sugar Co.
   Miranda Sugar Sales Co.
   New Tuinucu Sugar Co.
   Punta Alegre Sugar Co.
   United Fruit Co.

Banks, resolution 2
   Chase Manhattan Bank
   First National City Bank of New York
   First National Bank of Boston

Resolution 3
   Burrus Flour Mills, flour milling.
   Reynolds International de Cuba S.A., regional office.
   Moore Business Forms de Cuba, business forms.
   West Indies Perlite Manufacturing Corp., building materials.
   Manufacturers General Electric S.A., electrical supplies.
   Union Light Power Co. of Cuba.
   Cia. Antilante de Lanchajes S.A.
   Petroleo Cruz Verde S.A., petroleum exploration
   Cia. Cubana de Minas y Minerales S.A., minerals
   Bethlehem Cuba Iron Mines & Co., iron ore.
   Havana Coal co., Co-1.
   Regla Coal & Co. of Cuba S.A., coal.

1.4 List of companies contained in Memorandum of Marshall Diggs for which Mario Kohly brought suit against the government of Fidel Castro and for which he acted as representative and agent.

Firestone Tire & Rubber Co. of Cuba S.A., rubber tires.
Cia. Embotelladora Coca-Cola, S.A., beverages.
Minimax Supermercados, S.A., supermarkets.
Schering Pharmaceuticals of Cuba, pharmaceuticals.
Abbott Laboratories de Cuba, pharmaceuticals.
E.R. Squibb & Sons, pharmaceuticals.
Cuban American Line Supply Co.
Insurance companies:
  Pan American Life Insurance Co.
  Cia. de Seguros de Ingenios, S.A.
  United States Life Insurance Co.
  American Insurance Co.
  Commercial Insurance of Newark, N.J.
  The Home Insurance Co.
  Insurance Co. of North America.
  Johnson & Higgins, S.A.
  Seguros Frenkel de Cuba, S.A.
  American Insurance Underwriters of Cuba, S.A.
  Occidental Life Insurance Co.
  American National Insurance Co.
  The Employer's Fire Insurance
  Firemen's Insurance Co. of Newark.
  Great American Insurance Co.
  The Hanover Fire Insurance Co.
  Hartford Fire Insurance Co.
  Maryland Casualty Co.
  National Union Fire of Pittsburgh.
  Phoenix Insurance Co. of Hartford.
  Queen Insurance Co., Ltd., of American.
  Saint Paul Fire & Marine Insurance.
  Security Insurance Co. of New Haven.
  The Unity Fire & General Insurance.
  United States Fire Insurance Co.
  Eagle Fire Co. of New York
  American Surety Co.
  American International Insurance Co.
  National Fire Insurance of Hartford.
Machinery, motor vehicles, accessories, and parts:
  Power Machinery Co. S.A.
  Power Equipment, S.A.
  International Harvester of Cuba.
  W.M. Anderson Trading Co., S.A.
  Willys Distributors, S.A.
  Agencia de Tractores y Equipos.
  Iberia Machinery Co., S.A.
  Autos Volkswagen de Cuba, S.A.
  Piezas y Accessorios K.W., S.A.
  The United Shoe Machinery Co.
  Remington Rand de Cuba, S.A.
  La Antillana, Cia. Comercial de Creditos, S.A.
  Otis Elevator Co.
  Fiberglass Distributors, Inc.
  Compania de Ensamblaje de Aires Acondicionados, A.S.

Sun Oil Co., petroleum exploration.
Kewanee Inter-American Oil Co., petroleum exploration
Cuban Gulf Oil Co., petroleum exploration.
Atlantic Refining Co., petroleum exploration.
ATESA Drilling Co.
Exploration Incorporated kayflex
Haliburton Oil Well Cementing Co.
John Bros. Co.
Productos Shulton de Cuba, S.A., toilet articles.
Max Factor Co., cosmetics.
Cuba Nickel Co., S.A., Nickel Processing Corp., U.S. Government-owned
nickel plants.
Cuban Air Products Corp., oxygen equipment.
Orientes Products Corp.
Servicios de Gomas Pioneer, S.A. (Pioneer Tire Co.), tire recapping.
Compania Gas Liquido, S.A., liquid petroleum gas.
Gas Popular de Cuba, S.A., liquid petroleum gas.
H.D. Rosen Co., S.A.
Polyplasticos Industriales, S.A.
Sika Industrio-Quimica, S.A.
Home Products of Cuba, Inc.
Peison Rossi & Cia.
Armco International Corp., iron and steel products.
Mohawk Iron & Steel Corp., iron and steel products.
Fundacion MacFarlane, S.A. (J. MacFarlane and family), foundry.
Fundacion MacFarlane, S.A. (J. MacFarlane and family), foundry.
Reynolds Aluminum Co. of Cuba, aluminum foil, etc.
Manufacturers Kawneer de Cuba, S.A. (the Kawneer Co.), aluminum products.
Productos de Cobre de Cuba, S.A. (Phelps-Dodge Corp.), copper wire.
Ventanas del Caribe S.A., aluminum windows.
National Paper & Type Co. of Cuba, S.A., paper and paper products.
Compania Papelera Flamingo, S.A., paper and paper products.
Cuban American Metls Distributors, Inc.
International Carbon & Ink, S.A., paper.
Industrias Metalicas y Electricas S.A.
Palm Clothing Co., clothing.
Cia. Nacional de Huntos, S.A.
Elliot Knitting Mills, Inc., of Cuba, S.A., textiles.
Exquisite Form Brassiere of Cuba, S.A., clothing.
Tejidos Mina, S.A., textiles.
Fabricantes de Colchones Americanos, S.A., bedding.
Cia. Onix de Cuba, S.A.
Consolidated Textile Mills, Inc., textiles.
Arrocera Texita S.A., rice mills.
Cia. de Refresco Canada Dry, S.A., beverages.
Pan American Standard Brands, Inc., yeast.
Nuba Grapefruit, Inc.
Rancho Products Corp.
Alquizar Pineapple Co., Inc., pineapple.
General Distributors, S.A.
Supermercados Eklon S.A., supermarket.
F.W. Woolworth Co., merchandising.
Sears, Roebuck & Co., merchandising.
Compania de Ferrocarril de Puerto Padre, railway.
Armour & Co., fertilizers.
Cia. de Cemento Cubana Portland (Lone Star Cement Co.), cement producer/
Cia. de Vidrio Owens-Illinois, S.A. (Owens-Illinois Glass Co.), glass
containers.
Continental Can Corp., metal containers.
Cia. Goodrich de Cuba (Goodrich Rubber Co.), rubber tires.

Gold Seal Hosiery, hosiery.
Tejidos Soltex, textiles.
Ribbon Fabric Co. of Cuba, S.A.
Swift & Co., meatpacking.
Los Precios Fijos, S.A.
Ferrocarriles Consolidados de Cuba, S.A. (consolidated railways of Cuba).
Readers Digest (printing presses leased to expropriated firm).

IV.   U.S. AFFILIATES, SUBSIDIARIES AND FIRMS OWNED BY U.S. CITIZENS, WHICH
                    HAVE BEEN INTERVENED

   Cia. Antillana de Acero (10 percent U.S. owned), manufacturing iron and
steel rods.
     Cia. Concordia Textile (U.S. pres. in Cuba), textiles.
     Cia. Industrial de Goma (U.S. pres. in Cuba), rubber products.
     Cia. Pepsi-Cola de Cuba (Pepsi-Cola International), soft drink bottles.
     Goodyear de Cuba (Goodyear Rubber Tire Co.), tires and tubes.
     U.S. Rubber Co. Ltd., rubber shoes and products; tires and tubes.
     Moa Bay Mining Co. (Freeport Nickel-Sulphur), nickel and cobalt.

By now, Castro has formally taken or informally deprived this country
and its citizens of control of all the property which we directly or
indirectly owned in Cuba, has stopped any payment from Cuba on debts
of the local enterprises involved or on debts of the Government, and
has blocked transfer of any bank accounts or other assets we might
attempt to take out of Cuba.

BACKGROUND OF SENOR MARIO GARCIA KOHLY

Mario Garcia Kohly is a Cuban citizen, 62 years of age, born n Cuba in 1901, the son of Mario Garcia-Kohly and Margarita Antiga-Castelio.

His mother was a Cuban whose ancestors came from Barcelona, Spain.

His father was a Cuban who distinguished himself as an orator and writer on the Cuban political situation. He was made the Cuban Ambassador to Spain in 1913 by Menocal and continued to serve in this capacity for 23 years through the regimes of Zayas and Machado before his resignation in 1935.

After spending his boyhood in Cuba and Spain, Kohly attended the Clark High School in 1915 and 1916 in the United States, followed by one year at Columbia University in 1917.

He remained in New York after his year at Columbia and entered into a joint venture with a German named Westhauser. This venture was a credit information business called the New York Credit Exchange which, at the time, was the strongest competitor of Dun & Bradstreet. In 1921 he sold his interest in the business to Westhauser for $25,000 and returned to Cuba, representing the Thulen Signal Company and distributing its products, automobile signals. In the same year, 1921, he sold his agency to a man named Perrira and returned to the United States where he met his wife in Tampa, Florida.

Kohly's wife is Doris Baker Buhr Kohly who was born in Westfield, Pennsylvania.

He remained in Tampa until 1927 and engaged in the real estate business in his own name, the Kohly Avenue Development being one of his projects.

(more)

1.5 Summary of Mario Kohly's biographical data.

In 1927 he returned to Cuba for a visit with his family before going to Spain where he formed the Sam Milk Company which manufactured paper milk cartons and, in addition, formed a cooperative of 8,000 milk producers in the Province of Santander.

Batista Sent Kohly to Jail

In 1936 Sr. Kohly ran for Congress in the Unionist Party after the downfall of General Machado, but he was unsuccessful due to the power of the Batista machine, in control at the time, and the fact that Sr. Kohly made public speeches against Batista's usurpation of powers not rightfully his, against the graft and corruption in the Batista machine, etc. During such a public speech Mr. Kohly was pulled off the grandstand by Batista's soldiers and taken to jail. He was released and not charged, however, due to the popular support he received from the townspeople of Regla (where the speech was given) and due to the intervention on his behalf of Mayor Blanco.

After this brief and unsuccessful overture in politics, Sr. Kohly returned to the business world of Cuba forming a brokerage business which included transactions in real estate, mortgages, and insurance. From this he went into finance, putting together syndicates for the financing of large government projects such as the French Key Project of building roads to the seaports, land reclamation projects, small housing projects, etc., culminating in 1956 with the financing of the Hilton Hotel. He was working on an 80 million dollar project, Canal Via Cuba, when Castro began his activity.

On January 1, 1959, Castro took over the government of Cuba, and on January 9, 1959, Sr. Kohly was arrested by Castro. Upon his release from prison, he obtained a false passport and escaped to the U. S.

-30-

(1)

RELACION DE ORGANIZACIONES Y DELEGACIONES ASISTENTS
AL GRAN CONGRESO DE UNIDAD CUBANA

ORGANAZACION	DELEGACION
1. ORGANIZACION REVOLUCIONARIA CUBANA	CARMELINA BONAFONTE Margot Trujillo Jose Perez Benitoa Cucu Hernandez Ramon Jimenez Maseda
2. AMERICAN LEGION CUBAN VETERANS	MONEULLOA Manry G. Farr Marco A. Martinez Manuel Arquez Tulio Prieto
3. BLOQUE DE ASOCIACIONES ANTICOMUNISTAS CUBANAS	HECTOR GARCIA Reinaldo Miyares Almeida
4. VANGUARDIA DEMOCRATICA CRISTIANZ	ENRIQUE VILLAREAL Jesus Angulo Clemente Pedro Garcia Fadin Ana Villareal Dr. Manuel Alonso
5. MOVIMIENTO DE ABOGADOS LATINO- AMERICANOS ANTICOMUNISTAS	ANTONIO OTERO DALMAU Rene de Cardenas Emilio Bonich Castro Mier Urbano Herminio R. Fuentes
6. ACCION REVOLUCIONARIA DEMOCRATICA DE AMERICA	JESUS ARTIGA CARBONEL Mario Guerra Tomas Sanchez
7. RESISTENCIA AGRAMONTE	ERENESTO ROSSELL LEYTE VIDAL Eliseo Guerra Romero Carlos Guas Decall Ernesto Rosell Faulino
8. CUBA LIBRE	BALBINA BATISTA BORREGO Gudelia Quintana Garcia Delia Lay Tereau Antonio Mata Dora Lauzerique
9. CONFEDERACION DE ORGANIZACIONES DE DA MAS ANTICOMUNISTAS	CUCU HERNANDEZ Margarita Ramos Esperanza Capote Zenaida Capote Maria L. Bonafonte
10. JUVENTUD DEMOCRATICA CUBANA	ALFREDO CASTELLANOS Blas Elias Jenovevo Perez Valdes Abelardo Valdes Mario Pascual
11. COL EGIO NACIONAL DE GRADUADOS DE EN 6. SOCIALES. POL, Y ECON.DE CUBA	JOSE R. COSCULLUELA Miguel Rodriguez Callet Juan Clemente Zamora Andres Quintia Manuel Secades
12. PARTIDO LIBERAL	RAFAEL GUAS INCLAN Carmelo Urtiaga Padilla Ernesto Rosell Amleto Battisti Ernesto Perez Carrillo
13. ORGANIZACION FINERA	ANDRES SAR-ALVAREZ Casimiro Machado Torrez

2.3, 4.3, 4.7 Complete listing of 115 anti-Castro Cuban organizations operative in the Uinted States and Cuba under the aegis of umbrella organization, *United Organizations for the Liberation of Cuba* of which Mario Garcia Kohly was president. All delegates are listed.

(2)

ORGANIZACIONS	DELEGACIONES
14. FRENTE PANAMERICANO ANTICOMUNISTA	RENE DE CARDENAS Francisco Ramos Montejo Rigoberto Batista
15. LEGION ANTICOMUNISTA DE PUERTO RICO	FERMIN ALVAREZ SILVA
16. CONFERERACION DE TRABJODORES DE CUBA	EUSEBIO MUJAL BARNTOL Jesus Artigas Carbonel Arquinindes Pexidor Ramon Martin
17. FEDERACION NACIONAL DE TRABAJODRES FERROVIARIOS	JAVIER BOLAMOS PACHECO Angel Morilla Felipe Balbuena Pedro de la Vega
18. FEDERACION NACIONAL DE TRABAJODERES METALURGICOS	FRANCISCO ROJAS Jose Tenreiro
19. FEDERACION NACIONAL DE TRAJODORES MINEROS	FAUSTO WATERMAN Joel Chavez Roberto Vazquez
20. FEDERACION NACIONAL DE TRABAJADORES LICOREROS Y CERVECEROS	SATURINO ESTEVEZ Manuel Medina Nicolas Mancito
21. FEDERACION NACIONAL DE TRABAJODERS DEL COMERCIO	HECTOR BODELO Humberto Vidal Teresa Quinoa Paul Rodriquez Humberto Zurbaran
22. FEDERACION NACIONAL DE TRABAJADORES DE LA MEDICINA	RAMON MARTIN Nicolas Mancito Manuel Medina Roberto Valdes Rosendo Reyes
23. FEDERACION AEREA DE CUBA	AMADO CABRE R A Manuel Pederro
24. FEDERACION NACIONAL DE TRANSPORTE	FACUNDO POMAR SOLER Ricardo Torres Fidel Cordero Wilfredo Fernandez Jose Valdes
25. SECTOR AEREO CUBANO	TEDDY WHITEHOUSE Guillermo Alexander Carlos M. Pirri Llorca Manrique Alonso Bonada Arturo Pajardo Cordero
26. FEDERACION NACIONAL DE TRABAJADORES AZUCUREROS	ROLANDO LEONARD Raul Valdivia Mario Cruz Rivero Pedro Llorente Bienvenido Figueroa

(3)

ORGANIZACIONS	DELEGACIONES
27 FEDERACION OBRERA DEL RAMO DE LA CONSTRUCCION	PASCUAL RUEDOLO Pelayo Vigil
28. FEDERACION DE ARTISTAS Y DE ESPECTA-CULOS PUBLICOS	CESAR POMAR Daniel Talavera Alberto Pineiro Berta Lazo Enrique Arteaga
29. COMANDOS DE LIBERACION ANTI-COMUNISTAS COMETAS A B y C.	ANTONIO PASTOR PAEZ Miguel Alpizar
30. ASOCIACION NACIONAL DE PEQUENOD INDUSTRIALES DE CUBA	LUCIANO BRANA Mariano Jordan Fran Perez Perez Armando Urrutia Luis Larraudi
31. COLEGIO NACIONAL DE PROCUPADORES CUBANOS EN EL EXILIO	JOSE IGNACIO CORTES LARA Maria Teresa Marina de Pino Donso Felix Benite Ochoa Gerardo Suarez Garcia Gabriel Mendez Basilio
32. PARTIDO NECIONALISTA CHINO DE CUBA EN EL EXILIO	ALFONSO CHIONG
33. COLEBIO NACIONAL DE ECONOMISTAS DEMOCRATICOS	ALBERTO ARREDONDO Julio Figueroa Alberto Diaz Masvidal Emilio Rodriguez Oscar Morales
34. FRENTE ANTI-COMUNISTA CRISTIANO CUBANO	RICARDO JIMENEZ NUNEZ Julio del Real Garcia Jim More Francisco del Rey Felipe Roloff
35. CENTINELAS DEL CARIBE	LORENZO M. DIAZ Marcelino Rodriguez Carlos Gonzalez Vincinte Collazo Flores Antonio de Pina Varona
36. CUBA NUEVA	FEDERICO DE LA CRUZ MUNOZ Eladio Paz Torriente Manuel A. Ricardo Seina Baz Trespalacios Demetrio Omar Perez
37.HERMANDAD DE MUJERES ANTI-COMUNISTAS	VIOLETA MAZA
38. ORGANIZACION CUBANA ANTI-COMUNISTA DE NEW YORK	PEDRO ALOMA KESELL
39. UNIDAD PINARENA	MANUEL BENITEZ VALDES Gonzolo Padron Reinaldo Rodriguez Raimundo Corvo Julio Fernandez Pinelo

(4)

ORGANIZACIONES	DELEGACIONES
40. FRENTE DE LIBERACION NACIONAL	HUMBERTO NUNEZ ESPINOSA Enriqou Rodriguez Nunez Marta Jimenez Nunez Jose Ramirez Sains Elio Luque Castro
41. UNIDAD DE CUBANOS ANTI- COMUNISTAS	RAMON LAZO Jose A. Kuan Avelino Acosta Angel Acosta Camilo Gonzalez Chavez
42. ACCION REVOLUCIONARIA DEMOCRA- TICA CUBAN	CLEMENTE MORALES LLANES Mena Vazquez Rafael Rosell Pedro Garcia Jorge L. Martinez Dominguez
43. MODEMBNTO DE LIBERACION DEMOCRATICO REVOLUCIONARIO (LIDERE)	FELIPE VIDAL SANTIGO Federico Sainz de la Maza Jose Boveda Alberto Salomon Francisco Gil
44. CONFEDERACION NACIONAL DE PROFESIONALES NO UNIVERSITARIOS	ISRAEL DEL VALLE Manuel Marin Vila Omart Pedro Manuel Garcia Elvira Corral
45. FEDERACION DE CONSTRATISTAS UNIDOS DE CUBA	TOMAS PEREZ YANES
46. PARTIDO REVOLUCIONARIO CUBANO AUTENTICO	ARMANDO GARCIA SIGFREDO Eduardo Suarez Rivas Alejandro Ramos Isauro Valdes Dr. Perez Munoz Orquidia Marroqui (Suplente)
47. MOVIMIENTO 24 DE FEBREO	ARMANDO LEMUS CASTILLO Ramon Mas Carrido Juan G. Alvarez Jose Hernandez Gonzalez Jose Ismael Martinez
48. JUNTA ANTI-COMUNISTA DE CUBA	AURELIA SILVA Sergio Fernandez Francisco Valdes Gomez Eduardo Arias Lopez
49. CHRISTIAN ANTI-COMUNIST GROUP	MANUEL PEREZ DAVILA Orlando Caraballo
50. UNION DE MUJERES ABTI-COMUNI- STAS DE CUBA	YOLANDA PARET Dora Causa Carmen Ianz de Roloff Carmen Hernandez Lupe Sala
51. LEGION NACIONAL DE EX- CAMBATIENTES DE LA SEGUNDA GUERRA MANDIAL	RAIMOND PELAEZ Pedro del Iino Rolando Cruart
52. ASOCIACION DE GARTULARIOS AUX- ILIARES Y EMPLEADOS DE NOTARIA Y BUFETES	JOSE FARAFAR BELLO Adolfo Capo Cesar Alonso Maresa Domingo Ruiz Adolfo Perez Prieto

(5)

ORGANIZACIONES	DELEGACIONES
53. JUVENTUD AUTENTICA REVOLUCION- aria clandestina	GERARDO BARRERAS Felix Martinez Orlando Reyes Jose Manuel Brito Javier de la Vega
54. FRENTE UNIDO REVOLUCIONARIO DE EDUCADORES LIBRES	JOSE UTRERA Victor San Emeterio Erena Campos
55. ACCION Y SABOTAJE GERARDO DUNDORA	ARNABDI OEREZ TORRON Manuel Gonzalez Miguel Reigada Valdes Olga Garcia Vazquez Roberto Castellon
56. FRENTE UNIDO DE OBREROS CUBANOS	FIDEL CORDERO Roberto Miyares Oscar Oliva Jesus Alverez
57. DIRECTORIO REVOLUCIONARIO DE LIBERACION ANTI-COMUNISTA	ALFONSO MARQUET Alfredo Sotolongo Morales Eliseo Guerra Romero Adalberto Moenck Sotolongo Jose Manuel Gonzalez
58. ASOCIACION DE CONTADORES CUBANOS	JULIO CURRAIS Oscar Roger Carlos M. Tamayo Rafael Lorie Vals Armando Fernandez Lopez
59. CIRCULO DE ESTUDIOS "JOSE MARTI"	AGUSTIN CAIO Ifraelio Garcia Rojas Maria Ramos Gerardo Suarez Jr. Juan V. Travieso Iena
60. FEDERACION NACIONAL DE LA QUIMICA INDUSTRIAL	ALBERTO HERNANDEZ Orlga Hernandez Pablo Ramirez
61. ASOCIACION DE ABOGADOS CUBANOS	OVIDIO MANALICH RODRIGUEZ Emilio Cancio Bello Antonio Anillo Sarmiento Santiago Rosell Ferea Ramiro Manalich Rodriguez
62. MOVIMIENTO ANTI-COMUNISTA FEMENINO DE CUBA	ESTRELLA RUBIO BENAVENTE Daysy Garcia Lidian Cruz Alcovert Marta Dulzaides Valoez
63. FEDERACION OBRERA MARITIMA NACIONAL	MARTIN SALABARRIA Mario Alverez Ernesto Mestre J. Sabatier Gerardo Piloto
64. FEDERACION NACIONAL DE BARBEROS Y PELUQUEROS	DOMILIANO VAZQUEZ
65. FEDERACION NACIONAL DE BARBEROS Y PELUQUEROS	DOMILIANC VAZQUEZ

(6)

ORGANIZACIONES	DELEGACIONES
66. ASOCIACION DE AUTENTICOS	RUBEN DE LEON Juam Amador Rodriguez Jose Gomez Morodo Francisco Morales Yanes
67. MOVIMIENTO CRISTIANO DE LIBERACION	REINALDO LOPEZ LIMA Emilio Palomo Rolando Amador Francisco Sayas Castro Miguel Lopez Lima
68. ACCION CUBANA	BERNABE SANCHEZ CULMELL Tirso Dominguez Luis H. Vidana Armando Montes Ernesto Robledo
69. ASOCIACION DE PROPIETARIOS DE FAR MACIAS DE DUBA EN EL EXILIO	FEDRO ENRIQUE OLIVER
70. FEDERACION NACIONAL DE TRABA- JADORES DE LAS PLANTAS DE LUZ GAS Y AGUA DE CUBA	CARLOS FARETS Omar Guerra
71. FEDERACION NACIONAL DE TRABA- JADORES RES DEL CALZADO	ALDO BARRIOS Ramon Arencibia
72. FEDERACION NACIONAL DE TRABA- JADORES CINEMATROGRAFICOS	MANUEL SOLE Jose Perez
73. FEDERACION NACIONAL DE TRABA- JADO RES GRAFICOS DE CUBA	ARQUIMIDES TEXIDOR
74. FEDERACION NACIONAL DE MUSICOS DE CUBA	WILFREDO GARCIA CURBELO
75. SECCION FEMENINA C.T.C.	JUANITA LEON Z. Sariol Berta Villalba Elena Escarpeter (Vda de Calixto Sanchez)
76. MOVIMIENTO ANTI-COMUNISTA CUBA NO	JESUS DIAZ ALVAREZ Armando Alvarez Graciela Hernandez Rilde Rojas Jose M. Lopez
77. ASOCIACION DE MADRES CUBANAS EN EN EXILIO	GARDENIA ESPINOSA Concepcion Gonzalez Luisa Sarrainz Estela More Aida Caro Teresa Sarmiento (suplenta)
78. ACCION ANTI-COMUNISTA	JOSE M. QUIÑONEZ Alberto Marrero Ramon Gonzalez
79. CRUZADA UNIDAD REVOLUCIONARIA ANTI-COMUNISTA	JOSE C. VILLALOBOS Reinaldo Gavilongo Fedro Martinez
80. ORGANIZACION REVOLUCIONARIA LA VOZ CUBANA ANTI-COMUNISTA	NIRSO PIMENTEL Jose Cabrera Teresa Sarmiento

(7)

ORGANIZACIONES	DELEGACIONES
81. FAMILIARES DE PRESOS POLITICOS	PEDRO MANUEL FROMETA Lorenzo Mata Carlos Martinez
82. MOVIMIENTO DEL PUEBLO LIBRE	ANTONIO MARTENEZ FRAGA Humberto Quinonez CarlosMarquez Sterling Hector de la Torre Roberto Fernandez Herrero Juan Casanova (suplente) Herminio Fuentes
83. JUNTA CIVICA MILITAR CRISTIANA	JOSE PINEIRO PAEZ Francisco Perez Abreu Eugenio Sanchez Torrento Rogelio Fernandez Mata
84. FRENTE NACIONAL DEMOCRATICO TRIPLE "A"	AURELIANO SANCHEZ ARANGO Leopoldo Morffi Machado Orlando Garcia Vazquez Fernando Melo Fontanil Mario Villar Roses
85. MOVIMIENTO DEMOCRATICO DE LIBERACION	DR. GOODWALL MACEO SANTURION Carlos Bustillo Rodriguez Mario Fernandez Lopez Mario Valdes Acosta Alberto Valdes Acosta
86. COLEGIO NACIONAL DE LOCUTORES DE CUBA	MANUEL RODRIGUEZ FERNANDEZ Eduardo Gonzalez Rubio Jose A. Yeyille Juan Amador Rodriguez Jose A. Lopez (JOALO)
87. ORGANIZACION AUTENTICA OA	DR. JOSE F. IRIARTE Osvaldo Mardonez Placido Gonzalez Miguel Echegarrua Miguel Roque
88. LIGA ANTI-COMUNISTA DE CUBA	SALVADOR DIAZ VERSON
89. GRITOMDE YARA	ANTONIO CENDON FERREIRO Ignacio Fernandez Rodriguez Eloy de Armas Jose Fernandez Rodriguez Dr. Domingo Alvarez Guedes
90. FRENTE ORIENTAL DE LIBERACION	DR. ISRAEL M. SOTO BARROSO Dr. Fernando del Busto Victoriano Perez Almaguer Alnfoso Perez Cruz Francisco Moro Rueda
91. JUNTA REVOLUCIONARIA ANTI- COMUNISTA DE PINAR DEL RIO	ELFIDIO GARCIA TURURI Gerardo Capo Mendoza Juan Martinez Raimundo Corbo Cesar Paget
92. BLOQUE RADICAL ANTI-COMUNIS- TA	EDUARDO HERNANDEZ D'ABRIGEON Pedro Vidaurreta Nicasio E. Bercomo Julio Powel

(8)

ORGANIZACIONES	DELEGACIONES
93. MOVIMIENTO DE RECUPERACION DEMOCRATICA DE CUBA	ARMANDO PORTOCARRERO Nelson Carrazco Ernest o Lopez Leonardo Artiles Robecto Ilerlo Jubier
94. UNION PATRIOTICA ANTI-COMUNSTA	FELIX HERNANDEZ TELLAECHE Ramon Granda Fuentes Antolin del Collado Manol in del Busto Gilberto Ceballos Alvarez
95. CLUB MARTI DE TAMPA DE CUBANOS ANTI-COMUNISTAS	RADIO CREMATA Enrique Munoz Isabel Beristain Jose Cueva Enrique Gonzalez Francisco Martinez Jose R. Suarez Angel M. Cremata
96. ORGANIZACIONES REVOLUCIONARIAS UNIDAS	RAUL VALDIVIA Francisco Choa Hermida Juan Montalvo Saladriga Carlos Manuel Fernaandez F. Ramon O. Hermida Antorcha
97. ACCION REVOLUCIONARIA CONSTITU-CIONAL VENEZUELA	CARLOS ROMERO Pedro Oscar Rodriguez Luis Dulzaires
98. ORGANIZACIONES AUTONOMAS CLANDES-TINAS LEGION DE LA CRUZ VERDE	CARLOS A. BERDURA SIXTO A. QUINTERO Erasmo A. Garateix Lucia A. Latimer Miguel Alvarez Iglecias
99. MOVIMIENTO ANTI-COMUNISTA CUBANO	PEDRO SALVA MONTERO Hector Torres Jose J. Larraz Otoniel Pena
100. COLEGIO MEDICO VETERINARIO DE CUBA E.	FAUSTO WATERMAN Rafael del Pino Pacheco Araseli San German
101. COLEGIO DE PROF. DE EDUC. FISC. Y DEPORTES	LUIS COBIELLA Hilda Calsadilla Jaime J. Servera
102. AGRUPACION MEDICA ANTI-COMUNIS-TA CUBANA (A.M.A.C.)	ALFREDO NOGEIRA MANUEL ARIUDIA JOSE PADRO JIMENEZ
103. COLEGIO DE EDUCADORES CUBANOS EN EL EXILIO	ISOLINA DIAS Roberto Toledo Eugenio Sanchez Torrente Julia Elisa Consuegra Leovigildo Gonzalez Mesa
104. ACCION CIVICA ANTI-COMUNISTA (A.C.A.)	ERNESTO AZUA PONT Jaime Calvo R. Canals Emilio Areaga Jose M. Menendez

(9)

ORGANIZACIONES	DELEGACIONES
105. JUVENTUD ANTI-COMUNISTA DE AMERICA A.C.A.	ENRIQUE FERNANDEZ PARAJON Oscar Gonzalez Elijio Contreras Carlos Quiros Antonio Fernandez
106. SALVEMOS A CUBA (S.A.C.)	ROBERTO RODRIGUEZ Clara Cortada Antonio Clemente Gillermina L. de Fernandez Juan Pelaez
107. LEGION ESTUDIANTIL CATOLICA (L.E.C.)	ARMANDA RUIZ Ernesto A. Calzadilla Felix C. Gonzalez Alfredo P. Cardenas Pedro Nodarse
108. ACCION CRISTIANA DE HOMBRES LIBRES (A.C.H.L.)	JOSE LOPEZ VILADOY Herminio Navarro Julio A. Martin Tomas Jardines
109. FRATERNIDAD PATRIOTICA DE CUBA (F.P.C.)	MARIA MANCITO Luis Lopez Alberto Ra,oerez Felipe Mendoza Bernardo Villegas
110. ARTISTAS UNIDOS POR CUBA LIBRE (A.U.C.L.)	EDUARDO OCANA Lorenzo Bermudez Rigoberto Diaz Pedro Garcia
111. ASOCIACION DE AGENTES EMPRESA-RIOS DE CUBA	JOSE M. FUENTEVILLA Mario Aguero Ramiro Obrador
112. FEDERACION ESTUDIANTIL UNIVERSI-TARIA LIBRE	ANTIONIO ANILLO SARMIENTO Maria Matilde Causa Luis Isaias Rodriguez Raul Pozo Guillermo Mozquera
113. FRENTE ANTI-COMUNISTA DE AMERICA LATINA	SANTIAGO REY PERNA
114. ASOCIACION NACIONALISTA BUBANA	SANTIAGO GONZALES NARANJO
115. BLOQUE DE ORGANIZACIONES ANTI-COMUNISTAS	HECTOR GARCIA

M E M O R A N D U M

Gentlemen:

After having organized the CUBAN LIBERATORS, composed in its majority
of ex-Army, Navy and Aviation men, all of them Cubans residing in
exile and a large underground in Cuba, also among the ex-Army, I came
to Washington, D.C. on the tenth of June this year in the vain hope
of being able to obtain the arms necessary with which to equip my men
and overthrow the communist regime of Fidel Castro.

Since the above date I have been told that this support would come at
once as there was the desire on the part of various government members
to have the Cuban situation cleared up before the elections. As of
two weeks ago I have been told that nothing can be done until after the
elections but I have been given to understand that immediately after
the elections I would receive the necessary support and help to oust
Castro.

I have been advised that the major companies whose properties were confiscated in Cuba have been told by the State Department to keep hands
off Cuba until after the elections.

Mr. Thompson, representing the C.I.A. and upon request of Mr. Nixon
through his military aid, General Cushman, called on me at Marshall
Diggs' office and requested or at least suggested that I join with two
communist front organisations operating now in Miami whom he claimed
were well financed. I explained to Mr. Thompson that I could not join
with either organization as they were both communist fronts organised
in part by Castro himself, by the Communist Party and by the President
of Venezuela, Romulo Betancourt.

Since that date after such an offer was made to me I have felt completely
ostracised here in Washington while these communist fronts continue to
receive the direct support of the C.I.A. and the State Department and
the American Embassy in Havana as proven by the following facts:

"The FRONT, as this communist organization is known, has been receiving
arms and money on their own admission from C.I.A. and the State Department. They have allowed to recruit openly in the City of Miami without
ever being molested. Arms have been dropped in Cuba to particians of
this communist Front. At the request of Tory Varona, coordinator of the
Front, the American Embassy in Havana expedites the issuing of visas in
hours that normally would take a year. Men belonging to my organization
have been contacted by the American Embassy in Havana and have been issued
special passports to come to the United States and told to contact the
C.I.A. office in Miami. Upon doing so, they have been told to join the
FRONT and later to return to that Office where they will be given the
instructions as to whom to see in the State Department so they may
receive the funds and coordinate their return to Cuba as an invasion force".

2.5 October 18, 1960 memorandum of Mario Kohly describing
organization and deployment of Cuban exiles and resident Cubans in
United States and Cuba.

MEMORANDUM

There is only one reasonable explanation to Fidel Castro's actions and his attitude towards the United States, his constant agressions and insults, his many threats to take over the U.S. Base in Guantanamo and his executions and imprisonment of American citizens: his desire to achieve fame and glory.

According to Castro's own remarks he would consider he had failed miserably as the new Bolivar if he should be put out of Cuba by Cubans in open revolt against his regime. It is his greatest desire and ambition to provoke the United States by all means possible into armed intervention by the U.S. Marines.

Castro will continue his harassment of Americans until such time as American public opinion will force the President of the United States to declare open warfare or intervention in Cuba. By so doing both Castro and his communist organization will be able to claim before all the Latin American countries and the world in general that the Cuban does not repudiate communism or the 26 of July Movement that brought communism in Cuba but that it was the American Imperialism that overthrew his regime against the will of the Cuban people. This he will be able to prove because it is a well known fact to any observer of Latin American psychology that the strong nationalistic feeling which has been whipped up against the United States by Castro will make the Cubans fight and resist any direct intervention by U.S. Marines, thus, another "Hungary" will have been provoked and Khruschev will have been justified in the massacre of the Hungarian people.

There is only one way in which this can be prevented and that is to have a force of Cubans, preferably a force of ex-Army men who are already trained (such as we the CUBAN LIBERATORS have) so they be thrown into Cuba at a moment's notice thus avoiding the need of United States direct intervention.

Of the approximate six thousand men which CUBAN LIBERATORS can now count in the United States and over 12,000 men in Cuba, I am afraid we are going to lose a great many who are falling into the hands of COMMUNIST ORGANIZED FRONTS in Miami for the sole purpose of dispersing them into camps in Mexico, Guatemala and other Latin American countries so as to make it impossible for us to strike with sufficient power in the short time that we may be called to do so once Castro's provocations cause a further worsening of relations and a wave of public indignation in the United States.

In order to keep our Organization together fund should be made available at once so as to keep the key men in eating money and in touch with their subordinates and in a position to help those more needy. Men must be brought back from their camps in Latin America and kept under control in Miami. Their families must be fed. The hunger and misery of these men who want to fight for freedom are undergoing is appauling. Immediate help must be obtained.

Mario Garcia Kohly
Executive Director
CUBAN LIBERATORS

Washington, D. C.
18 October 1960

IN THE CIRCUIT COURT OF THE
ELEVENTH JUDICIAL CIRCUIT
OF FLORIDA, IN AND FOR DADE
COUNTY, FLORIDA   AT LAW

NO. 60-L-2257 - Christie

HARRIS AND COMPANY ADVERTISING:
INC., a Florida corporation
                                    :
                    Plaintiff,
                                    :
v.   FINAL JUDGMENT FOR PLAINTIFF
                                    :
REPUBLIC OF CUBA,
                                    :
                    Defendant.
                                    :

THIS CAUSE having come on this day for trial, after due notice,
the Court having heard testimony from witnesses for the parties and
arguments of counsel, having found that plaintiff's Amended Complaint has
been proven by competent evidence and that defendant has no good and meri-
torious defense thereto, having found that the following properties of the
defendant and/or its government-owned and/or government operated instru-
mentalities attached prior to judgment, to wit:

> 1 C-46 #CVC153, as equipped (stored at Air International,
> 1 C-46 #CVC644, as equipped Miami International Airport,
> 1 C-46 #CVC787, as equipped Miami, Florida)
>
> 1 C-46 #CU-C1-45, as equipped (stored at Marathon Aviation,
>   Inc., Marathon, Florida)
>
> Approximately one million pounds of insecticides, fertilizer
> and miscellaneous supplies (stored at Eagle, Inc., Pier #2,
> Miami, Florida)
>
> 1 B-26 #FAR933, as equipped (stored at American Air Motors,
> Miami International Airport, Miami, Florida).

are rapidly deteriorating, subject to decay, subject to high storage fees,
and will not sell for their full value if held for a period of Thirty days, by
reason of which plaintiff has moved for a shortened sale thereof, plaintiff
having requested the Court to enter Final Judgment in its favor, and the
Court being fully advised in the premises, it is therefore

2.7 Lawsuit brought by Kohly against Republic of Cuba in exercising his
representative responsibilities of U.S. corporations with holdings in Cuba.

Article 2.—For the purposes of reconstructing and functioning of the Confederation of Labor of Cuba the following persons appointed to the corresponding posts shall be recognized as the provisional committee for administration:

In Charge of General Matters: David Salvador Manso
In Charge of Organization: Octavio Louit Venzán
In Charge of Finances: José Pelló Jaén
In Charge of Representation before Official and Employer Organizations: Antonio Torres Chedebau
In Charge of Documents and Correspondence: Conrado Bécquer Díaz
In Charge of Propaganda: José María de la Aguilera Fernández
In Charge of Foreign Relations: Reinol González Gonzáles
In Charge of Internal Relations: Jesús Soto Díaz
In Charge of Legal Matters: José de J. Plana del Paso

The Committee for Provisional Administration of the Confederation of Labor of Cuba, above mentioned, shall have legal personality (corporate) adequate to govern and administer said confederation and to represent it before Official and Employer Organizations, all in accordance with the rights and powers conferred by the By-laws and Regulations of the said Confederation of Labor of Cuba upon its board of administration.

Article 3.—The Committee for Provisional Administration of the Confederation of Labor of Cuba shall appoint provisional revolutionary administrative committees for the Federations of Industries and Provincial Federations, the Provisional Administrative Committees of the same to be composed of the following officers: In Overall Charge: In Charge of Organization; In Charge of Finances; In Charge of Representation before Official and Employer Organizations, and In Charge of Documents and Propaganda.

The persons who are appointed to perform the mentioned offices in the Federations of Industries and Provincial Federations, and in the Syndicates, Unions and Guilds, shall be endowed with adequate legal personality to govern and administer said labor organizations, and to represent them before Official and Employer Organizations. All of this in accordance with the powers conferred upon the Administrative Boards by the By-laws and Regulations.

Article 5.—The persons in charge of Organization and of Documents in the Confederation of Labor of Cuba shall file with the Office on Labor Organizations in the Ministry of Labor, through certified document, the legal status of those persons holding offices on the Provisional Administrative Committees of the Federations of Industries and Provincial Federations and of the Syndicates, Unions and Guilds, and shall issue the credentials for these persons, to be communicated to the respective employers.

Article 6.—The provisional administrative committees for the Syndicates, Unions and Guilds shall not call general elections until a period of ninety business days has elapsed from the date of effectiveness of this Law, after which they will have a period of forty-five days in which to call and hold said elections.

Article 7.—A period of ten week days, which cannot be extended, computed from the date of publication of this Law in the OFFICIAL GAZETTE of the Republic, is granted to all administrators and officials of Labor Organizations who functioned as such on the thirty-first of December of nineteen hundred fifty-eight, in order that they may return and deliver all documents and property of any kind, belonging to the labor organizations in which they held office.

Article 8.—The Minister of Labor is charged with the execution of the present Law and of enacting interpretative and regulatory resolutions regarding same. All laws and decrees contrary to its observance are repealed.

Therefore I order that the present Law in all of its parts be observed and executed.

Issued in the Presidential Palace, in Havana, on the twentieth of January of nineteen hundred fifty-nine.

(Signed) MANUEL URRUTIA LLEO.
José MIRÓ CARDONA,
Prime Minister.
MANUEL FERNÁNDEZ GARCÍA,
Minister of Labor.

Mr. SOURWINE. While you were attending the convention of the Cuban Confederation of Labor in Havana last month, did you meet any delegates from the German Democratic Republic?

2.9 José Miro Cardona's signature as Cuba's Prime Minister in House Select Committee on Internal Security document of January 23, 1959.

EXCERPT OF STATEMENT MADE BY MARIO KOHLY, JULY 1975.

Summary

          The tape you are about to hear is the last statement
made by Mario Garcia Kohly, Sr. It is one side of a half hour
tape that he made just four weeks prior to his death. On it you
will hear Kohly state that the understanding he had with the
Central Intelligence Agency was that Miro Cardona, Tony Verona,
Manuel Artimes, and the rest of the Cuban Revolutionary Front group
that was being held incommunicado down in Miami would be eliminated
after a successful invasion at the Bay of Pigs. He made this deal
with then Vice President Nixon who was the CIA Action Officer in
the White House and whom the Bay of Pigs was originally developed
under.

          For this agreement that Kohly would take over the
island after a successful invasion, Kohly pledged his 42,000 man
underground internal Cuban organization as well as his 300 to 400
man guerrilla army which was fully armed and ready to go in the
Escambrey Mountains and which was to join up with the Bay of Pigs
invaders. In addition, he was to supply all the necessary information his underground had gained on the missile installations then
being installed in Cuba. When the Front group realized they were
being held incommunicado at Opa Locka, one of the members, Tony
Verona, climbed through a bathroom window and called Washington
and the Administration.

          Kohly states in this last statement of his that Castro
was responsible for the death of John F. Kennedy. This statement
is designed to completely smokescreen the fact that the Cuban
exiles had a participation in the assassination. This will come
out at a later date, but it is not relative to the fact that the

2.16 Statement of Mario Kohly, Sr. in July 1975, four weeks prior to his
death. This statement describes the tenets of Mario Kohly's agreement with
Richard M. Nixon which was called *Operation Forty*.

Kohly
2.

CIA was deliberately condoning the assassination of as many as
five people which they held prisoner in Miami on April 17, 1961.

Kohly Transcript

On the other tape I started to give an account of how
I learned that the treacherous action had been played upon us by
President Kennedy in stopping the air support after the boys had
already started for Cuba. There was no way of advising them
because there was radio silence at all times. The true account of
how I learned is this.

I was working at Marshall Diggs office at ten o'clock
at night preparing some reports to be transmitted to Cuba which
we had made arrangements with my son in Miami to transmit messages
from myself here to him and from him to the underground in Cuba.
We did this through portable radios -- he's quite a radio expert.
And I ran out of cigars -- out of smokes -- while I was in Marshall
Diggs office that night. Just before returning home, I stopped by
the Mayflower to buy some. I went in there to the cigar stand and
who did I run into but ex-Senator Owen Brester of Maine who had
been introduced to me sometime previously by Marshall Diggs and we
had become pretty good friends. Brewster had been trying to get me
on the phone, but I had refused to answer the phone just figuring it
was my wife calling me to get home early or some of my girl friends
and not my wife.

Then, Brewster was very angry and said, "Why don't you
answer your phone? I've got a most important message for you.
I've been trying to get you all evening."

Kohly
3.

So after due apologies and so forther, I asked what
the message is.

He said, "Mario, quick, have you any way of contacting
the underground in Cuba?"

He knew that I was working very closely with them and I
said, "Yes. I have ways of contacting them."

He said, "Look. Tell them right away that the air
support has been called off. Kennedy has double crossed the Cuban
exiles."

I was shocked also to a point of immobility for a
second. Then I excused myself, thanked him, and went to the phone
and called my son up long distance from the office of Marshall Diggs
and told him that the message must go through to Cuba at once,
saying 'do not cooperate in operations unless you see the eagle
flying.' The boys would know what that was because it was a prearranged signal in case of any such events. We had taken every
precaution. I had been somewhat suspicious of the Kennedy Administration's sincerity, while at all times under the CIA's operations
most of the time. So I had made contingency plans to communicate
to the underground in case we did get double crossed. Thus, in
effect, the message was sent and the lives of better than 42,000
men were saved who would have cooperated with the invasion and who
would have been slaughtered -- which apparently was exactly what
was intended to happen. So the Cuban people are eternally grateful
to Owen Brewster (of late) as well as myself for having given them
the advance information which saved the lives of the Cuban underground.

My part in the Cuban invasion plans were limited to some

Kohly
4.

extent. I had arranged to recruit or to enlist better than
300 boys who on a set signal once we took over the island would
meet with me and arrange for the overthrow of the CIA inspired
council with Miro Cardona and the rest of them. If this had
been successful they would have been eliminated almost at once
and I would have come into Cuba and taken over.

This can be confirmed through Mr. Sourwine in the U.S.
Senate who called me one day to meet with one of the troopers or
rather a group of troopers who had come out of the Bay of Pigs
alive and to come back to the States and it was this trooper who
very discretely divulged our plans to Owen Brewster and stated that
each one of them was wearing a yellow hankerchief around their collar
to show who was who and to know each other so that at the proper
time they could communicate. Yellow was chosen because it fitted
in with the uniforms and would not attract attention as they were
current army handkerchiefs or bandanas, whatever you wish to call
them.

Comment

The excerpt you have just heard was from the last
statement made by Mario Garcia Kohly, president de facto in exile
of Cuba and leader of the United Organizations for the Liberation
of Cuba, less than four weeks before his death on August 5, 1975.
The original of this tape is in the safety deposit box of the law
firm of Adelberg, Adelberg & Rudow, 10 Light Street, Baltimore,
Maryland.

AFFIDAVIT:

I, Anthony M. Eaton, presently residing at 710, Park
Avenue, Baltimore, Maryland,21201.,U.S.A., do hereby
attest and affirm, in support of the confidential memorandum
hereto attached and witnessed, that, to the best of my
knowledge and belief the facts stated therein are correct
and factual, and further, that I shall be prepared to provide
further details, together with the reasons for such knowledge
on my part to any properly constituted body in closed session
bearing in mind the currently enforceable Official Secrets Act
extant in the United Kingdom. I shall hold myself at the disposal
of Mr. Robert D. Morrow and any other person who he shall
designate as being the proper authority to which to provide
such information and shall use my best efforts to provide
other persons with relevant testimony at such time as they may
be required.

ANTHONY M. EATON.

STATE OF MARYLAND.
County of _Baltimore_   ,ss:

I HEREBY CERTIFY that on _3rd_ July 1976., before me, the
subscriber, a notary public of the State of Maryland, in and for
the _County of Baltimore_ personally appeared Anthony M. Eaton and
acknowledged the forgoing Affidavit and the attached, witnessed
memorandum to be his act and hand.

WITNESS my hand and notorial seal, the day and year last mentioned
above.

Notary Public.

3.1 Affidavit of Anthony M. Eaton dated June 3, 1976, confirming British
Royal Air Force's knowledge of Soviet missiles in Cuba in the fall of 1960 and
Soviet non-compliance with agreement between JFK and Khruschev after the
Missile Crisis in October 1962.

7/15/76

Commission...
notary Public

STRICTLY CONFIDENTIAL AND PRIVATE

Memo

TO: Robert D. Morrow
FROM: Anthony M. Eaton
DATE: 3 June 1976
SUBJ: Cuban Missiles and Their Relevant Dates

        As I told you during our recent conversations,
my knowledge of the missiles (USSR) existance in Cuba began in
late 1960, either September or October of that year when overflights
were made from the Bahamas by the R.A.F. and pictures taken which
clearly indicated IRBM implacements being set up in several
locations. This information was passed by the Joint Services
Committee of the SIS to the Joint Services Intelligence Bureau in
Northumberland Avenue and then to the Foreign Office for passage to
the U.S. State Department. I am informed by the British Embassy
that the matter is one upon which there can be "No comment" and that
any such information would still be covered by the Official Secrets
Act under which, as a British subject, I am still liable.

        At a future date, shortly after the "missiles of October,"
I was approached by one of the staff of "Jane's Fighting Ships" and
informed that by his calculations, the ships provided by the USSR
for the ostensible removal of missiles, were not loaded with
missiles. His calculated results rested on the ship displacement,
weight and dimensions of the missiles, and the likely ballast loading
when the ships reached Cuba. These results were checked by several
other authorities using news and military photographs and they also
decided that few, if any, missiles were, in fact, removed.

        Several sources of such evidence can still be reached; but,
due to the Official Secrets Act, great care will have to be
exercised as no one wants to be charged under the various provisions
therein.

ORANGE COUNTY HEALTH DEPARTMENT
832 WEST CENTRAL BOULEVARD • POSTOFFICE BOX 3187 • TEL: 849-3335, ORLANDO, FLORIDA 32802

Department of Health and Rehabilitative Services
DIVISION OF HEALTH

CERTIFICATE OF DEATH
FLORIDA

STATE FILE NO.
REGISTRAR'S NO. 75 811

DECEASED — NAME: John Adrian O'Hare SEX: Male DATE OF DEATH: March 23, 1975

RACE: White AGE — LAST BIRTHDAY: 49 DATE OF BIRTH: Nov. 14, 1925 COUNTY OF DEATH: Orange

CITY, TOWN, OR LOCATION OF DEATH: Orlando INSIDE CITY LIMITS: Yes HOSPITAL OR OTHER INSTITUTION: Florida Hospital

STATE OF BIRTH: New York CITIZEN OF WHAT COUNTRY: USA MARRIED, NEVER MARRIED, WIDOWED, DIVORCED: Married SURVIVING SPOUSE: Ethel Harriett Nelson

SOCIAL SECURITY NUMBER: 079-20-0739 USUAL OCCUPATION: Salesman KIND OF BUSINESS OR INDUSTRY: Visual Aids

RESIDENCE — STATE: Florida COUNTY: Orange CITY, TOWN, OR LOCATION: Orlando INSIDE CITY LIMITS: no STREET AND NUMBER: 2400 Falkner Road

FATHER — NAME: John A O'Hare MOTHER — MAIDEN NAME: Regina

INFORMANT — NAME: Thomas O'Hare MAILING ADDRESS: 2400 Falkner Road, Orlando, Florida 32810

PART I DEATH WAS CAUSED BY:
(a) Acute myocardial infarction, massive
(b) Acute thrombotic occlusion of the left coronary artery

PART II — OTHER SIGNIFICANT CONDITIONS: Severe mitral stenosis with ...

AUTOPSY: Yes IF YES WERE FINDINGS CONSIDERED IN DETERMINING CAUSE OF DEATH: Yes

PROBABLY ACCIDENT, SUICIDE OR HOMICIDE, OR UNDETERMINED: No

INJURY AT WORK: No

CERTIFICATION — PHYSICIAN:
HOUR OF DEATH: 10:05 P March 23, 1975 10:05 P.

CERTIFIER — NAME: R.G. Guzman, M.D., M.E., Dist. 9 DATE SIGNED: 5-24-75
MAILING ADDRESS: 1416 South Orange Avenue, Orlando, Florida 32806

BURIAL, CREMATION, REMOVAL: Burial CEMETERY OR CREMATORY — NAME: Glen Haven Mem Park LOCATION: Winter Park Florida

DATE: March 26, 1975 FUNERAL HOME — NAME AND ADDRESS: Cox-Parker F.H. 1350 W. Fairbanks Ave., Winter Park, Fla. 32789

REGISTRAR — SIGNATURE: Ella M. Laby DATE RECEIVED BY LOCAL REGISTRAR: MAR 25 1975

CERTIFIED COPY

I hereby certify the above to be a true and correct copy of the Local Registrar's record on file in the Orange County Health Department, Orlando, Florida.

W.N. Sisk, M.D.
County Health Officer and Local Registrar

Ella M. Laby
Chief Deputy Registrar

MAY 6 1975
Date Issued

WARNING: Not valid unless raised seal of the Orange County Health Department is affixed.

4.4 Death Certificate of John O'Hare, former CIA mercenary assassin under employ of Eladio del Valle, responsible for assassination of Manuel Rodriguez Quesada and Gilberto Rodriguez Hernandez, in September–October 1964. (See page 240, Chapter 14 for transcript extract.)

ALBION ARMS

PETERBOROUGH, ONTARIO

MAKE	CAL.	QUANTITY
GERMAN M.G.34	8 m/m	1,092 ✗
GERMAN M.G.42	8 m/m	961 ✗
ITALIAN BREDA	6.5 m/m	1,133 ✗
BRNO L.M.G.	8 m/m	123 ✗
STEYR L.M.G.	8 m/m	87
BREDA L.M.G.	6.5 m/m	50
FIAT L.M.G.	8 m/m	177

6.4 Weapons list containing make, caliber and quantity of weaponry
purchased by Mario Kohly's organization from Albion Arms in
Petersborough, Ontario. Actual purchase was made by author in Greece and
delivery performed with assistance of David Ferrie.

Black/16

Morrow:	I know. /He had to know Kovans fairly well to make that reply./
Black:	That is a bit girl /noticing a girl passing the table/.
Morrow:	That's right. I was noticing.
Black:	When's your new book coming out? Do you have a long way to go on it.
Morrow:	No. I have to deliver it October first.
Black:	You say the name of your book is Betrayal? What was that about?
Morrow:	That was about my experiences with the CIA as a contract agent back in 1959 through 1964 /I meant 1963/.
Black:	You know where I've heard your name. Now I can tell you have... I know three Bob Morrow's. I know a Bob Morrow who's a colonel in the Air Force and now living in California. I know a Bob Morrow who's father is chairman of the board of Lincoln National Life in Indianapolis. And I know that's not you, because I just saw him last week. You're the Bob Morrow that Don Mitchell talked to me about.
Morrow:	Don Mitchell?
Black:	Yeah. He was with the CIA up until this last year. I heard your name from him as if there was just one Bob Morrow.
Morrow:	Well, I'm probably the one. I was the one that did all the counterfeiting of Cuban pesos back in 1963.
Black:	Did you know my friend Johnny Roselli?
Morrow:	I sure did. /I said this because I had met Roselli twice during 1961./
Black:	Johnny stayed with me, you know, several times before he was killed. In fact I was the last person he talked to on Tuesday before they took him away.

8.2 Clandestinely taped luncheon meeting between Robert D. Morrow and Fred Black at Duke Zeibert's Restaurant in Washington, D.C. on May 24, 1977, wherein Black admits friendship with J. Roselli. (edited transcript)

Black/17

Morrow:	Jesus Christ!
Black:	I entertained Dade County homocide detectives and FBI agents once every two weeks, on the dot. This trip they won't see me, because I'm going to Florida on Thursday, so they'll call me and ask me if I've heard anything about it /the Roselli murder/.
Morrow:	Jack Anderson just expounded that he knew all about it.
Black:	I heard him on the AM...
Morrow:	Good Morning, America show.
Black:	Yeah. I'm seeing Jack /Anderson/ tomorrow morning at 10 o'clock.
Morrow:	Ask him... tell him I'd sure like to know who the hell it is /that killed Roselli/.
Black:	I don't think he knows anything; I think he's just talking.
Morrow:	Yes, bull shit. Because everything he's used about the Kennedy assassination has come around to exactly what I've put in the book /Betrayal/.
Black:	Is that right?
Morrow:	Yes.
Black:	I never understood how a reporter like Jack could say he knew all these things, when people like me for instance who don't amount to anything /he caught himself in mid-sentence/... and I was never in anything except in business... why I wouldn't think of going to Jack and telling him anything that I didn't want published in the newspaper. So, why anybody else would, I don't know. I think a lot of their work /meaning Jack Anderson's/ is pure conjecture.
Morrow:	There's no question about it.
Black:	I know that Wadden /Black's attorney; friend of Tom Downing/

Black/18

spoke to Roselli and Anderson together on several occasions.
But knowing Wadden the way I do, I know he wouldn't let
Roselli give him the time of day.

Morrow: Did you know Johnny Roselli spent quite a bit of time here in
            Washington back in 1961?

Black: No. I didn't know him in those days. I only met him, Roselli...
            when Ed Morgan /Roselli's Washington attorney who told Earl
            Warren about the assassination attempts on Castro in 1961/
            introduced me to him back in... I guess, my last trial was
            back in 1968... just prior to my last trial, in early 1968, I met
            him at the Desert Inn /in Las Vegas/. I'd never met him
            before. I knew who he was for years, but I'd never met him
            /Roselli and Clifford Jones were close associates, so Black
            had to know him/.

Morrow: Well, I met him right here in Washington in 1961... twice; and
            Sam Giancana once.

Black: I never met Giancana. But, as I say, I knew Johnny very well.
            And I know Johnny's family.

Morrow: Did you know Marshall Diggs?

Black: That's a familiar name.

Morrow: The attorney... back in the old days.

Black: Yeah, yeah. I knew him. He's dead, isn't he?

Morrow: Oh, yes.

Black: And also another fellow that knew Johnny real well that I've
            known for thirty years is Joe Shimon.

Morrow: Joe... Shimon?

Black: Shimon. Yeah. He's /an/ ex-police instructor here.* He was
            always very close to Roselli, Mayheu,** and that whole crowd....

Black/19

* Shimon actually ran an organization known as the International
Police Academy on R Street in Washington, D.C., according to Ross
Allen Schoyer who once worked with Shimon in 1958 and 1959. The I.P.A.
was a CIA front organization that specialized in training foreign operators
such as the Iranian Secret Police in dirty tricks and other gestapo-type
operations.

** Meaning Robert Maheu who was an FBI agent under Guy Banister
in the late 40's; then when working for Howard Hughes became assassination coordinator for the CIA/Mafia attempts on Castro.

Black: /Black then addressed the waiter who had come to the table./
(cont.)   Maurice, could you get us another drink and I'm going to
            have that goulash.

Morrow: Make that two...

Black: ... and he's going to have the same thing.

Morrow: ... and a glass of iced tea with it. Can I finish this first
            /meaning my second drink/?

Black: Sure. Joe's /meaning Joe Shimon/ retired now; but I had
            lunch with him a couple of weeks ago. The same people that
            badger me about Roselli, badger Joe. And I can truthfully
            say that in all the time that I knew Roselli about the only
            thing he ever told me that might have been the least bit spicy
            was he told me that he knew Judith Exner. And that's the
            only thing he ever told me.

Morrow: So did a lot of people /know Judith Exner/.

Black: Yeah. And I never even knew who she was until I read it in
            the paper.

Morrow: Did you know Jack Kennedy at all?

Black: Who?

Morrow: Jack Kennedy.

Black: Oh, yes. I knew him when he was a Congressman and knew
            him when he was a Senator. A lot of his friends were very

Black/20

good friends of mine. The only person who hated me
was Bobby... /that/ was his brother.

Morrow: Join the club. Bobby hated my guts.

Black: Well, he told me he was going to put me in the penitentiary.

Morrow: I'll tell you what he told me. He told me he was going to
have me strung up in a Guatemalean jail somewhere...
deported.

Black: Boy, he was something, wasn't he? Yeah, he told me that
/was going to put Black in jail/, and by god he did his best.
When he was murdered, shot, whatever happened to him
out in California, I think I was the first person in town
they /meaning the FBI/ checked on to see where I was because on my tape /according to Black they had bugged and
recorded his hotel room/, when they played them back, they
had two things /already on the FBI transcript/ they had
written out in long hand. One was that I had called him a
/expletive deleted/, and they had written that out in long
hand. And then another time I had said I would like to kill
the son-of-a-bitch if I had the chance. So those /remarks/
they wrote out in long hand, so naturally when he /RFK/
was killed, I was the first person they checked /on/ to see
where I was.

Morrow: Well, I unfortunately was noted for having the propensity of
calling him /expletive deleted/. That unfortunately didn't
go over too well.

Black: Inclined not to make you too popular with him. Well, I'm
anxious to see if Jack Anderson really does know anything
and if they /Anderson and company/ are going to name
Roselli's murderers. I bet they don't. I don't think he
knows anything about it.

Morrow: I think the same people that did in Mr. Roselli, did in Mr.
Carlos Prio Socarras and a fellow by the name of George
DeMohrenschildt.

Black: Which one is DeMohrenschildt?

Black/21

Morrow:	/I took a stab at this question to get his reaction./ Well, he was Oswald's CIA contact.
Black:	Did Bill Harvey die normally or was he killed?
Morrow:	I would suspect that Bill died of over weight primarily.
Black:	I never saw him, but I heard a lot about him.
Morrow:	/I understand/ he was a wild man.
Black:	That's what John /meaning Roselli/ said. But John liked him.
Morrow:	Well, he worked with him.
Black:	But John liked him, and he didn't like very many people.
Morrow:	I met Harvey twice, and that was /when he was/ over at the old CIA headquarters right off C Street. You must know Fred Blumenthal too?
Black:	I don't. Those are just names. Excuse me, I'll be right back. /He left for several minutes, obviously going to the men's room. After coming back, he continued/ Drink a couple glasses of that tea; and that will do it.
Morrow:	I think I'm about to do the same thing. /I needed to turn over the tape on the recorder in my pocket./
Black:	I had a kidney operation in May of last year.
Morrow:	Really?
Black:	Stones. Since that time I have had /problems/ in my control area. When I have to go, if I don't go I have a problem. I think you're going to like this /referring to the Hungarian goulash which had been delivered to the table while he was away/.
Morrow:	I haven't eaten here in years.

X10

<u>THE MURDER WEAPON.</u>

A RIFLE WAS DISCOVERED ON THE SIXTH FLOOR OF THE BOOK

DEPOSITORY BUILDING AT 1:22 P.M. ON NOVEMBER 22, 1963. THE

DALLAS AUTHORITIES TOLD THE PRESS LATER THAT DAY THAT THE

WEAPON WAS A 7.65 GERMAN MAUSER. DALLAS DISTRICT ATTORNEY WADE

REPEATED THIS INFORMATION AT A FORMAL TELEVISED PRESS CONFERENCE

AND IT WAS WIDELY PUBLICIZED. DEPUTY CONSTABLE SEYMOR WEITZMAN,

ON NOVEMBER 23, 1963, IN A NOTARIZED AFFIDAVIT, DESCRIBED THE

RIFLE HE AND DEPUTY SHERIFF BOONE FOUND AS "A 7.65 MAUSER,

BOLT ACTION EQUIPPED WITH A 4/18 SCOPE, A THICK LEATHER

BROWNISH BLACK SLING ON IT." IN A FILMED INTERVIEW IN APRIL

1974, ROGER CRAIG, A DEPUTY SHERIFF ALSO PRESENT WHEN THE RIFLE

WAS FOUND STATED:

        "I WAS STANDING NEXT TO WEITZMAN, HE WAS STANDING

        NEXT TO FRITZ, AND WE WEREN'T ANY MORE THAN SIX OR

        EIGHT INCHES FROM THE RIFLE, AND STAMPED RIGHT ON THE

12.13 Statement of The Honorable Thomas N. Downing before the House
Committee on Rules, Wednesday, March 31, 1976.
Extract: The Murder Weapon.

THE MURDER WEAPON - 2

BARREL OF THE RIFLE WAS 7.65 MAUSER. AND THAT'S

WHEN WEITZMAN SAID, 'IT IS A MAUSER,' AND POINTED

TO THE 7.65 MAUSER STAMP ON THE BARREL."

THIS DESCRIPTION OF THE RIFLE IS INCOMPATIBLE WITH THE

WARREN COMMISSION'S CASE AGAINST OSWALD. ALTHOUGH THE FBI

REPORTED THAT OSWALD OWNED A RIFLE IT WAS NOT SIMILAR TO THE

ONE REPORTEDLY FOUND ON THE BOOK DEPOSITORY SIXTH FLOOR.

ACCORDING TO THE FBI, THE RIFLE OSWALD HAD PURCHASED WAS A

MANNLICHER/CARCANO, 6.5 ITALIAN CARBINE. THIS RIFLE, WHICH

THE WARREN COMMISSION IDENTIFIED AS THE MURDER WEAPON, IS

AVAILABLE FOR EXAMINATION IN THE NATIONAL ARCHIVES. ANY

INDIVIDUAL, REGARDLESS OF HIS EXPERIENCE IN FIREARMS, CAN

CLEARLY SEE IT IS AN ITALIAN RIFLE BECAUSE STAMPED CLEARLY ON

THE RIFLE ARE THE WORDS, "MADE ITALY" AND "CAL. 6.5." IT IS

UNLIKELY THAT TWO POLICE OFFICERS UPON CLOSE INSPECTION WOULD

HAVE MADE SUCH A CASE OF MISTAKEN IDENTIFICATION.

THE MURDER WEAPON - 3

RECENTLY DECLASSIFIED CIA DOCUMENTS ADD FURTHER
EVIDENCE THAT "OSWALD'S" RIFLE WAS NOT THE RIFLE FOUND IN
THE BOOK DEPOSITORY. A CIA REPORT, DATED NOVEMBER 25, 1963,
STATES "ON NOVEMBER 22, 1963 LEE HARVEY OSWALD SHOT PRESIDENT
KENNEDY WHILE THE PRESIDENT WAS RIDING IN AN OPEN AUTOMOBILE
ON A DALLAS TEXAS STREET. THE RIFLE USED WAS A MAUSER ..."

A SECOND CIA REPORT DATED FIVE DAYS AFTER THE ASSASSINA-
TION STATES:

28 NOVEMBER 1963

INFORMATION ON THE WEAPON

PRESUMABLY USED IN THE

ASSASSINATION OF PRESIDENT KENNEDY

1. AS REGARDS ARTICLES APPEARING RECENTLY IN THE
ITALIAN AND FOREIGN PRESS CONCERNING THE PRESUMED USE OF AN
ITALIAN-MADE RIFLE IN THE SLAYING OF PRESIDENT KENNEDY, THE
FOLLOWING COMMENTS ARE MADE.

2. THE WEAPON WHICH APPEARS TO HAVE BEEN EMPLOYED IN
THIS CRIMINAL ATTACK IS A MODEL 91 RIFLE, 7.35 CALIBER, 1938
MODIFICATION.

3. THE DESCRIPTION OF A "MANNLICHER CARCANO" RIFLE IN
THE ITALIAN AND FOREIGN PRESS IS IN ERROR.

THE MURDER WEAPON - 4

     IT SHOULD BE CLEAR THAT THE INITIAL IDENTIFICATION OF

THE RIFLE AS A 7.65 MAUSER CLEARLY WAS NOT, AS THE COMMISSION

MAINTAINED, BECAUSE DEPUTY CONSTIBLE WEITZMAN "THOUGHT IT LOOKED

LIKE A MAUSER." SINCE THE COMMISSION'S CASE AGAINST OSWALD AS

THE LONE ASSASSIN IS BUILT ALMOST EXCLUSIVELY ON HIS OWNERSHIP

OF THE 6.5 MANNLICHER/CARCANO, THE IDENTIFICATION OF THE

MURDER WEAPON AS 7.65 MAUSER TENDS TO DISCREDIT THE ENTIRE CASE.

M E M O R A N D U M

Being the Head of the Cuban Government and having been recognized as such
by the Cuban Underground, I have been working actually and by all means possible
to bring about the downfall of the Communist occupation of my country (CUBA).

To accomplish the above we have shipped arms into Cuba and financed many
expeditions of Sea-Raiders. Due to the policy of the past Administration all our
efforts to overthrow Castro's Communist regime had met with little success. Our
ships have been confiscated and so have many of our arms. We tried to shift our
base of operations to the Bahamas, but the late President Kennedy obtained the
cooperation of the British in stopping our actions from the Bahama's base.

There was only one other way to fight Castro, that is from inside Cuba,
left open to us. To accomplish that we required large sums of money, Cuban currency, that could not be bought in the U.S. or even inside Cuba because of the
U.S. ban of Cuban currency. So I decided to print Cuban currency for use inside
the Island in the amount of 50 million dollars.

This is not a new idea. Mr. Morgenthau's father of the New York State
District Attorney, when he was Treasurer of the U.S., had currency printed in
this country to be used in all occupied countries.

There was the trouble of finding someone to make the plates, print the
money and extend credit for doing this work until such time as our success inside Cuba, through the use of this currency, would decide the American public
to send its donations to our cause. I had been negotiating with an attorney in
Annapolis by the name of Walter Scholz, who claimed to have many clients interested in seeing Cuba free and that he would, for a consideration, help me
raise funds. Because of his apparent interest in the cause of Cuban liberation,
I mentioned my plan of having Cuban money printed. He immediately offered to
locate a printer who could do this on credit. Some weeks later I heard from
Mr. Scholz who said he had located such a man and brought him to my home in
Arlington to meet me. This man said he could not finance the making of the
plates, but would finance the printing of the bills. I borrowed money, I had
the plates made up and met several times in N.Y. with the printer at his request.
Finally on the first of October I met him to deliver the plates only to find
that he was an informer or agent of the Government and I was arrested and charged
with counterfeiting Castro's money, possession of plates for that purpose and

13.8 Memorandum composed by Mario Kohly, Sr. explaining his rationale
in the creation and implementation of his second counterfeiting operation
and requesting a change of venue in the Federal proceedings against him in
the U.S. District Court for the Southern District of New York.

- 2 -

conspiring to sell these bills in the U.S. This last part of the charge is so
ridiculous, it is not even funny. Since there is no market anywhere in the
world for Cuban money except inside Cuba. Before meeting with the printer, I
had spent sometime in Miami making arrangements with ten of the largest Underground groups to supply them with better than 100,000.00 pesos each per week,
so that they could distribute it in Havana among the Underground. I have letters signed before Notary Publics by each one of these organizations to that
effect.

Immediately upon my arrest the District Attorney, Mr. Morgenthau, who
seems very interested in protecting Mr. Castro by every means possible, had the
newspapers specially Newsweek (owned by the Washington Post)smear me and slander
me in every way possible and ridiculing the possibility of using this money inside Cuba, saying that Castro would give us a very hard time, even if we had
been sincere in that attempt. It must be that he is a very great sympathizer
of Castro for the plates were made in Baltimore, my first meeting with the
printer who turned out to be an informer, who lived in New Jersey, was at my
home in Arlington, Va., and yet the appointment to pick me up and arrest me was
made at the Waldorf Hotel in New York City, so that Mr. Morgenthau could protect
his friend Castro.

This appointment in New York, made on the first of October, was very
timely for I had just announced a few days previous, and had told even the
printer-informer, that on the seventh of October I was giving a banquet at the
Shoreham Hotel for 50 Cuban leaders, 30 U.S. Congressmen and the representatives
of 10 European Exiled Organizations from behind the Iron Curtain, all of whom
had accepted and was to be headed by Monsignor Balkunas. Apparently this was
more than Mr. Morgenthau could stand as the purpose of the banquet was to show
my strength and support and require the recognition of a Cuban Government in
Exile against Castro.

It is my considered opinion that should this case be allowed to go to
trial the Administration of President Johnson will be greatly embarrassed as it
would show insincerity of purpose when they claim they   are   trying
to blockade Castro's economy and yet arrest and treat as a common criminal, a
Cuban leader, head of 96 exiled organizations, 16 Underground groups and whose

- 3 -

proclamation as President of Cuba in Exile has been published in the Congressional Record of October 1, 1962, by Congressman John R. Pillion of N.Y.

I have been refused to have my case transferred from N.Y. where I do not feel I can obtain a fair trial because of the negative propaganda by Mr. Morgenthau. Therefore I have asked for repeated postponements before pleading "not guilty" in the hopes of avoiding this embarrassment to the Administration of President Johnson, whom I have met personally and admire greatly. In the hopes he will have this case dismissed before I have to go to trial and the indignant press such as the New York Times, Erie Times, and Buffalo News and others publish something that may hurt the present Administration at the coming elections.

Exhibit 11
Nixon Letter to Judge Weinfeld on Kohly

NIXON, MUDGE, ROSE, GUTHRIE & ALEXANDER
(MUDGE, STERN, BALDWIN & TODD)
20 BROAD STREET
NEW YORK, N.Y.

March 9, 1965

The Honorable Edward Weinfeld
United States District Judge
Federal Courthouse
Foley Square
New York, New York

Dear Judge Weinfeld:

I am writing, at the request of his counsel, in behalf of Mario Kohly who, I understand, has been convicted of violating a statute prohibiting the unauthorized printing of foreign currency and sentenced to a one year term of imprisonment. While I have no personal knowledge of the particular circumstances of the case, I am advised that Kohly is a person of good repute and believe that the acts which led to his conviction, although unlawful, were not motivated by any desire for personal gain but rather from a dedication to his country.

As one who has followed the Cuban problem closely, I believe it is possible that, in the face of a difficult, dangerous and changing situation, the complexities of United States policy toward the Castro regime, particularly as it has affected the exiles, might well have created an atmosphere in which a person such as Kohly could honestly, though mistakenly, believe that actions such as those for which he was convicted were not contrary to the interests of the United States. The situation of the Cuban exiles in this country in the years since the communization of Cuba has been, in many ways unique in our history. Their presence here cannot be dissociated from the active hostility of the Castro regime towards the United States, and the resulting antagonism on the part of the public, the press and

16.6 Letter from Richard Nixon to The Honorable Edward Weinfeld dated March 9, 1964.

The Honorable Edward Weinfeld   -2-   March 9, 1964

the government here towards Castro. The exiles have, in
consequence, from time to time, as your Honor knows, been
encouraged and aided by the United States in efforts to
overthrow the Cuban Government, and such efforts, in the
nature of things, have been covert and sometimes extra
legal. The patriotism, courage and energy of the exiles
in attempting to mount a counterrevolution have been in
the past, and may in the future again be regarded as
advantageous to the interests of the United States as well
as those of Cuba.

It appears to me that to the extent compatible
with the public interest, these unique circumstances ought
to be taken into account in determining the severity of the
penalty to be imposed on Kohly.

I trust that your Honor will understand that my
purpose in writing this letter is to aid the Court in its
consideration of the defendant's application for suspension
or reduction of the sentence imposed.

Very truly yours,

RMN:AGA

CC: Robert M. Morgenthau, Esq.
United States Attorney

UNITED STATES DISTRICT COURT

FOR THE SOUTHERN DISTRICT OF NEW YORK

- - - - - - - - - - - - - - - - x

UNITED STATES OF AMERICA,   :   No. 65 CR. 845

             Plaintiff, :

        -against-   :   MOTION FOR REDUCTION
                                              OF SENTENCE

MARIO KOHLY,   :

             Defendant. :

- - - - - - - - - - - - - - - - x

        Movant respectfully moves the Court, pursuant to
Federal Rule of Criminal Procedure 35, to modify the sentence
heretofore imposed in this proceeding by ordering that the
one-year term of the sentence run concurrently with the one-
year sentence previously imposed in No. 63 Cr. 988 or by sus-
pending the sentence.

        Movant was convicted in this Court in 1964 on two
counts of conspiracy (under 18 U.S.C. Sec. 371) to violate
18 U.S.C. Secs. 478-481, and unlawful possession of plates from
which the counterfeit notes of a foreign government could be
printed, and sentenced to one year in prison on each count,
the terms to run concurrently. An appeal was taken to the
Court of Appeals, which affirmed the conviction on February
26, 1965. A petition for a writ of certiorari was denied on
June 1, 1965.

        Thereafter movant, who had remained free on
bail, failed to surrender to commence serving the sentence.
He was taken into custody in January 27th, 1966, pleaded
guilty to a bail-jumping charge on March 18, and on March
25th was sentenced by your Honor to one year's imprisonment,
the term to run consecutively with the concurrent one-year
terms originally imposed.

16.8 Motion for Reduction of Sentence submitted to U.S. District Court,
Southern District of New York by law firm of Nixon, Mudge, Rose, Guthrie &
Alexander in the case of the United States of America vs. Mario Kohly.

NIXON, MUDGE, ROSE, GUTHRIE & ALEXANDER
(MUDGE, STERN, BALDWIN & TODD)

JOHN H. ALEXANDER
BLISS ANSNES
PETER W. ASHER
ARTHUR M. BECKER
MILTON BLACK
JOHN F. BROSNAN
GEORGE E. BUCHANAN
GOLDTHWAITE H. DORR
RICHARD S. FARROW
LEONARD GARMENT
RANDOLPH H. GUTHRIE
MATTHEW G. HEROLD, JR.
JOSEPH V. KLINE
WILLIAM B. LANDIS
RICHARD M. NIXON
RICHARD S. RITZEL
MILTON C. ROSE
NORMAN M. SEGAL
HARRY G. SILLECK, JR.
JAMES P. TANNIAN
JOHN WALLIS
ROBERT E. WALSH
GEORGE W. WHITTAKER

20 BROAD STREET

NEW YORK, N.Y.

April 21, 1966

HANOVER 2-6767
CABLE "BALTUCHIN"
—
WASHINGTON OFFICE
839-17th STREET, N.
WASHINGTON, D.C.
STERLING 3-8775
—
EUROPEAN OFFICE
12, RUE DE LA PAIX
PARIS 2ᵉ, FRANCE
742-05-99

Mrs. Margarita Garcia Kohly
730 Pennsylvania Avenue
Miami Beach, Florida

Dear Mrs. Garcia Kohly:

I have your letter of the 19th. I have also received your earlier letter, with which you enclosed a copy of Judge Murphy's decision, dated April 4, 1966, denying the applications for reduction of the sentence recently imposed on Mr. Kohly. I have also received a letter from your sister-in-law.

As I advised you I would, I attempted to talk to Judge Murphy about the case, but was advised by his staff that any applications to him should be made formally in accordance with the Rules of Criminal Procedure. My original purpose in attempting to see the Judge was of course materially changed by the fact that he had determined to consider the letters sent to him by you and by Mr. and Mrs. Kohly as applications for reduction of sentence and had denied them. In light of that fact, I was attempting to ascertain whether the Judge would entertain an additional application for reduction of sentence.

You may well imagine that the Court would not normally permit a succession of such applications after having denied the first. However, in view of the unusual circumstances in this case generally and of the informal nature of your personal applications to the Judge, it may just be possible that the Judge in his discretion would give consideration to a more formal application which we might now make and I am prepared to make such an application. However, I want to make it perfectly plain to you that Judge Murphy, having imposed the sentence and then having denied your applications after reconsidering the

16.9 Letter of Robert R. Thornton, Esq., to Mrs. Margarita Garcia Kohly, stating authorization by Richard M. Nixon of Nixon, Mudge, Rose, Guthrie & Alexander to represent Kohly without fees in New York court case.

Mrs. Margarita Garcia Kohly   -2-   April 21, 1966

matter, is unlikely to change his decision. Furthermore, it
would be within his discretion even to refuse to consider a
further application which we might now make.

To set your mind at rest regarding the press
of time in this matter, the Rules of Procedure provide that
reduction of sentence may be granted within a period of 60
days after sentence is first imposed. Therefore, we are
still well within the period if Judge Murphy should in his
discretion determine to consider a further application.

From your letter I gather that you may be under
a misapprehension as to the procedural steps which are possible.
As I informed you when you were here in New York, there is
no question of an appeal being taken to the Court of Appeals
or to the Supreme Court in this matter. The only remedy available is the application for reduction of the sentence imposed
on the bail jumping charge.

Before I undertake to make such an application as
I have discussed above, I will need direct authority from Mr.
Kohly himself to represent him. If he wishes that I do so,
will you please inform him that I would require a letter from
him to that effect. It may also be necessary for me to visit
him before making the application to the Court. Therefore, I
would like to know where he is and when he can be seen.

As I have already informed you, Mr. Nixon has
authorized me to offer my services in this matter without charge
to Mr. Kohly.

Very truly yours,

Robert R. Thornton

RRT:jg

AIR MAIL

THE SUN, BALTIMORE, WEDNESDAY MORNING, SEPTEMBER 29, 1971

Embattled GOP Candidate, Morrow, Calls For Unity

By BENTLEY ORRICK

Robert D. Morrow, the GOP candidate for president of the City Council, issued a "call for unity among Baltimore Republicans" yesterday, but conceded that "with all this fiasco" a joint campaign against the Democrats was unlikely.

In fact, Mr. Morrow said, he had "not even been consulted" about the choice of a replacement for the third citywide candidate's post, the comptroller nomination.

"I have no idea who they will pick," Mr. Morrow said. He said he has been brushed off by the GOP mayoral candidate, Dr. Ross Z. Pierpont, as a man with "personal problems."

Dr. Pierpont disassociated his candidacy from that of Mr. Morrow's because of Mr. Morrow's role in an abortive scheme to counterfeit Cuban pesos in 1963 and 1964.

Mr. Morrow and his wife were allowed to plead no contest and were given a year's probation on charges of making the plates for the counterfeit pesos. Mario Garcia Kohly, who calls himself the president of the Cuban Government in Exile, traveled to Baltimore last week to describe Mr. Morrow's role as patriotic and anti-communist, and in no way motivated by desire for personal monetary gain.

Mr. Kohly was sentenced to a year in jail for his part in this counterfeiting scheme—a sentence he said came about when "top officials" in the United States government refused to speak up for the plotters after earlier encouraging them secretly.

"The reaction to my press conference last week" with Mr. Kohly "indicates that the majority of Republicans and Democrats alike approves of my attempt to upset Fidel Castro's finances with the peso-counterfeiting plan. There is no reason why we Republicans should not close ranks and shoot for a victory in November," Mr. Morrow said.

Dr. Pierpont, meanwhile, sounded confident that the city Republican Central Committee would take his advice on naming a candidate for comptroller to replace Darl D. Chappell, who had resigned, citing embarrassment over the Morrow case.

Dr. Pierpont said he still planned to plump for a Negro Republican to give the ticket "racial balance," but the normally outgoing physician said that just who his choice was, would have to remain a secret.

Cool To Contest

The committee meets tonight but the city's two most politically involved black Republicans, Archie W. Jones, the city chairman, and Marshall W. Jones, Jr., an undertaker, both have cast cold water on the suggestion that one of them take on the incumbent, Hyman A. Pressman. Mr. Pressman led all candidates with 101,000 votes in the September 14 primary.

The committee has the option of leaving the nomination vacant and not contesting the comptroller election. The Republicans, outnumbered more than 5 to 1, are contesting only 8 of the 18 Council seats.

Dr. Pierpont said he is sticking by his decision to run separately from Mr. Morrow whom he unsuccessfully urged to resign. "But I wish him nothing but the best and if the Republican hierachy decides otherwise, we can reassess the position," he said.

"I have no squabble with Ross," Mr. Morrow said. He acknowleged that he had announced his break with the Pierpont ticket before Dr. Pierpont acted and said that was one reason he was making the gesture of asking for GOP unity.

"I'd certainly consider it," Mr. Morrow said when asked if he would again take a place on a Pierpont ticket. He said that in the meantime he is planning several "small, independent fund raising events" to pay for his campaign.

Epilogue.3 *Baltimore Sun*, September 29, 1971 article describing author's role in Cuban anti-Castro movement and press conference with Mario Kohly during author's campaign for City Council President.

Press Statement on Watergate for CREEP

ON JUNE 2, 1972, AFTER THE MARYLAND PRIMARY, MARIO GARCIA KOHLY, PRESIDENT DE FACTO OF CUBA IN EXILE, INFORMED ME THAT HE HAD BEEN APPROACHED BY TWO MEN CLAIMING THEY WERE WITH THE COMMITTEE TO RE-ELECT THE PRESIDENT.

THESE MEN WISHED TO ENLIST HIS ORGANIZATION'S HELP TO BREAK INTO THE WATERGATE COMPLEX TO UNCOVER WHAT THEY CLAIMED WAS A CASTRO / DEMOCRATIC PLOT TO EMBARRASS THE NIXON ADMINISTRATION BEFORE THE ELECTIONS.

KOHLY CAREFULLY CHECKED WITH HIS UNDERGROUND SOURCES IN CUBA AND DISCOVERED THAT THERE WAS NO DEAL MADE BETWEEN THE DEMOCRATS AND CASTRO BUT DID DISCOVER SUBSEQUENTLY THAT A LARGE SUM OF MONEY WAS IN A MEXICAN BANK FOR THE ALLEGED PURPOSE OF FUNDING THE WATERGATE BREAK-IN AND REPUTEDLY CONTROLLED BY THE DEMOCRATIC PARTY.

BECAUSE THE STORY DID NOT MAKE ANY SENSE THAT THE DEMOCRATS WOULD WANT TO BUG THEIR OWN HEADQUARTERS, HE DISMISSED THE MATTER UNTIL AFTER THE ACTUAL WATERGATE INCIDENT. WHEN HE DISCOVERED THAT AN OLD FRIEND, MR. FRANK STURGIS, WAS INVOLVED.

KOHLY HAS BEEN UNABLE, UPON REPEATED ATTEMPTS, TO REACH STURGIS TO INFORM HIM OF THIS POSSIBLE DEMOCRATIC INVOLVEMENT.

I HAVE SENT COPIES OF A LENGTHY STATEMENT OUTLINING MORE DETAILS TO THE F.B.I. AND MAILED COPIES TO U.S. ATTORNEY BEALL FOR TRANSMITTING TO THE FEDERAL GRAND JURY IN WASHINGTON.

Epilogue.4   Author's press statement on Watergate for CREEP regarding Democratic Party's attempt to uncover *Operation Forty* and Nixon's role therein.

On or about the third week of October, 1960, I
was with Mario Garcia Kohly when he informed me that he had
met with Vice President Nixon about a week before. He
stated to me that an agreement had been reached between he
(Kohly) and the Vice President for the elimination of Miro
Cardona and all the leftist Cuban Revolutionary Front
leaders in order that Kohly could immediately take over the
reins of power in Cuba, once a successful invasion by exiles being trained by the Central Intelligence Agency had
been accomplished. He stated that this agreement was made
once he had pledged to have his underground inside Cuba
support the invaders as well as committing his 300 to 400
man guerrilla army located in the Escambrey Mountains to
attack Castro's forces if necessary to support the landing.
He claimed Manuel Artimes and his followers were to be
assassinated by this force once a successful landing had
been completed. He also stated that the balance of the
Front leaders would be held incommunicado and turned over
to Kohly's exile groups for elimination once the invasion
had been successful or Kohly's guerrilla army had joined
the invasion forces. After this meeting between Kohly and
myself, I inquired of my case officer in the presence of
General Cabell if this was true and they confirmed it to
be so.

On the night of April 17, 1961, en route from Opa
Locka to Buckingham Field, I was told by my case officer
that the Front group was being held incommunicado at Opa
Locka pending the outcome of the invasion. The inference
was that they would never be heard from again.

                                 ROBERT D. MORROW

District of Columbia, ss:

I HEREBY CERTIFY that before me, the subscriber,
a Notary Public in and for the District aforesaid, personally
appeared ROBERT D. MORROW, who acknowledged the foregoing
statement to be true to the best of his knowledge, recol-
lection, and belief.

WITNESS my hand and Notorial Seal this 19th day of
July, 1976.

                          NOTARY PUBLIC

Epilogue.5 Affidavits of Robert D. Morrow and Mario Garcia Kohly, Jr.,
submitted to the House Rules Committee in July 1976, attesting to the
authenticity of *Operation Forty*'s existence and the role played by
Richard M. Nixon in its conception.

AFFIDAVIT:

IN OCTOBER 1960, IN A CONVERSATION BETWEEN MY
FATHER IN WASHINGTON, D.C. AND MYSELF IN MIAMI BETWEEN
TWO PREDESIGNATED PAY TELEPHONES, I WAS TOLD THAT VICE
PRESIDENT NIXON HAD AGREED TO THE ELIMINATION OF THE
LEFTIST APPROVED CUBAN REVOLUTIONARY FRONT LEADERS
AT A TIME WHEN THE ISLAND WOULD BE INVADED BY THE
EXILE GROUPS TRAINED UNDER THE DIRECTION OF THE
CENTRAL INTELLIGENCE AGENCY. THIS PROMISE WAS MADE IF
MY FATHER WOULD GUARANTEE THE USE OF HIS UNDERGROUND OR-
GANIZATION INSIDE CUBA AND HIS 300-400 MAN ARMED
GUERRILA FORCE IN THE ESCAMBREY MOUNTAINS.

JUST PRIOR TO THE INVASION IN APRIL 1961, MY
FATHER AGAIN NOTIFIED ME BY TELEPHONE TO EXPECT NEWS-
PAPER PUBLICITY REGARDING THE CUBAN REVOLUTIONARY FRONT
JOINING THE UNITED ORGANIZATIONS AS AN INTEGRAL·PART
AND THAT THE INVASION WAS TO TAKE PLACE WITHIN THE NEXT
FEW DAYS AND TO CONTACT COLONEL PEPE PINERO AND COLONEL
SANCHEZ MOSQUERA (WHO LATER BECAME AN AGENT FOR THE
CIA) AND TO TELL THEM THEY WERE NOT TO WORRY ABOUT THIS
ACTION AND INSTRUCTED ME TO EXPLAIN WHY, I.E., THEY
WOULD BE TAKEN CARE OF IMMEDIATELY UPON THE SUCCESSFUL
TAKEOVER OF CASTRO'S GOVERNMENT BY MY FATHER. I WAS

AFFIDAVIT
MARIO GARCIA KOHLY, JR.
PAGE TWO

ALSO TOLD THAT MANUEL ARTIMES AND AURELIANO SANCHEZ
ARRANGO WERE TO BE SHOT AS SOON AS THEY HAD WORD THAT
MIRO CARDONA AND THE REST OF THE CUBAN REVOLUTIONARY
FRONT GROUP BEING HELD IN COMMUNICATO AT OPA LOCKA HAD
BEEN ELIMINATED. WHEN KENNEDY CALLED OFF THE AIR
COVER FOR THE BAY OF PIGS INVASION, THESE PLANS WERE
ABORTED. LIKEWISE, WHEN SENATOR OWNE BREWSTER
INFORMED MY FATHER THAT THERE WOULD BE NO AIR COVER,
I WAS INSTRUCTED TO IMMEDIATELY PULL THE UNDERGROUND
AND ARMED FORCE FROM TAKING ANY SUPPORTIVE ACTION.

MARIO GARCIA KOHLY, JR.

STATE OF VIRGINIA
COUNTY OF ARLINGTON, SS:

I HEREBY CERTIFY THAT ON 15TH DAY OF JULY, 1976, BEFORE
ME, THE SUBSCRIBER, A NOTARY PUBLIC OF THE STATE OF
VIRGINIA, PERSONALLY APPEARED MARIO GARCIA KOHLY, JR.
AND ACKNOWLEDGED THE FOREGOING AFFIDAVIT TO BE HIS ACT
AND HAND.

WITNESS MY HAND AND NOTORIAL SEAL, THE DAY AND YEAR LAST
MENTIONED ABOVE.

My commission expires on
May 27, 1978.

NOTARY PUBLIC.

Select Committee on Assassinations Nondisclosure Agreement

I, ████████████████████ in consideration for being
employed by or engaged by contract or otherwise to perform
services for or at the request of the House Select Committee
on Assassinations, or any Member thereof, do hereby make the
representations and accept the obligations set forth below as
conditions precedent for my employment or engagement, or for
my continuing employment or engagement, with the Select Committee, the United States House of Representatives, or the
United States Congress.

1. I have read the Rules of the Select Committee, and I
hereby agree to be bound by them and by the Rules of the House
of Representatives.

2. I hereby agree never to divulge, publish or reveal by
words, conduct or otherwise, any testimony given before the .
Select Committee in executive session (including the name of any
witness who appeared or was summoned to appear before the Select
Committee in executive session), any classifiable and properly
classified information (as defined in 5 U.S.C. §552(b)(1)), or
any information pertaining to intelligence sources or methods as
designated by the Director of Central Intelligence, or any confidential information that is received by the Select Committee
or that comes into my possession by virtue of my position with
the Select Committee, to any person not a member of the Select
Committee or its staff or the personal staff representative of
a Committee Member unless authorized in writing by the Select
Committee, or, after the Select Committee's termination, by
such manner as the House of Representatives may determine or,
in the absence of a determination by the House, in such manner
as the Agency or Department from which the information originated may determine. I further agree not to divulge, publish
or reveal by words, conduct or otherwise, any other information
which is received by the Select Committee or which comes into
my possession by virtue of my position with the Select Committee,
for the duration of the Select Committee's existence.

3. I hereby agree that any material that is based upon or
may include information that I hereby pledge not to disclose,
and that is contemplated for publication by me will, prior to
discussing it with or showing it to any publishers, editors or
literary agents, be submitted to the Select Committee to determine whether said material contains any information that I
hereby pledge not to disclose. The Chairman of the Select Committee shall consult with the Director of Central Intelligence
for the purpose of the Chairman's determination as to whether
or not the material contains information that I pledge not to
disclose. I further agree to take no steps toward publication
until authorized in writing by the Select Committee, or after
its termination, by such manner as the House of Representatives

Epilogue.8 House Select Committee on Assassinations Nondisclosure
Agreement.

-2-

may determine, or in the absence of a determination by the
House, in such manner as the Agency or Department from which
the information originated may determine.

4. I hereby agree to familiarize myself with the Select
Committee's security procedures, and provide at all times the
required degree of protection against unauthorized disclosure
for all information and materials that come into my possession
by virtue of my position with the Select Committee.

5. I hereby agree to immediately notify the Select Committee of any attempt by any person not a member of the Select
Committee staff to solicit information from me that I pledge
not to disclose.

6. I hereby agree to immediately notify the Select
Committee if I am called upon to testify or provide information
to the proper authorities that I pledge not to disclose. I
will request that my obligation to respond is established by
the Select Committee, or after its termination, by such manner
as the House of Representatives may determine, before I do so.

7. I hereby agree to surrender to the Select Committee
upon demand by the Chairman or upon my separation from the
Select Committee staff, any material, including any classified
information or information pertaining to intelligence sources
or methods as designated by the Director of Central Intelligence,
which comes into my possession by virtue of my position with the
Select Committee. I hereby acknowledge that all documents
acquired by me in the course of my employment are and remain the
property of the United States.

8. I understand that any violation of the Select Committee
Rules, security procedures or this agreement shall constitute
grounds for dismissal from my current employment.

9. I hereby assign to the United States Government all
rights, title and interest in any and all royalties, remunera-
tions and emoluments that have resulted or may result from any
divulgence, publication or revelation in violation of this
agreement.

10. I understand and agree that the United States Government
may choose to apply, prior to any unauthorized disclosure by
me, for a court order prohibiting disclosure. Nothing in this
agreement constitutes a waiver on the part of the United States
of the right to prosecute for any statutory violation. Nothing
in this agreement constitutes a waiver on my part of any defenses
I may otherwise have in any civil or criminal proceedings.

-3-

11. I have read the provisions of the Espionage Laws,
Sections 793, 794 and 798, Title 18, United States Code, and
of Section 783, Title 50, United States Code, and I am aware
that unauthorized disclosure of certain classified information
may subject me to prosecution. I have read Section 1001, Title
18, United States Code, and I am aware that the making of a
false statement herein is punishable as a felony. I have also
read Executive Order 11652, and the implementing National
Security Council directive of May 17, 1972, relating to the
protection of classified information.

12. Unless released in writing from this agreement or any
portion thereof by the Select Committee, I recognize that all
the conditions and obligations imposed on me by this agreement
apply during my Committee employment or engagement and continue
to apply after the relationship is terminated.

13. No consultant shall indicate, divulge or acknowledge,
without written permission of the Select Committee, the fact
that the Select Committee has engaged him or her by contract
as a consultant until after the Select Committee has terminated.

14. In addition to any rights for criminal prosecution or
for injunctive relief the United States Government may have for
violation of this agreement, the United States Government may
file a civil suit in an appropriate court for damages as a
consequence of a breach of this agreement. The costs of any
civil suit brought by the United States for breach of this
agreement, including court costs, investigative expenses, and
reasonable attorney fees, shall be borne by any defendant who
loses such suit. In any civil suit for damages successfully
brought by the United States Government for breach of this
agreement, actual damages may be recovered, or, in the event
that such actual damages may be impossible to calculate, liquidate
damages in an amount of $5,000 shall be awarded as a reasonable
estimate for damages to the credibility and effectiveness of the
investigation.

15. I hereby agree that in any suit by the United States
Government for injunctive or monetary relief pursuant to the
terms of this agreement, personal jurisdiction shall obtain and
venue shall lie in the United States District Court for the
District of Columbia, or in any other appropriate United States
District Court in which the United States may elect to bring
suit. I further agree that the law of the District of Columbia
shall govern the interpretation and construction of this
agreement.

16. Each provision of this agreement is severable. If a
court should find any part of this agreement to be unenforceable,
all other provisions of this agreement shall remain in full force
and effect.

-4-

I make this agreement without any mental reservation or purpose of evasion, and I agree that it may be used by the Select Committee in carrying out its duty to protect the security of information provided to it.

Date: _July 19, 1977_

I am submitting a list of material and information which has already been given to the committee, or which I intend to give the committee in the near future. I intend to publish some of this information.

LOUIS STOKES, Chairman
Select Committee on Assassinations

Morrow: Mr. Jim Garrison, please.

Secretary: Just a moment, please......./rather garbled exchange between you
             and the secretary./

Garrison: Hello.

Morrow: Mr. Garrison?

Garrison: Yeah.

Morrow: I don't know whether you know me or not. I wrote a book on the
             same subject you had an investigation on.

Garrison: Yeah. A very interesting book. And you named some familiar
             characters.

Morrow: Yes. I thought you'd notice some.

Garrison: It looks like your book did pretty well.

Morrow: Well, it's doing quite well overseas as well.

Garrison: That's good.

Morrow: But I'm following it up and have gotten a lot deeper into the thing
             and, as you may or may not know, I worked with General Cabell back
             in the old days.

Garrison: Uhum.

Morrow: And the reason for my call was I understand around 1971 just prior
             to his death, you were thinking about an indictment against him.

Garrison: No. I was never thinking about an indictment of Cabell. There
             wasn't enough information to indicate that any action on his part.
             The only position I ever took on him, as a matter of fact, most of
             the things I know about him are really pretty good. He was
             apparently a strong, effective character. I have just made the
             point, that I would make again

Epilogue.9 Transcript of telephone interview conducted by author with Jim
Garrison on August 8, 1977 regarding CIA and Bay of Pigs personnel's role
in Kennedy assassination.

Garrison/2

although I no longer try to communicate with the press
because I think it's hopeless -- they get everything backwards.
You've probably been through that by now. It's hopeless.
But I make the point of the way the Warren Commission looked
into it so... well, on purpose. Because they had to well aware
that it was a segment of the Agency, although I think quite
obviously, what you would call a marginal segment -- contract
employee type. I find the best way to describe them, the cluster
involved, as those involved in the Bay of Pigs, so to speak.

Morrow: There's no question about that.

Garrison: I think the agency made a serious mistake. As I told a friend or
two with the Agency -- we all have friends with the Agency --
and I have some who are under a pretty deep cover, but they
know I know they're with the Agency and so we... I've told them
that the Agency made a mistake of judgment when it made the
decision to go along with the rest of the government -- in fact,
they probably helped persuade the rest of the government -- to
cover-up the involvement of this segment in order to protect its
reputation. Because actually it had participated in unearthing
it, it could have acquired a lot of credit. And by now, most
people sense that there was some role of the Agency involved;
and, instead of perceiving it in perspective, they're going to think
the whole Agency was, which was not the case. The point I usually
make about Cabell thought, is that the Warren Commission
instead of calling the people they should have questioned who could
have given insight and understanding, they called people like
Oswald's baby sitter and questioned her about when he was three
years old and questioned her for eighteen pages. Well, that's
crazy, you see. They should have called some people like
General Charles Cabell, where they had a split and he was in
charge of the Bay of Pigs. That doesn't mean he's involved. But
he'd certainly be a person you'd want to question. And, at the
very least, he might have some insight.

Morrow: Well, that's what I thought. That that was the interpretation you
would have taken.

Garrison: Positively. And I'm... you've got to understand that I'm kind of
pro-military. I'm a retired national guard officer with five
years active duty and eighteen years more in the national guard.
I retired a leutinent colonel. So, I'm not anti-military at all;

Garrison/3

but the press, I'm afraid to talk to them about something like that. They's take off and say Garrison charges Cabell with assassination.

Morrow: You know, it's a funny thing. I'm completely aware of what you're saying. And the interesting is that I've uncovered some information recently that indicates that a number of people -- not necessarily military, but a few were ex-military people in the Company did actually have some knowledge beforehand that this was going to happen.

Garrison: I think that's very possible. Like... even possibly in some cases... even up into the middle elements of operations. But I'm satisfied that in most~~xxasxx~~ those cases it would be just knowledge. And... I think if we had a magic eye and could see clearly at this moment, we'd find that there'd be some that had knowledge beforehand and, for one reason or another, didn't do nothing. And afterwards, virtually all of them had to sense what happened. And, by now, most of them would have to know. I mean people in the position let's say of a Richard Helms -- who I'm satisfied had nothing to do with it; but people with the kind of contacts and sources that he would have as head of domestic operations when that thing happened, it wouldn't be too many weeks afterwards before he knew with some precision.

Morrow: That somebody knew in the Company.

Garrison: What?

Morrow: That somebody did know in the Company.

Garrison: Yeah.

Morrow: There's no question about that.

Garrison: But I would not dare try and explain that to the press because you'd end up with the headlines... every time I try to indicate there was a marginal element involved, I'd read headlines, 'Garrison charges CIA assassinated Kennedy' and it's a

374 APPENDICES

Garrison/4

structure that simply is not the case. John McCone, the head
of the CIA regarded Kennedy as a son. So I just stopped trying
to communicate with them

Morrow: Why, the only other thing that I thought about while I had you
on the phone if I could have the privilege of asking you. Are
you familiar with a story that Richard Nixon was down in Dallas
at Clint Murchison's home the night before along with J. Edgar
Hoover?

Garrison: Well... I don't think Hoover was there. If he was, I don't know
anything about it. But it's a matter of record that Nixon was those
there. But, again, I'm going to take a conversative view of/things.
And there are such things as coincidences. He left by plane
about a half an hour, I think, before Kennedy arrived. And he was
there, if I remember correctly, in a connection with the Pepsi
Cola convention that his law firm represented.

Morrow: That's correct.

Garrison: And so you can... people can get excited and go off in the wrong
direction on something like that. We're not dealing with...
Nixon may not be a perfect individual, but... I don't think we're
dealing with people on that level with regard to the assassination.
That's not his cup of tea any more than it probably was General
Cabell's. The assassination of the president... General Cabell
might have had a different attitude toward him when he cut off
our oil and things like that. But, I regard the Nixon thing as of
no significance. I don't think he could possibly be involved. The
type of individual that's involved is definitely rabid characters
who were trained to assassinate even before the Bay of Pigs,
and after the Bay of Pigs used on raids. That's the group that
we're dealing with here.

Morrow: I'm aware of that.

Garrison: And I feel that the greatest likihood of success lies in the possibility
of a tangent position in the Agency itself. And, I think, it's not
beyond the realm of possibility. I think it's really possible that
the Agency may come to see that it won't be that expensive for it
to participate.

CENTRAL INTELLIGENCE AGENCY

WASHINGTON, D.C. 20505

Office of General Counsel

17 January 1989

James H. Lesar, Esquire
918 F Street, N.W.
Suite 509
Washington, D.C. 20004

Re: Assassination Archives and Research
     Center v. CIA, C.A. No. 88-2600 GHR
     (D.D.C. Dec. 21, 1988)

Dear Mr. Lesar:

I am writing to you on behalf of the Central Intelligence Agency (CIA) in connection with the above-referenced litigation. Pursuant to the Court Order dated December 21, 1988, we have completed our processing of documents responsive to your client's request.

As noted in the CIA's declaration filed with the Court on 3 September 1987, we are responding to item one of plaintiff's request—all CIA information on George Herbert Walker Bush which might reflect a relationship with him prior to his term as Director of the CIA—and the second part of item two—documents regarding the Kennedy assassination or its investigation that may have been sent to and reviewed by Mr. Bush while he was Director of Central Intelligence. The first part of item two—all records on the Kennedy assassination or its investigation which mention George Bush, to the extent that plaintiff's request seeks "all records" which mention George Bush—would not be searchable through CIA's indexing system, but rather, would require individual documents to be searched to determine if George Bush is mentioned. That would constitute research that we believe we are not obligated to undertake under the Freedom of Information Act.

This letter provides our determinations with respect to documents responsive to our search, as described above: two documents are released in full, 16 documents are released in part, and a number of documents are being withheld in their entirety. We have determined that those documents being withheld in their entirety must be denied pursuant to FOIA

Document listing provided by CIA pursuant to litigation between Assassination Archives and Research Center v. CIA (Dec. 21, 1988). Documents relate to George H. Bush's knowledge of author's activities with Cuban exile movement as CIA contract employee and his (Bush's) knowledge of Kennedy assassination investigation.

exemptions (b)(1), (b)(3), and (b)(5). The basis for exempting
the sanitized material from the 16 documents released in part
are as follows:

Document Number   Exemption
and Description   Basis

1.   1-page note, dated 14 June 1976.   (b)(3)
2. *no description given*
3&4.   1-page Routing and Record Sheet,   (b)(1), (b)(3)
        dated 9 July 1976, with attached
        2-page memorandum dated 9 July 1976,
        with attached 1-page Washington Star
        article, dated 8 July 1976.

5&8.   Document 8: 1-page Official Routing Slip,   (b)(1), (b)(3)
        dated 3 August 1976, with attachments:
        8-page text, undated; 2-page chronology
        dated 2 July 1971-23 July 1972; 3-page
        General Chronology, dated January 1960-
        22 November 1963; 1-page UPI News Service,
        dated 2 August.
        Document 8: 2-page memorandum, dated
        31 July 1976.

6.   2-page memorandum, dated 2 August 1976,   (b)(1), (b)(3)
        with attached 2-page article from
        "Midnight", dated 2 August 1976.

9.   3-page memorandum, dated 6 October 1976,   (b)(1), (b)(3)
        with attached Washington Star article,
        dated 1 October 1976.

10.   1-page Outgoing Message, dated   (b)(1), (b)(3)
        1 October 1976.

11&12. Doc. 12: 1-page note, dated 5 October 1976, (b)(3)
        with attached document 11.
        Doc 11: 1-page Official Routing Slip, dated
        2 October 1976, with attached: 1-page
        Washington Star article, dated 1 October 1976;
        and article dated 1 October.

14.   1-page memorandum, dated   (b)(3)
        15 September 1976.

17.   5-page memorandum, dated   (b)(1), (b)(3)
        15 September 1976.   (b)(5)

15.   2-page memo with attached 2-page   (b)(1), (b)(3)
        Washington Post article.   (b)(5)

16.   1-page Note, dated 15 September 1976.   (b)(3)

18a.   2-page Washington Star article, dated   (b)(3)
        22 October 1976.

20.   2-page letter, dated 5 December 1976,   (b)(3)
        with 2-page attachment.
The two documents released in full are document no. 18,
transcript of an interview of George Bush dated 19 July 1976,
and document no. 19, transcript of interview of George Bush on
Meet the Press on 22 February 1976.

     Exemption (b)(1) encompasses matters that are specifically
authorized under criteria established by the appropriate
Executive order to be kept secret in the interest of national
defense or foreign policy and which are, in fact, currently and
properly classified.

     Exemption (b)(3) pertains to information exempt from
disclosure by statute. The relevant statutes are subsection
102(d)(3) of the National Security Act of 1947, as amended, 50
U.S.C. §403(d)(3), which makes the Director of Central
Intelligence responsible for protecting intelligence sources
and methods from unauthorized disclosure and section 6 of the
Central Intelligence Agency Act of 1949, as amended, 50 U.S.C.
§403g, which exempts from the disclosure requirement
information pertaining to the organization, functions, names,
official titles, salaries, or numbers of personnel employed by
the Agency.

     Exemption (b)(5) pertains to information covered by common
law privileges. In this instance, exemption (b)(5) is asserted
for the deliberative process privilege.

     Your patience in this matter is appreciated.

                                    Sincerely,

                                    Cindy A. Ellis
                                    Attorney Advisor

Enclosures

cc: Nathan Dodell, Esquire (w/encs)
     Assistant U.S. Attorney

1 - Rosen
1 - Liaison
1 - Nasca

Date: November 29, 1963

To: Director
          Bureau of Intelligence and Research
          Department of State

From: John Edgar Hoover, Director

Subject: ASSASSINATION OF PRESIDENT JOHN F. KENNEDY
          NOVEMBER 22, 1963

          Our Miami, Florida, Office on November 23, 1963, advised
that the Office of Coordinator of Cuban Affairs in Miami advised
that the Department of State feels some misguided anti-Castro
group might capitalize on the present situation and undertake an
unauthorized raid against Cuba, believing that the assassination
of President John F. Kennedy might herald a change in U. S. policy,
which is not true.

          Our sources and informants familiar with Cuban matters in
the Miami area advise that the general feeling in the anti-Castro
Cuban community is one of stunned disbelief and, even among those
who did not entirely agree with the President's policy concerning
Cuba, the feeling is that the President's death represents a great
loss not only to the U. S. but to all of Latin America. These
sources knew of no plans for unauthorized action against Cuba.

          DEC-33   62-109060-1396

          An informant who has furnished reliable information in
the past and who is close to a small pro-Castro group in Miami
has advised that these individuals are afraid that the assassination
of the President may result in strong repressive measures being
taken against them and, although pro-Castro in their feelings,
regret the assassination.

          The substance of the foregoing information was orally
furnished to Mr. George Bush of the Central Intelligence Agency and
Captain William Edwards of the Defense Intelligence Agency on
November 23, 1963, by Mr. W. T. Forsyth of this Bureau.

          Director of Naval Intelligence

VHN:gci (12)

Memorandum of J. Edgar Hoover to Director of Intelligence and Research,
State Department, stating information relayed to George Bush regarding
anti-Castro exiles' sentiments on assassination of John F. Kennedy.

INDEX